Party-Appointed Experts in International Commercial and Investment Arbitration

International Arbitration Law Library

VOLUME 79

Editors

Professor Julian D.M. Lew QC has been involved with international arbitration for more than forty years as counsel, as arbitrator and as an academic. He is the founder and has been the Head of the School of International Arbitration, Centre for Commercial Law Studies, Queen Mary University of London since its creation in 1985. He is now an independent international arbitrator at 20 Essex Street, London.

Stavros Brekoulakis is the Michael & Laura Hwang Professor in International Arbitration at the National University of Singapore and a member of 3 Verulam Buildings (Gray's Inn). He is a leading academic in international arbitration and has led, or been involved in, several projects with ICCA, ICC Commission and ILA. He also acts as an independent arbitrator and has been appointed as a chairman, sole arbitrator, co-arbitrator and emergency arbitrator under all the major arbitration rules.

Introduction

Since its first volume published in 1993, this authoritative practitioner-oriented series has published in-depth and analytical works on niche aspects of international arbitration, authored by specialists in the field.

Objective

This authoritative and established series covering in-depth analyses of niche areas appeals to both practitioners and academics. The series includes specific monographs and PhD dissertations of high quality, which are practical and cover issues not fully explored in general texts.

Frequency

A volume is published whenever an interesting topic presents itself.

The titles published in this series are listed at the end of this volume.

Party-Appointed Experts in International Commercial and Investment Arbitration

Impact on Proceedings, Problems and Solutions

Ömer Faruk Kafali

Wolters Kluwer

Published by:
Kluwer Law International B.V.
PO Box 316
2400 AH Alphen aan den Rijn
The Netherlands
E-mail: lrs-sales@wolterskluwer.com
Website: www.wolterskluwer.com/en/solutions/kluwerlawinternational

Sold and distributed by:
Wolters Kluwer Legal & Regulatory U.S.
920 Links Avenue
Landisville, PA 17538
United States of America
E-mail: customer.service@wolterskluwer.com

ISBN 978-94-035-4889-0

e-Book: ISBN 978-94-035-4899-9
web-PDF: ISBN 978-94-035-4909-5

Table of Contents

List of Symbols and Abbreviations

§	Section
AAA	American Arbitration Association
ADR	Alternative Dispute Resolution
AF	Additional Facility
AO	Cap. 609 Arbitration Ordinance of Hong Kong
ARB	Arbitration
BCLP	Bryan Cave Leighton Paisner Law Firm
BGE	Bundesgericht (Swiss Federal Court)
BGH	Bungdesgerichtshof (German Federal Supreme Court)
BIT	Bilateral Investment Treaty
CCP	Code of Civil Procedure
CEPANI	Belgian Centre for Arbitration and Mediation
CETA	EU-Canada Comprehensive Economic and Trade Agreement
CIArb	Chartered Institute of Arbitrators
CJEU	Court of Justice of the European Union
Co.	Company
CPR	UK Civil Procedure Rules 1998
DCF	Discounted Cash Flow
DIS	Deutsche Institution für Schiedsgerichtsbarkeit e. V. (German Arbitration Institute)
EAA	English Arbitration Act of 1996
ECT	Energy Charter Treaty
EUVIPA	EU-Vietnam Free Trade Agreement
EWHC	High Court of England and Wales, the High Court of Justice

FTA	Free Trade Agreement
GAI	Generative Artificial Intelligence
GAR	Global Arbitration Review
GmbH	Gesellschaft mit beschränkter Haftung (Limited Liability Company)
HKIAC	Hong Kong International Arbitration Centre
HMK	Hukuk Muhakemeleri Kanunu (Turkish Code of Civil Procedure No. 6098)
IBA	International Bar Association
ICC	International Chamber of Commerce
ICCA	International Council for Commercial Arbitration
ICJ	International Court of Justice
ICrC	International Criminal Court
ICSID	International Centre for Settlement of Investment Disputes
IIA	International Investment Agreement
Inc.	Incorporation
Int'l	International
ISDS	Investor-State Dispute Settlement
ISTAC	Istanbul Arbitration Centre
ITLOS	International Tribunal for the Law of the Sea
ITOTAM	İstanbul Ticaret Odası Tahkim ve Arabuluculuk Merkezi (Istanbul Chamber of Commerce Arbitration and Mediation Centre)
LCIA	London Court of International Arbitration
m.	*Madde* (article)
ModG	*Modellgesetz* (UNCITRAL Model Law)
MÖHUK	*Milletlerarası Özel Hukuk ve Usûl Hukuku Hakkında Kanun* (Turkish Private International Law Act No. 5718)
MPI	Max-Planck Institute
MTK	Milletlerarası Tahkim Kanunu (Turkish International Arbitration Act No. 4686)
NAFTA	North American Free Trade Agreement
NJW	Neue Juristische Wochenschrift
NYC	United Nations (New York) Convention on the Recognition and Enforcement of Foreign Arbitral Awards dated 1958
OLG	*Oberlandesgericht* (Higher Regional Court)
PCA	Permanent Court of Arbitration
PILA	Private International Law Act
PRC	People's Republic of China

Pub.	Publication
R	Rule
Rep	Report
SA/S.A.	*Sociedade Anonima* (Joint-Stock Company)
SCC	Stockholm Chamber of Commerce
Sch	*Schiedsverfahren* (Arbitration)
SchiedsVfG	*Schiedsverfahrens-Neuregelungsgesetz* (Arbitration Amendment Act)
SchiedsVZ	Zeitschrift für Schiedsverfahren (German Arbitration Journal)
SHIAC	Shanghai International Economic and Trade Arbitration Commission
SIAC	Singapore International Arbitration Centre
SICC	Singapore International Commercial Court
SPILA	Swiss Private International Law Act of 1989
TIAL	Turkish International Arbitration Law No. 4686
UK	United Kingdom
UN	United Nations
UNCITRAL	United Nations Commission on International Trade Law
UNCTAD	United Nations Conference on Trade and Development
UNIDROIT	International Institute for the Unification of Private Law
US	United States of America
USMCA	United States-Mexico-Canada Agreement
VIAC	Vienna International Arbitral Centre
VSCA	Victoria Supreme Court of Appeal
WTO	World Trade Organization
YCA	Yearbook Commercial Arbitration by ICCA
ZPO	Zivilprozessordnung (German Code of Civil Procedure)

Introduction

1 INTRODUCTION TO THE PROBLEM

In adjudication, legal disputes are resolved by judges or arbitrators, considering the facts of the case (*Vakıâ, Sachverhalt*) and ascertaining the relevant legal rules for the specific case. This act of the adjudicator is called *a subsumption*.[1]

The establishment of facts[2] is the first step in any case, without regard to its criminal, civil, or international law character. Judges and arbitrators need facts and the law to perform their decision-making duty.[3] This is also true for international commercial arbitration[4] and international investment arbitration[5] disputes.[6]

1. Pekcanıtez, Atalay, and Özekes, *Medenî Usûl Hukuku Ders Kitabı*, 356; Erdönmez, 'Pekcanıtez Usûl', 795; Arslan et al., *Medenî Usul Hukuku*, 165; Tanrıver, *Medenî Usûl Hukuku*, 2021, I:409; Spitzer, 'Der Sachverständigenbeweis Im Österreichischen Zivilprozess', 28; Bernardino, 'The Discursive Construction of Facts in International Adjudication'; Özbek, *Tahkim Hukuku*, II:1349–1350; Kurkela, Turunen, and Conflict Management Institute, *Due Process in International Commercial Arbitration*, 141; Lew, 'The Need for Expert Evidence?', 246; Yılmaz, *HMK Serhi*, 2013, 371.
2. In this book, the phrase 'establishment of facts' is used rather than finding the facts, or fact-finding. For a critical evaluation of the term 'facts' used in international adjudication, *see* Bernardino, 'The Discursive Construction of Facts in International Adjudication'.
3. Kurkela, Turunen, and Conflict Management Institute, *Due Process in International Commercial Arbitration*, 174; Lew, 'The Need for Expert Evidence?', 246; Amaral, 'Burden of Proof and Adverse Inferences in International Arbitration: Proposal for an Inference Chart', 1; Feutrill and Rubins, 'The Preparation of Expert Evidence in International Commercial Arbitration: Practical Aspects', 314.
4. The term 'International commercial arbitration' in this thesis refers to the resolution of a commercial dispute between real and legal persons from two different states through arbitration. The term 'commercial' should be given a wide interpretation to cover not only matters arising from all contractual or non-contractual relationships of a commercial nature, but also ordinary relationships between non-commercial real or legal persons.
5. The term 'international investment arbitration' in this thesis refers to the resolution of a dispute between a real or legal person who is qualified as an investor according to the relevant legal instrument (Licence, Statute, Bilateral Investment Treaty or Multilateral Investment Treaty) and a state via arbitration. For more details, *see* Dolzer, Kriebaum, and Schreuer, *Principles of International Investment Law*.
6. Knoblach, *Sachverhaltsermittlung in Der Internationalen Wirtschaftsschiedsgerichtsbarkeit*, 41.

With the rightly established facts, the corresponding legal position can be determined (*Da mihi um, dabo tibi ius*).[7,8] The arbitrator's duty can only be diligently fulfilled if the facts have been concretely established.[9]

The facts in an arbitration case are mainly derived from the parties' submissions.[10] In addition, if the relevant procedure allows so, facts may be inquired by the arbitrators.[11]

In principle, the parties to a dispute need to prove the disputed relevant facts.[12] Proof is the act of convincing the arbitrator that the facts underlying the party's claim are genuine and honest.[13] In addition to the facts, the law is also subject to proof in international disputes. To prove the facts, the parties must provide evidence.[14] Evidence in arbitration cases mainly consists of documents, witnesses, expert opinions and sight or subject inspections.[15]

Facts are generally determined based on contractual terms, documents related to a contract and its performance such as price, delivery terms. Additionally, entity (private) records, public records, meeting notes and correspondence between parties are of essence.[16] If the matters of the case are related to scientific, technical, or complex legal knowledge, experts are used to understand the facts and enable the arbitrators to obtain a better understanding thereof.[17] The opinion of experts is a means of obtaining

7. Give me the facts and I will give you the law.
8. Kurkela, Turunen, and Conflict Management Institute, *Due Process in International Commercial Arbitration*, 142.
9. Grando, *Evidence, Proof, and Fact-Finding in WTO Dispute Settlement*, 10–11.
10. Pekcanıtez and Yeşilirmak, 'Tahkim', 2704.
11. For German and UK law *see* Knoblach, *Sachverhaltsermittlung in Der Internationalen Wirtschaftsschiedsgerichtsbarkeit*, 42–43; For UK, also *see* Nairn, Szymanski, and Lekakis, 'National Report for England and Wales (2021 through 2023)', 29. Pekcanıtez and Yeşilirmak, 'Tahkim', 2704; Postacıoğlu and Altay, *Medeni Usul Hukuku Dersleri*, 1045.
12. Kurkela, Turunen and Conflict Management Institute, *Due Process in International Commercial Arbitration*, 142–143; Sourgens, Duggal and Laird, *Evidence in International Investment Arbitration*, 24; Marriott, 'Evidence in International Arbitration', 281; Hacıbekiroğlu, *Milletlerarası Tahkim Hukukunda Deliller ve Delillerin Degerlendirilmesi*, 10.
13. Atalay, 'İspat', 1585–1586; Atalay, 'Delil Kavramı Üzerine', 129; Arslan et al., *Medenî Usul Hukuku*, 405; Alangoya, Yıldırım, and Deren-Yıldırım, *Medeni Usul Hukukunun Esasları*, 294.
14. Atalay, 'Delil Kavramı Üzerine', 130; Atalay, 'Pekcanıtez Usûl', 2021, 1730; Yeğengil, *Tahkim (L'Arbitrage)*, 302; Akıncı, *Milletlerarası Tahkim*, 342; Ağırman, *Milli & Milletlerarası Tahkim*, 455; Redfern et al., 'The Standards and Burden of Proof in International Arbitration', 318.
15. Lew, Mistelis, and Kröll, *Comparative International Commercial Arbitration*, 564; Lew, 'The Need for Expert Evidence?', 246; Yeşilirmak, *Türkiye'de Ticari Hayatın ve Yatırım Ortamının Iyileştirilmesi Için Uyuşmazlıkların Etkin Çözümünde Dogrudan Görüşme, Arabuluculuk, Hakem-Bilirkişilik ve Tahkim: Sorunlar ve Çözüm Önerileri*, 114–115; Wach and Petsch, 'Der Sachverständigenbeweis Im Schiedsverfahren: Grenzen Der Gestaltungsfreiheit von Parteien Und Schiedsgericht', 91; Hacıbekiroğlu, *Milletlerarası Tahkim Hukukunda Deliller ve Delillerin Degerlendirilmesi*, 18; Akıncı, *Milletlerarası Tahkim*, 342; Korkmaz, 'Güncel Tartışmalar Ekseninde Tahkimde Tanık Delilinin Güvenilirliği', 647; Bacanlı, 'Bir Alternatif Uyuşmazlık Çözüm Yolu Olarak Istanbul Tahkim ve Arabuluculuk Merkezi (ISTAC) Tahkim Yargilamasinda Delillerin Ibrazı ve Değerlendirilmesi', 96; Hobér and Sussman, *Cross-Examination in International Arbitration*, 24–25.
16. Lew, 'The Need for Expert Evidence?', 247.
17. Kurkela, Turunen, and Conflict Management Institute, *Due Process in International Commercial Arbitration*, 169; Karadaş, *Ulusal (İç) Tahkim*, 182.

evidence that helps an arbitral tribunal establish the facts of a case or understand complex issues.[18]

A significant part of disputes in international commercial and investment arbitration[19] involve more and more factual situations that require special or technical knowledge.[20] Moreover, complex legal issues may need to be critically opined on.

As a matter of fact, if arbitral tribunals want to assess facts to apply the corresponding legal rules correctly, the opinion of an architect and engineer in a construction dispute or an accountant in a financial dispute will be required unless the arbitrator has the required knowledge or understanding of the relevant subject.[21]

As statistics show, a significant portion of arbitrators across the globe are lawyers with extended knowledge in one or more industries.[22] Nevertheless, this knowledge rarely goes beyond a general understanding of industry-related issues.[23] Thus, at this stage, arbitrators will need to use the experts' opinions in the form of a report while

---

18. Weigand and Baumann, *Practitioner's Handbook on International Commercial Arbitration*, para. 1.281; Mosk, 'The Role of Facts in International Dispute Resolution (Volume 304)', 41. 'Sometimes the determination of facts is based on opinions – for example, the opinions of experts.'; Meier, 'Germany', 1, para. 5.
19. This argument is not exclusive to arbitration; it could also apply to other international courts and tribunals.
20. Born, *International Commercial Arbitration*, 2448; Blackaby et al., *Redfern & Hunter on International Arbitration*, para. 6.135.Schneider and Scherer, 'Art. 184', 2096; Wach and Petsch, 'Der Sachverständigenbeweis Im Schiedsverfahren: Grenzen Der Gestaltungsfreiheit von Parteien Und Schiedsgericht', 92; Khodykin and Mulcahy, *A Guide to the IBA Rules on the Taking of Evidence in International Arbitration*, 281; Proske, *Expert Witness Conferencing in Schiedsverfahren*, 1; Balkar, *Milletlerarası Ticari Tahkim ve Etik*, 165; Feutrill and Rubins, 'The Preparation of Expert Evidence in International Commercial Arbitration: Practical Aspects', 307.
21. Blackaby et al., *Redfern & Hunter on International Arbitration*, para. 6.133; Schütze, Tscherning, and Wais, *Handbuch Des Schiedsverfahrens: Praxis Der Deutschen Und Internationalen Schiedsgerichtsbarkeit*, 222; Akıncı, *Milletlerarası Tahkim*, 339; Abdel Wahab, 'Party Appointed Experts in International Commercial Arbitration', 181; Knoblach, *Sachverhaltsermittlung in Der Internationalen Wirtschaftsschiedsgerichtsbarkeit*, 189; O'Malley, *Rules of Evidence in International Arbitration*, 174; Ziya Akıncı and Ejder Yılmaz in Akıncı and Ekmen, 'Tartışmalar', 200–201; Can and Tuna, *Milletlerarası Tahkim Hukuku*, 412; Ağırman, *Milli & Milletlerarası Tahkim*, 459, 461; Geisinger, 'Advocacy in International Commercial Arbitration: What For?', 15; Meier, 'Germany', 3.1.2, para. 4; Borris et al., 'New York Convention, Article V [Grounds for Refusal of Recognition and Enforcement of Arbitral Awards]', para. 191; Ashford, *Handbook on International Commercial Arbitration*, 295; For instance, LMAA has a number of expert arbitrators in maritime dispute, *see* Erdoğan and Meral, 'Londra Deniz Ticareti Hakemleri Birliği(LMAA) Tahkimi İlişkin Genel Bir Değerlendirme', 1073.
22. Blackaby et al., *Redfern & Hunter on International Arbitration*, para. 6.135; Can and Tuna, *Milletlerarası Tahkim Hukuku*, 412; Industries such as energy, environment, intellectual property; ICC, ICC Arbitration and ADR Commission Report Resolving Climate Change Related Disputes through Arbitration and ADR, 2019, 19, para. 5.8 https://iccwbo.org/wp-content/uploads/sites/3/2019/11/icc-arbitration-adr-commission-report-on-resolving-climate-change-related-disputes-english-version.pdf (accessed 24 September 2025); In the construction industry, engineers and architects who have appropriate arbitral practice training, are also being appointed as arbitrators; O'Malley, *Rules of Evidence in International Arbitration*, 174; Abdel Wahab, 'Party Appointed Experts in International Commercial Arbitration', 183; Reiner and Aschauer, 'ICC Rules', 135; Knoblach, *Sachverhaltsermittlung in Der Internationalen Wirtschaftsschiedsgerichtsbarkeit*, 48–49; Uluç, *Corruption in International Arbitration*, 163.
23. Khodykin and Mulcahy, *A Guide to the IBA Rules on the Taking of Evidence in International Arbitration*, 281; Munday, *Cross & Tapper on Evidence*, 541.

resolving the issues in the case and rendering the award because they will not have the relevant expertise to decide on the matter.[24]

Despite being able to research themselves from various sources or ask a fellow from the corresponding field, arbitrators are expected to rely on something other than their personal information, save for exceptional situations.[25] In most arbitration laws and in practice, it is mandatory for an award to include reasoning.[26] Since arbitrators must indicate, *inter alia*, the *ratio* on which the award is based, a firm ratio is sometimes only possible with the help of an expert opinion.[27]

Therefore, it is clear that experts assist arbitral tribunals in the adjudication process and, even indirectly, have the potential to imperatively influence the proceedings and impact their outcome.[28]

It is even argued that after the selection of arbitrators, choosing an expert is the second most crucial aspect of arbitral proceedings.[29] The 2022 Queen Mary and Pinsent Masons survey revealed that 76% of the respondents selected technical expertise (tribunal/counsel/experts) as the most crucial procedural element once an arbitration commenced.[30]

A diligent arbitral tribunal would care about the personality and qualifications of the expert. For this reason, there is a strong argument that the experts and their reports

24. Lew, 'The Need for Expert Evidence?', 246; *see* Wilske and Gack, 'Expert Evidence in International Commercial Arbitration', 88; Proske, *Expert Witness Conferencing in Schiedsverfahren*, 1; for the same view for quantum issues *see* Jones, 'Redefining the Role and Value of Expert Evidence', 39. *See* Lee, 'Selecting the Expert Witness as an Arbitrator in Patent Arbitrations'.
25. Reiner and Aschauer, 'ICC Rules', 135; Schäfer and Wilson, 'ICC Bulletin', 2009, 20:23 ff.; This can cause problems as in *Adem Dogan v. Turkmenistan*, ICSID Case No. ARB/09/9, Decision on Annulment, 15 January 2016, para. 240 available at https://jusmundi.com/en/document/decision/en-adem-dogan-v-turkmenistan-decision-on-annulment-friday-15th-january-2016 (accessed 3 December 2022): 'Indeed, the Tribunal offered contradictory reasons when it rejected the FMV standard for lack of sufficient evidence to assign value to the Claimant's investment, and then applied its own artificial valuation method not supported by evidence.'
26. Direnisa, 'Hukuk Muhakemeleri Kanunu Çerçevesinde Tahkimde Hakem Kararlarının Gerekçesi Üzerine Düşünceler', 1551; Tanrıver, *Medenî Usûl Hukuku*, 2022, II:420; Kalpsüz, *Türkiye'de Milletlerarası Tahkim*, 142.
27. Schütze, Tscherning, and Wais, *Handbuch Des Schiedsverfahrens: Praxis Der Deutschen Und Internationalen Schiedsgerichtsbarkeit*, 222.
28. Respondents in the recent 'Evidence in International Arbitration Report' released on 6 September 2023, overwhelmingly (82%) considered that experts have a significant impact on the outcome of the case. *See* Australian Centre for International Commercial Arbitration and FTI Consulting, 'Evidence in International Arbitration Report'; Tanrıver, *Hukukumuzda Bilirkişilik*, 26; Wach and Petsch, 'Der Sachverständigenbeweis Im Schiedsverfahren: Grenzen Der Gestaltungsfreiheit von Parteien Und Schiedsgericht', 98; O'Malley, *Rules of Evidence in International Arbitration*, 168; Oetiker, 'Commentary on Art. 26-30 Swiss Rules of Arbitration', 313; Weiss and Bürgi Locatelli, 'Der Vom Schiedsgericht Bestellte Experte-Ein Überblick Aus Sicht Eines Internationalen Schiedsgerichts Mit Sitz in Der Schweiz', 499.
29. Moses, *The Principles and Practice of International Commercial Arbitration*, 197; Pitkowitz and Kathan-Spath, 'The Arbitrator and the Arbitration Procedure, The Vienna Propositions for Streamlining Arbitral Proceedings: Keeping Pace with New Developments and User Expectations', 145.
30. '2022 International Arbitration Survey: Future of International Energy Arbitration Survey Report', 32.

should be impartial, independent, and objective, just as arbitrators or judges themselves are. However, as will be demonstrated below, in most scenarios, meeting these requirements is a challenging task for experts appointed by the parties.

As in litigation, in international commercial arbitration, experts are either appointed by the arbitral tribunal ex officio or, upon request, by the parties. International commercial arbitration is a field in which civil and common law legal traditions collide, and question marks appear in some areas.

Currently, in international arbitration proceedings, on average, experts are involved in two-thirds of arbitrations, and there is a tendency to rely more on party-appointed experts.[31] Experts are appointed by the parties in 90% of arbitrations and 10% of arbitrations by the tribunal.[32] In particular, the expert opinion submitted by the parties leads to some problems (*party-appointed experts*).[33]

Where the experts are appointed by parties, realistically, the relevant party selects an expert who will strengthen their hand in terms of their case.[34] Naturally, there is a beneficial relationship because the party will directly pay the expert. It is likely that this situation causes the expert to preserve his/her opinion and, as argued by practitioners and scholars, engage in some advocacy, which could lead to the expert not being impartial or independent and the report not being objective.[35]

Blackaby et al. assert that 'one of the most unsatisfactory features of procedure in international commercial arbitration is the prevailing practice whereby the parties present conflicting expert evidence on matters of complex technical opinion'.[36]

31. For statistical proof *see* '2012 International Arbitration Survey: Present and Preferred Practices in the Arbitral Process', 26; Ünüvar, 'Experts: Investment Arbitration'; O'Malley, *Rules of Evidence in International Arbitration*, 145; Wilske and Markert, *Beck'scher Online-Kommentar ZPO*, § 1049 paras 9–10; Abdel Wahab, 'Party Appointed Experts in International Commercial Arbitration', 182; Webster and Bühler, *Handbook of ICC Arbitration: Commentary, Precedents, Materials*, 445; For reasons *see* Webster and Bühler, *Handbook of UNCITRAL Arbitration*, 421, 449, para. 29-04; Trittmann and Kasolowsky, 'Taking Evidence in Arbitration Proceedings Between Common Law and Civil Law Traditions', 330–340; Jones, 'Ineffective Use of Expert Evidence in Construction Arbitration', 2; Proske, *Expert Witness Conferencing in Schiedsverfahren*, 26.
32. '2012 International Arbitration Survey: Present and Preferred Practices in the Arbitral Process', 29; In another recent survey, 96% of respondents argued for a right to rely on party-appointed expert evidence in 'BCLP 2021 Survey', 9 ('BCLP Survey'); For similar results *see* IBA Arbitration Guidelines and Rules Subcommittee, 'Report on the Reception of the IBA Arbitration Soft Law Products', (International Bar Association, 2016), para. 45. (https://res.cloudinary.com/lbresearch/image/upload/v1474620896/soft_law_products_report_238116_954.pdf (accessed 24 September 2025)); Similarly Kurkela, Turunen, and Conflict Management Institute, *Due Process in International Commercial Arbitration*, 170.
33. To be dealt with in detail in Chapter 4; For critiques *see* Mosk, 'The Role of Facts in International Dispute Resolution (Volume 304)', 21.
34. The BCLP Survey shows that party-appointed experts are preferred in arbitration because parties and their representatives know more about the dispute and are more comfortable selecting the appropriate expert to assist them and the tribunal on the expertise required issues. The BCLP Survey was conducted with 289 international respondents, of whom the majority (75%) were from a common law background, and 44% were experts in various fields. *See* 'BCLP 2021 Survey', 17; Knoblach, *Sachverhaltsermittlung in Der Internationalen Wirtschaftsschiedsgerichtsbarkeit*, 280–281.
35. Kesikli, 'Milletlerarası Ticari Tahkimde Delillerin Değerlendirilmesi', 214.
36. Blackaby et al., *Redfern and Hunter on International Arbitration*, para. 6.138.

The use of party-appointed experts is deemed a crucial part of international arbitration and not something that can be ostracised from the procedure.[37] Contrary to procedural rules specific to evidence at state courts, the absence of regulations regarding the burden of proof, the standard of proof, the admissibility of or the weight to be given to expert opinion, and factors affecting admissibility or weight are the reasons for issues.[38]

A common framework that predictably regulates the use of party-appointed experts and their roles and duties in the process is needed.[39] Due to the problems described above, the focus is to improve and strengthen the effective use of party-appointed experts through rules and methods.

In the United Nations Commission on International Trade Law (UNCITRAL) Model Law, statutory laws of states, ICSID Convention and Rules, UNCITRAL Arbitration Rules, and the rules of many arbitral institutions, provisions are minimal and mostly non-existent.[40]

Some of the arbitration institutions like the ICC, German Arbitration Institute (DIS) and Belgian Centre for Arbitration and Mediation (CEPANI) stand out in the world of international dispute resolution in terms of the level of a certain degree of specific rules governing expert nomination, selection and appointment, the factors to consider in selecting them and the procedures to be followed to ensure their use. Additionally, the Chartered Institute of Arbitrator's Protocol for the Use of Party-Appointed Experts Witnesses in International Arbitration (CIArb Protocol) and the IBA Rules on the Taking of Evidence in International Arbitration (IBA Rules) and the DIS Practice Note on the Use of Experts in Arbitration (DIS Practice Note) also merit special attention for its detailed rules on party-appointed experts, which are important and widely used in international disputes.[41]

There must be coherence in practice governing different aspects of expert use and clarity in the rules and practices to be followed in this respect.[42] The main aim of establishing rules and methods is to ensure the neutrality and objectivity of the experts and cost-efficiency in the proceedings, thereby leading to a more qualified result.[43] In

37. Nessi, 'Expert Witness: Role and Independence', 72; Roney, 'Cross-Examination of Experts', 111.
38. Mbengue and Das, 'Rules Governing the Use of Experts in International Disputes', 451; Yıldızlı, *Uluslararası Tahkimde Zararın Degerlendirilmesi*, 122.
39. Nessi, 'Expert Witness: Role and Independence', 72; Ünüvar, 'Experts: Investment Arbitration', para. 57.
40. Patocchi, Paolo Michele and Niedermaier, 'UNCITRAL Rules', 1183 fn. 529; Blackaby and Wilbraham, 'Practical Issues Relating to the Use of Expert Evidence in Investment Treaty Arbitration', 656; Waincymer, *Procedure and Evidence in International Arbitration*, 945; Abdel Wahab, 'Party Appointed Experts in International Commercial Arbitration', 191; Nessi, 'Expert Witness: Role and Independence', 101; Jones, 'Redefining the Role and Value of Expert Evidence', 24.
41. Only 35 % of practitioners share the view, that the IBA Rules provide sufficient protection against party-appointed experts not being objective, in 'BCLP 2021 Survey', 9.
42. de Chazournes et al., 'The Expert in the International Adjudicative Process: Introduction to the Special Issue', 339.
43. Wach and Petsch, 'Der Sachverständigenbeweis Im Schiedsverfahren: Grenzen Der Gestaltungsfreiheit von Parteien Und Schiedsgericht', 92; Nessi, 'Expert Witness: Role and Independence', 101; Jones, 'Ineffective Use of Expert Evidence in Construction Arbitration', 4.

this regard, some non-binding rules and methods have been proposed to overcome the flaws related to experts. For example, the expert's impartiality and objectivity declaration, the experts joining together to prepare a joint opinion instead of a unilateral written report by each expert or expert conferencing.

However, more than non-binding rules and methods are required to ensure the effective functioning of the expert mechanism. In the absence of formal rules of evidence in arbitration, the lack of a code of conduct and the procedures governing experts vary between cases, which leads to critics even discussing the legitimacy of arbitration as a dispute resolution mechanism between investors and states.[44] Hence, much more detailed legal provisions are needed in arbitration laws to strengthen the framework.

In addition, a mandatory examination procedure is required to prove that the rules and methods are working correctly. The arbitral tribunal and the parties will perform this procedure during the hearing phase. First, the arbitral tribunal should always examine the experts' competencies and experience and whether they understand the issues of dispute in the case, the facts and the subject for which a statement of expertise is sought. Subsequently, in the cross-examination process, the attorneys of the parties will cross-examine the expert presented by the opposing party and their opinion and will want to create a negative opinion before the arbitral tribunal regarding the competence, impartiality, and objectivity of the expert and, ultimately, the opinion he[45] presented. Thus, it is necessary to conduct an examination when party-appointed experts have been relied upon.

At its 38th session, the United Nations Commission on International Trade Law (UNCITRAL) Working Group III requested the Secretariat to consider how possible work on 'damages and compensation' could be undertaken, stressing the role of experts (A/CN.9/1004, paragraph 104). Accordingly, the Working Group declared, among others, 'to consider whether to undertake work on the development of *treaty provisions, guidelines, or standards* for tribunals to address the following issues ... viii. The issue of the selection of experts and their ethical regime ...'.

Thus, the question this book will try to answer is as follows: 'What principles, rules or methods can solve the issues arising out of the use of party-appointed experts?'

Considering the sources encountered in international arbitration, only some provisions refer to party-appointed experts, and no clear duties and obligations are codified in institutional rules and national laws. Thus, remedies against experts appointed by the parties are limited, and tribunals are left with the challenging task of assessing their competence to decide such issues, as well as assessing disqualification requests or, primarily, the weight of two different professional opinions. This leads to both parties' efforts being wasted and the tribunal being placed in a difficult position, which in the end results in timely and costly judgments.[46]

---

44. *See* Hodgson and Stewart, 'Experts in Investor-State Arbitration: The Tribunal as Gatekeeper', 458.
45. For better readability, the male form is used in the text. Nevertheless, all information in this document refers to members of both genders on equal terms.
46. Knoblach, *Sachverhaltsermittlung in Der Internationalen Wirtschaftsschiedsgerichtsbarkeit*, 282.

2 AIM

This book aims to examine the importance and impact of both tribunal-appointed and party-appointed experts in the realm of international arbitration proceedings (*Chapters 1–2*), identify the problems resulting from the use of party-appointed experts in international arbitration proceedings (*Chapter 3*), examine the already proposed solutions to the issues (*Chapter 4*), and critically assess which solutions would overcome the shortcomings to the problems encountered in practice, especially to the problems that lead to inefficiency of the proceedings (*Chapters 4–5*).

In particular, this thesis aims to achieve the following objectives:

- Determining the underlying reasons that lead to problems in practice originating from the use of party-appointed experts.
- Suggesting solutions to the issues in practice arising from the use of party-appointed experts.
- Contributing to the more effective use of party-appointed experts in international arbitration proceedings.
- Preventing the annulment of arbitral awards and the denial of recognition and enforcement of arbitral awards due to issues relating to party-appointed experts.

3 SCOPE AND LIMITS

This thesis discusses both tribunal-appointed and party-appointed experts who have an essential place in international commercial and investment arbitration, their qualifications, functions and roles, impact on proceedings, problems and possible solutions within the scope of modern international commercial and international investment arbitration rules and practice. In principle, a comparison between court-appointed and tribunal-appointed experts and the use of experts before courts is not included in the scope of this study. The liability of experts in international arbitration will also not be examined.

The author is conscious that experts are being encountered in the proceedings at domestic courts in litigation, and many other international courts and tribunals such as the Court of Justice of the European Union (CJEU),[47] World Trade Organization (WTO),[48] International Court of Justice (ICJ),[49] Permanent Court of Arbitration (PCA), International Criminal Court (ICrC), the International Tribunal for the Law of the Sea

47. *See* Van Damme, 'The Assessment of Expert Evidence in International Adjudication', 402.
48. *See* Valles, 'Different Forms of Expert Involvement in WTO Dispute Settlement Proceedings', 367–378; Plant, 'Expert Evidence and the Challenge of Procedural Reform in International Dispute Settlement', 464–472.
49. *See* Bennouna, 'Experts Before the International Court of Justice: What For?', 345–351; White, *The Use of Experts by International Tribunals*, 109; *see* Corfu Channel (*United Kingdom of Great Britain and Northern Ireland v. Albania*) where the court made use of, among other, naval experts. https://www.icj-cij.org/en/case/1 (accessed 3 June 2022).

(ITLOS),[50] and Iran-United States Claims Tribunal, however, will in principle not include those aspects, as it would enlarge the thesis to a multi-volume study. Nevertheless, references will be made in the footnotes as deemed fruitful since similarities can be drawn and applied uniformly in international dispute resolution.[51] For convenience reasons, while referring to investment and commercial arbitration, the term 'international arbitration' will be used.

The relationships of the experts with the arbitral tribunal and the parties, their role in the proceedings, and their contribution to the formation of the arbitral award will be evaluated, considering various legislations, arbitration rules, and soft law instruments. Additionally, problems in practice will be discussed, and solutions will be proposed. Furthermore, after the arbitral award, the effect of the expert and the expert opinion on set-aside and recognition and enforcement procedures will also be examined.

In this direction, international rules and practices, as well as legislation, case law, and practices of many jurisdictions, such as Türkiye, Germany, Switzerland, England, the USA, France, and Singapore, will be analysed and examined within the scope of the study. In this respect, the court practices of experts in countries subject to different legal systems will be mentioned only in a limited way and to the extent necessary in order to understand the notion of experts, analyse similarities and draw conclusions to propose solutions to the problems.

4 RESEARCH METHODOLOGY

In this study, more than one research method was used, such as theoretical, comparative, and qualitative research. In this context, sources and elements of international arbitration proceedings, like statutes of states, international arbitration rules, court and arbitration decisions, guidelines, surveys, and doctrinal works, will be used.

Considering, researching and analysing all these data sets, the problems and elements that will serve a more effective and efficient use of experts will be determined theoretically and practically. In other words, possible issues in laws and rules will be determined from the relevant texts, expert-sourced problems in the arbitration practice will be determined by court decisions and arbitral awards published in free and paid databases, and suggestions will be presented to these problems both on the basis of norm (i.e., principles, guidelines, rules) and practice (i.e., method).

5 LITERATURE REVIEW AND GAP ANALYSIS

Among others, *Schneider, Jones, and Kantor have been addressing the issues of* international arbitration experts for more than 30 years.

50. *See* Gautier, 'Experts Before ITLOS: An Overview of the Tribunal's Practice'.
51. Mbengue and Das, 'Rules Governing the Use of Experts in International Disputes', 434.

Kantor argued that 'no protocol or code can regulate the ability of a party to hire an expert who is just a good actor or actress'[52] and 'who is able to appear objective while delivering fundamentally partisan evidence'.[53]

Although the IBA Rules and the CIArb Protocol have concretely tried to prevent the problems over the years, they have left unanswered how an expert can, in fact, be independent and not merely show independence.[54] The IBA Rules require the report to contain a statement on the party-appointed expert's independence. It is not clear from the language of Article 5 whether any lack of independence in that regard would disqualify or discredit the conclusions submitted by the party-appointed expert.

Thus, there appears to be a significant disagreement on certain aspects of the use of party-appointed experts in the arbitral procedure, while certain vital legal concepts relevant to experts have different meanings for different individuals involved in the same legal system. Disagreements range from the roles played by party-appointed or tribunal-appointed experts, the use of invisible experts, admissibility, the burden of proof and the merits of methods such as cross-examination to the definitions of terms such as independence, impartiality and neutrality.

52. Kantor, 'A Code of Conduct for Party-Appointed Experts in International Arbitration: Can One Be Found?', 335.
53. Kantor, 335.
54. Jones, 'Ineffective Use of Expert Evidence in Construction Arbitration', 7.

CHAPTER 1

Use of Experts in International Arbitration

1.1 OVERVIEW

The *civil* and *common law* divide clearly emerges once again regarding the usage of experts in international arbitration.[55] As naturally expected, arbitrators and counsel should bring their legal culture to proceedings.[56]

There are observable differences in the use of experts, depending on the tradition. There may even be various usages within the tradition.[57]

55. *See* Lew, 'The Need for Expert Evidence?', 246–247; Punwar and Appel, 'Weighing the Evidence: Experts and Witnesses Versus Documentary Evidence', 153.
56. Wilske and Gack, 'Expert Evidence in International Commercial Arbitration', 77; Lew, Mistelis, and Kröll, *Comparative International Commercial Arbitration*, 554; Kaufmann-Kohler, 'Globalization of Arbitral Procedure', 1330; Baker and Greenwood, 'In Search of an Exemplary International Construction Arbitration' 181; Bernard, 'The Conduct of the Hearings' 636; Newman and Klieman, *Take the Witness: The Experts Speak on Cross Examination*, 55; Risse and Haller, 'Die "IBA-Regeln" Zur Beweisaufnahme in Der Internationalen Schiedsgerichtsbarkeit' 118; Lew, Mistelis, and Kröll, *Comparative International Commercial Arbitration*, 554; Uluç, *Evidence-Taking in National and International Arbitration: The Reconciliation of Civil Law and Common Law Traditions*, 25; Allen, Jr., 'Overview: The Common Law Systems', 20; Kurkela, Turunen, and Conflict Management Institute, *Due Process in International Commercial Arbitration*, 173; Geisinger, 'Advocacy in International Commercial Arbitration: What For?', 9.
57. 'On the other hand, one must acknowledge the danger of supposing that there is a single, uniform "common law approach" to anything. The daily local practice experience of the Edinburgh attorney is likely to share little with that of her counterpart in Walla Walla. And even within the framework of a single jurisdiction and a single specialty practice area, each case is unique. Just as one can never step twice into the same river, no lawyer in any jurisdiction, whether grounded in civil or common law, will or can behave in precisely the same way in two different matters. The realisation that varying responses may be possible not only in different cases but also within a single case means that it is not really credible to speak confidently about an unswerving "French approach" or "American approach" in any given procedural arena' *See* Allen, Jr., 'Overview: The Common Law Systems', 15; *see* for details of court practices of court and party-appointed experts in various countries Proske, *Expert witness conferencing in Schiedsverfahren*, 13–25; Aygül, *Milletlerarası Ticarî Tahkimde Tahkim Usûlüne Uygulanacak Hukuk ve Deliller*, 265.

In the *common law* legal tradition, which is followed by states like Australia, England,[58] Singapore and the United States, expert opinion is generally adduced in an adversarial system where the parties bring their experts.[59] The appointment of a court- or tribunal-appointed expert is relatively rare.[60] Some jurisdictions also allow court- or tribunal-appointed experts.[61]

In this approach of expert usage, the party engages early with an expert, provides all necessary documents, instructs the expert, outlines issues to be addressed, prepares the expert for testimony and examination, and pays his fee.[62]

This kind of expert is preferred over tribunal-appointed experts primarily to have greater control of the evidence since the party is consciously engaging a specific expert whom they believe would have a positive impact on the claim and is preparing the expert for examination to ensure the party's arguments succeed.[63] Additionally, despite their opposing positions, the party-appointed experts bring divergent views,[64] and hence, the authors argue that this creates a better picture for the tribunal when rendering a decision.[65]

Civil law jurisdictions like Türkiye, Germany, Switzerland, Austria, and France, where the adjudicators bear to a certain degree of investigative responsibilities, adopt a lesser adversarial system of taking evidence than the stark adversarial approach in most common law countries.[66] In this approach, arbitrators are endowed with broad

58. Although it is part of the common law, the revised Code of English Civil Procedure has adopted a more civil law approach by encouraging single joint experts and promoting expert neutrality. *See* for details CPR 35 in justice.gov.uk/courts/procedure-rules/civil/rules/part35; Yazıcı-Tıktık, 'HMK m. 293'teki Uzman Görüşü Kurumu Ile Anglo-Sakson Hukuk Sistemindeki Uzman Tanık Kurumunun Karşılaştırılması', 84.
59. Allen, Jr., 'United States', 289; Waincymer, 'Advocacy Training in International Commercial and Investment Arbitration', 61; Schiau, 'An Arbitration Dilemma', 335; Punwar and Appel, 'Weighing the Evidence: Experts and Witnesses Versus Documentary Evidence', 158.
60. Allen, Jr., 'Overview: The Common Law Systems', 19.
61. Elsing and Townsend, 'Bridging the Common Law-Civil Law Divide in Arbitration', 59–65; Lim, 'Tribunal-Appointed Experts in International Arbitration', 208; Jones, 'Ineffective Use of Expert Evidence in Construction Arbitration', 1; Knoblach, *Sachverhaltsermittlung in Der Internationalen Wirtschaftsschiedsgerichtsbarkeit*, 274; Proske, *Expert Witness Conferencing in Schiedsverfahren*, 13; Yazıcı-Tıktık, 'HMK m. 293'teki Uzman Görüşü Kurumu ile Anglo-Sakson Hukuk Sistemindeki Uzman Tanık Kurumunun Karşılaştırılması', 80; *see* Toraman, 'Anglo-Amerikan Hukukunda Mahkeme Tarafından Tayin Edilen Bilirkişiler Court-Appointed Experts in Anglo-American Law'; Allen, Jr., 'United States', 289.
62. Liebscher, Mosimann and Schmidt-Ahrendts, 'Handbuch Schiedsgerichtsbarkeit', 403; Proske, *Expert Witness Conferencing in Schiedsverfahren*, 28.
63. Knoblach, *Sachverhaltsermittlung in Der Internationalen Wirtschaftsschiedsgerichtsbarkeit*, 282, Proske, *Expert Witness Conferencing in Schiedsverfahren*, 27, 48; Hoffmann and Shetty, 'Evidence and Hearings', 215.
64. Lew, Mistelis, and Kröll, *Comparative International Commercial Arbitration*, 577–578.
65. Jones, 'Party Appointed Expert Witnesses in International Arbitration: A Protocol at Last', 154; Knoblach, *Sachverhaltsermittlung in Der Internationalen Wirtschaftsschiedsgerichtsbarkeit*, 283.
66. Yeşilirmak, *Türkiye'de Ticari Hayatın ve Yatırım Ortamının Iyileştirilmesi Için Uyuşmazlıkların Etkin Cözümünde Dogrudan Görüşme, Arabuluculuk, Hakem-Bilirkişilik ve Tahkim: Sorunlar ve Cözüm Önerileri*, 114; Reiner, 'Austria', 67.

powers.[67] As a result, court- or tribunal-appointed experts are the leading practice in this approach.[68]

Although arbitral statutes and rules foresee the appointment of party-appointed experts, in countries like Germany and Switzerland, these are seen as part of the party's own submissions and have far less value, in contrast to a court or tribunal-appointed expert.[69]

International arbitration is a melting pot where different legal traditions collide and merge to a certain degree, at least in some aspects.[70] As a result, both tribunal and party-appointed experts are foreseen in the UNCITRAL Model Law, international agreements, arbitration rules and guidelines and are applied in practice.[71] As a result, common law tools such as the use of party-appointed experts and cross-examination became ordinary procedures even in international arbitration cases where the tribunal and parties both have a civil law background.[72]

The numbers show that experts are appointed more regularly in common lawyers' arbitrations (77%) than in civil lawyers' arbitrations (57%).[73] Stakeholders in international arbitration find party-appointed experts more effective (43%), whereas a slightly smaller number (31%) finds tribunal-appointed experts more effective. In support of the former, some argue that tribunal-appointed experts are exceptional in ICC Arbitration practice.[74] Consistent with domestic litigation practice and culture, more civil lawyers (43%) than common lawyers (19%) found tribunal-appointed experts more effective.[75]

67. Reiner, 'Austria', 21.
68. Poudret and Besson, *Comparative Law of International Arbitration*, 560; For instance, in Türkiye and France, experts are being appointed from a formally qualified list of independent experts; Proske, *Expert Witness Conferencing in Schiedsverfahren*, 14. Austria *see* Reiner, 'Austria', 75; Waincymer, 'Advocacy Training in International Commercial and Investment Arbitration', 61.
69. Lim, 'Tribunal-Appointed Experts in International Arbitration', 208; Wilske and Gack, 'Expert Evidence in International Commercial Arbitration', 79.
70. Wilske and Gack, 'Expert Evidence in International Commercial Arbitration', 81; Van Houtte, 'Party-Appointed Experts and Tribunal-Appointed Experts'; Jones, 'Ineffective Use of Expert Evidence in Construction Arbitration', 1; Knoblach, *Sachverhaltsermittlung in Der Internationalen Wirtschaftsschiedsgerichtsbarkeit*, 45.
71. Aygül, *Milletlerarası Ticarî Tahkimde Tahkim Usûlüne Uygulanacak Hukuk ve Deliller*, 271; Proske, *Expert Witness Conferencing in Schiedsverfahren*, 25; Yıldızlı, *Uluslararası Tahkimde Zararın Degerlendirilmesi*, 122.
72. Proske, *Expert Witness Conferencing in Schiedsverfahren*, 27; Atlı, 'Uluslararası Tahkim Sempozyumu', 142; Patocchi arguing in the same direction in Uşan, *Uluslararası Tahkim Sempozyumu 25–26 April (Nisan) 2019*, 194.
73. '2012 International Arbitration Survey: Present and Preferred Practices in the Arbitral Process', 29. The interviewees who preferred tribunal-appointed experts said that party-appointed experts often act as partisan advocates for the party who appointed them, which regularly results in the appointment of a third (tribunal-appointed) expert. According to them, a system whereby an expert is appointed by the tribunal from the outset would bring a more neutral expert opinion, as well as save time and money; *see* Lim, 'Tribunal-Appointed Experts in International Arbitration', 207–208.
74. Varga, *Beweiserhebung in Transatlantischen Schiedsverfahren: Eine Suche Nach Kompromissen Zwischen Deutscher Und US-Amerikanischer Beweisrechtstradition*, 212.
75. Hodgson and Stewart, 'Experts in Investor-State Arbitration: The Tribunal as Gatekeeper', 457; Nessi, 'Expert Witness: Role and Independence', 73–74.

A survey shows that parties and lawyers with knowledge of the dispute are better placed than the tribunal in selecting appropriate experts.[76] Some argue even that tribunal-appointed experts are exceptional in ICC Arbitration practice.[77]

Appointed either by the tribunal or by the parties in international arbitration, experts can be categorised based on the subject on which they provide expertise as technical (scientific), legal and quantum (valuation) experts.

The general function of experts is to provide a well-reasoned, objective, and impartial opinion.[78] Each of these experts clarifies disputed or related issues that have a material outcome of the case, which the arbitrators are not able to do due to a lack of special and technical knowledge. Thus, they support arbitral tribunals in the decision-making process.[79]

Like witnesses of fact, experts are being directly and cross-examined.[80]

1.2 DEFINITION

In international arbitration, there is no universally agreed-upon definition of what constitutes an expert or expert evidence.

The *Merriam-Webster Dictionary* defines an expert as 'one with the special skill or knowledge representing mastery of a particular subject'.[81] The *Oxford Dictionary* defines an expert as 'a person with special knowledge, skill or training in something'.[82] The *Cambridge Dictionary* defines an expert as 'a person with a high level of knowledge or skill relating to a particular subject or activity'.[83] The *Black's Law Dictionary* defines an expert as 'a person that had knowledge and skills learned over years of experience in a subject'. Their opinions can be helpful in problem-solving.[84]

Taking into account these definitions, an expert differentiates himself from a non-expert with a high level of special knowledge, skill, training, or experience in a particular subject or activity.

Experts are, in essence, qualified, impartial, objective and reputable individuals or organisations who have special training, education, skills or knowledge and experience

---

76. 'BCLP 2021 Survey', 17.
77. Varga, *Beweiserhebung in Transatlantischen Schiedsverfahren: Eine Suche Nach Kompromissen Zwischen Deutscher Und US-Amerikanischer Beweisrechtstradition*, 212.
78. de Chazournes et al., 'Uses of Experts Before International Courts and Tribunals', 492, 495.
79. Wach and Petsch, 'Der Sachverständigenbeweis Im Schiedsverfahren: Grenzen Der Gestaltungsfreiheit von Parteien Und Schiedsgericht', 95; O'Malley, *Rules of Evidence in International Arbitration*, 171; Abdel Wahab, 'Party Appointed Experts in International Commercial Arbitration', 182; Knoblach, *Sachverhaltsermittlung in Der Internationalen Wirtschaftsschiedsgerichtsbarkeit*, 265.
80. Wilske and Gack, 'Expert Evidence in International Commercial Arbitration', 79.
81. Merriam-Webster.com Dictionary, 'expert', https://www.merriam-webster.com/dictionary/expert (accessed 3 July 2022).
82. *Oxford Learner's Dictionaries*, 'expert', https://www.oxfordlearnersdictionaries.com/definition/english/expert_1 (accessed 3 July 2022).
83. *Cambridge Dictionary*, 'expert', https://dictionary.cambridge.org/dictionary/english/expert (accessed 3 July 2022).
84. The *Law Dictionary*, 'expert', https://thelawdictionary.org/expert/ (accessed 3 July 2022).

falling within their expertise and can be consulted for the resolution of a dispute before a court and/or tribunal.[85] Experts in arbitration are an essential means that present information and opinion on matters that (generally) fall outside the expertise of counsel and the tribunal.[86]

In the international arbitration context, an expert is someone who gives his opinion on specific matters before an adjudicated case to help the arbitrators solve the issues in a case with the help of the given opinion.[87]

Experts explain special factual situations in which the arbitrator cannot rely on his own knowledge derived from the case.[88] The expert contextualises the facts and evidence.[89]

Experts should not only have extended experience and track records in the field but also have a good understanding of how to engage adjudicative bodies and how to prepare a proper, readable opinion directed at an average adult person.[90]

A negative definition also helps reinforce the understanding; thus, stating what an expert is conceptually not might diminish confusion. Since an expert does not, in principle, identify, clarify, or interpret the law, opine on how the law is to be applied to the facts, take into account, and weigh the evidence, he is not an adjudicator.[91] Additionally, the expert does not frame legal claims, develop legal arguments, or present evidence, which is the role of the legal counsel. Hence, he is not a lawyer representing the client in the case.[92]

Although experts are highly likely to testify before an arbitral tribunal, the expert is not a witness. A witness is a person who makes representations to adjudicators about the veracity of facts.[93] Notwithstanding the frequent use of the term 'expert witness', the roles of a witness and an expert are distinct and should not be confounded.[94] The witness will testify on knowledge of the fact that he/she has been witness to through his sense organs, whereas the expert will state an opinion based on his experience and knowledge on a particular matter.[95]

---

85. Tanrıver, *Hukukumuzda Bilirkişilik*, 25; *see* Cayan, *Medeni Usul Hukukunda Bilirkişilik Müessesesi*, 3 ff.; Van Damme, 'The Assessment of Expert Evidence in International Adjudication', 402; Mosk, 'The Role of Facts in International Dispute Resolution (Volume 304)', 126.
86. Bor, 'Expert Evidence', 503; Lew, 'The Need for Expert Evidence?', 247.
87. O'Malley, *Rules of Evidence in International Arbitration*, 145.
88. Tanrıver, *Hukukumuzda Bilirkişilik*, 25.
89. Flett, 'When Is an Expert Not an Expert?', 355.
90. *See* Blackaby and Wilbraham, 'Practical Issues Relating to the Use of Expert Evidence in Investment Treaty Arbitration', 662.
91. Flett, 'When Is an Expert Not an Expert?', 354.
92. Flett, 354.
93. *See also* Alvarez, 'The Search for Objectivity: The Use of Experts in Philip Morris v Uruguay', 411.
94. *See* Taşdemir, 'İngiliz ve Amerikan Medenî Yargılamasında Uzman Tanıklık'.
95. Alvarez, 'The Search for Objectivity: The Use of Experts in Philip Morris v Uruguay', 411–412; Akıncı, *Milletlerarası Tahkim*, 341; *see* Sandifer, *Evidence Before International Tribunals*, 382–402.

1.3 GENERAL FUNCTION, ROLE, AND POSITION OF EXPERTS

Experts are primarily appointed to clarify disputed issues that have a material outcome to the case, which the arbitrators are not able to do due to a lack of special and/or technical knowledge and thus support tribunals in the decision-making process.[96] Experts generally do not relate to the direct reconstruction of past events, although they may elucidate causes and effects and can establish facts.[97] The parties' confidence factor in the final award can be greatly enhanced by the belief that crucial issues have been given the benefit of exposure and analysis by an expert.[98]

If the arbitrator on its own can access the required knowledge to decide the matter, no expert is needed, with the condition that parties have been given a fair opportunity to address the issues on which the arbitral tribunal relies.[99] However, this does not mean that the arbitrator should act as both expert and arbitrator ('in camera expertise proceeding').[100] The contrary position would mean outsourcing the adjudicatory

96. Lew, 'The Need for Expert Evidence?', 249; Wach and Petsch, 'Der Sachverständigenbeweis Im Schiedsverfahren: Grenzen Der Gestaltungsfreiheit von Parteien Und Schiedsgericht', 95; *see* D'Aspremont and Mbengue, 'Strategies of Engagement with Scientific Fact-Finding in International Adjudication'; O'Malley, *Rules of Evidence in International Arbitration*, 171; Abdel Wahab, 'Party Appointed Experts in International Commercial Arbitration', 182; White, *The Use of Experts by International Tribunals*, 163; Kamya-Lukoda, 'Role of Expert Witnesses in Construction Arbitration: Delay and Disruption and Quantum Issues', 79; Jones, 'Ineffective Use of Expert Evidence in Construction Arbitration', 1; Proske, *Expert Witness Conferencing in Schiedsverfahren*, 3.
97. Erdoğan and Üçüncü, 'Bilirkişilik Kurumu ve Bilirkişi Raporunun Delil Değerine İlişkin Bazı Sorunlar', 359–360; Kurkela, Turunen, and Conflict Management Institute, *Due Process in International Commercial Arbitration*, 169; Meier, 'Germany', 1, para. 5.
98. Allison and Holtzmann, 'The Tribunal's Use of Experts', 282.
99. Wach and Petsch, 'Der Sachverständigenbeweis Im Schiedsverfahren: Grenzen Der Gestaltungsfreiheit von Parteien Und Schiedsgericht', 95; O'Malley argues that even if an arbitrator is an expert in a field relating to the dispute since the role of the arbitrator is evaluating the evidence and not producing it, he cannot act as an expert itself. *See* O'Malley, *Rules of Evidence in International Arbitration*, 175–176. Similarly, Theune, 'DIS Rules', 266; The ICC Commission on Arbitration and ADR foresees in its report on 'Resolving Climate Change Related Disputes through Arbitration and ADR' that any technical knowledge or understanding by a non-lawyer arbitrator who is an expert in other scientific or technical fields would nevertheless need to be provided to the parties for comment on the relevant matter, before being applied in making any award or decision. *See* 'ICC Commission Report on Resolving Climate Change Related Disputes through Arbitration and ADR', 20, para. 5.8; Khodykin and Mulcahy, *A Guide to the IBA Rules on the Taking of Evidence in International Arbitration*, 290; Knoblach, *Sachverhaltsermittlung in Der Internationalen Wirtschaftsschiedsgerichtsbarkeit*, 218; *see* Ashford, *The IBA Rules on the Taking of Evidence in International Arbitration*, 110, para. 5.2.
100. Theune, 'DIS Rules', 266; Lachmann, *Handbuch Für Die Schiedsgerichtspraxis*, para. 1533; Knoblach, *Sachverhaltsermittlung in Der Internationalen Wirtschaftsschiedsgerichtsbarkeit*, 219; Khodykin and Mulcahy, *A Guide to the IBA Rules on the Taking of Evidence in International Arbitration*, 286; Schäfer and Wilson, 'ICC Bulletin', 2021, 65:

> If the dispute involves specialized knowledge other than the applicable law (which falls squarely within the tribunal's duties) and only one member of a three-arbitrator tribunal possesses the required expert knowledge, the situation becomes more complex because of the need to avoid a de facto in camera expertise proceeding. In other words, unless the parties expressly agree, it is neither expected nor recommended that one arbitrator will perform an independent expert investigation or evaluation on which the other arbitrators would rely in making their decision. Many problems exist with this

mandate[101] and harm not only the cost-efficiency of the proceedings but also the right to due process.[102] This should, however, be differentiated if the specific arbitrator was chosen intentionally as someone who is an expert on a subject, e.g., construction engineering.[103]

The expert should assist the arbitral tribunal in making a proper legal decision.[104] The experts' role must not be considered in isolation, but is always relative to the overriding competence and function of the arbitral tribunal.[105]

Experts may assist an arbitral tribunal in identifying the proper sources and offer additional support for a factual assertion, opine on conflicting legal rules and evidence, help the tribunal in selecting from the available facts or evidence and express views on the burdens of proof along with the weight of other evidence relative to applicable legal standards.[106] (Tribunal-appointed) experts may evaluate and summarise the opinions of party-appointed experts and add further interpretations for the tribunal.[107]

Furthermore, the expert can be the original source of facts in the sense that the expert observed, assessed and organised the facts after an inspection on site.[108] The expert can be relied upon in support of the validity and general acceptance of using a specific (scientific) methodology and of the results of its application to the facts in the case.[109]

While this is a general rule and application, there are circumstances in which experts play other roles. For instance, some party-appointed experts may assist the pleadings of the case even before the proceedings begin.[110]

---

approach, not the least of which is that it reduces the parties' ability to comment on, ask questions about and, if appropriate, challenge what the expert has done.

101. Liebscher, Mosimann, and Schmidt-Ahrendts, 'Handbuch Schiedsgerichtsbarkeit', 403.
102. Alvarez, 'The Search for Objectivity: The Use of Experts in Philip Morris v Uruguay', 412; Zuberbühler et al., *IBA Rules of Evidence*, 154; O'Malley, *Rules of Evidence in International Arbitration*, 167.
103. Knoblach, *Sachverhaltsermittlung in Der Internationalen Wirtschaftsschiedsgerichtsbarkeit*, 219; Schütze, 'Beweisaufnahme Nach Civil Law', 31, 33; Musielak and Voit, *ZPO*, § 1042, para. 22.
104. Senogles, 'Some Views from the Crucible: The Perspective of an Expert Witness on the Adversarial Principle', 363.
105. White, *The Use of Experts by International Tribunals*, 164.
106. Tanrıver, *Hukukumuzda Bilirkişilik*, 25; Alvarez, 'The Search for Objectivity: The Use of Experts in Philip Morris v Uruguay', 418; White argues that the expert should not identify which facts are relevant and significant nor assess and weigh them. White, *The Use of Experts by International Tribunals*, 165.
107. Van Damme, 'The Assessment of Expert Evidence in International Adjudication', 402; O'Malley, *Rules of Evidence in International Arbitration*, 174.
108. Tanrıver, *Hukukumuzda Bilirkişilik*, 25; Van Damme, 'The Assessment of Expert Evidence in International Adjudication', 402; O'Malley, *Rules of Evidence in International Arbitration*, 186; Özbek, *Tahkim Hukuku*, II:1448.
109. Proske, *Expert witness conferencing in Schiedsverfahren*, 3; Van Damme, 'The Assessment of Expert Evidence in International Adjudication', 403.
110. Lew, Mistelis, and Kröll, *Comparative International Commercial Arbitration*, 578; Parlett, 'Parties' Engagement with Experts in International Litigation', 441.

The expert is appointed not only to present the position of the appointer but also sometimes to oppose the counterparty's expert opinion or even the opinion of the tribunal-appointed expert.[111]

Experts (ought to) only present their professional opinions in cases. It would be inappropriate to accept that the expert's conclusions are the truth or even the fact itself, but the tribunal will establish the facts based on the expert's opinion and might even draw separate conclusions based on legitimate reasons.[112]

Therefore, the presence of an expert does not in itself mean that the arbitrator will directly, without weighing and assessing the opinion, incorporate the opinion into the award. This would delegate its function as an adjudicator to an expert, which is not permitted in international arbitration.[113] The arbitrator will have the final word on how to assess the facts and disputed issues and whether or not to rely on the expert's opinion.[114] Arbitrators will perform subsumption, not experts.[115]

Investment arbitrators, counsel and experts generally have the view that, regardless of whether the experts are acting on the instruction of the party or the tribunal, the expert's duty is owed to the tribunal in both cases.[116]

Despite practical differences, there is an overall consensus on the principle that the general function of experts is to provide a well-reasoned, independent, and impartial opinion.[117] Nevertheless, there are positions in which the party-appointed expert's additional role is to support the appointing party in its arguments.[118]

---

111. Wach and Petsch, 'Der Sachverständigenbeweis Im Schiedsverfahren: Grenzen Der Gestaltungsfreiheit von Parteien Und Schiedsgericht', 94–95.
112. Bennouna, 'Experts Before the International Court of Justice: What For?', 345–346.
113. Blackaby et al., *Redfern and Hunter on International Arbitration (Student Version)*, para. 6.135; Wach and Petsch, 'Der Sachverständigenbeweis Im Schiedsverfahren: Grenzen Der Gestaltungsfreiheit von Parteien Und Schiedsgericht', 97; Zuberbühler et al., *IBA Rules of Evidence*, 154; Oetiker, 'Commentary on Art. 26-30 Swiss Rules of Arbitration', 312; Schneider, 'Technical Experts in International Arbitration', 452; White, *The Use of Experts by International Tribunals*, 164.

    See Suez, *Sociedad General De Aguas De Barcelona S.A. And Vivendi Universal S.A. v. Argentine Republic* (ICSID Case No. ARB/03/19) Decision On Argentina's Application For Annulment, para. 306:

    > endogenous factors amounted to a 'significant' contribution within the meaning of Article 25(2)(b) and thus excluded the state of necessity defense. This, however, is a legal assessment on which neither of the economic expert reports could opine. In fact, if the Tribunal had looked for guidance on this legal question in any of the expert reports, it could have been found to have committed the same annullable error that the Enron committee found, i.e., deference to an economic expert report where the tribunal should have made its own legal assessment of a requirement under international law.

114. Wach and Petsch, 'Der Sachverständigenbeweis Im Schiedsverfahren: Grenzen Der Gestaltungsfreiheit von Parteien Und Schiedsgericht', 97; Lörcher, 'Liber Amicorum Karl-Heinz Böckstiegel', 485.
115. Tanrıver, 'Hukuk Yargısı Bağlamında Bilirkişilikle Ilgili Temel Problemler ve Cözüm Arayışları', 576.
116. de Chazournes et al., 'Uses of Experts Before International Courts and Tribunals', 492, 495.
117. de Chazournes et al., 492, 495.
118. de Chazournes et al., 492, 495.

1.4 TYPES OF EXPERTS

In this section, the various types of experts encountered in international arbitration are categorised, and information on their qualifications and peculiarities is provided.

Experts can be categorised based on the appointing authority (section 1.4.1) or on the subject (section 1.4.2) on which they will give an opinion.

Based on the appointing authority, experts are either appointed/chosen by the parties (section 1.4.1.1) or appointed by the arbitral tribunal (section 1.4.1.2). Based on the subject on which the expert will provide an opinion, they can be classified as technical/scientific experts (section 1.4.2.1), legal experts (section 1.4.2.2), and quantum (valuation) experts (section 1.4.2.3).

Generally speaking, in international arbitration, more than one category of experts is used in a single case.[119]

1.4.1 Based on the Appointing Authority

1.4.1.1 Party-Appointed Experts[120]

The common law system is heavily adversarial in nature, meaning that the parties to the case bear the primary responsibility to establish the facts of the case. Although found in the civil law system, party-appointed experts are a main characteristic element of this legal culture.[121] International arbitration practice prefers the use of party-appointed experts.[122]

1.4.1.1.1 Definition

A party-appointed expert is a person or organisation appointed by a party in order to report on specific issues determined by the party (IBA Rules Definitions).[123]

As the definition indicates, this type of expert is an expert in the sense of the definition made in section 1.2 of Chapter 1;[124] however, he or she is instructed and

119. Kalpsüz, *Türkiye'de Milletlerarası Tahkim*, 92.
120. As party-appointed experts will be comprehensively discussed in the next chapter, only the definition and function of party-appointed experts are discussed here.
121. Nessi, 'Expert Witness: Role and Independence', 75.
122. Feutrill and Rubins, 'The Preparation of Expert Evidence in International Commercial Arbitration: Practical Aspects', 307.
123. Pekcanıtez, 'Özel Uzman', 397; Kesikli, 'Milletlerarası Ticari Tahkimde Delillerin Değerlendirilmesi', 212; For definitions in Turkish law *see* Elyıldırım, *Hukuk Yargılamasında Uzman Görüşü*, 30–31; Aygül, *Milletlerarası Ticarî Tahkimde Tahkim Usûlüne Uygulanacak Hukuk ve Deliller*, 271; Schneider, 'Technical Experts in International Arbitration', 447; Hacıbekiroğlu, *Milletlerarası Tahkim Hukukunda Deliller ve Delillerin Degerlendirilmesi*, 124; Hobér and Sussman, *Cross-Examination in International Arbitration*, 22.
124. *See* pages 14-15.

compensated by the party to the dispute.[125] This distinguishes it from a tribunal-appointed expert and has a different legal nature.[126]

Parties in international arbitration practice generally desire to have control over experts from selection until cross-examination.[127] This is why parties appoint their own expert.[128] Parties, by choosing their expert, can put forward their case on why the evidence of their expert should be preferred to that of their counterparty.[129] This brings much scepticism about their objectivity and impartiality, which is expected from experts.[130]

Party-appointed experts are criticised for not being objective and 'cherry-picking' facts and information to ensure support for the party appointing them.[131]

1.4.1.1.2 Function and Role

As it is the general function of experts in general, party-appointed experts are to present the arbitral tribunal with an opinion on certain expertise required in technical, scientific or legal circumstances, plus helping the parties to construct and substantiate their arguments.[132] Another function of the party-appointed expert is to use it in negotiating and settling the dispute, even before the initiation of the arbitral proceedings.[133]

The reasons why party-appointed experts are preferred over tribunal-appointed experts can be that the parties seek support for their arguments, and they help to construct the pleadings of the case, even before the proceedings start.[134]

Party-appointed experts are also appointed by the parties to convince the tribunal that disputed facts occurred as they allege, having a representative nature of the facts[135]

125. Özbek, 'Uzman Görüşünün Yargılamada Değerlendirilmesi', 67.
126. O'Malley, *Rules of Evidence in International Arbitration*, 145; Atalay, 'Pekcanıtez Usûl', 2021, 2958.
127. Schiau, 'An Arbitration Dilemma', 335–336; Hobér and Sussman, *Cross-Examination in International Arbitration*, 20.
128. O'Malley, *Rules of Evidence in International Arbitration*, 145.
129. Bennouna, 'Experts Before the International Court of Justice: What For?', 346.
130. Abdel Wahab, 'Party Appointed Experts in International Commercial Arbitration', 190.
131. Flett, 'When Is an Expert Not an Expert?', 356.
132. Knoblach, *Sachverhaltsermittlung in Der Internationalen Wirtschaftsschiedsgerichtsbarkeit*, 274; Proske, *Expert witness conferencing in Schiedsverfahren*, 29; Roney, 'Cross-Examination of Experts', 111.
133. Proske, *Expert witness conferencing in Schiedsverfahren*, 29.
134. Elyıldırım, *Hukuk Yargılamasında Uzman Görüşü*, 61–62; Atalay, 'Pekcanıtez Usûl', 2021, 1958; Pekcanıtez, 'Özel Uzman', 399; Tanrıver, *Hukukumuzda Bilirkişilik*, 31; Akil, 'Bilirkişi-Uzman Tanık Ayrımı', 173; Karslı, *Medeni Muhakeme Hukuku*, 622; Sarısözen, 'Özel Bilirkişi (Uzman Görüşü)', 1703; Cayan, *Medeni Usul Hukukunda Bilirkişilik Müessesesi*, 10; Arslan et al., *Medenî Usul Hukuku*, 472. Özbek, 'Uzman Görüşünün Yargılamada Değerlendirilmesi', 136; Budak and Karaaslan, *Medenî Usul Hukuku*, 2022, 311; Lew, Mistelis, and Kröll, *Comparative International Commercial Arbitration*, 578; Parlett, 'Parties' Engagement with Experts in International Litigation', 441; Proske, *Expert Witness Conferencing in Schiedsverfahren*, 29.
135. *See* Atalay, 'Delil Kavramı Üzerine', 131–132.

and thus having an evidence-like function. The party-appointed expert may be appointed to affect, for or against, the tribunal-appointed expert's opinion.[136]

1.4.1.2 *Tribunal-Appointed Experts*

Tribunal-appointed experts are seen more often in countries following the civil law legal culture, as principally, the inquisitorial approach is accepted to establish facts in this system.

The inquisitorial system primarily burdens the court or tribunal to engage in the fact-establishing process.[137] That's why civil law adjudicators tend to rely on the experts appointed by them and give less weight to expert opinions provided by the parties.[138]

1.4.1.2.1 *Definition*

A Tribunal-Appointed Expert is a person or organisation appointed by the Arbitral Tribunal in order to report to it on specific issues determined by the arbitral tribunal.[139] These specific issues are matters that should be explained to the arbitral tribunal, since the tribunal requires guidance due to a lack of special knowledge, so that it can decide on the dispute.[140]

The tribunal-appointed expert is an independent natural or legal person who is engaged by the arbitral tribunal to act in the present case for the sake of clarifying the missing knowledge that is needed for the tribunal to adjudicate the case and render an award.[141] The tribunal-appointed expert has expertise in one more area and is expected to inform the tribunal in those areas in due course of the proceedings.

1.4.1.2.2 *Legal Basis*

The power of the tribunal to appoint experts is based on the UNCITRAL Model Law, international agreements, arbitration laws, arbitration rules, parties' agreements, and soft law instruments.[142]

---

136. Webster and Bühler, *Handbook of UNCITRAL Arbitration*, 454; Elyıldırım, *Hukuk Yargılamasında Uzman Görüşü*, 64; Toraman, *Medeni Usul Hukukunda Bilirkişi İncelemesi*, 87. Pekcanıtez, 'Özel Uzman', 407; Ağırman, *Milli & Milletlerarası Tahkim*, 464.
137. Nessi, 'Expert Witness: Role and Independence', 74.
138. Khodykin and Mulcahy, *A Guide to the IBA Rules on the Taking of Evidence in International Arbitration*, 282.
139. IBA Rules, Definitions.
140. O'Malley, *Rules of Evidence in International Arbitration*, 169; In an ICC case where the tribunal was composed of a lawyer with knowledge on Hungarian law, the tribunal rejected the appointment of an expert on that matter. *See Importer in the UK v. Exporter in Hungary*, Final Award, ICC Case No. 5418, 1987, in Van Den Berg, *ICCA Yearbook Commercial Arbitration 1988*, XIII:102.
141. O'Malley, *Rules of Evidence in International Arbitration*, 169; For appropriateness for legal persons to be an expert *see* Schneider, 'Technical Experts in International Arbitration', 456.
142. *See* Lim, 'Tribunal-Appointed Experts in International Arbitration', 209–210; Dayınlarlı, *Milletlerarası Tahkim Rehberi*, 80–81. Dayınlarlı, *UNCITRAL Kurallarına göre Uzlaşma ve Tahkim*, 100; Demir Gökyayla, 'Tahkimde Taraflarca Getirilme İlkesi ve Delil İkamesi', 85.

UNCITRAL Model Law Article 26(1), EUVIPA Chapter 3 section A Article 3.52,[143] TIAL Article 12(A),[144] Turkish CPC Article 431,[145] ICC Arbitration Rules Article 25(2),[146] and IBA Rules Article 6 and Prague Rules on the Efficient Conduct of Proceedings in International Arbitration Article 6.1 ('Prague Rules') is an example of an explicit provision granting the tribunal the authority to appoint experts.

Even if there are no provisions in the applicable statute or the arbitration rules, the parties may agree to empower the arbitral tribunal to appoint such an expert expressly in the arbitration agreement or during the proceedings. Nevertheless, even in the case of a lack of express authorisation, it is widely accepted that the tribunal has the inherent power to appoint an expert if the circumstances require it.[147]

It is also possible that the parties mutually wish to derogate from the tribunal's power to appoint an expert despite the applicable law to the arbitration and the rules foreseeing the possibility.[148] Since UNCITRAL Model Law Article 19 and many of the following statutory provisions regulate party autonomy as a fundamental principle in conducting the proceedings, parties can expressly exclude the power of the tribunal to appoint experts.[149] In such a scenario, tribunals shall refrain from appointing experts.[150] Such an agreement risks not establishing the facts and proving arguments,

143. 'The Tribunal, at the request of a disputing party or, after consulting the disputing parties, on its own initiative, may appoint one or more experts to report to it in writing on any factual issue concerning environmental, health, safety, or other matters raised by a disputing party in the proceedings.'

144. 'A) The arbitral tribunal may; 1. appoint one or more experts to report to it on specific issues to be determined by the arbitral tribunal'.

145. '1) The arbitrator or arbitral tribunal may decide on:
    a) The selection of one or more experts to report on the issues it has determined;
    b) The parties making the necessary explanations to the expert and providing the relevant documents and information;
    c) The conduct of an inspection.

    (2) Unless otherwise agreed, upon the request of one of the parties or if deemed necessary by the arbitrator or arbitral tribunal, the experts shall attend the hearing to which they are summoned after submitting their written or oral reports. At this hearing, the parties may question the experts and may have their own specially selected experts heard on the matter of the dispute.'

146. 'The arbitral tribunal may decide to hear witnesses, experts appointed by the parties or any other person, in the presence of the parties, or in their absence provided they have been duly summoned.'

147. Oetiker, 'Commentary on Art. 26-30 Swiss Rules of Arbitration', 309; Nessi, 'Expert Witness: Role and Independence', 80; Khodykin and Mulcahy, *A Guide to the IBA Rules on the Taking of Evidence in International Arbitration*, 327–328.

148. Konrad and Hunter, 'LCIA Rules', 466; Oetiker, 'Commentary on Art. 26-30 Swiss Rules of Arbitration', 311.

149. Zuberbühler et al., *IBA Rules of Evidence*, 156; Poudret and Besson, *Comparative Law of International Arbitration*, 560; Oetiker, 'Commentary on Art. 26-30 Swiss Rules of Arbitration', 311; for circumstances for disregarding such agreement *see* Berger and Kellerhals, *International and Domestic Arbitration in Switzerland*, 497.

150. Khodykin and Mulcahy, *A Guide to the IBA Rules on the Taking of Evidence in International Arbitration*, 328.

which the parties must endure. Nevertheless, the parties could still be able to engage with a party-appointed expert.[151]

When analysing the above provisions that foresee the appointment of tribunal-appointed experts, two conditions enable (or even require) the tribunal to appoint an expert when there is a: (1) specific technical issue; and (2) the opinion of an expert is necessary.[152] Both conditions must be present at the same time, as the contrary approach would violate the duty of the tribunal to assess, weigh the evidence and render its decision.[153]

An arbitral tribunal should explicitly inform the parties, consult them on whom to appoint and then appoint an expert.[154] This would be in line with the international arbitration culture, where proceedings are generally planned and conducted with the participation and views of the parties discussed in case management conferences. The tribunal-appointed expert is appointed and constructed by the arbitrators and paid, in principle, by both parties under arbitration costs.[155] In the arbitration proceedings, the

151. Oetiker, 'Commentary on Art. 26-30 Swiss Rules of Arbitration', 311; If the party-appointed experts are not able to help the tribunal understand the expert-required issue, the parties risk, in such an occasion, that the tribunal rules against the party bearing the burden of proof. If not precluded by the parties, the claiming party might have succeeded in its claim if the tribunal had been able to appoint an independent expert to clarify the matter.

152. Lim, 'Tribunal-Appointed Experts in International Arbitration', 216; Khodykin and Mulcahy, *A Guide to the IBA Rules on the Taking of Evidence in International Arbitration*, 285; ICC, 'ICC Arbitration Commission Report on Controlling Time and Costs in Arbitration', para. 62; Schäfer and Wilson, 'ICC Bulletin', 2021, 64.

153. *See Contractor (European Country), Contractor (Middle Eastern Country) v. Owner (Middle Eastern Country)* (Final Award), ICC Case No. 4629, 1989 in Van Den Berg, *ICCA Yearbook Commercial Arbitration 1993*, XVIII:15: 'The arbitral tribunal "may appoint one or more experts, define their Terms of Reference, receive their reports and/or hear them in person" (Art. 14(2) Rules of the ICC). The arbitrators are at liberty to decide whether such an appointment is necessary for the solution of the case. Such an expert may be useful or even necessary for technical questions. In the present situation, such utility is in no way established. On the contrary, the questions which are typically in the field of activity of an expert have already been covered by the [first expert's] report. This report describes the work done by the defendant party and is necessary for the determination of the payment claimed by the claimants. Other questions such as the ones quoted by respondent are to be resolved by the arbitrators. Moreover, it is their duty to interpret the contractual documents and evidence filed by the parties. Appointing a second expert would lead to a replacement of the arbitrators by an expert. Therefore, independently from the question of the cost of an expertise, the request of respondent is to be dismissed.'

154. O'Malley, *Rules of Evidence in International Arbitration*, 166–167; *Reiner/Aschauer* argues that in practice, some tribunals engaged an unofficial or behind-the-scenes expert, described as *a phantom expert*. This approach is problematic because of procedural fairness and the probable delegation of adjudication authority. For an internal advisor, explicit consent is required. *See* Reiner and Aschauer, 'ICC Rules', 136; Parlett, 'Parties' Engagement with Experts in International Litigation', 445; Plant, 'Expert Evidence and the Challenge of Procedural Reform in International Dispute Settlement', 470; 'BCLP 2021 Survey', 4; Patocchi, Paolo Michele and Niedermaier, 'UNCITRAL Rules', 1182; Dayınlarlı, *Milletlerarası Tahkim Rehberi*, 81; Dayınlarlı, *UNCITRAL Kurallarına göre Uzlaşma ve Tahkim*, 100.

155. Zuberbühler et al., *IBA Rules of Evidence*, 171; The tribunal might rule according to the applicable law to the arbitration procedure that the losing party shall bear, among other costs, expert expenses.

arbitral tribunal concludes a work contract with the expert on behalf of the parties so that the fee claim is directed at the parties.[156]

1.4.1.2.3 Qualifications, Function, and Role

Before officially appointing and assigning the expert to his task, the expert should submit to the tribunal and the parties a curriculum vitae indicating qualifications and proving that he has the required expertise to fulfil the assigned duty.[157]

In addition to expertise, the expert must be impartial and unbiased, like an arbitrator, and must submit a declaration thereto, generally before the appointment.[158] This declaration must indicate that he is independent of the parties, their attorneys, advisers and the tribunal and disclose any existing facts or circumstances that may give rise to doubts as to his independence and impartiality.[159]

The independence and impartiality requirement of tribunal-appointed experts should be understood very strictly in contrast to that of party-appointed experts. The expert can be challenged, and the appointment is terminated if there are justifiable doubts that the expert lacks those qualifications.[160] Any partiality exercised by the tribunal-appointed expert may be interpreted as corrupt and, under the New York Convention and the UNCITRAL Model Law, may be a ground for a challenge to the enforcement of the arbitral award.[161]

In fact, independence is a prerequisite for having a neutral expert opinion. Impartiality, however, serves for objectivity. Both conditions are indispensable for a tribunal-appointed expert, even without explicit provisions in arbitration laws or rules.[162]

---

156. BGH NJW 1965, 298; Lörcher, 'Liber Amicorum Karl-Heinz Böckstiegel', 487; Musielak and Voit, *ZPO*, § 1049, para. 8; Wilske and Markert, *Beck'scher Online-Kommentar ZPO*, § 1049, para. 2.1. For the view that the claim should be against the arbitrator, *see* Münch, *Münchener Kommentar Zur ZPO*, § 1049, para. 22.
157. Zuberbühler et al., *IBA Rules of Evidence*, 161.
158. Tanrıver, *Hukukumuzda Bilirkişilik*, 31; Tanrıver, *Medenî Usûl Hukuku*, 2022, II:463; Abdel Wahab, 'Party Appointed Experts in International Commercial Arbitration', 190; Mbengue and Das, 'Rules Governing the Use of Experts in International Disputes', 434; Lim, 'Tribunal-Appointed Experts in International Arbitration', 212, 221; White, *The Use of Experts by International Tribunals*, 183; Patocchi, Paolo Michele and Niedermaier, 'UNCITRAL Rules', 1184; Nessi, 'Expert Witness: Role and Independence', 74; Some Arbitration rules refer to the arbitrators' requirement of independence and impartiality for tribunal-appointed experts; Webster and Bühler, *Handbook of UNCITRAL Arbitration*, 450; *see* that this is not strictly required under UK Arbitration Knoblach, *Sachverhaltsermittlung in Der Internationalen Wirtschaftsschiedsgerichtsbarkeit*, 272.
159. Zuberbühler et al., *IBA Rules of Evidence*, 162; Born, *International Commercial Arbitration*, 2035; Fouchard, Gaillard, and Goldman, *Fouchard, Gaillard, Goldman on International Commercial Arbitration*, 579; Angoura, *The Impartiality and Independence of Arbitrators in International Commercial Arbitration*, 121.
160. Wach and Petsch, 'Der Sachverständigenbeweis Im Schiedsverfahren: Grenzen Der Gestaltungsfreiheit von Parteien Und Schiedsgericht', 101; O'Malley, *Rules of Evidence in International Arbitration*, 181–182; Knoblach, *Sachverhaltsermittlung in Der Internationalen Wirtschaftsschiedsgerichtsbarkeit*, 271–272.
161. Uluç, *Corruption in International Arbitration*, 163–164.
162. Lim, 'Tribunal-Appointed Experts in International Arbitration', 221.

The BGH decided that a tribunal-appointed expert can only be challenged if the violation of its duty of disclosure raises doubts about his impartiality.[163]

When the expert is appointed by the tribunal, his central role is to translate technical issues that are foreign to the tribunal to facilitate the tribunal members' understanding (*evidentiary role*).[164]

Some scholars argue that experts are also appointed to summarise (technical) evidence, present evidence in an understandable form, and express comments on claims (*advisory role*).[165] The function of this expert is to assist the adjudicator in understanding complex facts or evidence.[166] The tribunal-appointed expert will assist the tribunal.[167] However, this does not mean that experts will weigh the evidence and arrive at conclusions.[168]

If the parties have relied on experts and the tribunal needs to be convinced more or, as in the case of valuation issues, feels a need for consultation, it may appoint an expert to bridge the gap.[169] Although this is highly likely to be helpful for the tribunal in finally awarding damages, it comes with the cost of a prolonged case outcome since the tribunal-appointed expert will need to read through the whole case file, perhaps consisting of a room full of pages.[170] This approach has been used in various cases.[171]

163. *See* German Federal Court of Justice (BGH), I ZB 46/18, BGH. 'Verletzt ... ein Sachverständiger seine Offenbarungspflicht, kann sich daraus ein selbständiger Grund für seine Ablehnung nur ergeben, sofern der Verstoß für sich bereits Zweifel an seiner Unparteilichkeit weckt.'
164. Tanrıver, *Medenî Usûl Hukuku*, 2022, II:463.
165. Schneider, 'Technical Experts in International Arbitration', 450; *see* for critics Hofmann and Kunz, 'Commentary on the Swiss Rules, Article 27 [Tribunal-Appointed Experts]', 727; Oetiker, 'Commentary on Art. 26-30 Swiss Rules of Arbitration', 314; O'Malley, *Rules of Evidence in International Arbitration*, 186; Schäfer and Wilson, 'ICC Bulletin', 2021, 70; *see also* IBA Rules Art. 3(8) for review of documents requested for document production by an independent expert.
166. de Chazournes et al., 'Uses of Experts Before International Courts and Tribunals', 495; Zuberbühler et al., *IBA Rules of Evidence*, 159.
167. Wach and Petsch, 'Der Sachverständigenbeweis Im Schiedsverfahren: Grenzen Der Gestaltungsfreiheit von Parteien Und Schiedsgericht', 96; Lörcher, 'Liber Amicorum Karl-Heinz Böckstiegel', 485; Oetiker, 'Commentary on Art. 26-30 Swiss Rules of Arbitration', 313; Wilske and Gack, 'Expert Evidence in International Commercial Arbitration', 89; for the perspective in Public International Law *see* Bennouna, 'Experts Before the International Court of Justice: What For?'; Hodgson and Stewart, 'Experts in Investor-State Arbitration: The Tribunal as Gatekeeper', 457. Dwyer, *The Judicial Assessment of Expert Evidence*, 195.
168. O'Malley, *Rules of Evidence in International Arbitration*, 170; Tanrıver, *Medenî Usûl Hukuku*, II:463.
169. Blackaby and Wilbraham, 'Practical Issues Relating to the Use of Expert Evidence in Investment Treaty Arbitration', 664.
170. For critics, *see* Blackaby and Wilbraham, 664; Ağırman, *Milli & Milletlerarası Tahkim*, 462.
171. *See Suez, Sociedad General de Aguas de Barcelona SA and Vivendi Universal SA v. Argentine Republic*, ICSID Case No. ARB/03/19, Award (9 April 2015) paras 7–18; *Perenco Ecuador Limited v. Republic of Ecuador*, ICSID Case No ARB/08/6, Interim Decision on the Environmental Counterclaim (11 August 2015) paras 585 ff.; *Abaclat and Others v. Argentine Republic*, ICSID Case No ARB/07/5, Procedural Order No 15 (20 November 2012) paras 11 ff.; *See*, for instance: 'the expert evidence from both sides does not provide a sufficient degree of confidence as to the actual conditions in the Blocks. The Tribunal considers that there are too many gaps and conflicts between [the parties'] evidence on these key issues' and appointed an expert. (*Perenco Ecuador Limited v. Ecuador*, Interim Decision on the Environmental Counterclaim, 2015, paras 581 ff.).

1.4.1.2.4 Legal Nature and Binding Forces

The tribunal-appointed expert and its report are generally accepted as a means of evidence.[172] The tribunal-appointed expert is neither a witness, since he will not testify on facts that were sensed with the organs, nor a fourth arbitrator, who will participate in the deliberations and have a vote. The tribunal-appointed expert is an assistant to the tribunal,[173] either by producing evidence or facilitating the understanding of technical matters beyond the knowledge of the arbitral tribunal.[174]

The tribunal is not strictly bound by the expert's opinion and will freely appraise the report and may come to a different conclusion in the award.[175] The tribunal may partially or fully adopt the expert's findings if they are in line with the facts and evidence in the record, logic and legal rules.[176] For due process concerns, the tribunal, either in rejecting the conclusions of the expert or totally accepting them in the award, shall state the reasons for it.[177]

However, significant weight is generally given in practice to tribunal-appointed experts due to their nature, in contrast to party-appointed experts.[178]

1.4.1.2.5 Appointments and Challenges

As stipulated earlier, the principal practice in international arbitration is the use of party-appointed experts.[179] Nevertheless, Arbitration rules give the arbitral tribunal broad authority to retain one or more experts directly after consulting the parties (e.g., ICC Arbitration Rules Article 25(3)).[180]

172. Zuberbühler et al., *IBA Rules of Evidence*, 170; Schäfer and Wilson, 'ICC Bulletin', 2021, 75.
173. Proske, *Expert witness conferencing in Schiedsverfahren*, 14; Budak and Karaaslan, *Medenî Usul Hukuku*, 2022, 311; Ruhlmann and Gutkes, 'France', 141.
174. O'Malley, *Rules of Evidence in International Arbitration*, 167; Lim, 'Tribunal-Appointed Experts in International Arbitration', 212; Oetiker, 'Commentary on Art. 26-30 Swiss Rules of Arbitration', 314; Weiss and Bürgi Locatelli, 'Der Vom Schiedsgericht Bestellte Experte-Ein Überblick Aus Sicht Eines Internationalen Schiedsgerichts Mit Sitz in Der Schweiz', 499; Proske, *Expert Witness Conferencing in Schiedsverfahren*, 14; Uluç, *Corruption in International Arbitration*, 163–164; Commentators argue that the participation of the expert could raise important issues regarding the right to be heard and should be avoided, unless it is impossible to adapt the expert's findings properly and decide the dispute. *See* Schneider, 'Technical Experts in International Arbitration', 464.
175. Zuberbühler et al., *IBA Rules of Evidence*, 170; Oetiker, 'Commentary on Art. 26-30 Swiss Rules of Arbitration', 313; Uluç, *Corruption in International Arbitration*, 164; *See* ICC Case No. 14079, Procedural Order May 2007, in ICC International Court of Arbitration, 'Procedural Decisions in ICC Arbitration', 11.
176. O'Malley, *Rules of Evidence in International Arbitration*, 199.
177. O'Malley, 200; *See* ICC Case No. 12131 (2006) (Partial Award) in Webster and Bühler, *Handbook of ICC Arbitration: Commentary, Precedents, Materials*, 448.
178. O'Malley, *Rules of Evidence in International Arbitration*, 167.
179. *See* Chapter 1 section 1.1.
180. ICC Arbitration Rules Art. 25(3): 'The arbitral tribunal, after consulting the parties, may appoint one or more experts, define their terms of reference and receive their reports. At the request of a party, the parties shall be given the opportunity to question at a hearing any such expert.'

The tribunal-appointed expert is generally appointed after the parties have submitted their initial briefs and the tribunal has become aware of the need for ex officio[181] or the parties have asked for the appointment of an independent expert, and this was welcomed by the tribunal.[182]

A mere request to appoint an expert from the parties should not be welcomed without[183] the determination of the tribunal that the expert is necessary for deciding on the merits of the case and that it will materially affect the outcome.[184] If the tribunal determines that no appointment of an expert is required, it can deny appointing an expert; however, it should stipulate this with clear reasoning in a procedural order or the award.[185]

The arbitral tribunal can also appoint an expert, even if none of the parties has asked the tribunal to do so. For instance, if there is an asymmetry of information and evidence between the parties, unequal access to evidence and information cannot be adequately addressed through the directions of the tribunal.[186] If, however, all parties object to the tribunal's appointment of an expert, the tribunal should refrain from doing so because at least one party must pay an advance on the expert's costs.[187]

An arbitral tribunal is free to nominate and appoint an appropriate expert; however, it may ask the parties to propose a joint name or a list of experts.[188] The tribunal could also ask the parties to nominate potential experts or request that an institution, such as the ICC International Centre for Expertise or any professional institution or professional chamber, recommend an expert.[189] Not only natural persons but also legal entities could be appointed, which will indeed identify one or more real-person experts who will be responsible for delivering the opinion.[190]

Each of these appointment methods can be used, depending on the circumstances of the case and the attitude of the parties involved. It can be a challenging task for the

181. *Webster/Bühler* stated that this phenomenon is rare in ICC practice. *See* Webster and Bühler, *Handbook of ICC Arbitration: Commentary, Precedents, Materials*, 445.
182. Zuberbühler et al., *IBA Rules of Evidence*, 154; Lim, 'Tribunal-Appointed Experts in International Arbitration', 213; Oetiker, 'Commentary on Art. 26-30 Swiss Rules of Arbitration', 310; Nessi, 'Expert Witness: Role and Independence', 74; Schäfer and Wilson, 'ICC Bulletin', 2021, 64; Proske, *Expert Witness Conferencing in Schiedsverfahren*, 15.
183. Schütze, *Zivilprozessordnung Und Nebengesetze: Großkommentar*, 11:592.
184. Wilske and Gack, 'Expert Evidence in International Commercial Arbitration', 90–91.
185. Webster and Bühler, *Handbook of ICC Arbitration: Commentary, Precedents, Materials*, 445.
186. Lim, 'Tribunal-Appointed Experts in International Arbitration', 214; Haugeneder, 'The Arbitration Agreement and Arbitrability, Party-Appointed and Tribunal-Appointed Experts in International Arbitration', 181, 191–192.
187. Schäfer and Wilson, 'ICC Bulletin', 2021, 70.
188. Schütze, *Zivilprozessordnung Und Nebengesetze: Großkommentar*, 11:591; Parlett, 'Parties' Engagement with Experts in International Litigation', 448; Zuberbühler et al., *IBA Rules of Evidence*, 157; Özbek, *Tahkim Hukuku*, II:1450.
189. Oetiker, 'Commentary on Art. 26-30 Swiss Rules of Arbitration', 312; Webster and Bühler, *Handbook of ICC Arbitration: Commentary, Precedents, Materials*, 446; Khodykin and Mulcahy, *A Guide to the IBA Rules on the Taking of Evidence in International Arbitration*, 331.
190. Zuberbühler et al., *IBA Rules of Evidence*, 157; Tanrıver, *Medenî Usûl Hukuku*, 2022, II:463.

tribunal to appoint an independent and impartial person who is an expert in the required subject matter.[191]

Although not directly chosen by the parties, the panel should be given the opportunity to comment on the qualifications, independence and impartiality of the tribunal-appointed expert, the questions to be asked and his findings.[192]

The Parties shall lay forth any objections they have within a time frame ordered by the tribunal (UNCITRAL Arbitration Rules Article 29(2), IBA Rules Article 6(2)).[193] Although there are generally no express provisions for the grounds of challenge to tribunal-appointed experts in significant arbitration rules, such as the ICC, LCIA or SIAC, in practice and in some arbitration rules, such as HKIAC Article 25(5) or Swiss Rules Article 28(1), the same reasons for challenge of arbitrators apply analogously.

It is contentious whether a tribunal has the duty to appoint an expert if the circumstances require one.[194] Some arbitral tribunals have held that the appointment of a tribunal-appointed expert is not appropriate merely because there is a gap in the evidentiary record as a result of the relevant party failing to adduce a party-appointed expert as the one carrying the burden of proof.[195] Some other tribunals also argued that it would not be fair or equal treatment to appoint a tribunal-appointed expert if doing so would effectively assist the one party in establishing its case and not enlighten the dispute in general.[196]

However, the Swiss Federal Tribunal stipulated in an older judgment that even in the absence of a request from a party, the arbitrator who does not have special knowledge must appoint an expert if clarification on certain specific technical problems is required for the resolution of the dispute.[197] However, in its latter judgments, the Supreme Court

191. *See* Wilske and Gack, 'Expert Evidence in International Commercial Arbitration', 92; Khodykin and Mulcahy, *A Guide to the IBA Rules on the Taking of Evidence in International Arbitration*, 332.
192. O'Malley, *Rules of Evidence in International Arbitration*, 184; Mbengue and Das, 'Rules Governing the Use of Experts in International Disputes', 434; Khodykin and Mulcahy, *A Guide to the IBA Rules on the Taking of Evidence in International Arbitration*, 336; Özbek, *Tahkim Hukuku*, II:1450.
193. Lim, 'Tribunal-Appointed Experts in International Arbitration', 221.
194. Berger and Kellerhals, *International and Domestic Arbitration in Switzerland*, 495; Zuberbühler et al., *IBA Rules of Evidence*, 154; Weiss and Bürgi Locatelli, 'Der Vom Schiedsgericht Bestellte Experte-Ein Überblick Aus Sicht Eines Internationalen Schiedsgerichts Mit Sitz in Der Schweiz', 484.
195. Oetiker, 'Commentary on Art. 26-30 Swiss Rules of Arbitration', 315; Schneider, 'Technical Experts in International Arbitration', 451; Derains and Schwartz, *A Guide to the ICC Rules of Arbitration*, 279; *Sanders*, stating in Sanders, 'Commentary On UNCITRAL Arbitration Rules', 204: 'In the civil law tradition, the trier of facts takes an active role in determining matters requiring expertise, including readily appointing its own expert on technical matters. In the common law approach, the parties are primarily responsible for presenting their cases, including the presentation of expert witnesses. Although the trier of facts can appoint its own experts, or special masters, usually the parties present their cases at their own risk; that is, they suffer the consequences of failing to make out their cases and the court rarely steps in.'
196. Lim, 'Tribunal-Appointed Experts in International Arbitration', 216–217; O'Malley, *Rules of Evidence in International Arbitration*, 169.
197. *See* 'Parties Not Indicated, Tribunal Fédéral, 1ère Cour Civile'; *see also* BGE 132 III 83: 'Es ist willkürlich, ohne Beizug eines unabhängigen gerichtlichen Sachverständigen auf eine bestrittene Parteibehauptung abzustellen, wenn der Sachrichter nicht über die notwendige Sachkunde verfügt (3.5).'

has changed its view and declared that such a duty exists only if a party requests the appointment of a tribunal-appointed expert.[198] *O'Malley* argued that if a party requests an expert in a timely manner, with reasons and advances in the costs, the tribunal should appoint an expert.[199]

The tribunal will draft a terms of reference and take the views of the parties regarding the content of it, specifically on the required qualifications of the expert, duties and issues to be answered, time schedule, responsibilities and powers of the expert and scope of the opinion and the remuneration.[200] When the parties agree on the expert and the conditions in the terms of reference, the document should be signed by the parties and the expert.[201]

Upon the appointment of the expert, a complex legal relationship comes into existence.[202] Despite an appointment by the tribunal, a contractual relationship between the parties and the expert is deemed to have been created if the parties advance the fees of the experts.[203]

Nevertheless, in contrast to party-appointed experts who receive direct remuneration from the appointing party, tribunal-appointed experts do not directly receive remuneration from the parties, which inherently leads to their independence and impartiality, save other circumstances which could aggrieve these notions.[204]

In international arbitration practice, the parties equally pay the advanced costs for the expert.[205] If a party withholds the payment of the advanced fee, the other party is requested to pay the other party's fee instead. If both parties do not advance the payment, then the tribunal will have to decide without any expert opinion and consider the burden of proof rules applicable to the dispute. In such cases, the parties cannot argue that the right to be heard is violated.

198. Scherer, 'Saudi Modern Foods Factory v. Pavan Mapimpianti S.p.A., Federal Supreme Court of Switzerland, 1st Civil Law Chamber, 10 June 1996', 769–770; Scherer, 'X. S.A.L., Y. S.A.L. et A. v. Z. Sàrl, Federal Supreme Court of Switzerland, 1st Civil Law Chamber, 4P.115/2003, 16 October 2003', 377–378; *see also* Chapter 2, section 2.7.1 regarding the admissibility of expert evidence in relation to the duty to appoint.
199. O'Malley, *Rules of Evidence in International Arbitration*, 177; similarly, Webster and Bühler, *Handbook of UNCITRAL Arbitration*, 449.
200. Zuberbühler et al., *IBA Rules of Evidence*, 159–160; Schneider, 'Technical Experts in International Arbitration', 458; Oetiker, 'Commentary on Art. 26-30 Swiss Rules of Arbitration', 315; O'Malley, *Rules of Evidence in International Arbitration*, 178; Reiner and Aschauer, 'ICC Rules', 136; Lim, 'Tribunal-Appointed Experts in International Arbitration', 223; Webster and Bühler, *Handbook of ICC Arbitration: Commentary, Precedents, Materials*, 447; Webster and Bühler, 449; Dayınlarlı, *UNCITRAL Kurallarına göre Uzlaşma ve Tahkim*, 100; For matters to be mentioned in the terms of reference *see* Schäfer and Wilson, 'ICC Bulletin', 2021, 73.
201. Webster and Bühler, *Handbook of UNCITRAL Arbitration*, 451.
202. Zuberbühler et al., *IBA Rules of Evidence*, 158; Weiss and Bürgi Locatelli, 'Der Vom Schiedsgericht Bestellte Experte-Ein Überblick Aus Sicht Eines Internationalen Schiedsgerichts Mit Sitz in Der Schweiz', 496–497; Lörcher, 'Liber Amicorum Karl-Heinz Böckstiegel', 486.
203. For details of the contractual nature, *see* Zuberbühler et al., *IBA Rules of Evidence*, 158; Schütze, Tscherning, and Wais, *Handbuch Des Schiedsverfahrens: Praxis Der Deutschen Und Internationalen Schiedsgerichtsbarkeit*, 224; Reiner and Aschauer, 'ICC Rules', 135.
204. Lim, 'Tribunal-Appointed Experts in International Arbitration', 212.
205. Oetiker, 'Commentary on Art. 26-30 Swiss Rules of Arbitration', 459.

If it appears from circumstances, after consulting with the parties, that the expert is not in a position to fulfil his obligations to provide an opinion so that the arbitrators can resolve the issues, he/she can be released from this task.[206]

The procedure applicable to the challenge of tribunal-appointed experts is comparable to that of arbitrators.[207] A challenge shall be brought by showing justifiable doubts about independence, impartiality, or expertise, and it shall not be arbitrarily limited to reasons of which the party becomes aware after the appointment has been made.[208]

Major reasons for challenges of tribunal-appointed experts are: (i) the lack of expertise/qualifications; (ii) prior or present personal or professional relationship between the expert and one of the parties;[209] (iii) adverse opinions expressed by the expert towards one of the parties before the report was finalised;[210] and (iv) financial (or other) interest of the expert in the outcome of the case in favour of a party.[211]

1.4.1.2.6 Duties and Powers

The expert's primary duty is to provide an opinion on the matters stipulated in the terms of reference, generally in the form of a written report, and testify if asked by the tribunal or the parties.[212]

Parties should be included in the process of determining the mandate of the tribunal-appointed expert so that they have an opportunity to clearly state the matters that fall under the expertise of the expert they want the expert to address.[213] In practice, this is done through terms of reference drafted by the tribunal. The draft terms of

206. Zuberbühler et al., *IBA Rules of Evidence*, 158; Oetiker, 'Commentary on Art. 26-30 Swiss Rules of Arbitration', 313.
207. *See, e.g.*, Swiss Rules Art. 28(1): 'The arbitral tribunal, after consulting with the parties, may appoint one or more experts to report to it, in writing, on specific issues. Articles 12 and 13 [challenge of an arbitrator] shall apply mutatis mutandis.'; Lim, 'Tribunal-Appointed Experts in International Arbitration', 222; Nessi, 'Expert Witness: Role and Independence', 75; Webster and Bühler, *Handbook of UNCITRAL Arbitration*, 450.
208. Lim, 'Tribunal-Appointed Experts in International Arbitration', 216, 222; O'Malley, *Rules of Evidence in International Arbitration*, 182; Haugeneder, 'The Arbitration Agreement and Arbitrability, Party-Appointed and Tribunal-Appointed Experts in International Arbitration', 187; Patocchi, Paolo Michele and Niedermaier, 'UNCITRAL Rules', 1184; Nessi, 'Expert Witness: Role and Independence', 74; Khodykin and Mulcahy, *A Guide to the IBA Rules on the Taking of Evidence in International Arbitration*, 336; Knoblach, *Sachverhaltsermittlung in Der Internationalen Wirtschaftsschiedsgerichtsbarkeit*, 269.
209. *See* German Federal Court of Justice (BGH), VI ZB 31/16, BGH, paras 6 ff.; Higher Regional Court (OLG) of Frankfurt am Main, 1 U 104/96, 28 April 2005, para. 3.
210. Higher Regional Court (OLG) of Saarland, 5 W 42/08-16, 11 March 2008, para. 26.
211. Nessi, 'Expert Witness: Role and Independence', 75; Khodykin and Mulcahy, *A Guide to the IBA Rules on the Taking of Evidence in International Arbitration*, 300.
212. Knoblach, *Sachverhaltsermittlung in Der Internationalen Wirtschaftsschiedsgerichtsbarkeit*, 270; Tanrıver, *Medenî Usûl Hukuku*, 2022, II:463; Özbek, *Tahkim Hukuku*, II:1451.
213. Tanrıver, *Medenî Usûl Hukuku*, 2022, II:463; Khodykin and Mulcahy, *A Guide to the IBA Rules on the Taking of Evidence in International Arbitration*, 332.

reference are generally circulated from the tribunal to the parties for comments before it is officially issued.[214]

The terms of reference for the expert are a vital tool for all participants in the case to orient themselves. The expert is to prepare the report according to the conditions and questions set forth in it. General matters that should be included in the expert's terms of reference are as follows:

- Identification of the case (name of institution, applicable rules, case ID, names and addresses of arbitrators, parties and the expert).
- Issues related to the organisation, preparation, delivery and presentation of the expert report.
- Definition of the questions/issues that the expert should address.
- The scope and limits of the expert's duties and rights (such as preparing the report, being available for examination at the hearings, disclosing all information for potential conflict of interest and keeping all information and documents confidential that he is entrusted with).
- Identification of information (documents, evidence, etc.) that is or should be provided to the expert on which the expert should base his/her report.
- The procedure by which the expert may contact the parties and collect further information and evidence that the expert may require in order to prepare the report.
- Rules for communication between the expert, the parties and the tribunal.
- An express statement of the parties' right to comment on the report and to examine the expert at an oral hearing.
- Remuneration, any advanced payment, and any cost-related issues.
- Statement of the power of the tribunal to adjust and review the terms of reference.[215]

The official terms of reference should be sent to both the experts and the parties (IBA Rules Article 6), ICC Arbitration Rules Article 25(3), UNCITRAL Arbitration Rules Article 29(2). The terms of reference should be signed by the tribunal, the parties and the expert(s).[216]

In order to produce the expert opinion, the expert will rely on submissions and evidence submitted by the parties. These documents should be transmitted to the expert(s) from the parties in whole form or so as to include all necessary details.[217]

However, the expert may need additional information or explanations from both parties. Therefore, with the order of the arbitral tribunal, the parties should provide any

214. Khodykin and Mulcahy, *A Guide to the IBA Rules on the Taking of Evidence in International Arbitration*, 333.
215. Khodykin and Mulcahy, 334–335; Schäfer, Verbist, and Imhoos, *ICC Arbitration in Practice*, 490; Schneider, 'Technical Experts in International Arbitration', 446.
216. Khodykin and Mulcahy, *A Guide to the IBA Rules on the Taking of Evidence in International Arbitration*, 334–335.
217. Tanrıver, *Medenî Usûl Hukuku*, 2022, II:463; Oetiker, 'Commentary on Art. 26-30 Swiss Rules of Arbitration', 316.

information or to provide access to any documents, goods, samples, property, machinery, systems, processes or site for inspection, but only those that are relevant to the case and material to its outcome (UNCITRAL Arbitration Rules Article 29(3), IBA Rules Article 6(3), Swiss Rules Article 28(2), SIAC Arbitration Rules Rule 26(1)(b), Prague Rules Article 6(2)(d)).[218]

The documents do not need to be provided and do not automatically become part of the case file unless consent is provided for by the affected party.[219] Goods or samples do not need to be handed over because proprietary rights can be violated.[220] Nevertheless, this does not mean that the parties have no right to information or to attend inspections, which would infringe on the right to be heard.[221]

Where the expert will conduct a site visit, the parties and their representatives are normally invited to attend the visit. If the experts perform tests or other experiments, the parties and their representatives will be given an opportunity to participate in or observe that process.[222]

If there is any objection to the relevance, materiality or appropriateness of a request by the expert, the tribunal shall decide such controversies (UNCITRAL Arbitration Rules Article 29(3)). If the concerned party does not adhere to the request of the expert or the order of the tribunal to provide access to the materials, the only weapon in the hand of the tribunal, not the expert, would be an adverse inference to the interests of that party.[223] Nevertheless, if the affected party insists on access to the relevant documents or materials, it may request assistance from a competent state court.[224]

Parties have the right to receive a copy of the expert opinion, review, comment, and respond to the expert's opinion during hearings.[225] If the parties have any comments or questions about the (main) report, the expert should clarify the issues with an additional report.[226] The UNCITRAL Model Law Article 26(2) provides:

> Unless otherwise agreed by the parties, if a party so requests or if the arbitral tribunal considers it necessary, the expert shall, after delivery of his written or oral report, participate in a hearing where the parties have the opportunity to put

218. Zuberbühler et al., *IBA Rules of Evidence*, 164; Oetiker, 'Commentary on Art. 26-30 Swiss Rules of Arbitration', 316; Lim, 'Tribunal-Appointed Experts in International Arbitration', 222; Webster and Bühler, *Handbook of UNCITRAL Arbitration*, 452; Knoblach, *Sachverhaltsermittlung in Der Internationalen Wirtschaftsschiedsgerichtsbarkeit*, 190.
219. Oetiker, 'Commentary on Art. 26-30 Swiss Rules of Arbitration', 317.
220. Zuberbühler et al., *IBA Rules of Evidence*, 164; Oetiker, 'Commentary on Art. 26-30 Swiss Rules of Arbitration', 317.
221. Lörcher, 'Liber Amicorum Karl-Heinz Böckstiegel', 492.
222. Zuberbühler et al., *IBA Rules of Evidence*, 163.
223. Lörcher, 'Liber Amicorum Karl-Heinz Böckstiegel', 492; Eberl, *Beweis Im Schiedsverfahren*, 133; Musielak and Voit, *ZPO*, § 1042, para. 27; Knoblach, *Sachverhaltsermittlung in Der Internationalen Wirtschaftsschiedsgerichtsbarkeit*, 229.
224. Zuberbühler et al., *IBA Rules of Evidence*, 165.
225. Knoblach, *Sachverhaltsermittlung in Der Internationalen Wirtschaftsschiedsgerichtsbarkeit*, 190–191; Lim, 'Tribunal-Appointed Experts in International Arbitration', 225; Webster and Bühler, *Handbook of UNCITRAL Arbitration*, 445; Özbek, *Tahkim Hukuku*, II:1451.
226. Parlett, 'Parties' Engagement with Experts in International Litigation', 448; Zuberbühler et al., *IBA Rules of Evidence*, 157.

questions to him and to present expert witnesses in order to testify on the points at issue.[227]

In contrast, EAA section 37(2) does not expressly provide directly for a right of examination and instead refers to the parties' opportunity to comment on the expert's opinion, which nevertheless may extend to the right to examine a tribunal-appointed expert at a hearing.[228]

Similarly, *Voser and Mueller noted* that, in civil law jurisdictions, the right to be heard only requires that the parties have the right to submit comments in writing to the expert's opinion and not the absolute right to examine the expert.[229]

Ex parte communications should be prevented since this could lead to serious doubt about the independence and impartiality of the expert, and if the expert has to communicate with one party, the arbitral tribunal should make sure that the counterparty is informed about this communication, specifically its contents and purpose.[230]

The costs and expenses of party-appointed experts may be included in the arbitration costs. For instance, under Article 38(1) of the ICC Arbitration Rules, the costs of the arbitration can include the amounts paid by the party-appointed experts. Under Article 38(4) of the ICC Arbitration Rules, the arbitral tribunal has the discretion to decide the costs to be awarded, which party or parties shall bear them, and in what proportion.[231]

1.4.2 Based on Subject Matter

An expert opinion, either submitted by the parties or as a result of the tribunal appointing an expert, can be presented on a wide range of different subjects. These subjects can be categorised as technical/scientific experts, legal experts, and valuation (quantum) experts.[232]

One may question whether treating legal and quantum experts who are not under the scope of scientific experts is appropriate. However, as will be demonstrated, not only are there differences in the subject, but the degree and weight of evidence might also slightly change due to their nature.

For instance, in *Compañía de Aguas v. Argentina,*[233] the tribunal concluded that 'the settling of damages is not an exact science'.[234] For sure, this is a valid argument since

227. Similar TIAL Art. 12(A)(2), ZPO § 1049(2), UNCITRAL Arbitration Rules Art. 29(5), ICC Arbitration Rules Art. 25(3), LCIA Arbitration Rules Art. 21(4).
228. Lim, 'Tribunal-Appointed Experts in International Arbitration', 226.
229. Voser and Mueller, 'Appointment of Experts by the Arbitral Tribunal: The Civil Law Perspective', 80.
230. Schäfer and Wilson, 'ICC Bulletin', 2021, 74.
231. Schäfer and Wilson, 70.
232. Born, *International Commercial Arbitration*, 2449; Hodgson and Stewart, 'Experts in Investor-State Arbitration: The Tribunal as Gatekeeper', 454; O'Malley, *Rules of Evidence in International Arbitration*, 145.
233. *Compañiá de Aguas del Aconquija S.A. and Vivendi Universal S.A. v. Argentine Republic*, ICSID Case No. ARB/97/3 (formerly *Compañía de Aguas del Aconquija, S.A. and Compagnie Générale des Eaux v. Argentine Republic*). Available online: https://www.italaw.com/cases/309 (accessed 7 January 2023).
234. *See, e.g., Compañía de Aguas v. Argentina*, para. 8.3.16.

the level of objectivity presentable and testable in scientific opinions is different from expertise in law and valuation. In particular, in the latter ones, there can be multiple views/positions and methods on the subject which could be applied to the specific case, and this is not the same as determining the boiling level of water at sea level.

According to statistics, financial/accounting experts are used most frequently (46%), followed by technical (35%) and industry-specific experts (17%), whereas legal experts are used least frequently (13%).[235]

1.4.2.1 Technical/Scientific Experts

Technical expertise is often required as a substantive area relevant to the case that is usually outside the competence of the tribunal, such as construction, oil and gas, mining, intellectual property, environment or other areas of science.[236] In addition, planning/delay analysis, market practice, technology and forensic analysis of evidence such as handwriting, photographs or other data might become necessary.[237]

When deciding on a legal dispute between the parties, the tribunal has a mandate to conduct scientific fact-finding if the case calls for it.[238] For instance, if a host state in an investor-state dispute argues that it declined to renew the licence of the investor to operate because it harmed the environment, it has to prove this via an opinion by one or more biologists.[239] The unexplained failure to present scientific evidence can lead to adverse inferences.[240]

For instance, in *Bear Creek Mining Corporation v. Peru*, the investor claimant submitted a technical expert opinion for the technical review of the investor's projects located in Peru.[241]

---

235. '2012 International Arbitration Survey: Present and Preferred Practices in the Arbitral Process', 29.
236. Blackaby and Wilbraham, 'Practical Issues Relating to the Use of Expert Evidence in Investment Treaty Arbitration', 661; Hodgson and Stewart, 'Experts in Investor-State Arbitration: The Tribunal as Gatekeeper', 455; Mosk, 'The Role of Facts in International Dispute Resolution (Volume 304)', 128; Jones, 'Ineffective Use of Expert Evidence in Construction Arbitration', 2; Spitzer, 'Der Sachverständigenbeweis Im Österreichischen Zivilprozess', 28.
237. *See Tethyan Copper Company Pty Limited v. Islamic Republic of Pakistan*, Award, 12 July 2019, ICSID Case No ARB/12/1 available at www.italaw.com (accessed 24 September 2025); *See* Cosar, 'Fraudulent Evidence: Investment Arbitration', para. 30, 59; Bor, 'Expert Evidence', 503; Mosk, 'The Role of Facts in International Dispute Resolution (Volume 304)', 75; Kamya-Lukoda, 'Role of Expert Witnesses in Construction Arbitration: Delay and Disruption and Quantum Issues', 82.
238. Donoghue, 'Expert Scientific Evidence in a Broader Context', 382.
239. Erdoğan and Üçüncü call these in old Turkish 'ehl-i hibre', *see* Erdoğan and Üçüncü, 'Bilirkişilik Kurumu ve Bilirkişi Raporunun Delil Değerine İlişkin Bazı Sorunlar', 363; *see Methanex Corporation v. United States of America* (Final Award on Jurisdiction and Merits, 3 August 2005, ad hoc UNCITRAL Tribunal under NAFTA Ch 11), available at www.italaw.com (accessed 24 September 2025); *Chemtura Corporation v. Government of Canada* (Award, 2 August 2010, ad hoc UNCITRAL Tribunal under NAFTA Ch 11) www.italaw.com (accessed 19 June 2022).
240. Donoghue, 'Expert Scientific Evidence in a Broader Context', 385; O'Malley, *Rules of Evidence in International Arbitration*, 159.
241. *Bear Creek Mining Corporation v. Republic of Peru*, ICSID Case No. ARB/14/21, available at https://www.italaw.com/cases/2848 (accessed 19 June 2022).

Technical and scientific experts are the least problematic with respect to their value to the tribunal and the potential for biased opinions. Their opinion must rely on some objective facts, defined best practices, or industry standards, which make their view objectively testable.[242]

1.4.2.2 Legal Experts

One would naturally expect that there is no need for legal experts in proceedings because arbitrators as adjudicators[243] and legal counsel of the parties would already have extensive knowledge on matters of law.[244] Acting as a legal expert (before courts) is even clearly forbidden by a statutory provision in Türkiye.[245]

A tribunal is expected to know the applicable law to the dispute on its own without having to rely on the parties' legal pleadings.[246] This principle is expressed as *Iura Novit Curia* or *Iura Novit Arbiter (la cour sait le droit)*. Accordingly, in international arbitration, arbitrators should be aware of the applicable law.[247]

However, in international arbitration and even sometimes domestic litigation, a legal expert can be required, especially if there is a foreign (domestic) law issue with which the arbitrators are not familiar.[248]

The legal expert will help the tribunal assess the legal knowledge.[249] Legal experts may help in identifying the applicable legal authorities and sources and interpreting

242. Lew, 'The Need for Expert Evidence?', 247; Hodgson and Stewart, 'Experts in Investor-State Arbitration: The Tribunal as Gatekeeper', 455.
243. Ünüvar, 'Experts: Investment Arbitration', para. 56; Bacanlı, 'Bir Alternatif Uyuşmazlık Cözüm Yolu Olarak Istanbul Tahkim ve Arabuluculuk Merkezi (ISTAC) Tahkim Yargilamasinda Delillerin Ibrazı ve Değerlendirilmesi', 98.
244. Spitzer, 'Der Sachverständigenbeweis Im Österreichischen Zivilprozess', 28; Feutrill and Rubins, 'The Preparation of Expert Evidence in International Commercial Arbitration: Practical Aspects', 315; *see VM Solar Jerez GmbH, M Solar Verwaltungs GmbH, Solarizz Holding Verwaltungs-GmbH, M Solar GmbH & Co. KG, Solarizz Holding GmbH & Co. KG and Helmut Vorndran v. Kingdom of Spain*, ICSID Case No. ARB/19/30, Decision on the Proposal to Disqualify All Members of the Tribunal (18 October 2022), para. 23.
245. The HMK Art. 266(1) and Turkish Law on Experts (No. 6754) Art. 10(4) prohibit lawyers to be (court-appointed) experts, *see* Tanrıver, *Medenî Usûl Hukuku*, 2021, I:409–11; Elyıldırım, *Hukuk Yargılamasında Uzman Görüşü*, 113–115; Akıncı, *Milletlerarası Tahkim*, 340–341, fn. 459; Budak and Karaaslan, *Medenî Usul Hukuku*, 2022, 309; Özbek, *Tahkim Hukuku*, II:1448; *Atalı* argues that legal court-appointed experts impact the proceedings in a positive way and should be allowed, *see* Atalı, '6754 Sayılı Bilirkişilik Kanunu ve Hukuki Konularda Bilirkişilik', 3278 ff.
246. Cordero-Moss, 'Iura Novit Curia', 111.
247. Pekcanıtez, Atalay, and Özekes, *Medenî Usûl Hukuku Ders Kitabı*, 624; Pekcanıtez and Yeşilirmak, 'Tahkim', 2705; Tanrıver, *Medenî Usûl Hukuku*, 2022, II:431; Özbek, *Tahkim Hukuku*, II:1363.
248. O'Malley, *Rules of Evidence in International Arbitration*, 174; Centner, *Iura Novit Curia in Internationalen Schiedsverfahren: Eine Historisch-Rechtsvergleichende Studie Zu Den Grundlagen Der Rechtsermittlung*, 112; Jones, 'Ineffective Use of Expert Evidence in Construction Arbitration', 2. Can and Tuna, *Milletlerarası Tahkim Hukuku*, 417; Harris and Ali, 'Better Never Than Late?', 271.
249. Wach and Petsch, 'Der Sachverständigenbeweis Im Schiedsverfahren: Grenzen Der Gestaltungsfreiheit von Parteien Und Schiedsgericht', 96; Schütze, *Das Internationale Zivilprozessrecht in Der ZPO: Kommentar*, 70–71.

and construing those materials.[250] Although applying the relevant legal principles to the facts is the duty of the arbitrators, legal experts also opine on how to apply the relevant rules to the present facts.[251]

Legal experts present a particular challenge to the arbitral tribunal because their opinions can be closely intertwined with advocacy. Legal experts typically provide views on international law, international investment law, or the domestic law of the investor or host state in investor-state arbitration.

1.4.2.2.1 International Law Experts

In international practice, arbitrators appearing in an international investment case are expected to be the foremost experts in international and investment law.[252] In international investment disputes, submitting a report from a party-appointed expert whose expertise is in international law is not plausible because the expert presents views on points of law; it would instead make sense to have him as a co-counsel.[253] A well-established tribunal will hardly be impressed that the relevant person is appointed as an expert and will know how to weigh the statements. It would be more suitable to have him as a counsel or even to classify and treat the expert in that manner. Nevertheless, international law experts should not be excluded in advance. However, less weight can be attributed where the tribunal does not find it relevant.[254]

However, international law experts are frequently used in international investment law disputes. For instance, in the famous Yukos case, *inter alia*, the provisional application of the Energy Charter Treaty (ECT), possibly with regard to the jurisdiction of the Arbitral Tribunal vis-à-vis cases lodged against Russia, was an issue for which an expert opinion was submitted.

In *Phillip Morris v. Uruguay,*[255] international law experts provided an opinion on the meaning of international intellectual property law, the interpretation of fair and equitable treatment, arbitrary treatment, and the requisites and burdens of proof applicable to denials of justice under customary international law.[256]

When determining the content of the law, according to the principle of *the iura novit arbiter,* the arbitrator must exhaust all sources of knowledge. If, despite every effort, the arbitrator is not able to access the relevant information, he or she shall use a legal

250. Feutrill and Rubins, 'The Preparation of Expert Evidence in International Commercial Arbitration: Practical Aspects', 315.
251. Feutrill and Rubins, 315.
252. Hodgson and Stewart, 'Experts in Investor-State Arbitration: The Tribunal as Gatekeeper', 455.
253. Blackaby and Wilbraham, 'Practical Issues Relating to the Use of Expert Evidence in Investment Treaty Arbitration', 655, 661.
254. Freyer, Newman, and Hill, 'Assessing Expert Evidence', 430, 441; Almost all respondents (93%) in a survey share this view in 'BCLP 2021 Survey', 9.
255. *Philip Morris Brands Sàrl, Philip Morris Products S.A. and Abal Hermanos S.A. v. Oriental Republic of Uruguay,* ICSID Case No. ARB/10/7 available at https://www.italaw.com/cases/460 (accessed 9 December 2023); Alvarez, 'The Search for Objectivity: The Use of Experts in Philip Morris v Uruguay', 414–418.
256. Alvarez, 418; Ünüvar, 'Experts: Investment Arbitration', para. 53.

expert. This is natural because the arbitrator should try to render an award that should be safe from annulment and subject to enforcement, if necessary.[257]

1.4.2.2.2 (Domestic) Foreign Law Experts

Although arbitrators should also be appointed based on their knowledge of the relevant domestic law, legal experts are more often employed to present opinions on the application of domestic law.[258] Some have pointed to the particular circumstances of investment arbitration, with respect to the need to understand procedural and substantive areas of domestic law in jurisdictions unfamiliar to the arbitrators, as a way of accounting for the practice of resorting to legal experts.[259]

It is expected that an arbitral tribunal, or at least one of the members appointed by the parties or the court, has an extended knowledge of the law applicable to the dispute. However, given the nature of complex multi-party arbitrations in practice, it is highly likely that the tribunal requires assistance in understanding specific provisions of foreign law that it is not familiar with.[260] In addition, if an amended legal provision is so far back that it is hard for the arbitrator to have a firm understanding, then a legal expert might be helpful.[261] In such cases, legal experts can be appointed by the tribunal, or the parties can also rely on such experts.[262]

In English courts, applicable foreign law is proven by reference to expert evidence.[263] The Singapore International Commercial Court Practice Directions also allow the use of foreign law experts.[264]

Generally speaking, in countries following the civil law approach, courts have considerable authority to apply foreign law and ascertain its content.[265] In international arbitration, the responsibility for ascertaining foreign law is generally divided between the parties and the tribunal. However, a different approach can be adopted depending on both the counsel and the arbitrators in each case.

---

257. Centner, *Iura Novit Curia in Internationalen Schiedsverfahren: Eine Historisch-Rechtsvergleichende Studie Zu Den Grundlagen Der Rechtsermittlung*, 112; It is even possible that eight legal experts do not suffice to determine the applicable legal rules, *see*, for example, BGH, II ZR 49/90, 21 January 1991, paras 5–11.
258. Blackaby and Wilbraham, 'Practical Issues Relating to the Use of Expert Evidence in Investment Treaty Arbitration', 661.
259. Blackaby and Wilbraham, 660.
260. Khodykin and Mulcahy, *A Guide to the IBA Rules on the Taking of Evidence in International Arbitration*, 287.
261. Centner, *Iura Novit Curia in Internationalen Schiedsverfahren: Eine Historisch-Rechtsvergleichende Studie Zu Den Grundlagen Der Rechtsermittlung*, 98.
262. Schütze, 'Der Beweis Des Anwendbaren Rechts Im Schiedsverfahren Und Die Feststellung Seines Inhalts', 154.
263. Khodykin and Mulcahy, *A Guide to the IBA Rules on the Taking of Evidence in International Arbitration*, 287; Similarly for International Arbitration, *see* Hobér and Sussman, *Cross-Examination in International Arbitration*, 26.
264. Singapore International Commercial Court Practice Directions, Rule 26(2). https://www.judiciary.gov.sg/docs/default-source/amendments-docs/2022/sicc-pd_2022_v1.pdf?sfvrsn=4d986e38_2 (accessed 10 August 2022).
265. International Law Association Committee on International Commercial Arbitration, 'Ascertaining the Contents of the Applicable Law in International Commercial Arbitration', 163 ff.

Aktepe Artık argued that although it is generally possible for a non-lawyer arbitrator or arbitral tribunal to appoint a legal expert, the appointment of a legal expert should not be allowed in the presence of a legal arbitrator. Appointing a legal expert if the sole arbitrator is a lawyer or if there is a legal arbitrator in the arbitral tribunal is not considered an appropriate solution, considering that it will cause an increase in trial costs and that the parties have chosen the arbitrator on the grounds that he is an expert on the subject of the dispute. When it is remembered that the law requires that if the arbitrator consists of more than one person, at least one of them must be a lawyer with five years or more seniority in his field, it would not be suitable for the arbitrator, who is already assumed to be an expert, to appoint another person who is an expert to make legal evaluations.[266]

For instance, in *Yukos v. Russia*, legal expert opinions were submitted for, *inter alia*, constitutional legal aspects of the conclusion and application of the international treaties of Russia and the arbitrability of taxation-related issues under Russian law.[267] Similarly, in *Joshua Dean Nelson v. The United Mexican States*, the disputing parties adduced expert reports concerning Mexican and US civil and administrative law, specifically regarding corporations and bankruptcy law.[268]

In a mining dispute filed against Peru, multiple expert opinions were acquired from both the claimant investor and the respondent host state. The opinions were related to Peruvian law provisions in the mining sector.

To over-rely on domestic law experts is dangerous because there might be multiple views on a domestic law issue.[269] In addition, lawyers are often poor experts because they can easily cross the line between being in the shoes of an expert and advocating for the appointing party.[270] In addition, there is always the opportunity to engage with local co-counsel, who are naturally expected to know and have the capacity to make arguments on local law.

The tribunal does not have to appoint a natural person directly but can choose to acquire knowledge from a university or institution such as the Max-Planck Institute (MPI) for International and Comparative Law or the MPI for International Procedural Law.

The crucial point here is that the tribunal shall not, in any case, delegate its adjudication duty and authority to the legal expert.[271]

266. Aktepe Artık, *Medeni Usûl Hukukunda Hakem Kararlarının İptali Sebepleri*, 380.
267. Ünüvar, 'Experts: Investment Arbitration', para. 48; *Yukos Universal Limited (Isle of Man) v. The Russian Federation*, UNCITRAL, PCA Case No. 2005-04/AA227 https://www.italaw.com/cases/1175 (accessed 24 September 2025).
268. *Joshua Dean Nelson and Jorge Blanco v. United Mexican States*, ICSID Case No. UNCT/17/1, para. 165. https://www.italaw.com/sites/default/files/case-documents/italaw11557_0.pdf (accessed 17 August 2023).
269. Hodgson and Stewart, 'Experts in Investor-State Arbitration: The Tribunal as Gatekeeper', 455; Khodykin and Mulcahy, *A Guide to the IBA Rules on the Taking of Evidence in International Arbitration*, 287.
270. Blackaby and Wilbraham, 'Practical Issues Relating to the Use of Expert Evidence in Investment Treaty Arbitration', 661.
271. Schütze, 'Der Beweis Des Anwendbaren Rechts Im Schiedsverfahren Und Die Feststellung Seines Inhalts', 155; Oetiker, 'Commentary on Art. 26-30 Swiss Rules of Arbitration', 313.

Again, in *Phillip Morris v. Uruguay*, Uruguayan law experts expressed views about whether the implemented law, which allegedly deprived the investor, extended the police power to protect health, protected the use of trademarks, considered trademarks as property, or enabled contradictory decisions by national courts.[272]

1.4.2.3 Quantum (Valuation/Damages) Experts

After a tribunal concludes that one or more parties are liable for damages or the tribunal needs to evaluate the value of a specific asset, set of goods or a company, quantum (valuation) experts are the type of experts that are needed. Quantum or valuation experts are cost engineers, accountants, and financial experts and are indispensable, especially when it is hard or not possible for the arbitral tribunal to calculate the damages or compensation in a case.[273]

In some cases, it may be readily determinable for the tribunal, based on the records, to calculate the claim of the claiming party. However, this is only occasionally the case. How should it be expected from an average arbitrator when a melting furnace that was ordered and just installed explodes in a facility, and fire surrounds and damages a whole facility that becomes inoperable for months? Not only the price for the furnace but also the installation work, all other damaged equipment, and the financial loss due to inoperability have to be calculated.

In addition, when licences have been illegally ceased or the facilities of an investor projected to operate for decades in the relevant state have been expropriated, the expected income must be calculated. Thus, the tribunal will have to consult the opinions of one or more experts to award compensation.

Quantum experts are the expert type mostly faced in arbitration due to the overwhelming incapacity of fiscal skills of arbitrators, which is a result of the lack of fiscal curricula in legal education.[274]

Quantum experts are expected to bridge the gap between arbitral tribunals, which decide on the liability but cannot determine the exact amount to be awarded. However,

---

272. Alvarez, 'The Search for Objectivity: The Use of Experts in Philip Morris v Uruguay', 418; Ünüvar, 'Experts: Investment Arbitration', para. 53; O'Malley, *Rules of Evidence in International Arbitration*, 173.
273. Simmons, 'Valuation in Investor-State Arbitration: Toward a More Exact Science', 208 ff.; White, *The Use of Experts by International Tribunals*, 128; Abdel Wahab, 'Party Appointed Experts in International Commercial Arbitration', 183.
    In investor-state arbitrations, generally, if the investor prevails partially or fully on his or her claims, damages are awarded. An UNCTAD study reviewing cases concluded in 2014 found that only 2% of cases concluded that year found a breach, but did not award damages to the investor. UNCTAD, 'Recent Trends in IIAs and ISDS' (2015) 8 http://unctad.org/en/PublicationsLibrary/webdiaepcb2015d1_en.pdf (accessed 5 July 2022). Similar statistics were found for cases concluded in 2015, *see* UNCTAD, 'Investor-State Dispute Settlement: Review of Developments in 2015' (2015) http://investmentpolicyhub.unctad.org/Upload/ISDS%20Issues%20Note%202016.pdf (accessed 11 July 2022).
274. Ünüvar, 'Experts: Investment Arbitration', para. 61; Tuna, *Alternative Dispute Resolution in Energy Industries*, 209.

as observed in practice, this function is not always easily fulfilled due to the availability of multiple calculation approaches and models for the same occasion.[275]

For instance, the 'income-based approach', which estimates the value of a business based on discounted cash flow (DCF), the 'market-based approach', which compares the subject of valuation to that of other similar businesses and the 'assets-based approach' which is based on the idea that an asset is worth no more than it would cost to replace all of its constituent parts.[276]

Especially when it comes to investment arbitration, quantum experts present the greatest challenge in increasingly high-stakes cases because they generally present widely divergent estimates of damages that tribunals struggle to understand and make use of, but are indispensable in order to reach a final determination of a damages award.[277] Tribunals have also been criticised for decisions on damages that lack a sufficient explanation of how the valuation was determined or the usage of inconsistent methodologies to synthesise divergent expert valuations.[278]

Simmons rightly argued that the negative consequences of inaccurate and opaque valuations could extend to the entire arbitral system.[279] Such weaknesses in reasoning can lead to challenges in awarding and, in some instances, annulment of damages awards.[280]

1.5 INTERIM CONCLUSION

Experts are qualified, impartial, objective, and reputable individuals or organisations who have special training, education, skills, or knowledge and experience that falls within their expertise. They can also be consulted for the resolution of a dispute before a court or arbitral tribunal to resolve disputes.[281]

275. Blackaby and Wilbraham, 'Practical Issues Relating to the Use of Expert Evidence in Investment Treaty Arbitration', 661; O'Malley, *Rules of Evidence in International Arbitration*, 173; *see* the proposals from Jones to overcome the challenges, Jones, 'Ineffective Use of Expert Evidence in Construction Arbitration', 13–14. O'Malley, Rules of Evidence in International Arbitration, 173; Jones, 'Ineffective Use of Expert Evidence in Construction Arbitration', 13–14.
276. Giray, *Milletlerarası Yatırım Tahkiminde Kamulaştırmadan Dogan Tazminat ve Tazminatın Hesaplanmasında Kullanılan Yöntemler*, 222 ff.; Trenor, *The Guide to Damages in International Arbitration*, 184 ff.; Yıldızlı, *Uluslararası Tahkimde Zararın Degerlendirilmesi*, 122.
277. Blackaby and Wilbraham, 'Practical Issues Relating to the Use of Expert Evidence in Investment Treaty Arbitration', 663; *see*, for instance, the ad hoc Committee found in *Maritime International Nominees Establishment v. Republic of Guinea*, ICSID Case No. ARB/84/4, Decision on Annulment, 14 December 1989, para. 6.107 the tribunal's decision on quantum 'inconsistent and in contradiction with its analysis of damages theories' and annulled the award.
278. Simmons, 'Valuation in Investor-State Arbitration: Toward a More Exact Science', 208.
279. *See* Simmons, 208 ff.
280. Hodgson and Stewart, 'Experts in Investor-State Arbitration: The Tribunal as Gatekeeper', 456; *Venezuela Holdings, BV and others v. Bolivarian Republic of Venezuela*, ICSID Case No ARB/07/27, Decision on Annulment (2017); *Occidental Petroleum Corporation and others v. Republic of Ecuador*, ICSID Case No ARB/06/11, Decision on Annulment (2015); *Mar Int'l Nominees Establishment v. Guinea*, ICSID Case No ARB/84/4, Decision on Annulment (1989).
281. Tanrıver, *Hukukumuzda Bilirkişilik*, 25; *see* Cayan, *Medeni Usul Hukukunda Bilirkişilik Müessesesi*, 3 ff.; Van Damme, 'The Assessment of Expert Evidence in International Adjudication', 402; Mosk, 'The Role of Facts in International Dispute Resolution (Volume 304)', 126.

Civil law and common law have developed different approaches to the use of experts in dispute resolution. Despite the differences in traditions, international arbitration practice overwhelmingly favours the use of party-appointed experts. One of the reasons that parties choose arbitration over other forms of dispute resolution is to have freedom and control over evidence.

Primarily, experts are used to clarify disputed issues that have a material outcome to the case, which the arbitrators are not able to understand. Thus, experts support tribunals in the decision-making process. In some situations, the expert can be the original source of facts in the sense that the expert observed, assessed and organised the facts after an inspection on site.[282] Parties to a dispute may even engage experts before proceedings to receive help in constructing the pleadings of the case.[283]

Experts can be categorised based on the appointing authority or on the subject on which they will give an opinion. Based on the appointing authority, experts are either appointed by the parties or appointed by the arbitral tribunal. Based on the subject on which the expert will provide an opinion, they can be classified as technical/scientific experts, legal experts and quantum (valuation) experts. In most international arbitration cases, more than one category of experts is used in a single case.[284]

Technical expertise is often required as a substantive area relevant to the case that is normally outside the competence of the tribunal, such as construction, oil and gas, mining, intellectual property, environment or other areas of science, such as planning/delay analysis, market practice, technology and forensic analysis.[285]

Arbitrators in international arbitration cases may be from different countries. However, there may be foreign law issues that the arbitrators are not familiar. In such situations, legal experts are useful to understand the applicable law.[286] Legal experts typically provide opinions on international law, international investment law, or the domestic law of the investor or host state in investor-state arbitration.

Damages or losses of profits are the most common remedies in international arbitration. In some cases, damages and loss of profits are easily determinable for the tribunal based on the records. However, in most cases, complex calculations are required. After a tribunal concludes that one or more parties are liable for damages or

282. Tanrıver, *Hukukumuzda Bilirkişilik*, 25; Van Damme, 'The Assessment of Expert Evidence in International Adjudication', 402; O'Malley, *Rules of Evidence in International Arbitration*, 186; Özbek, *Tahkim Hukuku*, II:1448.

283. Lew, Mistelis, and Kröll, *Comparative International Commercial Arbitration*, 578; Parlett, 'Parties' Engagement with Experts in International Litigation', 441.

284. Kalpsüz, *Türkiye'de Milletlerarası Tahkim*, 92.

285. Blackaby and Wilbraham, 'Practical Issues Relating to the Use of Expert Evidence in Investment Treaty Arbitration', 661; Hodgson and Stewart, 'Experts in Investor-State Arbitration: The Tribunal as Gatekeeper', 455; Mosk, 'The Role of Facts in International Dispute Resolution (Volume 304)', 128; Jones, 'Ineffective Use of Expert Evidence in Construction Arbitration', 2; Spitzer, 'Der Sachverständigenbeweis Im Österreichischen Zivilprozess', 28.

286. Abdel Wahab, 'Party Appointed Experts in International Commercial Arbitration', 183; Foster, 'The Role of Adjudicators and the Role of Experts', 147; Kalpsüz, *Türkiye'de Milletlerarası Tahkim*, 92; Ağırman, *Milli & Milletlerarası Tahkim*, 460; Özbek, *Tahkim Hukuku*, II:1458; Schneider and Scherer, 'Art. 184', 2098; Centner, *Iura Novit Curia in Internationalen Schiedsverfahren: Eine Historisch-Rechtsvergleichende Studie Zu Den Grundlagen Der Rechtsermittlung*, 111–112; Ahrens, *Der Beweis Im Zivilprozess*, 29, 459.

the tribunal needs to evaluate the value of a specific asset, set of goods or a company, quantum (valuation) experts are the type of experts, such as cost engineers, accountants and financial experts.[287]

287. Simmons, 'Valuation in Investor-State Arbitration: Toward a More Exact Science', 208 ff.; White, *The Use of Experts by International Tribunals*, 128; Abdel Wahab, 'Party Appointed Experts in International Commercial Arbitration', 183.

In investor-state arbitrations, generally, if the investor prevails partially or fully on his or her claims, damages are awarded. An UNCTAD study reviewing cases concluded in 2014 found that only 2% of cases concluded that year found a breach but did not award damages to the investor. UNCTAD, 'Recent Trends in IIAs and ISDS' (2015) 8 http://unctad.org/en/PublicationsLibrary/webdiaepcb2015d1_en.pdf (accessed 5 July 2022). Similar statistics were found for cases concluded in 2015; *see* UNCTAD, 'Investor-State Dispute Settlement: Review of Developments in 2015' (2015) http://investmentpolicyhub.unctad.org/Upload/ISDS%20Issues%20Note%202016.pdf (accessed 11 July 2022).

CHAPTER 2
Party-Appointed Experts

2.1 LEGAL BASIS

Besides limitations in a few jurisdictions, overwhelmingly, international conventions, statutory provisions of countries and arbitration rules permit the parties to appoint and rely on their own experts,[288] sometimes explicitly and sometimes implicitly, relying on the party autonomy principle.

Nevertheless, unlike rules applicable to tribunal-appointed experts, the most prominent arbitration rules mentioned below in section 2.1.2 do not address the role, qualifications, or ethical duties of party-appointed experts.

2.1.1 International Treaties

Although international conventions are not expected to include rules on experts and their procedures, some regional and bilateral treaties have provisions that authorise parties to rely on party-appointed experts. Below, some examples of these are analysed.

2.1.1.1 The United States-Mexico-Canada Agreement

The United States-Mexico-Canada Agreement (*USMCA*) is a comprehensive convention with provisions, *inter alia,* on free trade and investment. The USMCA entered into force on 1 July 2020, replacing the North American Free Trade Agreement (*NAFTA*).

288. Starting from this section to the end of this script, the terms 'party-appointed expert', 'party expert' and 'expert' are used interchangeably, referring to the same concept. Where explanations related to specifically tribunal-appointed experts are provided, this will be explicitly specified.

USMCA Chapter 14, Article 14.D.11, permits the appointment of party-appointed experts:

> Without prejudice to the appointment of other kinds of experts when authorized by the applicable arbitration rules, a tribunal, on request of a disputing party or, unless the disputing parties disapprove, on its own initiative, may appoint one or more experts to report to it in writing on any factual issue concerning scientific matters raised by a disputing party in a proceeding, subject to any terms and conditions that the disputing parties may agree.

2.1.1.2 Comprehensive Economic and Trade Agreement

The Comprehensive Economic and Trade Agreement (*CETA*) between Canada, the European Union, and its Member States is a progressive trade agreement between the EU and Canada, which entered into force provisionally in 2017.[289]

In addition, indirectly, the agreement also enables the disputing parties to rely on their own experts. Chapter 8 Article 8.37(1) provides that '[a] disputing party may disclose to other persons in connection with the proceedings, including witnesses and experts, such unredacted documents as it considers necessary in the course of proceedings under this Section'.

2.1.2 Arbitration Rules

UNCITRAL Arbitration Rules and leading institutional arbitration rules generally provide provisions for experts. However, these are not specific and leave a large margin for determination by the arbitral tribunal.

2.1.2.1 ICSID Arbitration Rules

On 21 March 2022, the Administrative Council of the ICSID approved extensive amendments to its Regulations and Rules. There are various provisions in the ICSID Arbitration Rules (as well as the Additional Facility Rules) regarding the use of party-appointed experts. ICSID Arbitration Rule 38 regulates the adducing of witness and (party-appointed) expert evidence. ICSID Arbitration Rule 38(7) provides that Rule 38 paragraphs (1)–(5) regarding witnesses shall apply, with necessary modifications, to evidence given by a party-appointed expert.

Accordingly, the provisions provide that a party intending to rely on evidence given by an expert shall file a written statement by that expert, which shall identify the expert, contain the expert report, and be signed and dated (ICSID Arbitration Rule 38(1)).

The party-appointed expert may be called for examination at a hearing in which the tribunal determines how the examination will be conducted, but in any case, before the

289. https://policy.trade.ec.europa.eu/eu-trade-relationships-country-and-region/countries-and-regions/canada/eu-canada-agreement_en (accessed 28 September 2023).

tribunal, by the parties, and under the control of the chair of the tribunal (ICSID Arbitration Rule 38(2–4)). The expert shall be examined in person unless the arbitral tribunal determines that another means, such as video conferences, of examination is appropriate in the circumstances (ICSID Arbitration Rule 38(5)). The experts must make the following declaration before giving evidence: 'I solemnly declare upon my honour and conscience that my statement will be in accordance with my sincere belief.' (ICSID Arbitration Rule 38(8)). The ICSID Additional Facility Rules on the subject (Rule 48) are similar to the Arbitration Rules with respect to experts.

Phillip Morris v. Uruguay is an example case where party-appointed experts were heavily relied upon, including experts on law, on the marketing of cigarettes and on public health.[290]

Additionally, in ICSID Arbitration practice, the tribunal (president) may wish to retain an assistant for additional support. Such an assistant may only be appointed with the prior consent of both parties to the dispute. The parties should be informed about the assistant's *curriculum vitae*, tasks to be performed, and fee-related issues.[291]

For instance, in *Coropi Holdings et al. v. Serbia,*[292] the tribunal retained a Public International Law professor. The tribunal ruled in the First Procedural Order as follows:

> it would benefit the overall cost and time efficiency of the proceedings if the Tribunal had an assistant. By letter of 6 March 2023, the presiding arbitrator, with the approval of the other Members of the Tribunal, proposed that Professor Philippa Webb be appointed as Assistant to the Tribunal.
>
> Professor Webb will (i) undertake only such specific tasks as are assigned to her by the presiding arbitrator, such as the marshalling of evidence, research of specific issues of law, organisation of case documents, monitoring of the case correspondence, and similar matters; (ii) assist the Tribunal during its deliberations; (iii) undertake such tasks in support of the ICSID Secretary of the Tribunal as the Secretary of the Tribunal and the presiding arbitrator may consider appropriate. Professor Webb will not undertake any functions incumbent upon a Member of the Tribunal, nor duplicate the tasks of the ICSID Secretary of the Tribunal.
>
> Professor Webb shall be subject to the same confidentiality obligations as the Members of the Tribunal and sign a declaration to that effect.
>
> The Parties approved the appointment of Professor Webb as Assistant to the Tribunal.
>
> Professor Webb shall receive: (a) US$ 250 for each hour of work performed in connection with the case or pro rata; and (b) reimbursement of reasonable expenses related to the hearing on the same basis as applies to Members of the

290. *See Philip Morris Brands Sàrl, Philip Morris Products S.A. and Abal Hermanos S.A. v. Oriental Republic of Uruguay*, ICSID Case No. ARB/10/7, Award, 8 July 2016, https://www.italaw.com/sites/default/files/case-documents/italaw7417.pdf (accessed 9 December 2023); Alvarez, 'The Search for Objectivity: The Use of Experts in Philip Morris v Uruguay', 413.
291. *See* https://icsid.worldbank.org/resources/content/arbitrators/tribunal-assistants (accessed 20 September 2023).
292. *Coropi Holdings Limited, Kalemegdan Investments Limited and Erinn Bernard Broshko v. Republic of Serbia*, ICSID Case No. ARB/22/14.

Tribunal. The fees and expenses of Professor Webb will be paid from the advance payments made by the parties.[293]

2.1.2.2 *UNCITRAL Arbitration Rules*

UNCITRAL Arbitration Rules are a comprehensive set of procedural rules upon which parties may agree to conduct arbitral proceedings arising out of their relationship. They are widely used in investment, commercial, ad hoc, and administered arbitrations.

The UNCITRAL Arbitration Rules explicitly stipulate that parties may rely on their own experts. Unless otherwise directed by the arbitral tribunal, statements by an expert (Expert Report) may be presented in writing and signed by them (UNCITRAL Arbitration Rules Article 27(2)). The provision states that experts could be any individual party or any individual related to a party; however, there is nothing specific about the qualification of party-appointed experts.[294]

The tribunal may require experts to attend hearings but may also allow attendance by video conference, or the proceedings can be conducted on the basis of documents and other materials (UNCITRAL Arbitration Rules Article 17(3)).[295]

2.1.2.3 *ICC Arbitration Rules*

The ICC Arbitration Rules do not have detailed provisions for party-appointed experts. The ICC Arbitration Rules provide for party-appointed experts in a provision that regulates the hearing. Accordingly, the arbitral tribunal may decide to hear experts appointed by the parties in the presence of the parties or in their absence, provided they have been duly summoned (ICC Arbitration Rules Article 25(2)).[296]

2.1.2.4 *Istanbul Arbitration Centre (ISTAC) Arbitration Rules*

The ISTAC Arbitration Rules foresee the appointment of party-appointed experts under a simple provision. ISTAC Arbitration Rules Article 29(3) provides that:

> [t]he Sole Arbitrator or Arbitral Tribunal may hear the experts appointed by the parties, as well as, after consulting with the parties, if it deems necessary, may appoint an expert and define the scope of duty. At the hearing, the Sole Arbitrator or Arbitral Tribunal or the parties, may directly ask questions to any such expert(s).

---

293. *Coropi Holdings Limited, Kalemegdan Investments Limited and Erinn Bernard Broshko v. Republic of Serbia*, ICSID Case No. ARB/22/14, Procedural Order No. 1, 31 March 2023 (para. 8).
294. Hodgson and Stewart, 'Experts in Investor-State Arbitration: The Tribunal as Gatekeeper', 459.
295. Bor, 'Expert Evidence', 505; Mbengue and Das, 'Rules Governing the Use of Experts in International Disputes', 445.
296. Reiner and Aschauer, 'ICC Rules', 135; Bor, 'Expert Evidence', 506.

2.1.2.5 *Istanbul Chamber of Commerce (ITOTAM) Arbitration Rules*

Contrary to other institutional rules, the ITOTAM Arbitration Rules are rather detailed when it comes to provisions concerning experts. Article 28(2) stipulates that the arbitral tribunal may require the parties to submit their expert reports and evidence together with their translations in the language or languages agreed upon by the parties or determined by the arbitral tribunal.

Article 34(1) foresees that the arbitral tribunal may decide to hear party-appointed experts in the presence of the parties or in their absence only if such parties have been duly summoned but failed to appear without stating any valid excuse.

Article 35 is a great example that regulates the framework of party-appointed experts. Article 35(1) explicitly states that the arbitral tribunal, instead of appointing itself an expert, may request the parties to bring an expert opinion. This is a novel provision since, as will be elaborated on in the coming chapters, it diminishes the problem of an arbitral award being set aside on the ground that the tribunal did not appoint an expert.

According to Article 35(2), the parties and the arbitral tribunal may examine experts at the hearing. Article 35(3) regulates the binding nature of expert evidence. The provision stipulates that the arbitral tribunal will freely evaluate both the party-appointed and tribunal-appointed expert opinions.

Finally, Article 53(2) obliges experts involved in the arbitration administered by ITOTAM to keep the arbitral proceedings confidential.

2.1.2.6 *The LCIA Arbitration Rules*

The LCIA Arbitration Rules have detailed provisions regarding party-appointed experts, which it refers to as 'witnesses'. The tribunal has exercised broad discretion in relation to experts in the rules.

Before any hearing, the Arbitral Tribunal may order any party to inform in writing the identity of each expert that the party wishes to rely on, as well as the subject matter, content and relevance to the issues of that expert's opinion and testimony (LCIA Arbitration Rules Article 20(2)).[297]

In principle, the expert will provide a written opinion, either as a signed statement or a document. However, the tribunal can direct the expert otherwise (LCIA Arbitration Rules Article 20(3)).

The Arbitral Tribunal will decide the time, manner, and form in which the written materials shall be exchanged between the parties and presented to the Arbitral Tribunal, and it may allow, refuse, or limit the written and oral testimony of experts (LCIA Arbitration Rules Article 20(4)).

One of the essential powers of the tribunal is that if it orders the other party to secure the attendance of that expert and the expert refuses or fails to attend the hearing without good cause, the tribunal can infer adversely and limit the weight of the written

297. Bor, 'Expert Evidence', 506.

expert opinion or exclude all or any part thereof altogether, as it considers appropriate in the circumstances (LCIA Arbitration Rules Article 20(5)).[298]

The LCIA Arbitration Rules allow expert shopping, which means that any party or its authorised representatives can interview any potential expert for the purpose of presenting an opinion to the tribunal, subject to the mandatory provisions of any applicable law, rules of law and any order of the arbitral tribunal otherwise (LCIA Arbitration Rules Article 20(6)).

LCIA Arbitration Rules do not require a sharp independence and impartiality requirement for the party-appointed expert and allow any individual who is even a party to the arbitration or was, remains or has become an officer, employee, owner, or shareholder of any party or is otherwise identified with any party, to become a party-appointed expert, subject to any order by the Arbitral Tribunal otherwise (LCIA Arbitration Rules Article 20(7)).

Subject to the mandatory provisions of any applicable law, the tribunal can administer any appropriate oath or affirmation to any expert at any hearing before the oral testimony of that expert (LCIA Arbitration Rules Article 20(8)).

The rules permit the examination of the expert by the tribunal and by each of the parties under the control of the tribunal (LCIA Arbitration Rules Article 20(9)).

Finally, Article 30.1 of the LCIA Arbitration Rules establishes that the confidentiality obligation is not only on the tribunal or the parties but also extends to party-appointed experts.

2.1.2.7 SIAC Arbitration Rules

Before any hearing, the Tribunal may require the parties to give notice to the identity experts whom the parties intend to produce, the subject matter of their testimony, and its relevance to the issues (SIAC Arbitration Rules 25.1).

The Tribunal may allow, refuse, or limit the appearance of experts to give oral evidence at any hearing (SIAC Arbitration Rules 25.2). The experts who provide oral testimony may be questioned by each of the parties, their representatives and the Tribunal in the manner that the Tribunal may determine (SIAC Arbitration Rules 25.3).

The Tribunal may direct the testimony of experts to be presented in written form, either as signed statements or sworn affidavits or any other form of recording. Subject to Rule 25.2, any party may request that such expert attend for oral examination. If the witness fails to attend an oral examination, the Tribunal may place such weight on the written testimony as it thinks fit, disregard such written testimony, or exclude such written testimony altogether (SIAC Arbitration Rules 25.4).

It is permitted for any party or its representatives to interview any experts or potential experts (that may be presented by that party) prior to their appearance to give oral evidence at any hearing (SIAC Arbitration Rules 25.5).

298. *See* Amaral, 'Burden of Proof and Adverse Inferences in International Arbitration: Proposal for an Inference Chart', 27.

The SIAC Investment Arbitration Rules of 2017 have a different provision than the SIAC Arbitration Rules of 2016. Accordingly, the written statement of the claimant and respondent shall include any expert report supporting the claim or defence (SIAC Investment Arbitration Rules 17.2.c. and 17.3.c.).

2.1.2.8 Swiss Rules

The Swiss Rules are rather conservative regarding the explicit regulation of party-appointed experts. The rules only directly prescribe provisions for tribunal-appointed experts in Article 28.

Nevertheless, tacit provisions can be found in Articles 26 and 27. Article 26(2) foresees that, at any time during the arbitration proceedings, the arbitral tribunal may require the parties to produce documents, exhibits, or other evidence within a time limit set by the arbitral tribunal. Party-appointed experts could be 'other evidence' in the sense of this provision.

Article 27(1) of the Swiss Rules states that at any stage of proceedings, the tribunal may hold a hearing for the presentation of evidence by experts or for oral argument.

Article 27(4) foresees that, before a hearing and within the time limit set by the arbitral tribunal, expert evidence may be presented in the form of written statements or reports. Experts may be heard and examined at the hearing. The arbitral tribunal may direct that experts be concerned through means that do not require their physical presence at the hearing, such as videoconference (Article 27(5)).

2.1.2.9 German Arbitration Institute (DIS, *Deutsche Institution für Schiedsgerichtsbarkeit*) Arbitration Rules

The DIS Rules Arbitration Rules do not have an explicit provision that regulates party-appointed experts. However, the DIS Arbitration Rules allow for both party-appointed and/or tribunal-appointed experts. The 2018 DIS Arbitration Rules encourage the parties and the arbitral tribunal to consider early on in the proceedings how to best deal with possible expert input in the arbitration, including in Article 27.7 and Articles 28.1, 28.2 and 28.3, 32 as well as Annex 3A of the Rules.

Article 28 sets the ground rules according to which the arbitral tribunal may appoint an expert on its own initiative. Article 28 does not provide for comparable restrictions concerning the party-appointed experts. Especially, there is no requirement for impartiality and independence. The arbitral tribunal is, however, advised to safeguard a certain standard by conducting proper briefings or requesting confirmation that the witness is impartial and has no prior involvement in the respective dispute.[299]

According to DIS Arbitration Rules Article 28, the arbitral tribunal, if it deems necessary, appoints an expert. The arbitral tribunal's appointing competence is not ultimate but restricted under Article 28.3. The provision requires the arbitral tribunal's

299. Trittmann and Schardt, 'The Proceedings Before the Arbitral Tribunal, Article 28: Establishing the Facts', 464.

consultation with the parties before appointing an expert (Article 28(3)). The provision further requires that the expert appointed by the arbitral tribunal shall be impartial and independent of the parties. The arbitral tribunal is obliged to discuss with the parties in the case management conference or, in subsequent meetings, whether to employ experts and, if so, how to efficiently conduct the procedure as per Article 27.7.[300] Article 28.3 implements a mechanism to challenge such tribunal-appointed experts, similar to the challenge of arbitrators. The purpose of these limitations is said to safeguard due process and guarantee the validity of the award.

The DIS Arbitration Rules Annex 3 foresees measures for increasing the procedural efficiency of the arbitral proceedings. Accordingly, the arbitral tribunal is urged to discuss with the parties during the case management conference the length or the number of submissions of any expert reports provided by the parties (Annex 3A).

2.1.2.10 PCA Optional Rules for Arbitration of Disputes Relating to Natural Resources and/or the Environment

The PCA Optional Rules for Arbitration of Disputes Relating to Natural Resources and/or the Environment (PCA Environmental Rules) provide for the establishment of a specialised list of arbitrators who are considered to have expertise in the area of natural resources and the environment. The Environmental Rules also provide for the establishment of a list of scientific and technical experts who may be appointed as experts pursuant to these Rules. Parties to a dispute are free to choose the experts from these Panels.

The PCA Environmental Rules Article 24(4) provides that the arbitral tribunal may order:

> may request the parties jointly or separately to provide a nontechnical document summarising and explaining the background to any scientific, technical or other specialised information which the arbitral tribunal considers to be necessary to understand fully the matters in dispute.

2.1.3 UNCITRAL Model Law

The UNCITRAL Model Law foresees both tribunal-appointed and party-appointed experts. Accordingly, if the parties have not excluded in their agreement the power of the tribunal to appoint experts, the arbitral tribunal may appoint one or more experts (UNCITRAL Model Law Article 26(1)).

If a tribunal-appointed expert delivers his written or oral report and a party requests or the arbitral tribunal considers it necessary, the expert shall participate in a hearing where the parties have the opportunity to examine him and to present their party-appointed experts in order to testify on the points at issue, unless otherwise agreed by the parties (UNCITRAL Model Law Article 26(2)).[301]

300. Trittmann and Schardt, 465.
301. *Kesikli* argued that the UNCITRAL Model Law does not explicitly regulate party-appointed

Article 24(3) of the Model Law provides that any expert report or evidentiary document on which the arbitral tribunal may rely in making its decision shall be communicated to the parties.

2.1.4 Statutes

Statutes in various countries permit the usage of party-appointed experts with a clear provision in their provisions that regulate (international) arbitration.

States also have provisions in civil procedure laws regarding party-appointed experts; however, caution must be exercised when exporting the evidentiary practice of national courts to international arbitration, whether under common law or civil law.[302]

2.1.4.1 Türkiye

Turkish International Arbitration Law[303] Article 12(A)(2) and national arbitration provisions encoded in the Code of Civil Procedure[304] ('HMK') Article 431(2), as statutes based on the UNCITRAL Model Law, both provide the parties with the opportunity to appoint their experts.[305]

There are no detailed provisions similar to the Model Law other than the possibility of appointing experts:

> Unless otherwise agreed by the parties, if a party so requests or if the arbitral tribunal considers it necessary, the expert shall, after delivery of his written or oral report, participate in a hearing where the parties have the opportunity to put questions to him and to present expert witnesses in order to testify on the points at issue.

According to the provisions of the Turkish Code of Civil Procedure, the arbitrator or the arbitral tribunal may appoint experts to report on the issues they determine. However, the authority granted to arbitrators by this provision should not be perceived as an absolute obligation. Indeed, in Turkish judicial practice, not consulting an expert,

experts, *see* Kesikli, 'Milletlerarası Ticari Tahkimde Delillerin Değerlendirilmesi', 215.

302. Alvarez, 'The Search for Objectivity: The Use of Experts in Philip Morris v Uruguay', 422.
303. Law No. 4686 of 21 June 2001, published in OG No. 24453 of 5 July 2001. For the English version, *see* https://turkisharbitrationacademy.com/eng/laws (accessed 24 September 2025).
304. Law No. 6100 of 12 January 2011, published in Official Gazette No. 27836 of 4 February 2011.
305. Pekcanıtez, Atalay, and Özekes, *Medenî Usûl Hukuku Ders Kitabı*, 626; Kuru and Aydın, *Medenî Usul Hukuku El Kitabı*, II:1892; Pekcanıtez and Yeşilirmak, 'Tahkim', 2713; Yılmaz, *HMK Serhi*, 2021, 4:5482; Akıncı, *Milletlerarası Tahkim*, 339; Sanlı, *Uluslararası Ticari Akitlerin Hazırlanması ve Uyuşmazlıkların Cözüm Yolları*, 337; Sanlı, Esen, and Ataman-Figanmeşe, *Uluslararası Ticari Akitlerin Hazırlanması ve Uyuşmazlıkların Cözüm Yolları*, 787; Kalpsüz, *Türkiye'de Milletlerarası Tahkim*, 93; Karslı, *Medeni Muhakeme Hukuku*, 914; Karadaş, *Ulusal (İç) Tahkim*, 181–182; Özbek, 'Uzman Görüşünün Yargılamada Değerlendirilmesi', 75; Ekşi, *Hukuku Muhakemeleri Kanunu'nda Tahkim*, 170; Dayınlarlı, *Milletlerarası Tahkim Rehberi*, 33; Hacıbekiroğlu, *Milletlerarası Tahkim Hukukunda Deliller ve Delillerin Degerlendirilmesi*, 83; Yılmaz, *HMK Serhi*, 2013, 1758; Nomer, Ekşi, and Öztekin Gelgel, *Milletlerlarası Tahkim Hukuku*, I:27; Görgün, Börü, and Kodakoğlu, *Medenî Usûl Hukuku*, 741.

if required, is seen as a deficiency that leads to the reversal of a (first or second instance) court decision.[306] Contrary to the domestic litigation practice, Turkish arbitration practice favours the appointment of experts by the parties.[307]

2.1.4.2 Germany

The German arbitration law provisions are to be found in the tenth book of the Code of Civil Procedure (*ZPO*), which contains sections 1026 to 1066. The provisions are almost a literal adaptation of UNCITRAL Model Law Article 26, with a few deviations.

ZPO § 1049(2) foresees that parties can appoint their own experts as follows:

> Unless otherwise agreed by the parties, if a party so requests or if the arbitral tribunal considers it necessary, the expert shall, after delivery of his written or oral report, participate in an oral hearing where the parties have the opportunity to put questions to him and to present their own experts in order to testify on the points at issue.[308]

The wording of the article seems to permit a party-appointed expert only when: (i) the tribunal appointed an expert; (ii) during oral hearings (but not in the preliminary proceedings); and (iii) through mere statements on disputed questions (instead of a comprehensive written opinion).[309]

Wach/Petsch argued that expert evidence in German arbitration is only possible through a tribunal appointment. In principle, there is no party-appointed expert; at least, it is technically not 'expert evidence'.[310]

However, as § 1049 provides, parties can, in a hearing, put questions to the tribunal-appointed expert and present (party-appointed) expert witnesses in order to testify on the points at issue.[311] Nevertheless, the reasoning of the legislation allows discarding the treatment of party-appointed experts as 'expert evidence':

> The German legal system is not familiar with the option provided for in Article 26 (2) of the Model Law to provide 'party-appointed experts', so that a waiver of the provision on expert evidence would have left open how this question is to be assessed under the new law … However, there are no objections to the adoption

---

306. Aktepe Artık, *Medeni Usûl Hukukunda Hakem Kararlarının İptali Sebepleri*, 379.
307. Pekcanıtez and Yeşilirmak, 'Tahkim', 2713; Akıncı, *Milletlerarası Tahkim*, 339; For contrary view *see* Eroğlu, *Tahkimde Yargılamanın Yenilenmesi*, 146–147.
308. The original text: 'Haben die Parteien nichts anderes vereinbart, so hat der Sachverständige, wenn eine Partei dies beantragt oder das Schiedsgericht es für erforderlich hält, nach Erstattung seines schriftlichen oder mündlichen Gutachtens an einer mündlichen Verhandlung teilzunehmen. Bei der Verhandlung können die Parteien dem Sachverständigen Fragen stellen und eigene Sachverständige zu den streitigen Fragen aussagen lassen.' *See* https://www.gesetze-im-internet.de/zpo/__1049.html (accessed 4 October 2022).
309. Knoblach, *Sachverhaltsermittlung in Der Internationalen Wirtschaftsschiedsgerichtsbarkeit*, 274–275.
310. Wach and Petsch, 'Der Sachverständigenbeweis Im Schiedsverfahren: Grenzen Der Gestaltungsfreiheit von Parteien Und Schiedsgericht', 111; For the argument that § 1049 does include party-appointed experts, *see* Münch, *Münchener Kommentar Zur ZPO*, § 1049, para. 38, 39.
311. Schwab and Walter, *Schiedsgerichtsbarkeit*, Chapter 15, para. 19; Knoblach, *Sachverhaltsermittlung in Der Internationalen Wirtschaftsschiedsgerichtsbarkeit*, 186, 274–275: Schütze, *Zivilprozessordnung Und Nebengesetze: Großkommentar*, 11:595.

> of Article 26 (2) of the Model Law in this respect either because the statements of such an expert, due to his proximity to the party, do not carry comparable weight to the statements of the expert appointed by the court.[312]

Knoblach shares the contrary view and argues that the party-appointed expert should be appointable even: (i) if no expert has been appointed by the tribunal; (ii) at any time during the proceedings; and (iii) with a comprehensive written opinion.[313]

Parties may agree on a neutral and objective expert, who will be appointed by the arbitral tribunal.[314] According to § 1049(1) of the ZPO, parties may exclude (party-appointed or tribunal-appointed) experts from the proceedings with an express agreement, however, the arbitrator cannot order such exclusion.[315] This is not contradictory to the right to be heard envisaged in the German Constitution Article 103; since the parties have the autonomy to decide how to conduct the proceedings, and with the agreement of the parties not to have an expert, this exclusion affects the burden of proof and does not limit the right to be heard.[316]

If the tribunal considers issues to be unsolvable without expert opinion, it is obliged to appoint one, as per § 1042 paragraph 4 of ZPO.[317]

Wach/Petsch argued that, as soon as there is an agreement between the parties to appoint a joint expert, the tribunal cannot base its decisions on party-appointed experts' opinions.[318] This does not prevent the parties from submitting expert opinions but prevents the tribunal from relying solely on that advice rather than appointing itself as an expert.[319]

---

312. *See* Gesetzentwurf der Bundesregierung Entwurf eines Gesetzes zur Neuregelung des Schiedsverfahrensrechts (Schiedsverfahrens-Neuregelungsgesetz – SchiedsVfG):

> 'Hinzu kommt, daß die in Artikel 26 Abs. 2 ModG vorgesehene Möglichkeit der Beibringung von " Parteisachverständigen" dem deutschen Rechtssystem nicht geläufig ist, so daß ein Absehen von der Vorschrift über den Sachverständigenbeweis offengelassen hätte, wie diese Frage nach dem neuen Recht zu beurteilen ist ... Der "Parteisachverständige" ist dem deutschen Recht wie gesagt bislang fremd. Gegen die Übernahme des Artikels 26 Abs. 2 ModG auch insoweit bestehen jedoch keine Bedenken, weil den Ausführungen eines solchen Sachverständigen wegen seiner Nähe zur Partei kein den Ausführungen des vom Gericht bestellten Sachverständigen vergleichbares Gewicht zukommt.' available at https://dserver.bundestag.de/btd/13/052/1305274.pdf (accessed 29 September 2022).

313. Knoblach, *Sachverhaltsermittlung in Der Internationalen Wirtschaftsschiedsgerichtsbarkeit*, 275–276.
314. Wach and Petsch, 'Der Sachverständigenbeweis Im Schiedsverfahren: Grenzen Der Gestaltungsfreiheit von Parteien Und Schiedsgericht', 110.
315. Wach and Petsch, 106, 108; Schwab and Walter, *Schiedsgerichtsbarkeit*, Chapter 15, para. 19; Knoblach, *Sachverhaltsermittlung in Der Internationalen Wirtschaftsschiedsgerichtsbarkeit*, 266.
316. Thomas et al., *Thomas/Putzo ZPO*, § 1049 para. 2.
317. Wach and Petsch, 'Der Sachverständigenbeweis Im Schiedsverfahren: Grenzen Der Gestaltungsfreiheit von Parteien Und Schiedsgericht', 103.
318. Wach and Petsch, 'Der Sachverständigenbeweis Im Schiedsverfahren: Grenzen Der Gestaltungsfreiheit von Parteien Und Schiedsgericht', 111.
319. For the argument that ZPO § 1049 does preclude party-appointed experts, *see* Schlosser, *Kommentar zur Zivilprozessordnung: ZPO, Band 10: §§ 1025–1066*, § 1049, para.1.

As iterated, according to German law, party-appointed expert opinion is classified by some scholars as unique evidence that has no relation to 'expert evidence' according to ZPO § 1049.

2.1.4.3 Switzerland

Swiss International Arbitration provisions in the Federal Act on International Private Law (SPILA)[320] do not directly regulate the matter of evidence. Article 184 of the SPILA only states that '[t]he arbitral tribunal *takes the evidence* itself'.[321] (emphasis added)

Before Swiss courts in litigation, a private expert opinion (*Privat-gutachten*) was not considered evidence, but merely a party allegation.[322] However, in arbitration proceedings, the statements, opinions, and conclusions of an expert appointed by a party are considered evidence. *Berger and Kellerhals* argued that a party-appointed expert is essentially subject to similar treatment as fact witnesses.[323]

2.1.4.4 UK

The UK is one of the top countries leading in arbitration law and practice. The English Arbitration Act (EAA)[324] is a comprehensive code and the principal statute regulating both national and international arbitration for arbitrations seated in England or Wales.[325] In England, 'there are no overarching rules or standards for the evaluation or admissibility of evidence which parties are obliged to abide by in such an arbitration'.[326] The reason for this is largely due to leaving great discretion to parties and the tribunal on how to construct the arbitration.

The EAA section 37 stipulates that, unless otherwise agreed by the parties, the tribunal may appoint experts, legal advisers or assessors.[327] The provision entails that such an expert, legal adviser or assessor may attend the proceedings, and the parties

320. Federal Act on Private International Law (PILA) of 18 December 1987, available at https://www.fedlex.admin.ch/eli/cc/1988/1776_1776_1776/en (accessed 2 April 2022).
321. *See* Voser and Mueller, 'Appointment of Experts by the Arbitral Tribunal: The Civil Law Perspective', 73; Weiss and Bürgi Locatelli, 'Der Vom Schiedsgericht Bestellte Experte-Ein Überblick Aus Sicht Eines Internationalen Schiedsgerichts Mit Sitz in Der Schweiz', 479.
322. Berger and Kellerhals, *International and Domestic Arbitration in Switzerland*, 493; *see* Girsberger and Voser, *International Arbitration*, 287.
323. Berger and Kellerhals, *International and Domestic Arbitration in Switzerland*, 493–494.
324. Available online: https://www.legislation.gov.uk/ukpga/1996/23/contents (accessed 3 April 2023).
325. Nairn, Szymanski, and Lekakis, 'National Report for England and Wales (2021 Through 2023)', 1; Rawding, Fullelove, and Martin, 'International Arbitration in England: A Procedural Overview', 361; Flannery, 'The English Statutory Framework', 208.
326. Tirado, Petit, and Keen, 'Factual Evidence', 483.
327. Nairn, Szymanski, and Lekakis, 'National Report for England and Wales (2021 Through 2023)', 31; Knoblach, *Sachverhaltsermittlung in Der Internationalen Wirtschaftsschiedsgerichtsbarkeit*, 185; Rawding, Fullelove, and Martin, 'International Arbitration in England: A Procedural Overview', 382; Flannery, 'The English Statutory Framework', 213; *see also* 'Protocol for the Instruction for Experts to give evidence in Civil cases' published by the UK Civil Justice Council.

shall be given a reasonable opportunity to comment on any information, opinion or advice offered by any such person.[328]

Although the provision does not explicitly mention the opportunity for the parties to appoint their own experts, such a proposal is also not forbidden and should be permitted according to procedural fairness reasons.[329]

Section 33(a) of the EAA provides that parties have an opportunity to make a fair case. This is related to procedural fairness and indicates that parties may rely on expert evidence where appropriate.[330]

EAA section 34(2)(f) provides that it is for the tribunal to decide whether to apply strict rules of evidence (or any other rules) as to the admissibility, relevance or weight of any material (oral, written or other) sought to be tendered on any matters of fact or opinion, and the time, manner and form in which such material should be exchanged and presented.[331]

Although not directly applicable to arbitration, under the UK Civil Procedure Rules 1998 (CPR), Courts in the UK have broad discretion to restrict or exclude expert evidence.[332] In the UK, experts who are found to violate their duties may be subject to disqualification.[333] However, the EAA has the power to restrict expert evidence, in contrast to the CPR.[334]

Where English law governs the arbitration, the duties owed by a party-appointed expert are often considered those set out in the *Ikarian Reefer* case. The *Ikarian Reefer* case summarises the main obligations of the party-appointed experts. The case foresees that the expert's work should be an independent product, uninfluenced as to form or content by the exigencies of the adjudicative process.[335]

The attorney may prepare the expert, examine, and advise him/her on additional matters to be included in the report.[336]

Even in England, where the Woolf reforms introduced independence as a requirement for the party-appointed expert, the lack of impartiality of a party-appointed expert affects the weight of his/her opinion in the assessment of evidence more than the admissibility.[337]

328. Rawding, Fullelove, and Martin, 'International Arbitration in England: A Procedural Overview', 382; Nairn, Szymanski, and Lekakis, 'National Report for England and Wales (2021 Through 2023)', 29.
329. Bor, 'Expert Evidence', 504.
330. Bor, 504.
331. Rawding, Fullelove, and Martin, 'International Arbitration in England: A Procedural Overview', 381; Nairn, Szymanski, and Lekakis, 'National Report for England and Wales (2021 Through 2023)', 30.
332. Kesikli, 'Milletlerarası Ticari Tahkimde Delillerin Değerlendirilmesi', 212.
333. Hodgson and Stewart, 'Experts in Investor-State Arbitration: The Tribunal as Gatekeeper', 457; Nessi, 'Expert Witness: Role and Independence', 77–78.
334. Hodgson and Stewart, 'Experts in Investor-State Arbitration: The Tribunal as Gatekeeper', 457, fn. 22.
335. Referencing *Whitehouse v. Jordan*, [1981] 1 WLR 246 at p. 256, per Lord Wilberforce.
336. Knoblach, *Sachverhaltsermittlung in Der Internationalen Wirtschaftsschiedsgerichtsbarkeit*, 187.
337. Proske, *Expert Witness Conferencing in Schiedsverfahren*, 23.

2.1.4.5 USA

The USA has developed extensive procedures for the qualification of experts and allows judges to act as gatekeepers to exclude questionable expert testimony.[338] Party-appointed experts are classified under the category of witnesses according to the Federal Rules of Evidence Rule 702.[339]

Traditionally, in US law, the main role for obtaining and presenting expert opinion is given to the parties because the US adopts an adversarial system. In this system, the judge as a decision-maker should be impartial and passive; the proceedings are administered by the parties and their lawyers.[340] Experts are commonly produced and paid for by the parties. The court shall decide the admissibility of such evidence.

2.1.4.6 Singapore

The Singapore International Commercial Court (SICC) Practice Directions[341] contain certain rules for the provision of expert evidence. It provides rules regarding the appointment, method of obtaining evidence and examination.[342]

In cases where expert witnesses will be called to give evidence, counsel for each party intending to call experts shall write to all other parties and inform the other parties of the name(s) of the expert(s) in which that party intends to engage, set out the areas or issues which the expert(s) will be opine on and attach the curriculum vitae of the expert(s) (n. 87(1)). The counsel for each party is to inform all other parties of any objections to the experts that will be called (n. 87(2)). The Counsel may raise objections about the experts at or before a Case Management Conference (n. 87(3)).

As a default practice, experts are directed to meet before hearings to discuss their respective opinions and to determine where they are in agreement on the issues, and where they do not agree, the extent of their disagreement. If not directed by the court otherwise, the parties and their lawyers will not be permitted to attend these expert meetings. The experts will then be expected to prepare a joint expert report.

The report must set out a list of the issues, areas/issues where experts agreed, areas/issues where they disagree, reasons, nature and extent of their disagreement, and any other helpful information (n. 88(1)). Although this report per se does not bind

338. Hodgson and Stewart, 'Experts in Investor-State Arbitration: The Tribunal as Gatekeeper', 457.
339. Budak, 'Anglo: Amerikan Medeni Yargılama Hukukunda Bilirkişilik (Uzman Tanıklar)', 828–829; Demirkapı, 'Anglo: Amerikan Hukukunda Bilirkişilik Kurumunda Yeni Eğilimler', 50.
340. Mosk, 'The Role of Facts in International Dispute Resolution (Volume 304)', 21; Güvenalp, *Milletlerarası Tahkimde İddia ve Savunma Hakkının İhlali*, 64–65; Teomete Yalabık, 'Questioning Expert Witnesses in Litigation and International Arbitration: How to Prevent Partisan Expert Reports and "Battle of Experts"', 141.
341. Singapore International Commercial Court Practice Directions, https://www.judiciary.gov.sg/docs/default-source/amendments-docs/2022/sicc-pd_2022_v1.pdf?sfvrsn=4d986e38_2 (accessed 19 January 2023); O'Malley, *Rules of Evidence in International Arbitration*, 145.
342. For similar practice in Australian courts, *see* Jones, 'Redefining the Role and Value of Expert Evidence', 33; Federal Court of Australia, *Expert Evidence Practice Note*, 25 October 2016, https://www.fedcourt.gov.au/law-and-practice/practice-documents/practice-notes/gpn-expt (accessed 19 October 2022).

parties without express agreement, the court has the discretion to take cognisance of the experts' agreement (n. 88(2)).

Experts are generally expected to testify after fact witnesses and may be examined concurrently as a panel (expert conferencing) (n. 89(3)).

The SICC also established a specialist Technology, Infrastructure and Construction list dealing with complex disputes in these areas, which also contains similar provisions for experts.[343]

2.1.4.7 Hong Kong

Cap. 609 Arbitration Ordinance (AO)[344] is the arbitration law applicable to arbitration, whose place of arbitration is Hong Kong (AO Article 5(1)). The AO is based on the UNCITRAL Model Law, and the provisions for experts are thus the same. As stipulated above, the UNCITRAL Model Law foresees both tribunal-appointed and party-appointed experts. Accordingly, the arbitral tribunal may appoint one or more experts (UNCITRAL Model Law Article 26(1)). Additionally, the parties have the opportunity to present their party-appointed experts (UNCITRAL Model Law Article 26(2)).[345]

2.1.5 International Guidelines and Practices

As demonstrated in the first section of this chapter, international treaties, arbitration rules, the Model Law, and statutes of various countries usually have fewer provisions concerning party-appointed experts.

However, there is no confusion whether it is permissible for the parties to appoint experts in international practice. On the contrary, even the tribunal expects the parties to bring their experts.[346]

Professional organisations like the International Bar Association, CIArb as an international centre for the practice and profession of arbitration (and alternative dispute resolution), and LCIA as an arbitration institution have each developed some set of non-binding rules that foresee how to handle issues regarding party-appointed experts in more detail than statutes or arbitration rules.

Among them, the Chartered Institute of Arbitrator's Protocol for the Use of Party-Appointed Experts Witnesses in International Arbitration (CIArb Protocol)[347]

343. *See* Singapore International Commercial Court Practice Directions, Part XXIV Technology, Infrastructure and Construction List, https://www.judiciary.gov.sg/docs/default-source/amendments-docs/2022/sicc-pd_2022_v1.pdf?sfvrsn=4d986e38_2 (accessed 19 January 2023).

344. [1 June 2011] L.N. 38 of 2011 https://www.elegislation.gov.hk/hk/cap609?pmc=0&m=0&pm=1&xpid=ID_1438403520837_004 (accessed 19 January 2023).

345. *Kesikli* argued that the UNCITRAL Model Law does not explicitly regulate party-appointed experts, *see* Kesikli, 'Milletlerarası Ticari Tahkimde Delillerin Değerlendirilmesi', 215.

346. O'Malley, *Rules of Evidence in International Arbitration*, 145.

347. Chartered Institute of Arbitrators Protocol for the Use of Party-Appointed Expert Witnesses in International Arbitration, https://www.ciarb.org/media/zvijl3kx/7-party-appointed-and-tribunal-appointed-expert-witnesses-in-international-arbitration-2015.pdf (accessed 24 October 2025). The CIArb Protocol applies only to party-appointed experts, not to tribunal-appointed experts or single-joint experts.

from 2007 has been the most specific and comprehensive on the issue of rules concerning party-appointed experts.

Additionally, the Rules on the Taking of Evidence in International Arbitration (IBA Rules) have detailed provisions regarding the appointment and use of party-appointed experts in international arbitration. The 2013 IBA Guidelines on Party Representation in International Arbitration (IBA Guidelines) also have provisions that are more specific and directed towards counsel and their relationship to party-appointed experts.

Moreover, the UNCITRAL Notes on Organizing Proceedings (UNCITRAL Notes) from 2016 have some provisions, among others, related to experts and their usage.

These rules may be incorporated into the agreed procedural rules governing the conduct of a particular arbitration or may provide guidance to parties or tribunals concerning various aspects of expert evidence.

2.1.5.1 IBA Rules on the Taking of Evidence

The IBA Rules on the Taking of Evidence, which have their roots in 1983 and were modernised in 2020, are the most widely known and frequently used soft-law instrument in arbitral practice.[348] The IBA Rules are frequently consulted as non-binding guidelines.[349] The IBA Rules are not directly applicable unless the parties adopt them. As there are no detailed regulations on taking and evaluating evidence in the Arbitration Rules, it is evident that the IBA Rules fill a crucial gap in the submission and evaluation of evidence in the field of international arbitration. But in order to apply the IBA Rules, parties need to agree on their application or the arbitrators should set their application in the first procedural order.[350]

The IBA Rules, *inter alia*, provide a detailed description of the appointment procedure of a party-appointed expert, the contents of the expert report, and the examination of the party-appointed expert (Article 5).[351] However, they do not review the qualifications of experts or challenging experts. Rather, the focus is on the rights of parties to examine information drawn upon in the drafting of a report and to permit any party the opportunity to respond to a tribunal-appointed expert.

Although the IBA Rules are a result of good practices developed and generally accepted over the years, serious criticism in relation to party-appointed experts can be made. The IBA Rules are not clear on the duties that a party-appointed expert has, specifically, no explicit reference to the party-appointed expert's duty to assist the arbitral tribunal exists,[352] only a mere declaration of the expert to express his/her

348. '2015 International Arbitration Survey: Improvements and Innovations in International Arbitration', 35.
349. Mbengue and Das, 'Rules Governing the Use of Experts in International Disputes', 447.
350. Esen, 'Violation of the Right to a Fair Trial in Arbitration', 113.
351. Ünüvar, 'Experts: Investment Arbitration', paras 22–24.
352. Waincymer, *Procedure and Evidence in International Arbitration*, 946; Khodykin and Mulcahy, *A Guide to the IBA Rules on the Taking of Evidence in International Arbitration*, 304–305.

genuine belief is required.[353] Some authors criticise the independence requirement and say that it is unclear since the party-appointed expert is hired by one side, closely works with them to prepare the report, and is paid by that party.[354] Other authors have deemed the statement of independence as a mere self-assessment of limited value.[355]

Some realistically looked beyond the independence requirement and suggested that the focus should be on the 'impartiality' of experts, whether the expert is capable of reaching the same conclusion based on the same criteria, irrespective of the instructing party.[356]

2.1.5.2 IBA Guidelines on Party Representation in International Arbitration

The IBA Guidelines on Party Representation in International Arbitration were drafted with the idea of having a coherent practice of counsel from various jurisdictions, all with different professional cultures.

The Guidelines are not intended to displace applicable mandatory laws, professional or disciplinary rules or agreed arbitration rules that may be relevant or applicable to matters of party representation, but to accommodate legal and cultural differences among counsel of multinational backgrounds. The Guidelines foresee specialised practices and procedures that have been developed in international arbitration over time.

Relevant principles regarding party-appointed experts are provided for in the Guideline paragraphs 11, 20, 22, 24, and 25:

> 11. A Party Representative should not submit Expert evidence that he or she knows to be false. And in case, take remedial measures, which may include one or more of the following:
>   (a) advise the Expert to testify truthfully;
>   (b) take reasonable steps to deter the Expert from submitting false evidence;
>   (c) urge the Expert to correct or withdraw the false evidence;
>   (d) correct or withdraw the false evidence;
>   (e) withdraw as Party Representative if the circumstances so warrant.
> 20. A Party Representative may assist Experts in the preparation of Expert Reports.
> 22. A Party Representative should seek to ensure that an Expert Report reflects the Expert's own analysis and opinion.
> 24. A Party Representative may, consistent with the principle that the evidence given should reflect the Expert's own analysis or opinion, meet or interact with Experts in order to discuss and prepare their prospective testimony.
> 25. A Party Representative may pay, offer to pay, or acquiesce in the payment of:
>   (a) expenses reasonably incurred by an Expert in preparing to testify or testifying at a hearing;

353. Kantor, 'A Code of Conduct for Party-Appointed Experts in International Arbitration: Can One Be Found?', 332; Waincymer, *Procedure and Evidence in International Arbitration*, 945; Burianski and Lang, 'Bibliographic Reference "Challenges" to Party-Appointed Experts', 15:277.
354. Mbengue and Das, 'Rules Governing the Use of Experts in International Disputes', 447.
355. Samaras and Strasser, 'Managing Party-Appointed Experts in International Arbitration--Analysis of the Current Framework and Best Practice Proposals-', 314, 318.
356. Cerrahoglu Balssenn, 'Instructions to Party-Appointed Experts Should Focus on Impartiality', 28; Michell and Mandhane, 'The Uncertain Duty of the Expert Witness', 648.

(b) reasonable compensation for the loss of time incurred by a Witness in testifying and preparing to testify; and
(c) reasonable fees for the professional services of a Party-appointed Expert.

2.1.5.3 *CIArb Protocol and Guidelines*

The CIArb Protocol for the Use of Party-Appointed Experts Witnesses in International Arbitration is a single set of rules that provides a complete regime for adducing party-appointed experts in proceedings.

The CIArb Protocol identifies the issues to be dealt with by way of expert evidence, the qualification and identity of experts such as independence, what tests or analyses are required, the contents of the experts' opinions, privilege, meetings of experts and the manner of expert testimony.[357]

The CIArb Protocol further attempts to ensure an expert's credibility by specifically noting that the expert's duty is to assist the tribunal. Additionally, it expects the expert meeting and the preparation of a joint statement on the areas of agreement and disagreement between the party-appointed experts.[358]

The Protocol further provides that the tribunal can order the experts to confer and produce additional or revised expert reports or order a preliminary hearing with the experts before the main arbitration hearing.[359]

However, as with the other rules, it does not provide a mechanism for challenging experts' opinions. The Protocol is also criticised for following English judicial practice and may not have been widely adopted in international arbitration for that reason.[360]

Further, the International Arbitration Practice Guideline for the Party-appointed and Tribunal-appointed experts sets out the practice in international commercial arbitration on the appointment and use of party-appointed and tribunal-appointed experts.[361]

It provides guidance for: (i) Powers to appoint an expert (Article 1); (ii) Assessing the need for expert evidence (Article 2); (iii) Methods of adducing expert evidence (Article 3); (iv) Procedural directions of the expert(s) (Article 4); and (v) Testing the experts' opinions (Article 5).

In 2019, CIArb also published the Guidelines for Witness Conferencing in International Arbitration, which contains directions for the concurrent taking of evidence while still affording important flexibility to parties and tribunals in designing a procedure that befits their needs.[362]

357. CIArb Protocol Foreword.
358. Nessi, 'Expert Witness: Role and Independence', 79–80.
359. Bor, 'Expert Evidence', 507.
360. Khodykin and Mulcahy, *A Guide to the IBA Rules on the Taking of Evidence in International Arbitration*, 285.
361. CIArb International Arbitration Practice Guideline for the Party-appointed and Tribunal-appointed experts available at https://www.ciarb.org/media/zvijl3kx/7-party-appointed-and-tribunal-appointed-expert-witnesses-in-international-arbitration-2015.pdf (accessed 24 October 2025).
362. CIArb Guidelines for Witness Conferencing in International Arbitration 2019, https://www.ciarb.org/media/c54lce1z/13-witness-conferencing-april-2019.pdf (accessed 24 October 2025).

2.1.5.4 *Rules on the Efficient Conduct of Proceedings in International Arbitration (Prague Rules)*

The Prague Rules on the Efficient Conduct of Proceedings in International Arbitration (Prague Rules) were drafted with the intention to provide a framework and guidance for tribunals and parties, with the aim to increase the efficiency of arbitration 'by encouraging a more active role for arbitral tribunals in managing proceedings'.[363]

Like the IBA Rules, the Prague Rules are not intended to replace the arbitration rules provided by various institutions. However, they are designed to supplement proceedings through the agreement of the parties or as otherwise applied by arbitral tribunals.

The Prague Rules provide limited guidance on party-appointed experts. It stipulates that despite the tribunal appointing an expert, the parties are not precluded from appointing their expert and submitting a report, and this expert can testify and be examined at the hearings (Prague Rules Article 6.5.).

The rules foresee that the tribunal has the authority to order the tribunal-appointed expert and the party-appointed expert(s) 'to establish a joint list of questions on the content of their reports, covering the issues that they consider necessary to be reviewed' (Prague Rules Article 6.6.).

The rules also authorise the tribunal, after the hearings, to instruct both tribunal and party-appointed experts to issue a joint report which indicates a list of issues on which the experts agree, a list of issues on which the experts disagree and reasons why the experts disagree (Prague Rules Article 6.7.).

The complexity of arbitral disputes and the need for expert opinion are some reasons that proceedings are lengthy and expensive. The Prague Rules appear to offer only a weak solution to the difficulty presented by conflicting expert opinions in Article 6.6 and 6.7.

Article 6 should have regulated the idea that a proactive arbitrator should convene a conference to discuss the parties' views with the experts before the second round of submissions on the merits or, in any event, before the hearing.[364]

2.1.5.5 *UNCITRAL Code of Conduct for Arbitrators in International Investment Dispute Resolution*

The Secretariats of ICSID and UNCITRAL have collaborated on a draft Code of Conduct for Arbitrators in International Investment Disputes (IID). At its fifty-sixth session in July 2023, UNCITRAL adopted the Code of Conduct for Arbitrators in International Investment Dispute Resolution and the accompanying commentary.

The Code is intended to provide applicable principles and provisions addressing matters such as independence and impartiality, as well as the duty to conduct

363. Prague Rules Preamble; *see* Stampa, 'The Prague Rules', 221–244; Patocchi, 'Uluslararası Tahkim Sempozyumu', 147; For details and comparison with IBA Rules, *see* Mert and Türkmen, 'Milletlerarası Tahkimde Delil İkamesi Hakkında Prag Kuralları ve IBA Kuralları'nın Karşılaştırılması', 37 ff.

364. Patocchi, 'Uluslararası Tahkim Sempozyumu', 165.

proceedings with integrity, fairness, efficiency, and civility in International Investment Disputes.

Paragraph 1 of Article 4 sets out prohibitions for an individual while they are currently acting as an Arbitrator. Unless the disputing parties agree otherwise, an Arbitrator cannot act concurrently as a party-appointed expert (witness) in any other proceeding if the other proceeding addresses the same measure(s), the same or related party(parties), or the same provision(s) of the same treaty.

Article 4 paragraphs 2–4 set out the temporal scope of the prohibition for Arbitrators. They are prohibited from acting concurrently as a party-appointed expert in another IID proceeding and for a period of three years under paragraphs 2–3 and under paragraph 4, for a period of one year, following the end of his or her functions as an Arbitrator. This means that an individual who functions as a party-appointed expert in an IID proceeding must resign from that role before accepting an appointment as an Arbitrator.

The prohibition applies only if the other proceeding addresses the same measure(s), the same or related party(parties), or the same provision(s) of the same treaty. When any of these criteria are met, the arbitrator will be prohibited from acting as a party-appointed expert in another proceeding. The use of the term 'same' throughout Article 4 means that the elements under scrutiny in the IID must be identical and not merely similar. In other words, the threshold for a prohibition to be triggered is high.[365]

However, even when the above-mentioned circumstances are not met, an Arbitrator should not act as a party-appointed expert in another proceeding if that would lead to a breach of independence and impartiality.

2.1.5.6 The ALI/UNIDROIT Principles

The ALI/UNIDROIT Principles of Transnational Civil Procedure (ALI/UNIDROIT Principles), first published as a draft in 1996 and adopted in 2005 by the Governing Council of UNIDROIT, are standards for the adjudication of transnational commercial disputes.[366]

These principles aim to reconcile the differences between various national rules of civil procedure, considering the peculiarities of international disputes compared to purely domestic ones. The ALI/UNIDROIT Principles are accompanied by a set of Rules of Transnational Civil Procedure, which were not formally adopted by either UNIDROIT or ALI but constituted the Reporters' model implementation of these principles.

Article 22(4) of the ALI/UNIDROIT Principles provides that the court may appoint its own expert to provide evidence on any relevant matter for which expert opinion is

365. UNCITRAL, Commentary to the UNCITRAL Code of Conduct for Arbitrators in International Investment Dispute Resolution, 18, paras 32–36. https://uncitral.un.org/sites/uncitral.un.org/files/media-documents/uncitral/en/2318824e-coc_arbitrators_ebook_11june.pdf (accessed 24 October 2025).

366. Available online at: https://www.unidroit.org/english/documents/2005/study76/s-76-13-e.pdf (accessed 12 November 2022).

appropriate. This provision then continues to state that the parties have the right to present their own expert. Importantly, these experts, irrespective of whether they have been appointed by the court or a party, owe their duty only to the court. Article 26 of the Rules provides that court-appointed experts must be neutral and independent from the parties and from any other influence. Similarly, party-appointed experts are subject to the same standards of neutrality and independence as court-appointed experts.[367]

The ALI/UNIDROIT Principles (supplemented by the Rules) adopt an intermediate position between the common law and civil law systems discussed earlier. The court may then appoint experts, but the parties may also bring party-appointed experts, irrespective of whether the court has appointed its own expert. 'However, and this is the most salient feature of this set of rules, party- and court-appointed experts ultimately owe their duty exclusively to the court and are subject to the same standards and obligations in terms of independence.'[368]

2.1.5.7 UNCITRAL Notes on Organizing Arbitral Proceedings

In 1996, UNCITRAL adopted the Notes on Organizing Arbitral Proceedings (*UNCITRAL Notes*), which were modernised and updated in 2016.

The UNCITRAL Notes are non-binding in nature and are designed to assist arbitration practitioners by providing an annotated list of matters on which a tribunal may wish to formulate decisions during the course of arbitral proceedings, like language and place of arbitration, questions relating to confidentiality, as well as conduct of hearings and the taking of evidence and possible requirements for the filing or delivering of an award.[369]

Specifically, paragraphs 92–107 are related to issues concerning the use of both tribunal and party-appointed experts in arbitral proceedings. Notes are silent on the independence of party-appointed experts but provide indirect tools to the tribunal to test the experts.[370]

The Notes provide that the parties may appoint experts or even a joint expert to address the issues agreed upon by the parties.[371] The tribunal may invite the experts who address the same issues to submit a joint expert report, indicating points of agreement and disagreement with the realisation of an informal meeting (pre-hearing meeting), where experts may find common ground and take the time to discuss any specific issues.[372] The arbitral tribunal may consider requesting additional or responsive expert reports on the points of conflict.[373]

The arbitral tribunal should address the sequence and timing of the submission of expert reports and should clarify the nature and extent of communication between the

367. ALI/UNIDROIT Principles of Transnational Civil Procedure, 59.
368. Nessi, 'Expert Witness: Role and Independence', 79–80.
369. United Nations, 'UNCITRAL Notes on Organizing Arbitral Proceedings', 1.
370. Nessi, 'Expert Witness: Role and Independence', 85.
371. United Nations, 'UNCITRAL Notes on Organizing Arbitral Proceedings', paras 94, 98.
372. United Nations, paras 95, 97.
373. United Nations, para. 96.

parties or their representatives and their experts, as well as the potential disclosure of such communications.[374]

2.1.5.8 *ICC Arbitration Commission Report on Controlling Time and Costs*

The ICC Arbitration Commission Report on Controlling Time and Costs in Arbitration advises parties to arbitration to presume that expert evidence will not be required and to only depart from this presumption if there are key issues on which expertise is needed to assist the tribunal.[375]

The techniques foresee some advice for the use of experts. Clarifying the subject matter and scope of the opinions at an early stage for having the experts report on the same issues (n. 64), limiting the number of experts per party for any particular subject matter (n. 65), and the number of rounds of expert reports, including the simultaneous or sequential exchange of these reports (n. 66) and the use of a single expert, appointed either by the arbitral tribunal or jointly by the parties for efficiency reasons (n. 68) relate to the adducing of the expert opinion.[376]

There are also notes on the pre-hearing and hearing phases. A pre-hearing meeting of experts is recommended to narrow the issues on which they agree and disagree after they have exchanged reports (n. 67). Conflicting experts should be required by a specified date consistent with the timetable for the arbitration to conference and be questioned by the tribunal and by the counsel at the same time (n. 79).[377]

2.1.5.9 *ICCA Guidelines on Standards of Practice in International Arbitration*

These Guidelines were developed by a Task Force of experts in the practice of international arbitration with experience from diverse jurisdictions. The Task Force first surveyed professional standards, ethical rules, and civility guidelines from various jurisdictions.

The Guidelines aim to articulate prevailing expectations as to the standards of practice in international arbitration. Whether a participant's conduct violates these Guidelines will necessarily be a fact-specific enquiry based on the circumstances at hand. Although the Guidelines are not intended as mandatory rules, they may be incorporated by parties in their arbitration agreement, adopted by arbitral institutions, or included by arbitral tribunals in a procedural order or in the terms of reference where appropriate.[378]

374. United Nations, paras 99, 100.
375. Khodykin and Mulcahy, *A Guide to the IBA Rules on the Taking of Evidence in International Arbitration*, 304.
376. ICC, 'ICC Arbitration Commission Report on Controlling Time and Costs in Arbitration', 13.
377. ICC, 14.
378. ICCA Task Force on Standards of Practice in International Arbitration, 'Guidelines on Standards of Practice in International Arbitration', 1.

The Guidelines are organised into four sections: (i) general guidelines for all participants in international arbitration (counsel, arbitrators, staff of arbitral institutions acting in the particular case, tribunal secretaries, witnesses, experts, court reporters, interpreters, translators, etc.); (ii) guidelines for party representatives; (iii) guidelines for arbitrators; and (iv) guidelines for other participants. Each sub-section presents several general principles followed by explanatory remarks.[379]

Experts and fact witnesses must be honest in their testimony before an arbitral tribunal. Experts and fact witnesses shall not knowingly make any false submissions to the arbitral tribunal. If an expert or fact witness learns that he or she has previously made a false submission to the arbitral tribunal, he or she shall promptly correct such submission (Guideline IV.A). Experts and fact witnesses shall assist the arbitral tribunal and follow its directions. (Guideline IV.B)

2.1.5.10 Code of Best Practices in Arbitration from the Spanish Arbitration Club

The Spanish Arbitration Club (Club Español del Arbitraje) has revised its Code of Best Practices (*CBP*) dated 2005 in 2019. While the former CBP was aimed exclusively at arbitral institutions, the updated CBP contains recommendations not only for arbitral institutions but also for all professionals participating in the arbitration process, such as arbitrators, lawyers, experts, and funders.[380] The CBP is a good example of 'soft rules' in arbitration. The Regulation contains recommendations made by the Spanish Arbitration Club for the entire arbitration law community.

The recommendations include duties for experts, such as the requirement of objectivity and independence (paragraphs 133–135), disclosure (paragraphs 136, 139–145), loyalty (paragraphs 147–149), confidentiality (paragraphs 152–153) and provisions regarding the fees of experts (paragraphs 150–151).[381] Additionally, it contains recommendations for elements that should be included in the expert's report (paragraph 146), including a declaration for objectivity and independence and disclosure of information (paragraphs 137–138).

2.1.5.11 DIS Practice Note on the Use of Experts in Arbitration

Although the 2018 DIS Arbitration Rules are mainly silent on how to handle party-appointed experts, the DIS has issued a practice note on the use of experts in arbitration (DIS Practice Note).[382] The DIS Practice Note provides guidance to the parties and the arbitral tribunal on how to efficiently and effectively conduct the expert procedure. The DIS Practice Note foresees three checklists for the use of experts: (1) checklist for the

379. ICCA Task Force on Standards of Practice in International Arbitration, 2.
380. Club Español del Arbitraje, Code of Best Practices in Arbitration, 2019, 6.
381. Club Español del Arbitraje, Code of Best Practices in Arbitration, 45–49.
382. Available at https://www.disarb.org/fileadmin//user_upload/Foerderung_Vernetzung/DIS-Praxislabor_Praxisgruppe_Sachverstaendige_Practice_Note_Experts.pdf (accessed 4 April 2025).

use of experts in general; (2) checklist regarding party-appointed experts; and (3) checklist regarding tribunal-appointed experts.

2.1.5.11.1 *Checklist for the Use of Experts in General*

First, in the first case management conference or, if necessary, in additional case management conferences, the arbitral tribunal should discuss with the parties whether to employ experts and, if so, how to conduct the expert procedure efficiently. Reasons why issues may not require expert evidence can, for example, be: (i) that they are not disputed; (ii) that the arbitral tribunal does not consider expert opinion necessary because an issue is irrelevant to the case or immaterial to its outcome; (iii) that the arbitral tribunal may find that expert opinion is not required because the arbitral tribunal is sufficiently knowledgeable of the (technical, factual or legal) issue in dispute; or (iv) for any other reason.[383] Specifically, the parties and the arbitral tribunal are encouraged to consider and discuss the issues that will and that will not require expert opinion (a joint determination).[384]

The DIS Practice Note states that the issues for determination can be factual, legal, or even technical. These may include issues, for example, such as statutes of limitation or notification requirements and consequences of not meeting such requirements, but also more generally an early determination of which issues the arbitral tribunal considers relevant and material to the outcome of the case. The arbitral tribunal is advised to encourage the parties to agree on certain issues or resolve certain issues amicably with a view to rendering the expert procedure more efficient and effective. The overall amount in dispute of the claims that require expert opinion may be a factor to consider when seeking to find agreement on points of dispute.[385]

The parties and the arbitral tribunal should also consider whether a joint appointment of experts is possible, where each party nominates an expert, which then together are appointed by the arbitral tribunal as tribunal-appointed experts.

The issues to be considered and discussed between the parties and the arbitral tribunal according to the structure of the expert opinion procedure should include:

- at which stage(s) of the arbitration, expert evidence shall be adduced;
- potential limitations to the length and or number of expert reports;
- (if party-appointed experts are used) in which sequence expert reports shall be adduced;
- whether further case management conferences pursuant to Article 27.6 shall be added to the procedural timetable for the specific purpose of discussing expert evidence;
- possible joint expert reports of party-appointed experts (if any);
- meetings among party-appointed experts (if any) and at which stage(s) of the proceedings such meetings might take place;

383. DIS Practice Note, 3.
384. DIS Practice Note, 3.
385. DIS Practice Note, 4.

- (joint) communication(s) of party-appointed experts (if any) to the arbitral tribunal and the parties regarding points of agreement and/or disagreement and at which stage(s) of the proceedings such report(s) might be given;
- oral testimony of experts including the possibility of witness conferencing by the arbitral tribunal and/or counsel;
- how to coordinate the evidence of experts in different disciplines;
- in which form expert evidence shall be adduced;
- whether an expert determination according to the DIS Rules on Expert Determination or an expertise according to the DIS Rules on Expertise may be conducive.[386]

2.1.5.11.2 Checklist Regarding Party-Appointed Experts

In order to tackle the risk of party-appointed expert opinions not being responsive and not helpful to the arbitral tribunal, the arbitral tribunal is encouraged to consider and discuss a handful of matters.

First, the parties and the arbitral tribunal are advised to consider agreeing on a set of instructions for party-appointed experts. If the parties' views differ on principles or methodology, or if the parties disagree on the assumptions the experts shall base their reports on, they may wish to instruct the party-appointed experts to opine on different alternatives to provide the arbitral tribunal with the opportunity of informed analysis.[387]

Second, if disciplines are at stake where the party-appointed experts may apply different methodologies to the same issue, the parties and the arbitral tribunal may wish to agree on the applicable methodologies that the party-appointed experts shall apply in preparing their expert reports.[388] Again, where the parties and/or experts cannot agree, the party-appointed experts might be instructed to opine on alternatives.

Third, experts are expected to discuss which rules of professional conduct shall apply and what effects such rules may have on the expert procedure.[389]

Fourth, the parties and the arbitral tribunal should consider coordinating the expert procedure and document production (if any) when setting up the procedural timetable in order to ensure responsive expert reports based on the same set of facts and documents. If possible, parties may wish to agree on a joint set of documents and/or information to be provided to all party-appointed experts.[390]

Lastly, in case the expert opinion is in a language other than the language of the proceedings, the parties and the arbitral tribunal should agree on the modalities of translation and interpretation of any written report and/or oral testimony at a case management conference.[391]

386. DIS Practice Note, 4–7.
387. DIS Practice Note, 8.
388. DIS Practice Note, 8.
389. DIS Practice Note, 9.
390. DIS Practice Note, 9–10.
391. DIS Practice Note, 10.

2.1.5.11.3 Checklist Regarding Tribunal-Appointed Experts

The arbitral tribunal may appoint experts on its own initiative if it so deems necessary to establish the facts of the case, after consulting with the parties. Additionally, the parties may agree that, instead of or in addition to party-appointed experts, the arbitral tribunal shall appoint experts.[392]

In this respect, the parties and the arbitral tribunal are encouraged to consider and discuss:

- whether a tribunal-appointed expert should be appointed;
- how to structure the expert procedure with the tribunal-appointed expert in order to ensure the efficient and effective conduct of the same;
- which instructions and assumptions are provided to the expert and which methodology the expert should apply;
- whether and how the tribunal-appointed expert is allowed to communicate directly with the parties;
- how to ensure that the expert is independent and impartial;
- who ultimately has to bear the costs.[393]

2.1.5.12 Professional Codes of Conduct

An expert is a professional, however, acting as an expert in an arbitral proceeding is not a profession. Experts in international arbitration are mostly scientists, engineers, lawyers, and accountants. Any professional organisation, such as chambers, councils or bars, has generally established codes of conduct that set out ethical rules for its members serving as experts or witnesses in dispute resolution proceedings.[394] These codes must be adhered to while acting as an expert, whether party-appointed or tribunal-appointed.

2.2 LEGAL NATURE

The legal nature of a particular matter determines the regime and consequences applicable to that subject.

Regarding party-appointed experts in international arbitration, no common and settled understanding exists as to its legal nature.[395] Although one may easily draw analogies from domestic court applications, depending on the legal culture of the arbitrator, this should not be done in international arbitration.[396] Procedural rules

392. DIS Practice Note, 11.
393. DIS Practice Note, 11–13.
394. *See,* for instance, https://euroexpert.org/standards/code-of-practice/ (accessed 25 October 2025); Khodykin and Mulcahy, *A Guide to the IBA Rules on the Taking of Evidence in International Arbitration*, 304.
395. Knoblach, *Sachverhaltsermittlung in Der Internationalen Wirtschaftsschiedsgerichtsbarkeit*, 274.
396. Eijsvoogel, 'General Synthesis Report', 6; Can and Tuna, *Milletlerarası Tahkim Hukuku*, 412.

concerning evidence for litigation are usually not mandatorily applicable in arbitration, except if they are related to fundamental rights such as equality or right to be heard.[397]

Arbitrators are generally and naturally influenced by court proceedings simply as a matter of habit or tradition. Only the best arbitration lawyers have sufficient experience and wisdom to fully detach themselves from their own legal system when determining or influencing international arbitration procedures.[398]

Depending on the legal culture background, the major views are that party-appointed experts are classified as witnesses, judicial/adjudicatory assistants, expert evidence, party submission, or sui generis evidence.

The author's personal view is that party-appointed experts can be classified as a means of evidence.[399] Before the arguments for this position are elaborated, various views on the matter will be explained.

2.2.1 Witness Evidence

Party-appointed experts, especially in *common law* countries, are often called 'expert witnesses', relying on the fact that they give testimony before tribunals and courts and are examined by these and party representatives. This is also the case in some civil law countries, such as the Netherlands.[400] Thus, they are categorised as witness evidence.[401] The UNCITRAL Model Law Article 26(2) also specifically refers to party-appointed experts, but not tribunal-appointed experts, as witnesses.

The LCIA Arbitration Rules Article 20, SIAC Arbitration Rules Rule 25, and American Arbitration Association (AAA) R-35 regard experts explicitly as 'witnesses'. Again, the CIArb Protocol refers to party-appointed experts as 'witnesses'.

The ICC Commission Report on Issues for Arbitrators Regarding Experts also states: 'Regardless of which party or parties appoint them, party-appointed experts are witnesses – nothing more and nothing less.'[402]

Nevertheless, there is a difference in the content that a fact witness and an expert testify to; whereas a fact witness testifies based on their first-hand experience,

397. Yeşilirmak, *Türkiye'de Ticari Hayatın ve Yatırım Ortamının Iyileştirilmesi Için Uyuşmazlıkların Etkin Cözümünde Dogrudan Görüşme, Arabuluculuk, Hakem-Bilirkişilik ve Tahkim: Sorunlar ve Cözüm Önerileri*, 104; Akıncı, *Milletlerarası Tahkim*, 342; Kalpsüz, *Türkiye'de Milletlerarası Tahkim*, 92; Born, *International Commercial Arbitration*, 2364; Taşkın, *Tahkim Hukukunda Tahkim Anlaşması, Hakem Kurulu ve Tahkim Yargılaması*, 191; Akıncı, 'Usul Kurallarına Aykırılık ve Dinlenilme Hakkı', 50; Redfern et al., 'The Standards and Burden of Proof in International Arbitration', 323; For contrary argument *see* Kuru and Aydın, *Medenî Usul Hukuku El Kitabı*, II:1892; Ağırman, *Milli & Milletlerarası Tahkim*, 455; Ermenek, 'Tahkimde Hukuki Dinlenilme Hakkının Korunması', 36.
398. Eijsvoogel, 'General Synthesis Report', 6.
399. Proske, *Expert Witness Conferencing in Schiedsverfahren*, 26.
400. Boerstra and Bitter, 'The Netherlands', 199.
401. Knoblach, *Sachverhaltsermittlung in Der Internationalen Wirtschaftsschiedsgerichtsbarkeit*, 277; Proske, *Expert witness conferencing in Schiedsverfahren*, 20; Wiegand, 'Der Experte im Verfahren Erkenntnisse aus nationalen und internationalen Verfahren vor Schiedsgerichten und staatlichen Gerichten', 19; Hobér and Sussman, *Cross-Examination in International Arbitration*, 25.
402. Schäfer and Wilson, 'ICC Bulletin', 2021, 65.

observations, and knowledge that he has observed or heard with their sense organs, the expert presents his professional opinion on a particular matter relying on his experience or knowledge.[403] Thus, each testimony has different purposes. The fact witness only helps the tribunal establish the facts of the case. The experts generally help the tribunal better understand facts but generally do not establish them. The fact that a witness is generally not replaceable, whereas another expert can be found on almost every occasion.[404]

Thus, witnesses and experts appear to differ from each other. It would be inappropriate to categorise experts as witnesses, relying merely on the fact that they give testimony and are examined at the hearings.[405]

In civil law countries, party-appointed experts are not accepted as witnesses[406] but are approached on the basis of interchangeability. In other words, the contribution of an expert is based on the accessible experience and knowledge of his field of expertise, which many other experts might also have. In contrast, the witness's position is that he has a special bond with an incident, which, if it were the only witness, is inimitable.[407]

The approach in common law countries is also changing, as CPR Rule 35 and EAA section 37, for instance, no longer name experts 'expert witnesses' but as mere 'experts'.[408] The HKIAC Arbitration Rules Articles 2.9, 22.5, and 22.7 also differentiate between witnesses and experts.

2.2.2 Assistant

Some scholars argue that party-appointed experts are assistants to the tribunal during proceedings and that they owe their duty to the court or tribunal.[409] The CIArb Protocol Article 4(3) also states that '[a]n expert's duty, in giving evidence in the Arbitration, is to *assist* the Arbitral Tribunal to decide the issues in respect of which expert evidence is adduced' [emphasis added].

403. Zuberbühler et al., *IBA Rules of Evidence*, 136; Schneider, 'Technical Experts in International Arbitration', 446; Webster and Bühler, *Handbook of ICC Arbitration: Commentary, Precedents, Materials*, 440; Spitzer, 'Der Sachverständigenbeweis Im Österreichischen Zivilprozess', 42; Knoblach, *Sachverhaltsermittlung in Der Internationalen Wirtschaftsschiedsgerichtsbarkeit*, 274; Elyıldırım, *Hukuk Yargılamasında Uzman Görüşü*, 56, 81; Atalay, 'Pekcanıtez Usûl', 2021, 1887; Proske, *Expert Witness Conferencing in Schiedsverfahren*, 20; Özbek, *Tahkim Hukuku*, II:1448.
404. Knoblach, *Sachverhaltsermittlung in Der Internationalen Wirtschaftsschiedsgerichtsbarkeit*, 276.
405. Similarly, Knoblach, *Sachverhaltsermittlung in Der Internationalen Wirtschaftsschiedsgerichtsbarkeit*, 274, fn. 435.
406. Pekcanıtez, 'Özel Uzman', 399; Münch, *Münchener Kommentar Zur ZPO*,§ 1049, para. 39.
407. Wach and Petsch, 'Der Sachverständigenbeweis Im Schiedsverfahren: Grenzen Der Gestaltungsfreiheit von Parteien Und Schiedsgericht', 97–98.
408. Teomete Yalabık, 'Questioning Expert Witnesses in Litigation and International Arbitration: How to Prevent Partisan Expert Reports and "Battle of Experts"', 136; Yazıcı-Tıktık, 'HMK m. 293'teki Uzman Görüşü Kurumu Ile Anglo-Sakson Hukuk Sistemindeki Uzman Tanık Kurumunun Karşılaştırılması', 85.
409. Parlett, 'Parties' Engagement with Experts in International Litigation', 441; Mbengue and Das, 'Rules Governing the Use of Experts in International Disputes', 445; Elyıldırım, *Hukuk Yargılamasında Uzman Görüşü*, 33; Sarısözen, 'Özel Bilirkişi (Uzman Görüşü)', 1703.

The expert should provide independent assistance to the tribunal by way of an objective, unbiased opinion in relation to matters within his expertise, and the expert should never assume the role of an advocate.[410] However, it is not clear whether the duty to assist the tribunal places party-appointed experts in the legal status of assistants. This could be argued when referring to tribunal-appointed experts.[411] In essence, the primary role of the party-appointed expert is to assist the appointing party.[412] It seems that this attribution to party-appointed experts is made not to define their legal nature but rather their role in the proceedings.

2.2.3 Party Submission

Some civil law scholars have argued that the opinion submitted by an expert is a qualified party submission (*qualifizierter Parteivortrag*).[413] Many Turkish scholars hold similar views (*nitelikli taraf beyanı*).[414] It is considered a means to influence or shape the opinion of the adjudicator.[415]

Accordingly, the expert is obliged, regardless of his personal or professional conviction, to accept orders from the party that is paying the expert and to represent the position that is favourable to the party commissioning him insofar as this is within the scope of what is justifiable in the scientific field in question.[416] This view is supported by the fact that there are no legal remedies, such as a challenge to the expert, which tribunal-appointed experts can be.

Schneider argued that a party-appointed expert report cannot serve as a mere party argument.[417] Other Swiss scholars also accept that party-appointed experts are more than just a party submission for various reasons; party submissions are pleaded in

410. Bor, 'Expert Evidence', 511; Hwang and Chin, 'The Role of Witness Statements in International Commercial Arbitration', 652.
411. Tanrıver, *Hukukumuzda Bilirkişilik*, 26; *see* the HKIAC Arbitration Rules Art. 25, which attributes this position to tribunal-appointed experts.
412. Proske, *Expert witness conferencing in Schiedsverfahren*, 20.
413. Wach and Petsch, 'Der Sachverständigenbeweis Im Schiedsverfahren: Grenzen Der Gestaltungsfreiheit von Parteien Und Schiedsgericht', 111; Ahrens, *Der Beweis Im Zivilprozess*, 967, para. 39. Based on the argument that ZPO § 1049 is a peremptory norm of law; 'Procedural Efficiency in International Arbitration: Choosing the Best of Both Legal Worlds', 122; Patocchi, Paolo Michele and Niedermaier, 'UNCITRAL Rules', 1182.
414. Tanrıver, *Hukukumuzda Bilirkişilik*, 33; Pekcanıtez, 'Özel Uzman', 393; Atalay, 'Pekcanıtez Usûl', 2021, 1959; Yazıcı-Tıktık, 'HMK m. 293'teki Uzman Görüşü Kurumu Ile Anglo-Sakson Hukuk Sistemindeki Uzman Tanık Kurumunun Karşılaştırılması', 91; Karslı, *Medeni Muhakeme Hukuku*, 623; Hanağası, *Medeni Yargılama Hukukunda Silahların Eşitligi*, 420; Toraman, *Medeni Usul Hukukunda Bilirkişi İncelemesi*, 660; Alangoya, Yıldırım, and Deren-Yıldırım, *Medeni Usul Hukukunun Esasları*, 369–370; Tanrıver, *Medenî Usûl Hukuku*, 2021, I:1106; Elyıldırım, *Hukuk Yargılamasında Uzman Görüşü*, 34; Akil, 'Bilirkişi-Uzman Tanık Ayrımı', 174, 177; Eroğlu, *Tahkimde Yargılamanın Yenilenmesi*, 149; Özbek, *Tahkim Hukuku*, II:1464; *Budak/Karaaslan* state that if the expert opinion is on legal issues, this is part of the party submissions, but if it is related to factual issues, then it's a means of (non-binding) evidence ('*takdiri delil*'). *See* Budak and Karaaslan, *Medenî Usul Hukuku*, 2022, 311.
415. Atalay, 'Pekcanıtez Usûl', 2021, 1959.
416. Wach and Petsch, 'Der Sachverständigenbeweis Im Schiedsverfahren: Grenzen Der Gestaltungsfreiheit von Parteien Und Schiedsgericht', 95.
417. Schneider, 'Technical Experts in International Arbitration', 446.

briefs and not in expert reports, a party-appointed expert should actually appear at the evidentiary hearing, and the words of a party-appointed expert may still have a different weight than the arguments developed by counsel, even if the expert does not appear at the hearing. Thus, if the requirements are met, party-appointed experts should be treated as a means of evidence rather than party representatives.[418]

However, it has been suggested that the report of a party-appointed expert who does not appear at the evidentiary hearing, despite a request, might be taken into account by the arbitral tribunal as part of the party's written argument, but not as expert evidence, since the opportunity to testify and examination could not be realised.[419] The German Federal Supreme Court and the Swiss Federal Supreme Court[420] share this view.

2.2.4 Expert-Determination

The use of experts in international arbitration can be easily mismatched with expert-determination. Expert-determination is a concept where parties, by agreement, refer a quality or quantity dispute or an issue to an expert or a panel of experts and accept as conclusive the determination or findings made by such expert(s).[421] If parties explicitly grant the expert the power to render a binding decision on certain factual issues, this is called expert-determination.[422] However, expert opinion does neither strictly bind the tribunal nor the parties; expert-determination, depending on the applicable law, will have a binding effect and, thus, has to be differentiated.[423] Parties need to have an agreement to appoint a reliable third-party expert, to make a decision or formal determination on the issues referred to the expert, in order to classify it as an expert-determination.

Atalı/Ermenek/Erdoğan argue that if a party does not object to an expert report, which indicates opinions on factual issues, an expert-determination agreement comes

418. Zuberbühler et al., *IBA Rules of Evidence*, 148.
419. Zuberbühler et al., 148; Schneider, 'Technical Experts in International Arbitration', 447.
420. Swiss Federal Supreme Court, 4A_178/2015, Swiss International Arbitration Decisions, 11 November 2015, para. 2.6.
421. Yesilirmak, 'Expert Determination in Turkey', 306 ff.; Yeşilirmak, *Türkiye'de Ticari Hayatın ve Yatırım Ortamının Iyileştirilmesi Için Uyuşmazlıkların Etkin Cözümünde Dogrudan Görüşme, Arabuluculuk, Hakem-Bilirkişilik ve Tahkim: Sorunlar ve Cözüm Önerileri*, 24; White, *The Use of Experts by International Tribunals*, 163; *see* Tuna, *Alternative Dispute Resolution in Energy Industries*, 180–185.
422. Yeşilirmak, *Türkiye'de Ticari Hayatın ve Yatırım Ortamının Iyileştirilmesi Için Uyuşmazlıkların Etkin Cözümünde Dogrudan Görüşme, Arabuluculuk, Hakem-Bilirkişilik ve Tahkim: Sorunlar ve Cözüm Önerileri*, 28; Zuberbühler et al., *IBA Rules of Evidence*, 159.
423. Elyıldırım, *Hukuk Yargılamasında Uzman Görüşü*, 49; However, an expert-determination should also be differentiated from an arbitral award. 'In a case brought before a German court, the legal nature of a decision made in the form of an "expert opinion-arbitral award" had to be determined. The court considered not only the form and title of the document, but the nature and effect of the said decision. Although the document was presented as an "expert opinion", there was a final and binding decision capable to be enforced and expressly excluded any review of the merits by the courts. Therefore, the court concluded that the decision was an award and not an expert opinion.' *See* [Oberlandesgericht Stuttgart, Germany, 1 Sch 21/01, 23 January 2002], http://www.dis-arb.de/en/47/datenbanken/rspr/olg-stuttgart-case-no-1-sch-21-01-date-2002-01-23-id171 (accessed 24 September 2025) in UNCITRAL, *UNCITRAL Digest*, 127, para. 3; Reiner and Aschauer, 'ICC Rules', 136.

into existence that is binding on the tribunal.[424] However, the party-appointed expert's opinions are not binding on the tribunal.

2.2.5 Expert Evidence

Some Turkish scholars have also argued that although the party-appointed expert is an expert like the tribunal-appointed expert, this does not lead to the former sharing the legal nature of the latter.[425] The main reason for this view is that the party-appointed expert has no duty to be independent and cannot be challenged.[426] Some other scholars stress that the equality of arms principle might be violated if the party-appointed expert is accepted as expert evidence.[427]

However, *Can/Tuna argued* that the party-appointed expert in arbitration is, in the legal sense, a (tribunal-appointed) expert.[428]

Some German scholars argue, according to the German ZPO, that only tribunal-appointed experts can be categorised as expert evidence (*Sachverständigenbeweis*) and that party-appointed experts cannot be categorised as the same according to ZPO § 1049, especially with the ratio that they must be neutrals and could be challenged.[429]

2.2.6 Evidence Assessment Tool

In general, evidence is submitted to prove alleged facts that occurred before filing a case.[430] Evidence indicates that an alleged fact occurred, such as a document proving that one is a debtor or video footage showing that an accident occurred.

The expert opinion sometimes does not prove an alleged fact but enables the arbitrator to come to an opinion and derive a conclusion from other evidence, such as witness statements or documents.[431] Thus, some authors rightly argued that an expert opinion lacks the representative quality of a fact (*delilin vakıayı temsil değeri*). Hence,

424. Atalı, Ermenek, and Erdoğan, *Medeni Usul Hukuku*, 541.
425. Atalay, 'Pekcanıtez Usûl', 2021, 1959; Pekcanıtez, 'Özel Uzman', 398–404; Karslı, *Medeni Muhakeme Hukuku*, 624; Yazıcı-Tıktık, 'HMK m. 293'teki Uzman Görüşü Kurumu Ile Anglo-Sakson Hukuk Sistemindeki Uzman Tanık Kurumunun Karşılaştırılması', 92.
426. Atalay, 'Pekcanıtez Usûl', 2021, 1959; Yazıcı-Tıktık, 'HMK m. 293'teki Uzman Görüşü Kurumu Ile Anglo-Sakson Hukuk Sistemindeki Uzman Tanık Kurumunun Karşılaştırılması', 92; Tanrıver, *Hukukumuzda Bilirkişilik*, 33; Elyıldırım, *Hukuk Yargılamasında Uzman Görüşü*, 50–51; Pekcanıtez, Atalay and Özekes, *Medeni Usul Hukuku Ders Kitabı*, 439.
427. Karslı, *Medeni Muhakeme Hukuku*, 624; Hanağası, *Medeni Yargılama Hukukunda Silahların Eşitligi*, 422; Especially if one party adduces multiple experts *see* Proske, *Expert witness conferencing in Schiedsverfahren*, 43.
428. Can and Tuna, *Milletlerarası Tahkim Hukuku*, 412.
429. Wach and Petsch, 'Der Sachverständigenbeweis Im Schiedsverfahren: Grenzen Der Gestaltungsfreiheit von Parteien Und Schiedsgericht', 103, 109; Knoblach, *Sachverhaltsermittlung in Der Internationalen Wirtschaftsschiedsgerichtsbarkeit*, 277; For similar views *see* Spitzer, 'Der Sachverständigenbeweis Im Österreichischen Zivilprozess', 40.
430. Elyıldırım, *Hukuk Yargılamasında Uzman Görüşü*, 56.
431. Atalay, 'Delil Kavramı Üzerine', 135; Özbek, 'Uzman Görüşünün Yargılamada Değerlendirilmesi', 129; Elyıldırım, *Hukuk Yargılamasında Uzman Görüşü*, 56.

it should not be qualified as evidence but as an assessment tool while evaluating the evidence's credibility.[432]

2.2.7 Sui Generis Evidence

Article 5(1) of the IBA Rules states that a party-appointed expert is a 'means of evidence'. This indicates that party-appointed experts are not mere party submissions in international arbitration but have their own weight.[433]

Some Turkish scholars argue that party-appointed experts are a sui generis type of nonbinding evidence (*Takdiri Delil*).[434] *Pekcanıtez* even argued that party-appointed experts are not a means of evidence.[435] The main supporting argument of this view is that party-appointed experts are regulated within the sections of evidence in the HMK (Chapter 4 section 7).[436] This view is echoed by the authors of the *Münchener Kommentar zur Zivilprozessordnung,* who stipulate that party-appointed experts are a means of sui generis expert evidence (*eine eigene Beweisform des Sachverständigenbeweises*).[437]

Knoblach also argued that according to German arbitration law, a party-appointed expert's legal nature cannot be classified as the party-appointed expert in the court proceedings.[438] The author shares the view that party-appointed experts are a means of providing sui generis expert evidence.[439]

The authors of the *Münchener Kommentar zur Zivilprozessordnung* and *Schlosser* also shared the view that party-appointed experts are in no way mere party submissions but a means of evidence.[440]

Although the expert receives instructions, he will make evaluations based on scientific facts and methods, which will differentiate him from a counsel.[441]

---

432. Atalay, 'Delil Kavramı Üzerine', 135; Erdoğan and Üçüncü, 'Bilirkişilik Kurumu ve Bilirkişi Raporunun Delil Değerine İlişkin Bazı Sorunlar', 362; Elyıldırım, *Hukuk Yargılamasında Uzman Görüşü,* 60; Görgün, Börü, and Kodakoğlu, *Medenî Usûl Hukuku,* 560.
433. Zuberbühler et al., *IBA Rules of Evidence,* 136.
434. Kuru, *Medenî Usul Hukuku El Kitabı,* I:826, 829; Cayan, *Medeni Usul Hukukunda Bilirkişilik Müessesesi,* 10; Işık, 'Uzman Görüşü (Mütalaa)', 92; Öztek, 'Bilirkişi Raporunun Hâkimi Bağlamaması', 1624–1625; Arslan et al., *Medeni Usul Hukuku,* 472; Kesikli, 'Milletlerarası Ticari Tahkimde Delillerin Değerlendirilmesi', 213; *Bacanlı* and *Eroglu* classify party-appointed experts merely as 'evidence'. *See* Bacanlı, 'Bir Alternatif Uyuşmazlık Cözüm Yolu Olarak Istanbul Tahkim ve Arabuluculuk Merkezi (ISTAC) Tahkim Yargilamasinda Delillerin Ibrazı ve Değerlendirilmesi', 97; Similarly in France, *see* Reiner, 'Austria', 25.
435. Pekcanıtez, 'Özel Uzman', 395, 405.
436. Öztek, 'Bilirkişi Raporunun Hâkimi Bağlamaması', 1624; Parlett, 'Parties' Engagement with Experts in International Litigation', 441; Abdel Wahab, 'Party Appointed Experts in International Commercial Arbitration', 182; Cayan, *Medeni Usul Hukukunda Bilirkişilik Müessesesi,* 10; Toraman, *Medeni Usul Hukukunda Bilirkişi İncelemesi,* 663.
437. Münch, *Münchener Kommentar Zur ZPO,* § 1049, paras 38–39; Saenger, 'ZPO § 1049 Vom Schiedsgericht Bestellter Sachverständiger', para. 5; Schlosser, *ZPO,* § 1049, para. 1.
438. Knoblach, *Sachverhaltsermittlung in Der Internationalen Wirtschaftsschiedsgerichtsbarkeit,* 276–277.
439. Knoblach, 277.
440. Münch, *Münchener Kommentar Zur ZPO,* § 1049, para. 39; Schlosser, *ZPO,* § 1049, para. 1.
441. Kesikli, 'Milletlerarası Ticari Tahkimde Delillerin Değerlendirilmesi', 214.

As *Atalay* stated, any means of establishing an opinion on a factual allegation shall be treated as evidence (*geniş anlamda delil*) to the extent that it serves to establish the existence of that fact.[442]

Thus, as long as an expert opinion either establishes the facts or makes them clearer to understand, I consider party-appointed expert opinions as a means of evidence that the arbitrators will freely assess along with other evidence.[443] In case the party-appointed expert opinion is on legal issues, it can still be treated as evidence, but the arbitrators will have it easier to deny the points made in such opinion, compared to a scientific or technical experts' determination on matters.

2.3 RELATION TO FUNDAMENTAL RIGHTS

2.3.1 Right to Be Heard (Due Process)

The right to be heard is the right to impact proceedings and the outcome thereof. The right to be heard is accepted as a fundamental right and a sub-element of the right to a fair trial in many jurisdictions.[444] The right to be heard is not only applicable in the state judiciary but also in arbitral proceedings.[445]

The right to be heard in arbitration has been codified in many arbitration laws (HMK Article 423 and 439/2-f, SPILA Article 182, ZPO § 1042(1)).[446] The violation of the right to be heard is a ground for annulment and refusal of recognition and enforcement of an arbitral award in many jurisdictions such as Türkiye, Germany, Switzerland, the USA, France, and Belgium.[447]

---

442. Atalay, 'Pekcanıtez Usûl', 2021, 1731; Similarly Erdoğan and Üçüncü, 'Bir Davada Alınan Bilirkişi Raporunun Başka Davada Delil Değeri', 1512.
443. Yıldızlı, *Uluslararası Tahkimde Zararın Degerlendirilmesi*, 122.
444. Yeğengil, *Tahkim (L'Arbitrage)*, 294; Pekcanıtez, Atalay, and Özekes, *Medenî Usûl Hukuku Ders Kitabı*, 623. Pekcanıtez, 'Hukuki Dinlenilme Hakkı', 754, 760–762; Yılmaz, 'Hukukî Dinlenilme Hakkı', 1–2; Curschmann, 'Germany', 144.
445. Born, *International Commercial Arbitration*, 2326; Pekcanıtez and Yeşilirmak, 'Tahkim', 2703; Kuru and Aydın, *Medenî Usul Hukuku El Kitabı*, II:1891; Arslan et al., *Medenî Usul Hukuku*, 829; Postacıoğlu and Altay, *Medeni Usul Hukuku Dersleri*, 1044; Ekşi, *Hukuku Muhakemeleri Kanunu'nda Tahkim*, 158; Nomer, Ekşi, and Öztekin Gelgel, *Milletlerlarası Tahkim Hukuku*, I:23; Mavrantonakis, *Das Verbot Der Révision Au Fond Im Internationalen Handelsschiedsverfahren: Zur Bindung Des Staatlichen Gerichts an Die Schiedsgerichtlichen Sachverhaltsfeststellungen Und Zu Den Erforderlichen Ausnahmen*, 98; For German law *see* Bermann, *Recognition and Enforcement of Foreign Arbitral Awards: The Interpretation and Application of the New York Convention by National Courts*, 355; Wach and Petsch, 'Der Sachverständigenbeweis Im Schiedsverfahren: Grenzen Der Gestaltungsfreiheit von Parteien Und Schiedsgericht', 94–95; Khodykin and Mulcahy, *A Guide to the IBA Rules on the Taking of Evidence in International Arbitration*, 287; Proske, *Expert witness conferencing in Schiedsverfahren*, 41; Karslı, *Medeni Muhakeme Hukuku*, 910.
446. Oetiker, 'Commentary on Art. 26-30 Swiss Rules of Arbitration', 318; Görgün, Börü, and Kodakoğlu, *Medenî Usûl Hukuku*, 741.
447. Pekcanıtez and Yeşilirmak, 'Tahkim', 2765; Aslan, 'Tahkim Davalarında Hukuk, Dinlenilme Hakkı ve Kamu Düzeni', 21; Can and Tuna, *Milletlerarası Tahkim Hukuku*, 374; Işık, *MTK ve HMK Kapmasında Hakem Kararlarına Karşı İptal Davası*, 286 ff.; Özbek, *Tahkim Hukuku*, II:1357; *see* Swiss Federal Supreme Court, 4A_440/2010, Bundesgericht, para. 4.1.

According to the right to be heard, the parties have the right to be informed and must be given the opportunity to present their case in both its factual and legal aspects, and the arbitral tribunal must consider these statements.[448] The right to be heard has many sub-elements; *inter alia*, it includes being given all the statements, documents or other information which have been submitted to the arbitral tribunal, a copy of any communication by the other party to the tribunal, and of any expert report or other document on which the arbitral tribunal may rely in rendering its award.[449] However, this right must be exercised in due time and in accordance with the procedure. For instance, the Hong Kong court has accepted the right to comment on the report of a tribunal-appointed expert as a basic right.[450] However, the rejection of evidence or non-examination of it relating to a matter or facts that are not in dispute is not a violation of the right to be heard.[451]

To convince the arbitrator, the party seeking a claim must assert and lay down the relevant facts and, if necessary, prove them according to the burden of proof rules. If the factual circumstances require specialised or technical knowledge that the arbitrators do not possess, the party bearing the burden of proof must submit an expert opinion to prove its arguments.[452] The same is true for the counterparty to have the opportunity to respond to expert reports as a matter of due process.[453]

What would have occurred if the parties had not submitted an expert opinion but had instead asked the tribunal to appoint an expert? Is the tribunal bound by such a request? Or does the tribunal have the authority and discretion to reject such a request? This is a particularly vital matter because, in civil law countries, there is a tendency to rely more on tribunal-appointed experts.[454]

448. Pekcanıtez and Yeşilirmak, 'Tahkim', 2704, 2765; Bermann, *Recognition and Enforcement of Foreign Arbitral Awards: The Interpretation and Application of the New York Convention by National Courts*, 355; Lachmann, *Handbuch Für Die Schiedsgerichtspraxis*, 323, para. 1299; Esen, 'Violation of the Right to a Fair Trial in Arbitration', 100; Dülger, *Milletlerarası Tahkimde Hakemlerin Dogal Yetkileri*, 94; Özekes, *Medenî Usûl Hukukunda Hukukî Dinlenilme Hakkı*, 153; Aktepe Artık, *Medeni Usûl Hukukunda Hakem Kararlarının İptali Sebepleri*, 384; Curschmann, 'Germany', 144; Yılmaz, 'Hukukî Dinlenilme Hakkı', 26; Işık, *MTK ve HMK Kapmasında Hakem Kararlarına Karşı İptal Davası*, 288–292; Ermenek, 'Tahkimde Hukuki Dinlenilme Hakkının Korunması', 39–41; Özbek, *Tahkim Hukuku*, II:333; Kurkela, Turunen, and Conflict Management Institute, *Due Process in International Commercial Arbitration*, 142; Swiss Federal Supreme Court, 4A_440/2010, Bundesgericht, para. 4.1.
449. Pekcanıtez and Yeşilirmak, 'Tahkim', 2767; UNCITRAL, *UNCITRAL Digest*, 112; Güvenalp, *Milletlerarası Tahkimde İddia ve Savunma Hakkının İhlali*, 71; Yılmaz, 'Hukukî Dinlenilme Hakkı', 13; Güvenalp, 'Tahkimde Tarafların Eşitliği ve Hukuki Dinlenilme Hakkı', 111; Ağırman, *Milli & Milletlerarası Tahkim*, 388.
450. *Paklito Investment Limited v. Klockner East Asia Limited*, High Court – Court of First Instance, Hong Kong, 15 January 1993, [1993] 2 HKLR 39, http://www.hklii.hk/eng/hk/cases/hkcfi/1993/147.html. (accessed 9 January 2023).
451. Pekcanıtez and Yeşilirmak, 'Tahkim', 2767.
452. Wach and Petsch, 'Der Sachverständigenbeweis Im Schiedsverfahren: Grenzen Der Gestaltungsfreiheit von Parteien Und Schiedsgericht', 94.
453. Waincymer, *Procedure and Evidence in International Arbitration*, 424.
454. Parlett, 'Parties' Engagement with Experts in International Litigation', 441; Abdel Wahab, 'Party Appointed Experts in International Commercial Arbitration', 182.

If the arbitrators do not appoint an expert because they do not consider it necessary to resolve the case rightfully, there is no set-aside reason:

> Moreover, the arbitral tribunal may refuse to allow evidence without violating the right to be heard if the evidence is inadequate to satisfy the tribunal of the existence of a given fact, if the fact to be proven is already established, if it is irrelevant or if the court, by proceeding with an advance assessment of the evidence, reaches the conclusion that it is already satisfied and that further evidence based on the advance assessment sought by a party can no longer modify its views.[455]

In international arbitration, it is generally accepted that it is not an obligation on the tribunal to appoint an expert;[456] however, if the parties have not relied on experts and the dispute includes matters of knowledge outside the scope of expertise of the arbitrators, the tribunal has few options on how to engage this problem. It can either appoint an expert or decide according to the rules of burden of proof.

If mandatory information/opinion is required for the resolution of the dispute; the Swiss Federal Supreme Court is of the view that the tribunal should appoint an expert if requested according to the procedure and in a timely manner.[457] Nevertheless, not appointing an expert can only violate the right to be heard if it impacts the essence of the arbitral award.[458]

If both parties request so, the tribunal shall have due regard to such since the tribunal is bound by the applicable law to the arbitration and, in case of a lack of any imperative provisions, is bound by the parties' agreement. The arbitral tribunal has the discretion to act only if the parties have no agreement.[459] In addition, not providing any expert report or withdrawing it cannot violate the right to be heard.[460]

However, there is also the view that, according to the rules of burden of proof, the claiming party, in order to prove its argument successfully, has to rely on the evidence adduced on his side and failing to do so, i.e., not adduce a party-appointed expert report, it will fail to prove, and the claim should be dismissed, and no burden should be put on the tribunal.

If the tribunal has no power to appoint an expert and the parties do not adduce an expert report either, despite it being fundamental to resolve the issues in the case, the tribunal will decide the issues according to the presented evidence, and if it is not

455. Scherer, 'A. v. 1. B., 2. C., Federal Supreme Court of Switzerland, 1st Civil Law Chamber, 4A_335/2012, 30 January 2013'; Scherer, 'Society X. v. Z., Federal Supreme Court of Switzerland, 1st Civil Law Chamber, Case No. 4A_277/2017, 28 August 2017'.

456. UNCITRAL, *UNCITRAL Digest*, 116; Hacıbekiroğlu, *Milletlerarası Tahkim Hukukunda Deliller ve Delillerin Degerlendirilmesi*, 23; Narçin, '4686 Sayılı Milletlerarası Tahkim Uyarınca Deliller', 17.

457. Zuberbühler et al., *IBA Rules of Evidence*, 155; Özbek, *Tahkim Hukuku*, II:1456–1457.

458. Özbek, *Tahkim Hukuku*, II:1457.

459. Wach and Petsch, 'Der Sachverständigenbeweis Im Schiedsverfahren: Grenzen Der Gestaltungsfreiheit von Parteien Und Schiedsgericht', 102; Münch, *Münchener Kommentar Zur ZPO*§ 1042, para. 118.

460. Scherer, 'A. v. B. SA, Federal Supreme Court of Switzerland, 1st Civil Law Chamber, Case No. 4A_572/2015, 6 January 2016'.

possible to decide due to lack of essential knowledge, the tribunal should proceed on the basis of the principles on the burden of proof pursuant to the law applicable to the arbitration.[461]

According to German law, the wording of ZPO § 1049(2) seems to give discretionary power to the arbitral tribunal to appoint an expert at its own discretion, but if the facts cannot be established from the mere submission of the parties and the arbitral tribunal does not have such knowledge, the arbitral tribunal must appoint an expert, for the right to be heard reasons, even if there is no request from the parties to do so.[462] The tribunal could rely on its own expertise, provided that the parties are informed about the tribunal's intention in this matter and the parties have a right to submit comments on the opinion.[463]

The arbitral tribunal is free to assess the relevance of a particular fact in the decision. A wrong assessment generally does not infringe on the parties' right to be heard. It is only violated if the tribunal's assessment is solely intended to conceal that the tribunal did not engage with the parties' arguments in any way.[464] That is the case where the reasoning of the tribunal does not take note of or consider the arguments at all.[465] Additionally, the tribunal needs to give the counterparty an opportunity to comment or argue against the presented views.[466]

The issue with the CIArb Protocol is that if the parties have agreed on the application, the Protocol provides that the parties need to obtain permission from the tribunal before adducing the party-appointed expert.[467] The IBA Rules do not have similar provisions,[468] and international arbitration practice does not require any permission, as can be recognised from the arbitration rules.[469] The prior permission approach is criticised because it could affect the recognition and enforcement of the award in certain jurisdictions.[470] This does not, however, mean that the parties have full freedom to adduce experts, but the tribunal should have the discretion to exclude or limit the presentation of expert evidence.[471]

461. Zuberbühler et al., *IBA Rules of Evidence*, 156.
462. Wach and Petsch, 'Der Sachverständigenbeweis Im Schiedsverfahren: Grenzen Der Gestaltungsfreiheit von Parteien Und Schiedsgericht', 103.
463. Meier, 'Germany', 3.1.2, para. 4.
464. Pekcanıtez, 'Özel Uzman', 415; Pekcanıtez and Yeşilirmak, 'Tahkim', 2764, fn. 496; Işık, *MTK ve HMK Kapmasında Hakem Kararlarına Karşı İptal Davası*, 291.
465. Tanrıver, *Hukukumuzda Bilirkişilik*, 33; Rosenfeld, 'Country Report: Germany', 184; German Federal Court of Justice (BGH), I ZB 90/18, openJur; Bundesgerichtshof (German Federal Court of Justice), III ZR 169/90, Wolters Kluwer; German Federal Court of Justice (BGH), I ZB 1/16, SchiedsVZ at 317; German Federal Court of Justice (BGH), I ZB 7/15, 2016 SchiedsVZ at 339.
466. Tanrıver, *Hukukumuzda Bilirkişilik*, 34.
467. Parlett, 'Parties' Engagement with Experts in International Litigation', 442.
468. Freyer, Newman, and Hill, 'Assessing Expert Evidence', 433.
469. For example, *see* ICC Arbitration Rules Art. 25(2), SCC Arbitration Rules Art. 33, Swiss Rules Art. 27.
470. Khodykin and Mulcahy, *A Guide to the IBA Rules on the Taking of Evidence in International Arbitration*, 289.
471. Khodykin and Mulcahy, 290; Pekcanıtez and Yeşilirmak, 'Tahkim', 2764, fn. 496; Işık, *MTK ve HMK Kapmasında Hakem Kararlarına Karşı İptal Davası*, 291.

2.3.2 Equality

The principle of equal treatment of the parties means that all parties are given equal opportunity to present their claims and defences at all stages of proceedings. Equality is fundamental to arbitration, as in any dispute resolution procedure.[472]

These principles, which determine the limits of procedural rules, are also the basic criteria for the collection and evaluation of evidence. Equality has been regulated in the UNCITRAL Model Law (Article 18), and, among others, Turkish (TIAL Article 8/B/1), German (ZPO § 1042(1)), Swiss (SPILA Article 182(3)),[473] and English arbitration (EAA Article 33). It is also foreseen in many arbitration rules, like the UNCITRAL Arbitration Rules Article 17/1 and soft law elements, such as IBA Rules Article 9(2)(g).[474]

The equal opportunity for the parties to present and examine evidence is so important that it has a direct impact on the enforceability of the award. For example, if the time limits for filings and the time allocation at the hearings are different, the other party is not given the opportunity to present evidence against the claim, or if one party's witness is unreasonably treated, or if experts are not given equal opportunity to comment and be questioned, there is a high likelihood that the award will be annulled or denied enforcement due to a violation of the equality of the parties and their rights of defence (TIAL Article 15/A/1-g, UNCITRAL Model Law Article 34/2, MÖHUK Article 62/ç-d).[475]

As stressed in *CME Czech Republic B.V. v. The Czech Republic*, the tribunal shall safeguard each party's equal right to present their case, which includes cross-examining the parties' experts.[476]

For example, the fact that the number of expert reports submitted is not equal should not by itself mean that the principle of equality is violated. Additionally, the parties should be able to appoint an expert to support their own claims and defences, and the report of the expert they appoint should be taken into consideration by the arbitrators

472. Pekcanıtez, Atalay, and Özekes, *Medenî Usûl Hukuku Ders Kitabı*, 623; Kuru and Aydın, *Medenî Usul Hukuku El Kitabı*, II:1891; Yılmaz, *HMK Serhi*, 2021, 4:5464; Wach and Petsch, 'Der Sachverständigenbeweis Im Schiedsverfahren: Grenzen Der Gestaltungsfreiheit von Parteien Und Schiedsgericht', 99; Mavrantonakis, *Das Verbot Der Révision Au Fond Im Internationalen Handelsschiedsverfahren: Zur Bindung Des Staatlichen Gerichts an Die Schiedsgerichtlichen Sachverhaltsfeststellungen Und Zu Den Erforderlichen Ausnahmen*, 98; Ekşi, *Hukuku Muhakemeleri Kanunu'nda Tahkim*, 158; Can and Tuna, *Milletlerarası Tahkim Hukuku*, 373; Ağırman, *Milli & Milletlerarası Tahkim*, 387.

473. *See* Swiss Federal Supreme Court, 4A_440/2010, Bundesgericht, para. 4.1.

474. Pekcanıtez and Yeşilirmak, 'Tahkim', 2703; Arslan et al., *Medenî Usul Hukuku*, 829, 831; Dülger, *Milletlerarası Tahkimde Hakemlerin Dogal Yetkileri*, 94; Born, *International Commercial Arbitration*, 2337; Tanrıver, *Medenî Usûl Hukuku*, II:417, 461; Güvenalp, *Milletlerarası Tahkimde İddia ve Savunma Hakkının İhlali*, 405; Hanağası, *Medeni Yargılama Hukukunda Silahların Eşitligi*, 204–205; Kalpsüz, *Türkiye'de Milletlerarası Tahkim*, 142; Özekes, *Medenî Usûl Hukukunda Hukukî Dinlenilme Hakkı*, 222; Karslı, *Medeni Muhakeme Hukuku*, 909.

475. Hohler, 'Country Report: Switzerland', 380; Kaufmann-Kohler and Rigozzi, *International Arbitration: Law and Practice in Switzerland*, 279; Geisinger and Ducret, 'The Arbitral Procedure', 88; Narçin, '4686 Sayılı Milletlerarası Tahkim Uyarınca Deliller', 27; Yılmaz, 'Hukukî Dinlenilme Hakkı', 25.

476. *See CME Czech Republic B.V. v. The Czech Republic*, UNCITRAL, Final Award 14 March 2003, para. 80, available at https://www.italaw.com/cases/281 (accessed 30 August 2022).

in making the final decision. One of the parties may claim that the opinion of the expert appointed was not taken into account by the arbitrators and, therefore, he was deprived of the opportunity to have an equal influence on the final decision.[477]

The UNCITRAL Model Law Article 18 establishes the fundamental principles that in all arbitrations, each party must be treated with equality and be given a full opportunity to present their case. It is clear that Article 18's mandatory procedural guarantees of equal treatment and the right to be heard apply to and sometimes override both the parties' procedural autonomy and the arbitral tribunal's discretion.[478]

2.3.3 Party Autonomy

Party autonomy is the primary principle in international arbitration.[479] Party autonomy not only enables the parties to bring a dispute before an arbitral tribunal instead of a state court but also enables them to construct the proceedings according to their desire, subject to mandatory rules (UNCITRAL Model Law Article 19) and arbitration laws based on it (TIAL Article 8/A, ZPO § 1042(3)).[480]

Parties can adduce whatever evidence they believe would lead them to succeed. Therefore, they are free to adduce an expert opinion or not.[481] Accordingly, parties may waive the use of party-appointed experts.

While there can be situations where it is required to apply for leave to submit a party-appointed expert opinion, as is the case in the UK, in most jurisdictions, there is no need to obtain approval from the tribunal to submit a party-appointed expert opinion.[482]

In principle, the parties to an arbitration have the duty to furnish evidence and to introduce experts to assist the arbitral tribunal.[483] Unless the applicable law or rules

---

477. Güvenalp, 'Tahkimde Tarafların Eşitliği ve Hukuki Dinlenilme Hakkı', 121.
478. Born, *International Commercial Arbitration*, 2327.
479. Born, 2295; Pekcanıtez, Atalay, and Özekes, *Medenî Usûl Hukuku Ders Kitabı*, 624; Yeşilirmak, *Türkiye'de Ticari Hayatın ve Yatırım Ortamının Iyileştirilmesi Için Uyuşmazlıkların Etkin Cözümünde Dogrudan Görüşme, Arabuluculuk, Hakem-Bilirkişilik ve Tahkim: Sorunlar ve Cözüm Önerileri*, 104; Takavut, *Milletlerarası Ticari Tahkimde Usule İlişkin Konularda İrade Serbestisi*, 30–31; Fouchard, Gaillard, and Goldman, *Fouchard, Gaillard, Goldman on International Commercial Arbitration*, 502; Knoblach, *Sachverhaltsermittlung in Der Internationalen Wirtschaftsschiedsgerichtsbarkeit*, 47; Narçin, '4686 Sayılı Milletlerarası Tahkim Uyarınca Deliller', 26; Dülger, *Milletlerarası Tahkimde Hakemlerin Dogal Yetkileri*, 87; Akıncı, 'Usule Uygulanacak Kurallar ve Usule Aykırılığın Sonuçları', 3.
480. Pekcanıtez and Yeşilirmak, 'Tahkim', 2704; Yeşilirmak, *Türkiye'de Ticari Hayatın ve Yatırım Ortamının Iyileştirilmesi Için Uyuşmazlıkların Etkin Cözümünde Dogrudan Görüşme, Arabuluculuk, Hakem-Bilirkişilik ve Tahkim: Sorunlar ve Cözüm Önerileri*, 104; Yeğengil, *Tahkim (L'Arbitrage)*, 295–296; Kuru and Aydın, *Medenî Usul Hukuku El Kitabı*, II:1890; Arslan et al., *Medenî Usul Hukuku*, 829; Budak and Karaaslan, *Medenî Usul Hukuku*, 2019, 434; Knoblach, *Sachverhaltsermittlung in Der Internationalen Wirtschaftsschiedsgerichtsbarkeit*, 48; Karslı, *Medeni Muhakeme Hukuku*, 910; Ekşi, *Hukuku Muhakemeleri Kanunu'nda Tahkim*, 164; Ağırman, *Milli & Milletlerarası Tahkim*, 383, 455.
481. Lew, Mistelis, and Kröll, *Comparative International Commercial Arbitration*, 578; Khodykin and Mulcahy, *A Guide to the IBA Rules on the Taking of Evidence in International Arbitration*, 287; Akıncı, *Milletlerarası Tahkim*, 340.
482. Zuberbühler et al., *IBA Rules of Evidence*, 135; Roney, 'Cross-Examination of Experts', 112.
483. Schneider and Scherer, 'Art. 184', 2083. UNCITRAL, *UNCITRAL Digest*, 116, para. 1; Tanrıver,

provide otherwise, the tribunal does not engage in a fact-finding process and seeks evidence.[484] This is called the maxim of disposition or principle of party presentation (*taraflarca getirilme ilkesi, Verhandlungsgrundsatz, Verhandlungsmaxime*).

The maxim of disposition stipulates that the material of the case (i.e., the material facts and means of proof that form the basis of the claim and defence) must be brought before the tribunal by the parties to the case.[485] According to this principle, the arbitrator cannot ex officio consider the material facts not raised by one of the parties and, as a rule, cannot resort to any evidence ex officio.

Parties may completely exclude the usage of experts under an express agreement[486] if the relevant provision in the applicable law to the arbitration procedure allows such an agreement.

2.3.4 *Iura Novit Curia/Arbiter*

A court or tribunal is expected to know the applicable law to the dispute on its own without having to rely on the parties' legal pleadings.[487] This universal principle is found in law in all legal cultures.[488] Accordingly, in international arbitration, arbitrators should also be aware of the applicable law.[489]

However, when it comes to international disputes, multiple jurisdictions can be involved, and members of a tribunal may only be specialised in some branches of law, such as commercial law, civil law, or investment law in specific jurisdictions.[490] Thus, as it was demonstrated in Chapter 1 section 1.4.2.2.1, arbitrators cannot know every law, specifically foreign domestic law, which creates the need for legal experts. Nevertheless, this does not harm the principle or in itself lead to delegation of decision-making.

While some argue[491] that, even in situations where arbitrators have the desired knowledge of a particular legal field, expert opinions should still be allowed by

Medenî Usûl Hukuku, II: 423, 461; Born, *International Commercial Arbitration*, 2448; Bacanlı, 'Bir Alternatif Uyuşmazlık Çözüm Yolu Olarak Istanbul Tahkim ve Arabuluculuk Merkezi (ISTAC) Tahkim Yargilamasinda Delillerin Ibrazı ve Değerlendirilmesi', 97; Ağırman, *Milli & Milletlerarası Tahkim*, 388–389, 391; Demir Gökyayla, 'Tahkimde Taraflarca Getirilme İlkesi ve Delil İkamesi', 72; Kurkela, Turunen, and Conflict Management Institute, *Due Process in International Commercial Arbitration*, 175; Görgün, Börü, and Kodakoğlu, *Medenî Usûl Hukuku*, 736.

484. Kurkela, Turunen, and Conflict Management Institute, *Due Process in International Commercial Arbitration*, 175; Ermenek, 'Tahkimde Hukuki Dinlenilme Hakkının Korunması', 37.Schneider and Scherer, 'Art. 184', 2082; Ermenek, 'Tahkimde Hukuki Dinlenilme Hakkının Korunması', 37.
485. Tanrıver, *Medenî Usûl Hukuku*, 2022, II:423; Demir Gökyayla, 'Tahkimde Taraflarca Getirilme İlkesi ve Delil İkamesi', 72.
486. Proske, *Expert Witness Conferencing in Schiedsverfahren*, 26; Karadaş, *Ulusal (İç) Tahkim*, 174.
487. Cordero-Moss, 'Iura Novit Curia', 111.
488. Cordero-Moss, 111.
489. Pekcanıtez, Atalay and Özekes, *Medenî Usûl Hukuku Ders Kitabı*, 624; Pekcanıtez and Yeşilirmak, 'Tahkim', 2705; Tanrıver, *Medenî Usûl Hukuku*, 2022, II:431; Özbek, *Tahkim Hukuku*, II:1363.
490. Ünüvar, 'Experts: Investment Arbitration', para. 58.
491. Ünüvar, para. 59.

recognised specialists so that the tribunal becomes more informed, helping in a more accurate and consistent award.[492] The tribunal needs to allow parties to make submissions and express their views on the law, so that the right to be heard is not violated.[493]

In practice, domestic law experts are commonly used in ISDS. The *Philip Morris v. Uruguay* tribunal, for instance, did not apply the principle of *iura novit curia* to disqualify legal experts.[494] Legal experts certainly play a crucial role in identifying domestic laws relevant to disputes so that arbitrators can better understand and ascertain the law and integrate these rules into their awards.[495]

In Germany, although legal expert opinion is generally regarded as inadmissible evidence in arbitration law, exceptions are recognised where the arbitral tribunal lacks expertise and an expert is required and where fact and law are so closely intertwined that it is not reasonably possible to distinguish between them. The extent to which legal provisions can be the subject of proof is problematic. In German ordinary court proceedings, the principle of *iura novit curia* applies, meaning that legal provisions are generally not subject to proof, except for the law applicable in another state, customary law and statutes of evidence.

The legal situation in international arbitration proceedings in some countries is less clear. In particular, when lawyers are arbitrators, it may be necessary to consult experts to provide knowledge about the applicable law.[496]

2.3.5 Procedural Fairness, Flexibility, and Cost-Efficiency

The tribunal has a responsibility to conduct the proceedings fairly, and flexibility and cost-efficiency must be balanced.[497] In international commercial arbitration, procedural fairness is a vital right, which includes the right of each party to present its case.[498]

While parties enjoy great flexibility[499] to adduce party-appointed experts, permitting them to present expert evidence without any limits could adversely affect the proceedings in terms of cost-efficiency,[500] especially when it is unnecessary to have

492. Ünüvar, para. 59.
493. Güvenalp, *Milletlerarası Tahkimde İddia ve Savunma Hakkının İhlali*, 79.
494. Alvarez, 'The Search for Objectivity: The Use of Experts in Philip Morris v Uruguay', 418.
495. Ünüvar, 'Experts: Investment Arbitration', para. 57.
496. Knoblach, *Sachverhaltsermittlung in Der Internationalen Wirtschaftsschiedsgerichtsbarkeit*, 216–217.
497. Dülger, *Milletlerarası Tahkimde Hakemlerin Dogal Yetkileri*, 94; Tanrıver, *Medenî Usûl Hukuku*, 2022, II:432; Ağırman, *Milli & Milletlerarası Tahkim*, 392.
498. Plant, 'Expert Evidence and the Challenge of Procedural Reform in International Dispute Settlement', 464; Born, *International Commercial Arbitration*, 2327.
499. Knoblach, *Sachverhaltsermittlung in Der Internationalen Wirtschaftsschiedsgerichtsbarkeit*, 48.
500. Jones, 'Redefining the Role and Value of Expert Evidence', 23; Knoblach, *Sachverhaltsermittlung in Der Internationalen Wirtschaftsschiedsgerichtsbarkeit*, 282; Even if one party did not rely on party-appointed experts, it will after the other party adduces an expert. *See* Münch, *Münchener Kommentar Zur ZPO*, § 1042, para.19; Güvenalp, *Milletlerarası Tahkimde İddia ve Savunma Hakkının İhlali*, 83; Özekes, *Medenî Usûl Hukukunda Hukukî Dinlenilme Hakkı*, 112.

party-appointed experts or experts at all.[501] These are competing positions that must be discussed and agreed upon between the parties and the tribunal.[502] If the tribunal comprises members who were specifically appointed due to their expertise in specific matters, experts should not be required to take an active part in the proceedings.[503]

If a party insists on using a party-appointed expert where the tribunal takes the view that such evidence is not required, the tribunal might not prevent adducing the report but could exclude the oral testimony of the expert. Generally, in practice, even if one of the parties would not have relied on an expert, it will do so when the counterparty insists on using a party-appointed expert. The tribunal could decide adversely against the party when deciding on costs due to violations of cost-efficiency concerns.[504]

Adducing expert opinions in the far late stages of proceedings is a situation in which it might not be evaluated by the tribunal and could be disregarded.[505] However, if there is a recent development in which the parties have just been informed about a fact or evidence, expert opinion could be allowed in such a scenario.[506]

2.3.6 Tribunal's Duty to Enquire

Arbitrators, as the adjudicators in an arbitration case, have the primary authority and duty to administer and direct proceedings.[507] Establishing the facts of the case is also within the scope of this matter.

When it comes to the collection and presentation of evidence, it is mostly not clear where such authority and duty reach their limits. Do arbitrators have a duty to appoint experts if technical matters are beyond the understanding of the tribunal and the parties refrain from appointing experts?

Civil law jurisdictions such as Türkiye, Switzerland, Germany, and France require the judge to appoint a court-retained expert if there are technical matters beyond the judge's jurisdiction.[508] The rationale behind this approach is that the judge has the duty to enquire (*hâkimin davayı aydınlatma ödevi, Aufklärungspflicht).*[509]

However, domestic civil procedure rules applicable to litigation are, in principle, not applicable to arbitration.[510] In international arbitration, the parties are primarily

501. Proske, *Expert Witness Conferencing in Schiedsverfahren*, 32.
502. Khodykin and Mulcahy, *A Guide to the IBA Rules on the Taking of Evidence in International Arbitration*, 288.
503. Özbek, *Tahkim Hukuku*, II:1456.
504. Khodykin and Mulcahy, *A Guide to the IBA Rules on the Taking of Evidence in International Arbitration*, 288.
505. Güvenalp, *Milletlerarası Tahkimde İddia ve Savunma Hakkının İhlali*, 85–89.
506. Güvenalp, 89.
507. *See* UNCITRAL Arbitration Rules Art. 17 and ICC Arbitration Rules Art. 22; For details of the authority of arbitrators, *see* Dülger, *Milletlerarası Tahkimde Hakemlerin Dogal Yetkileri*.
508. Pekcanıtez and Yeşilirmak, 'Tahkim', 2768; Redfern et al., 'The Standards and Burden of Proof in International Arbitration', 326; 'Parties Not Indicated, Tribunal Fédéral, 1ère Cour Civile', 381.
509. For details, *see* Meriç, 'Hâkimin Davayı Aydınlatma Yükümlülüğü', 390 ff.; Karadaş, *Ulusal (İç) Tahkim*, 173.
510. Yeğengil, *Tahkim (L'Arbitrage)*, 296–297; Akıncı, *Milletlerarası Tahkim*, 342; Kalpsüz, *Türkiye'de Milletlerarası Tahkim*, 92; Born, *International Commercial Arbitration*, 2364;

responsible for bringing their evidence, and only a restricted principle of investigation (*sınırlı araştırma ilkesi, beschränkter Untersuchungsgrundsatz*) is applicable.[511] The Parties may decide otherwise, for instance, by agreeing on the application of the Prague Rules.[512] Accordingly, the facts relied upon must primarily be established by the parties (*taraflarca getirilme ilkesi, Verhandlungsgrundsatz*).[513]

However, in some cases, the facts presented by the parties may be ambiguous and unclear. It is difficult for an arbitrator to evaluate a case that he cannot understand. In this case, the arbitrator may intervene. Thus, although arbitrators generally have the authority to appoint a tribunal-appointed expert depending on the applicable rules to the arbitration, they are not ordinarily obligated to do so.[514] There are likely to be grey areas where an arbitral tribunal feels conflicted between the duty to uphold the right to be heard obligations and the duty to promote fairness and efficiency while at the same time supporting the duty to respect the autonomy of the parties. One of these situations is to deny the tribunal the ability to appoint its own expert.[515]

The arbitrators should express what may be relevant, determine how relevant facts can be established and give the necessary guidance and directives to the parties and their experts.[516] The arbitrators can ask party-appointed experts to clarify certain issues rather than directly appointing a tribunal expert.[517]

In a set-aside case before the Turkish courts, the plaintiff claimed that the application of the penal clause in the Contract would cause its economic ruin and that the decision to reject the appointment of a tribunal-appointed expert to determine this situation violated the right to be heard and was against public order. Nevertheless, the Court of Cassation has rightly accepted that this is a matter at the discretion of the arbitrators and does not constitute a reason for set-aside.[518]

Although there is no doubt that an arbitral tribunal shall not render a decision that it does not fully comprehend, it is also the parties who bear the burden of proof.

Taşkın, *Tahkim Hukukunda Tahkim Anlaşması, Hakem Kurulu ve Tahkim Yargılaması*, 191; Akıncı, 'Usul Kurallarına Aykırılık ve Dinlenilme Hakkı', 50; Redfern et al., 'The Standards and Burden of Proof in International Arbitration', 323; For contrary argument *see* Kuru and Aydın, *Medenî Usul Hukuku El Kitabı*, II:1892.

511. Curschmann, 'Germany', 143.
512. *Demir Gökyayla* argues that the Prague Rules do give wide Powers, nevertheless does not indicate that the ex officio principle is applicable, *see* Demir Gökyayla, 'Tahkimde Taraflarca Getirilme İlkesi ve Delil İkamesi', 78.
513. Tanrıver, *Medenî Usûl Hukuku*, 2022, II:461; Demir Gökyayla, 'Tahkimde Taraflarca Getirilme İlkesi ve Delil İkamesi', 72; Kurkela, Turunen, and Conflict Management Institute, *Due Process in International Commercial Arbitration*, 175; Swiss Federal Supreme Court, 4A_597/2013, Bundesgericht, para. 3.2.2.
514. Akıncı, *Milletlerarası Tahkim*, 339; *Akil*, referring to the view echoed in German literature, *see* Akil, 'Bilirkişi-Uzman Tanık Ayrımı', 175, fn. 20; Demir Gökyayla, 'Tahkimde Taraflarca Getirilme İlkesi ve Delil İkamesi', 86; Özbek, *Tahkim Hukuku*, II:1453. In the same direction in Italy, *see* Cavasola and Paton, 'Italy', 174.
515. Waincymer, *Procedure and Evidence in International Arbitration*, 391–392.
516. Kurkela, Turunen, and Conflict Management Institute, *Due Process in International Commercial Arbitration*, 176.
517. Ağırman, *Milli & Milletlerarası Tahkim*, 391; Kurkela, Turunen, and Conflict Management Institute, *Due Process in International Commercial Arbitration*, 156.
518. Turkish Court of Appeal, 11th Civil Chamber, Docket No. 2020/577, Decision No. 2021/618, 1 February 2021; Ağırman, *Milli & Milletlerarası Tahkim*, 462.

Therefore, the tribunal's duty of enquiry needs to be considered in conjunction with the maxim of disposition.[519]

In civil law country practice, the administration of evidence is concerned only with facts that have been sufficiently addressed by the parties.[520] Therefore, if the parties did not mention in their submission an issue that could lead to an expertise-required matter, the tribunal cannot, per se, engage in a fact-establishing process in this regard.

However, if the parties submitted expert opinions and there was room for elaboration, the tribunal could ask these experts supplemental questions. Then, if the tribunal determines one of the experts(s) to be more convincing, it can decide in favour of one or, alternatively, come to a totally different conclusion, provided that this is arguable under the circumstances of the case.

If the parties did not adduce expert opinions during the proceedings, the tribunal will decide on the basis of the presented file it has received (HMK Article 430/1-c).[521] In principle, the tribunal should not appoint a tribunal-appointed expert if the parties relied on their experts or did not explicitly ask for the appointment of an independent expert.

However, if the parties did not adduce expert opinions, the tribunal is not equipped with the expertise, and the issues unquestionably require it, the tribunal should appoint an expert. This is subject to the parties' agreement, the applicable law, or the arbitration rules empowering the tribunal to do so.[522] The contrary position could lead to the annulment of the award in some jurisdictions, with the rationale that the right to be heard is violated.[523]

As a result, the parties bear the primary responsibility for seeking and presenting evidence in international arbitration.[524] However, this is not absolute; if necessary, the tribunal has the authority to intervene and guide the parties (*Manuduktionspflicht*) and even appoint an expert.[525] Thus, the approach in international arbitration is a combination of both adversarial and inquisitorial methods.

If an expert is appointed by the tribunal, it is fundamental that the arbitrators may not properly delegate the responsibility for deciding either all or part of the dispute to an expert.[526]

However, an arbitral tribunal lacking its own expertise can base its award on the report of a party-appointed expert without relying on a tribunal-appointed expert if the tribunal designates why it finds the expert report (more) plausible and gives the other party the opportunity to comment.[527]

519. Dülger, *Milletlerarası Tahkimde Hakemlerin Dogal Yetkileri*, 95.
520. Reiner, 'Austria', 23.
521. Tanrıver, *Medenî Usûl Hukuku*, 2022, II:461.
522. Özbek, *Tahkim Hukuku*, II:1454–1456.
523. Özbek, II:1455; *see* for details Chapter 2, section 2.3.1.
524. Redfern et al., 'The Standards and Burden of Proof in International Arbitration', 324; Allen, Jr., 'Overview: The Common Law Systems', 17.
525. Redfern et al., 'The Standards and Burden of Proof in International Arbitration', 328.
526. Born, *International Commercial Arbitration*, 2448; Lew, 'The Need for Expert Evidence?', 253.
527. Borris et al., 'New York Convention, Article V [Grounds for Refusal of Recognition and Enforcement of Arbitral Awards]', para. 551; For a case in Germany *see* OLGOLG München, 34

2.3.7 Good Faith (Bona Fide)

The principles of good faith must be adhered to when exercising their rights and fulfilling their obligations. The rule of law does not protect the manifest abuse of a right.[528] In an arbitration proceeding, the parties and their representatives must act according to this notion during the procedure.[529]

Ideally, the parties are obliged to submit the facts of the case according to the subjective truth.[530] This principle also applies to experts and their opinions, but with minor differences.[531] The difference arises because of terminological reasons. Whereas the truth is related to factual circumstances, expert opinion, as the term suggests, is an opinion, and opinions are related to a conclusion considering the relevant facts.

Some authors argue that a party-appointed expert is under the responsibility to tell the truth when he testifies, similar to a fact witness.[532] As discussed in the preceding section, party-appointed experts should not be considered a witness but as a category on its own. Hence, the obligation to provide an expert opinion 'truthfully' does not fit experts.[533] This does not mean that the expert's opinion is manipulative or misleading. However, the expert's opinion might not possibly reflect the 'truth'. Thus, it would be logical to expect experts to provide their opinions according to their 'genuine belief'.

2.4 THE PERSONALITY AND QUALIFICATIONS OF PARTY-APPOINTED EXPERTS

There are many factors to consider when appointing an expert. An expert would be chosen on the basis of the candidate's professional experience, reputation, analytical skills and qualifications, arbitral practice, and academic track record, which are represented by high-quality research output and the expert's own opinions on such issues relevant to the dispute.[534] There is no uniform understanding of the threshold of the required experience. However, being knowledgeable about the arbitral process itself would naturally be beneficial.[535] 'A proposed expert witness who is unable or unwilling to fulfil this duty to the court is not properly qualified to perform the role of an expert.'[536]

Sch 10/11, 2012, 119383 openJur, paras 23–26. *See also* Van Den Berg, *ICCA Yearbook Commercial Arbitration 2012*, XXXVII:231, para. 20.

528. Ağırman, *Milli & Milletlerarası Tahkim*, 389.
529. Görgün, Börü, and Kodakoğlu, *Medenî Usûl Hukuku*, 736.
530. Pekcanıtez and Yeşilirmak, 'Tahkim', 2704; Tanrıver, *Medenî Usûl Hukuku*, II:430–431.
531. Wach and Petsch, 'Der Sachverständigenbeweis Im Schiedsverfahren: Grenzen Der Gestaltungsfreiheit von Parteien Und Schiedsgericht', 95.
532. Schäfer and Wilson, 'ICC Bulletin', 2021, 63.
533. For a contrary view, *see* Knoblach, *Sachverhaltsermittlung in Der Internationalen Wirtschaftsschiedsgerichtsbarkeit*, 278–279.
534. Abdel Wahab, 'Party Appointed Experts in International Commercial Arbitration', 193; Ünüvar, 'Experts: Investment Arbitration', para. 42.
535. Abdel Wahab, 'Party Appointed Experts in International Commercial Arbitration', 184; Ünüvar, 'Experts: Investment Arbitration', para. 45.
536. Supreme Court of Canada, *White Burgess Langille Inman v. Abbott and Haliburton Co.*, para. 53.

The credibility of an expert depends on many criteria. In an unpublished case administered by the Shanghai International Economic and Trade Arbitration Commission (SHIAC) in 2016, the sea shipper questioned the independence of the assessor, who was solely appointed by the cargo owner and pleaded inadmissibility of the assessment report as a whole. The sea shipper also argued that the assessor should be summoned to testify before the tribunal, which would be extremely unlikely in the competitive assessment industry. The tribunal allowed the evidence because it held that opinions given by a party-appointed expert should generally be treated as document evidence submitted by the filing party rather than as testimony from an individual witness.

Hence, the expert was not required to testify before the tribunal under the Chinese Procedural Code or the SHIAC Rules. The tribunal further noted the well-recognised credibility of the assessor in the industry and found the likelihood of the assessor falsifying the opinions to be extremely low, provided that there was no counter evidence showing probable credibility concern over the authenticity of the documented opinions or the assessor himself.

As for loss assessment, the arbitral tribunal noted that the sea shipper had engaged its own expert. Given that the credibility of such an expert was not known to the arbitral tribunal and that it was considered economically feasible to have such an expert testify before the tribunal, an oral hearing was convened to examine the opinions given by the sea shipper-appointed expert.[537]

The arbitrator, before digging into the opinion, will assess the credibility of the author, also called *Voir dire*.[538] The arbitrator will have a better understanding of whether he can rely on the findings and views stipulated in the opinion if he knows the (personal and) professional qualifications of the expert. This could be comparable to a situation where a restaurant is visited based on a chef's qualifications.

The arbitrator will take into account the personality, education, experience, and reputation of the expert to assess whether the expert's views are scientifically objective and trustworthy.[539] Thus, it is vital for the expert to be transparent, and provisions of the IBA Rules (Article 5(2)(a) and 5(2)(c)) aim to ensure it via a statement including the full name and address of the party-appointed expert, a statement regarding his present and past relationship (if any) with any of the parties, their legal advisors and the arbitral tribunal, a description of his background, qualifications, training and experience and his independence from the parties, their legal advisors and the arbitral tribunal.[540]

537. Zhihe and Tingwei, 'The Use of Expert Witness in Arbitration from the Perspective of SHIAC'.
538. Blackaby and Wilbraham, 'Practical Issues Relating to the Use of Expert Evidence in Investment Treaty Arbitration', 657.
539. Wach and Petsch, 'Der Sachverständigenbeweis Im Schiedsverfahren: Grenzen Der Gestaltungsfreiheit von Parteien Und Schiedsgericht', 97; Abdel Wahab, 'Party Appointed Experts in International Commercial Arbitration', 193.
540. Blackaby and Wilbraham, 'Practical Issues Relating to the Use of Expert Evidence in Investment Treaty Arbitration', 657.

According to *Wach and Petsch*, based on the overriding mandatory provision of ZPO § 1049, the expert must be neutral and not be paid or instructed by a party.[541] The authors even exclude this in case the expert declares that they adhere to 'expert rules of conduct'.[542]

It is difficult for the arbitrator to assess who does not know that issue to assess whether the opinion is or is not constructed unobjective.[543]

2.4.1 Independence

IBA Rules Article 5(2)(c) foresee that the expert report shall contain a statement of the expert's independence from the parties, their legal advisors and the Arbitral Tribunal. The CIArb Protocol Article 4 headline reads as 'Independence, Duty and Opinion', the article itself does not mention an independence requirement.[544] Neither the IBA Rules nor the CIArb Protocol are clear on how an expert can, in fact, be independent.[545]

Being independent can be defined as not being dependent, such as not being subject to control by others, not being affiliated with a larger controlling unit, not requiring or relying on something else, not looking to others for opinions or guidance in conduct, and not being bound by or committed to a party.[546]

According to the comprehensive empirical study conducted by the University of Geneva[547] with arbitrators, counsel, and experts, independence was mentioned as a must-have fundamental attribute of experts by all respondents.[548]

From the view of arbitrators and counsel, independence is the concept where the expert's position is assessed, whether it has objective links with the party.[549] However, experts view independence as acting in freedom and in the absence of control by the party.[550]

There are views that foresee that party-appointed experts should be independent.[551] The main reason for this view is grounded in a function similar to that of the tribunal-appointed expert.

541. Wach and Petsch, 'Der Sachverständigenbeweis Im Schiedsverfahren: Grenzen Der Gestaltungsfreiheit von Parteien Und Schiedsgericht', 110.
542. Wach and Petsch, 110.
543. Wach and Petsch, 110.
544. CIArb Protocol Art. 4(1): 'An expert's opinion shall be impartial, objective, unbiased and uninfluenced by the pressures of the dispute resolution process or by any Party.'
545. Jones, 'Ineffective Use of Expert Evidence in Construction Arbitration', 7.
546. Merriam-Webster.com Dictionary, 'independent', https://www.merriam-webster.com/dictionary/independent (accessed 6 July 2022).
547. *See* Mbengue and Das, 'Rules Governing the Use of Experts in International Disputes'; de Chazournes et al., 'Uses of Experts Before International Courts and Tribunals'.
548. de Chazournes et al., 'Uses of Experts Before International Courts and Tribunals', 492.
549. de Chazournes et al., 493.
550. de Chazournes et al., 495–496.
551. Lew, Mistelis, and Kröll, *Comparative International Commercial Arbitration*, 575; Kesikli, 'Milletlerarası Ticari Tahkimde Delillerin Değerlendirilmesi', 215; Schütze and Thümmel, *Schiedsgericht Und Schiedsverfahren*, 133, para. 21; Roney, 'Cross-Examination of Experts', 114; Club Español del Arbitraje, Code of Best Practices in Arbitration, Rule 39.

The expert is expected to be independent from the party and its agents and from the counsel representing the client. Actually, not the parties but the legal counsel generally determines the expert to be appointed. It is common for legal counsel and their law firms to reach out to experts whom they occasionally engage for cases. That is why IBA Rules Article 5(2)(c) have foreseen that experts should also be independent of legal advisors.[552]

As will be evaluated in Chapter 4, neither the IBA Rules nor the CIArb Protocol explain how a party-appointed expert can, in fact, be independent and not just show independence.[553] Although stipulated as requirements in soft laws, due to their status, party-appointed experts cannot and should not be expected to be independent, but their report can be an independent product.

2.4.2 Impartiality

Impartiality refers to the absence of bias or predisposition towards a party and ensures objectivity. 'The expert's opinion must be impartial in the sense that it reflects an objective assessment of the questions at hand.'[554]

Being dependent does not automatically mean that an expert should be partial. Contrary to independence, impartiality should be sought regarding party-appointed experts.[555]

In particular, regarding academic experts, published writings can speak on their behalf and should be checked to ensure that they contain no statements that are inconsistent with the client's case. It could directly discredit the expert and lead the tribunal to the conclusion of lacking impartiality if any contrary statements are found in the opinion.[556]

The same quantum experts are increasingly employed in multiple cases by the same counsel, leading to the perception of the expert as a 'hired gun'.[557] 'Their valuations and methodologies can be remarkably similar, or they can differ between cases depending on the party (investor or state) that retains them, leading to questions about the credibility of their opinions.'[558]

552. Khodykin and Mulcahy, *A Guide to the IBA Rules on the Taking of Evidence in International Arbitration*, 303.
553. Jones, 'Ineffective Use of Expert Evidence in Construction Arbitration', 7.
554. Supreme Court of Canada, *White Burgess Langille Inman v. Abbott and Haliburton Co.*, para. 32.
555. Akıncı, *Milletlerarası Tahkim*, 341; Tanrıver, *Hukukumuzda Bilirkişilik*, 31.
556. Blackaby and Wilbraham, 'Practical Issues Relating to the Use of Expert Evidence in Investment Treaty Arbitration', 658.
557. 51% of respondents agreed that party-appointed experts are hired guns or advocates in disguise, but 24% do not consider it as an issue in 'BCLP 2021 Survey', 9.
558. Hodgson and Stewart, 'Experts in Investor-State Arbitration: The Tribunal as Gatekeeper', 456.

2.4.3 Reputable Expertise

The main reason the relevant expert is appointed is his extensive knowledge and/or experience in the subject and the reputation he has because of that.[559] The expert's opinion should be distinguishable from a 'lay' opinion.[560] It is crucial to establish in any review that the expert is well-recognised in the relevant discipline through experience or academic work.[561] This must be objectively testable.[562] This criterion is probably the most vital in order to convince the tribunal and result in favour.[563] The reputation of an expert must be above any suspicion.[564]

Additionally, experts are expected to have advanced communication skills. They should be able to convey the matters requiring expertise in a manner and form that provides the arbitral tribunal a comprehensive yet concise understanding.[565]

2.5 THE RELATIONSHIP BETWEEN THE PARTY AND THE EXPERT

2.5.1 Appointment Procedure

There is no clear-cut, regulated procedure for appointing party-appointed experts.[566] Only some limited arbitration rules, such as the LCIA Arbitration Rules Article 20.1, address that before any hearing, the tribunal may order any party to give written notice of the identity of each expert that the party wishes to call, as well as the subject matter of his testimony, its content, and its relevance to the issues in the arbitration. Putting aside the potential difficulty in identifying the desired expert, once the name is determined, interviewing the potential expert is vital before conclusively deciding to work with him.[567] Experts may be recruited prior to the initiation of proceedings or after the request has been submitted.

The parties are free to choose the experts they consider. This freedom is set out in *Bridgestone v. Panama*:

559. Abdel Wahab, 'Party Appointed Experts in International Commercial Arbitration', 184; Elyıldırım, *Hukuk Yargılamasında Uzman Görüşü*, 107; Tanrıver, *Hukukumuzda Bilirkişilik*, 31; Sarısözen, 'Özel Bilirkişi (Uzman Görüşü)', 1709; Atalay, 'Pekcanıtez Usûl', 2021, 1959; Taşdemir, 'İngiliz ve Amerikan Medenî Yargılamasında Uzman Tanıklık', 86.
560. Tarman, 'Bilirkişilik Sözleşmesinin Hukuki Niteliği ve Bilirkişinin Üçüncü Kişiye Karşı Olan Sorumluluğu', 5–6.
561. Blackaby and Wilbraham, 'Practical Issues Relating to the Use of Expert Evidence in Investment Treaty Arbitration', 658; Elyıldırım, *Hukuk Yargılamasında Uzman Görüşü*, 108; Sarısözen, 'Özel Bilirkişi (Uzman Görüşü)', 1709.
562. Özbek, 'Uzman Görüşünün Yargılamada Değerlendirilmesi', 90.
563. Proske, *Expert Witness Conferencing in Schiedsverfahren*, 27; Moses, *The Principles and Practice of International Commercial Arbitration*, 197.
564. Nessi, 'Expert Witness: Role and Independence', 100.
565. Pitkowitz and Kathan-Spath, 'The Arbitrator and the Arbitration Procedure, the Vienna Propositions for Streamlining Arbitral Proceedings: Keeping Pace with New Developments and User Expectations', 161–162.
566. Kesikli, 'Milletlerarası Ticari Tahkimde Delillerin Değerlendirilmesi', 214.
567. Voser and Bell, 'Expert Evidence in Construction Disputes: Arbitrator Perspective', 229.

> Lawyers acting for a party to litigation or arbitration who are seeking the services of an expert witness will inevitably wish to discuss the case with the proposed expert before engaging him or her. The reason for this is that, before engaging an expert, it is sensible to check that the expert's opinion will support the party's case.[568]

The main purpose of the expert interview is to enable a detailed discussion on the personality, potential conflicts, and content of the expert's opinion; to provide the expert with details as to the issues in dispute; for the expert to ask further questions to confirm his or her expertise and availability; and for counsel to assess the candidate's abilities as an expert. There may also be some discussions regarding the expert's preliminary view on certain aspects of the case may also be discussed. The expert can potentially declare the views he cannot support and the areas he has no expertise in.[569] The expert does not have to accept the appointment.[570]

According to Article 5(1)(i) of the IBA Rules, the party that wants to rely on party-appointed expert evidence has to identify the related expert(s) within the time frame the arbitral tribunal considers appropriate, best with the memoranda of claim and answer.[571] This rule aims to prevent the strategic withholding of expert reports, contribute to the equality of arms, and promote time and cost-efficiency.[572]

The party (counsel) engaging the expert would definitely predetermine that the expert's opinion would support the party's position. This, however, does not mean that the expert is not independent. An expert could hold a view totally in line with scientific or technical standards. It would be absurd and naive to think that the counsel would leave the room entirely to the expert without hinting at the party's desired position.[573]

2.5.2 Terms of Appointment

It is also explicitly permissible for a party to interview a potential expert witness for presenting such person's testimony to the tribunal. Article 5(2)(b) of the IBA Rules requires a party-appointed expert to provide a description of the instructions under which he is providing his opinions and conclusions. It is vital for counsels to provide a set of clear instructions or terms of appointment for party-appointed experts.[574]

568. *Bridgestone Licensing Services, Inc. and Bridgestone Americas, Inc. v. Republic of Panama* (ICSID Case No. ARB/16/34), Ruling On Claimants' Application to Remove The Respondent's Expert Witness as to Panamanian Law, 13 December 2018, paras 27, 35.
569. Voser and Bell, 'Expert Evidence in Construction Disputes: Arbitrator Perspective', 230; Parlett, 'Parties' Engagement with Experts in International Litigation', 447.
570. Samaras and Strasser, 'Managing Party-Appointed Experts in International Arbitration--Analysis of the Current Framework and Best Practice Proposals-', 314.
571. Zuberbühler et al., *IBA Rules of Evidence*, 136; Khodykin and Mulcahy, *A Guide to the IBA Rules on the Taking of Evidence in International Arbitration*, 292.
572. Zuberbühler et al., *IBA Rules of Evidence*, 143; Khodykin and Mulcahy, *A Guide to the IBA Rules on the Taking of Evidence in International Arbitration*, 293.
573. Kesikli, 'Milletlerarası Ticari Tahkimde Delillerin Değerlendirilmesi', 216.
574. Blackaby and Wilbraham, 'Practical Issues Relating to the Use of Expert Evidence in Investment Treaty Arbitration', 659; *See* O'Malley, *Rules of Evidence in International Arbitration*, 178–180; Proske, *Expert Witness Conferencing in Schiedsverfahren*, 21.

After the counsel has a preliminary understanding of the expert, the counsel usually works closely with the expert to describe the terms of appointment or questions to be answered in the report. The expert is provided with necessary documents, such as counter-expert opinions and judicial decisions that must be considered, as well as other evidence on which to base his opinion. The expert needs to explicitly reference these documents when writing his opinion.

2.5.3 Submission of Report

The party-appointed expert produces a draft report that is refined by counsel and then submitted as evidence.[575] Parties generally submit the expert's report with their initial submissions. Although the party relying on an expert has to acknowledge this earlier, the expert report can be submitted later, again within the time ordered by the tribunal (Article 5(1)(ii) of IBA Rules). If submitted at a late stage of the proceedings, the party risks the evidence being inadmissible.[576] Nevertheless, the arbitral tribunal will, in principle, generally decide, with the procedural timetable, when and how to submit the expert's report, taking into account the relation of the report with other submissions made by the parties.[577]

Although expert reports could be exchanged simultaneously, the sequential exchange could help the tribunal understand the issues addressed in the report better, because experts will comment on the counter-expert's report, which is expected to lead to a more refined explanation of the issues in general.[578]

2.5.4 Rights of Party-Appointed Experts

2.5.4.1 Assistance of the Party Counsel

Although the expert is approached to assist the parties in making their case, the expert will also need the assistance of the parties and specifically their representatives during the preparation of the opinion and the hearings.[579] The 2013 IBA Guidelines on Party Representation provide some guidance: they provide in general terms that party

575. Parlett, 'Parties' Engagement with Experts in International Litigation', 447; Lim, 'Tribunal-Appointed Experts in International Arbitration', 224; Feutrill and Rubins, 'The Preparation of Expert Evidence in International Commercial Arbitration: Practical Aspects', 323.
576. ICC Case No. 12761: 'The technical opinion of the individuals who have not been identified as experts by the parties in their respective evidential proposal writs, or whose Expert Report has not been presented on the abovementioned date, will not be admissible.' In ICC Bulletin, 2010 Special Supplement: Decisions on ICC Arbitration Procedure, 74.
577. Khodykin and Mulcahy, *A Guide to the IBA Rules on the Taking of Evidence in International Arbitration*, 293; Zuberbühler et al., *IBA Rules of Evidence*, 137.
578. *See* United Nations, 'UNCITRAL Notes on Organizing Arbitral Proceedings', para. 99.
579. Abdel Wahab, 'Party Appointed Experts in International Commercial Arbitration', 188; Rifkind, 'Preparing the Witness for Cross-Examination', 143; Schwartz and Digón, 'Witness Statements: Use and Abuse', 764.

representatives may assist experts in the preparation of their reports but should seek to ensure that an expert's report reflects his or her own analysis and opinion.[580]

This assistance includes a proper explanation of all aspects and providing evidence regarding the case that the expert must refer to and consider. Additional information regarding the role of the expert in the hearings, during the testimony and examination, style, tactics for behaviour[581] and expectations should be provided. While the party representatives should not instruct on the specific view the expert should provide, they can instruct 'how' to develop it and its scope.[582] That's why, in practice, the draft expert report is sent to the party representatives for review and comments. These comments should only address issues such as relevance, language, structure, and form without intervening in the expert's opinions.[583]

2.5.4.2 Remuneration

The expert provides a service to the party that could qualify as a work contract or ordinary mandate under many jurisdictions.[584] This means that the expert will receive remuneration.[585] In principle, this should be paid by the appointing party and should be borne alone and not be considered for legal costs.[586] Nevertheless, arbitration rules give the tribunal great discretion in awarding arbitration and legal costs and expenses. For instance, ICC Arbitration Rules Article 38 states that the costs of the arbitration shall include, among others, reasonable legal and other costs incurred by the parties to the arbitration.[587] This means that the tribunal can order the payment of the party-appointed expert fee from the counterparty. In addition, the LCIA Arbitration Rules Article 28.3 foresee that:

> The Arbitral Tribunal shall also have the power to decide by an order or award that all or part of the legal or other expenses incurred by a party (the 'Legal Costs') be paid by another party. The Arbitral Tribunal shall decide the amount of such Legal

580. Parlett, 'Parties' Engagement with Experts in International Litigation', 449; IBA Guidelines on Party Representation in International Arbitration (2013), Guidelines 20 and 22. The IBA Guidelines are more detailed than the 2014 LCIA Guidelines, which provide that '[a] legal representative should not knowingly procure or assist in the preparation of or rely upon any false evidence presented to the Arbitral Tribunal or the LCIA Court': 2014 LCIA Guidelines, para. 5.
581. *See* Rifkind, 'Preparing the Witness for Cross-Examination', 144.
582. Abdel Wahab, 'Party Appointed Experts in International Commercial Arbitration', 189; Kent, 'Expert Witnesses in Arbitration and Litigation Proceedings', 4; Ehle, 'Practical Aspects of Using Expert Evidence in International Arbitration', 80.
583. Abdel Wahab, 'Party Appointed Experts in International Commercial Arbitration', 189.
584. Oetiker, 'Commentary on Art. 26-30 Swiss Rules of Arbitration', 312–313; Knoblach, *Sachverhaltsermittlung in Der Internationalen Wirtschaftsschiedsgerichtsbarkeit*, 266; Schütze, *Zivilprozessordnung Und Nebengesetze: Großkommentar*, 11:593.
585. Schiau, 'An Arbitration Dilemma', 337; for instance, *see* for very high expert expenses in the amount of USD 4,774,505.01 in *Tethyan Copper Company Pty Limited v. Islamic Republic of Pakistan* ICSID Case No. ARB/12/, para. 1855; *see* for critics related to high expenditure in Tuna, *Alternative Dispute Resolution in Energy Industries*, 129–130.
586. Centner, *Iura Novit Curia in Internationalen Schiedsverfahren: Eine Historisch-Rechtsvergleichende Studie Zu Den Grundlagen Der Rechtsermittlung*, 112.
587. Yeşilirmak, *ICC Tahkim Kuralları ve Uygulaması*, 129.

> Costs on a reasonable basis as it thinks appropriate. The Arbitral Tribunal shall not be required to apply the rates or procedures for assessing such costs practised by any state court or other legal authority.

An expert should not receive benefits that could affect his sincere views when drafting the report, such as a fee arrangement that depends on the outcome of the case or benefits other than his fee and expenses.[588] In order to prevent this, it is useful to stipulate the basis for the remuneration of the expert (CIArb Protocol Article 4(4)(c)).

2.5.5 Obligations of Party-Appointed Experts

The obligations of the party-appointed expert are not exhaustively dealt with in the statutory provisions. However, soft law instruments regulate certain obligations of party-appointed experts.

First and foremost, the party-appointed expert is bound not only by obligations towards the appointing party but also to the tribunal. Even though the engagement of the expert by a party puts pressure on the expert, specifically in the perspective of being continuously hired, partisanship will highly likely have an adverse effect, and if exposed by the tribunal, this would harm the expert's overall reputation and lower demand for his advice.[589] The obligation to the tribunal overrides, despite having received instructions and been paid by a party (CIArb Protocol, Article 7.1.).[590]

Every other obligation should be read, bearing in mind this primary mandate. The party-appointed expert is expected to provide, before or during the proceedings, a well-organised and clear written report on the issues it was referred to (section 2.5.5.1.). The expert will need to attend, if not decided otherwise by the tribunal, oral hearings for testimony and examination (section 2.5.5.2.). The expert, according to the terms of the agreement under which the party engaged him/her, the applicable law to the arbitration and the arbitration rules must keep confidential all information he is provided within the course of the arbitral proceedings (section 2.5.5.3.).

2.5.5.1 Providing an Opinion

When the expert engaged by the party accepts the mandate, his/her main obligation is to provide the engaging party with an independent, professional and objectively verifiable, clear written opinion in the form of a report that includes his/her views that enable the tribunal to understand the special or technical matter. The expert report should include some mandatory components, as detailed in section 2.6 of this chapter.

---

588. Bor, 'Expert Evidence', 513; Zuberbühler et al., *IBA Rules of Evidence*, 140; Abdel Wahab, 'Party Appointed Experts in International Commercial Arbitration', 189; Khodykin and Mulcahy, *A Guide to the IBA Rules on the Taking of Evidence in International Arbitration*, 300.
589. Nessi, 'Expert Witness: Role and Independence', 100–101; Can and Tuna, *Milletlerarası Tahkim Hukuku*, 414.
590. 'BCLP 2021 Survey', 4; Nessi, 'Expert Witness: Role and Independence', 75–76; Explicitly stipulated in English High Court Civil Procedural Rules (26 April 1999) R 35.3.2.

The *Ikarian Reefer* case summarises the main obligations of the party-appointed experts. The case foresees that the expert's work should be an independent product, uninfluenced as to form or content by the exigencies of the adjudicative process.[591] The expert should provide assistance to the court by way of objective, independent and unbiased professional opinion in relation to matters within his expertise without assuming the role of the party representative.[592]

The expert should also help the tribunal at the post-hearing stage when applying, for instance, interest rates on issues of quantum.[593]

2.5.5.2 Attendance at Hearings

Mostly, when the experts submit a report to the tribunal and the counter-party, their mandate is half completed since they are generally expected to take part in oral hearings, testify and be examined by their appointing party, the counterparty and the tribunal.[594] This can be agreed upon otherwise by the parties, or the expert can be exempted by the decision of the tribunal, especially if the expert evidence is immaterial.[595]

The expert must be prepared for testimony and examination and must adhere to the tribunal's orders during the hearings. Additionally, if requested by the tribunal, the expert shall confer and coordinate with the counter-party's expert to clarify the issues together and declare common understandings to facilitate the process for the arbitral tribunal.[596] However, it is considered under due process rights to examine the (opposing) expert when asked to.[597]

If the expert does not attend the hearing, despite the order of the tribunal to do so, the hearing can be discarded.[598]

2.5.5.3 Confidentiality

Although arbitration rules regulate a confidentiality obligation only towards tribunal-appointed experts,[599] a party-appointed expert shall also retain information that he

591. Referencing to *Whitehouse v. Jordan*, [1981] 1 WLR 246 at p 256, per Lord Wilberforce.
592. Bor, 'Expert Evidence', 511; Abdel Wahab, 'Party Appointed Experts in International Commercial Arbitration', 189; *see Polivitte Ltd v. Commercial Union Assurance Co Plc*, [1987] 1 Lloyd's Rep 379 at 386 per Mr Justice Garland and Re J, [1990] FCR 193 per Mr Justice Cazalet.
593. Jones, 'Redefining the Role and Value of Expert Evidence', 39–40.
594. Abdel Wahab, 'Party Appointed Experts in International Commercial Arbitration', 189; Khodykin and Mulcahy, *A Guide to the IBA Rules on the Taking of Evidence in International Arbitration*, 318; Knoblach, *Sachverhaltsermittlung in Der Internationalen Wirtschaftsschiedsgerichtsbarkeit*, 278; for details of testimony and examination *see* Chapter 2 section 2.8.
595. Webster and Bühler, *Handbook of ICC Arbitration: Commentary, Precedents, Materials*, 440–441; Schäfer and Wilson, 'ICC Bulletin', 2021, 64.
596. Abdel Wahab, 'Party Appointed Experts in International Commercial Arbitration', 190.
597. Webster and Bühler, *Handbook of ICC Arbitration: Commentary, Precedents, Materials*, 441.
598. For further analysis of not attending the hearings by the party-appointed expert, *see* section 2.9.1 in this chapter.
599. *See, e.g.*, Swiss Rules Art. 44(1): 'Unless the parties expressly agree in writing to the contrary, the parties undertake to keep confidential all awards and orders as well as all materials

receives in time of the proceedings confidential. The terms of reference probably indicate an obligation of confidentiality for the expert.

Whether written communications between party-appointed experts and counsel may be subject to disclosure is a rarely confronted issue. *Friedland/Brown De Vejar* stipulated that 'the overwhelming view among experienced international arbitrators is that, in the ordinary situation, production would not be warranted'.[600]

UNCITRAL note states that 'the arbitral tribunal may wish to clarify the nature and extent of communication between the parties or their representatives and their experts, and whether a party might be requested to disclose such communications'.[601]

The issue of disclosure is not dealt with in any rule of major arbitral institutions. However, international practice shows that there is a presumption of non-disclosure of counsel-expert communications other than the documents relied upon by the expert in forming his opinion, as well as the documents expressly referenced by the expert in the report.[602]

While counsel-expert communications may be relevant to assist in evaluating the credibility and impartiality of an expert,[603] few believe that rules allowing the disclosure of counsel-expert communications would promote greater independence and objectivity of party-appointed experts.[604] Allowing disclosure would result in increased costs and inefficiency by increasing the use of 'shadow' experts. In addition, experienced arbitrators are generally well-equipped to determine a lack of objectivity or bias.[605]

2.5.6 Powers of Party-Appointed Experts

The expert should have the opportunity to inspect any site, property, machinery or any other goods, samples, systems, processes or documents upon request by the parties or at the tribunal's discretion (IBA Rules Article 7).[606] The parties and their representatives are allowed to participate in such inspections.[607]

submitted by another party in the framework of the arbitration proceedings not already in the public domain, except and to the extent that a disclosure may be required of a party by a legal duty, to protect or pursue a legal right, or to enforce or challenge an award in legal proceedings before a judicial authority. This undertaking also applies to the arbitrators, the tribunal-appointed experts, the secretary to the arbitral tribunal, the members of the board of directors of the Swiss Arbitration Centre, the members of the Court and the Secretariat.'

600. Friedland and De Vejar, 'Discoverability of Communications Between Counsel and Party-Appointed Experts in International Arbitration', 162; Friedland and De Vejar, 'Discoverability of Communications Between Counsel and Party-Appointed Experts in International Arbitration', 3.
601. United Nations, 'UNCITRAL Notes on Organizing Arbitral Proceedings', para. 100.
602. Friedland and De Vejar, 'Discoverability of Communications between Counsel and Party-Appointed Experts in International Arbitration', 2 ff.
603. *See* Nessi, 'Expert Witness: Role and Independence', 95–96.
604. 'BCLP 2021 Survey', 9.
605. 'BCLP 2021 Survey', 9.
606. Kalpsüz, *Türkiye'de Milletlerarası Tahkim*, 94; Cosar, 'Fraudulent Evidence: Investment Arbitration', para. 30.
607. Ünüvar, 'Experts: Investment Arbitration', para. 28; Kalpsüz, *Türkiye'de Milletlerarası Tahkim*, 94.

In case the expert needs any documents from the counterparty and the party is not willing to provide the documents, the tribunal may order that the party provide the requested documents to the party-appointed expert.[608]

The party-appointed expert may question the tribunal-appointed expert on issues raised in his expert report, the parties' submissions, witness statements, or the expert reports made by the party-appointed experts pursuant to IBA Rules Article 6.5.

2.6 EXPERT OPINION

The positive impact of the party-appointed expert report on proceedings is strictly tied to two things: (1) the personality of the expert (Subjective Test); and (2) the content and quality of the opinion (Objective Test). The personality should show strong signs of impartiality, excellent education, comprehensive experience, and good reputation. The opinion should be independent, scientifically objective, and trustworthy.

The arbitral tribunal will make its own critical, informed and independent assessment of the expert's opinion, whether or not it will evaluate it as evidence while drafting the award.[609] However, it is not always easy to assess expert evidence, as possibly there will be either contradictory experts, too technical reports or poor reports that do not assist the tribunal in deciding on the matters of what the expert report actually was adduced for.

The tribunal should first make a subjective analysis of the expert and should have a deeper look at whether the expert is particularly challenged on his/her credibility and reliability. Then, arbitrators should conduct an objective analysis by analysing the content of the experts' report and weighing it.

The central problem in party-appointed experts is that experts can become highly likely mere advocates and produce partisan opinions, as was also acknowledged by the famous *The Ikarian Reefer* case before the UK courts: 'It is [not] an exaggeration to say that the parties seem to have become more intent on *winning the battle of the experts than on establishing the facts* upon which their respective cases were based.'[610] (emphasis added)

Thus, tribunals that have already suffered the required knowledge will have to differentiate between opposing experts.[611]

2.6.1 Content of the Opinion

Arbitration laws and rules generally do not indicate details about how the expert's opinion should be composed, such as form and style. UNCITRAL Model Law Article 26(2) stipulates that a tribunal-appointed expert may deliver a 'written or oral report'

608. Can and Tuna, *Milletlerarası Tahkim Hukuku*, 416.
609. Abdel Wahab, 'Party Appointed Experts in International Commercial Arbitration', 195; Hodgson and Stewart, 'Experts in Investor-State Arbitration: The Tribunal as Gatekeeper', 461.
610. Bor, 'Expert Evidence', 503; *See also* Knoblach, *Sachverhaltsermittlung in Der Internationalen Wirtschaftsschiedsgerichtsbarkeit*, 281.
611. Wilske and Gack, 'Expert Evidence in International Commercial Arbitration', 93.

(similar to TIAL Article 12(A)(2), ZPO § 1049(2)). Arbitration laws, such as the EAA or the PILA's Arbitration chapter, do not even stipulate these provisions.

The IBA Guidelines, the CIArb Protocol, and the CBP outline rules that experts should adhere to when drafting their opinions. These rules have been developed over time in practice and present a good example of what qualifications a well-established expert opinion should have.

Whether non-compliance with the contents of the report leads to issues regarding its admissibility or weight depends on the circumstances of non-compliance. Where the report lacks some formal basics, for instance, the full name and communication address of the expert, this could be overcome by rapid revision, but if the report lacks the methodology or clear conclusions, this could lead the tribunal to attribute less value to the report. Thus, full compliance with the subjects listed below would enable the expert's opinion to be given greater weight.[612]

In International arbitration, the memorial style of written submissions, in which parties submit their statements of claim and answer that contain factual evidence, legal arguments, and all documentary material relied upon, including expert opinions, is more common.[613]

2.6.1.1 Author(s)

As is the case for all documents having a legal impact, the author should provide communication details at the very beginning of the opinion. If there are multiple authors, such as when a joint report is produced, Article 5(2)(i) of the IBA Rules states that 'if the Expert Report has been signed by more than one person, [the Expert Report shall contain] an attribution of the entirety or specific parts of the Expert Report to each author'.[614] Otherwise, it will make the life of the tribunal and the opposing counsel more difficult to whom objections and questions at the cross-examination phase will be directed.[615] It is not possible to keep the names of the experts confidential.[616]

The name would also help the tribunal and the counter-party address issues of conflict of interest or grounds to challenge the expert, especially if there is any relationship with the tribunal or the counter-party.[617]

It is not infrequent for an expert in one area to indicate that the expert has relied upon the work of a person with expertise in preparing the expert's report. If the issue

612. Knoblach, *Sachverhaltsermittlung in Der Internationalen Wirtschaftsschiedsgerichtsbarkeit*, 191.
613. Jones, 'Redefining the Role and Value of Expert Evidence', 34.
614. Khodykin and Mulcahy, *A Guide to the IBA Rules on the Taking of Evidence in International Arbitration*, 310.
615. Blackaby and Wilbraham, 'Practical Issues Relating to the Use of Expert Evidence in Investment Treaty Arbitration', 660; Khodykin and Mulcahy, *A Guide to the IBA Rules on the Taking of Evidence in International Arbitration*, 311.
616. Esen, 'Violation of the Right to a Fair Trial in Arbitration', 114.
617. Khodykin and Mulcahy, *A Guide to the IBA Rules on the Taking of Evidence in International Arbitration*, 297.

relies on a substantive one, then the indirect source as a base for the report may affect the gravity of the opinions but not the admissibility.[618]

The work must be the product of the expert himself, and it cannot be influenced by any party or their counsel. However, the Counsel may (and always do) assist experts in developing and presenting the report in a way that is likely to be helpful in convincing the tribunal, consistent with the party's arguments.[619] This should not result in the counsel drafting the report and the expert having only a finishing touch and signature.[620]

The author should indicate a 'description of his or her background, qualifications, training and experience' with a detailed curriculum vitae, which will enable the reader to duly perceive and assess the report (IBA Rules Article 5(2)(a), CIArb Protocol Article 4(4)(a), CBP paragraph 146(a)).

2.6.1.2 Guarantee of Independence and Impartiality

It is vital for an expert's credibility to be as transparent as possible. This is why the expert should include a statement regarding his present and past relationship (if any) with any of the parties, their legal advisors and the arbitral tribunal and that the expert is independent[621] of these and is not biased (IBA Rules Article 5(2)(a), 5(2)(c), CIArb Protocol Article 4(1), 4(4)(b), 8(1)).[622] These requirements are important to prevent legal advisors from regularly appointing the same experts who render favourable opinions for the respective parties.[623]

Lack of independence or impartiality can have serious legal effects, such as annulment or refusal of recognition and enforcement of an award. Recently, an ICSID

618. Webster and Bühler, *Handbook of UNCITRAL Arbitration*, 424.
619. Bor, 'Expert Evidence', 514.
620. Proske, *Expert Witness Conferencing in Schiedsverfahren*, 30; Dave, 'Should Experts Be Neutrals or Advocates?', 152.
621. As will be elaborated in Chapter 3 section 3.2.1, I do not consider that a party-appointed expert as a person should be independent, but his/her opinion must be independent.
622. Blackaby and Wilbraham, 'Practical Issues Relating to the Use of Expert Evidence in Investment Treaty Arbitration', 657; Abdel Wahab, 'Party Appointed Experts in International Commercial Arbitration', 191; Khodykin and Mulcahy, *A Guide to the IBA Rules on the Taking of Evidence in International Arbitration*, 297.
    See, e.g., CIArb Protocol Art. 8: 'I understand that my duty in giving evidence in this arbitration is to assist the arbitral tribunal decide the issues in respect of which expert evidence is adduced. I have complied with, and will continue to comply with, that duty. (b) I confirm that this is my own, impartial, objective, unbiased opinion which has not been influenced by the pressures of the dispute resolution process or by any party to the arbitration. (c) I confirm that all matters upon which I have expressed an opinion are within my area of expertise. (d) I confirm that I have referred to all matters which I regard as relevant to the opinions I have expressed and have drawn to the attention of the arbitral tribunal all matters, of which I am aware, which might adversely affect my opinion; (e) I confirm that, at the time of providing this written opinion, I consider it to be complete and accurate and constitute my true, professional opinion. (f) I confirm that if, subsequently, I consider this opinion requires any correction, modification or qualification I will notify the parties to this arbitration and the arbitral tribunal forthwith.'
623. Zuberbühler et al., *IBA Rules of Evidence*, 138.

arbitral award[624] was annulled by the ICSID Ad Hoc Committee on the grounds that a party-appointed arbitrator and his former law firm had worked closely and multiple times with that party's damages expert and his firm, which was not expressly disclosed:[625]

> The Committee, thus, finds critical the fact that the other arbitrators had no knowledge of the relationship between Dr. Alexandrov and Mr. Lapuerta. Had this information been shared with them, either by Dr. Alexandrov or by Mr. Lapuerta and the Brattle Group, it may have affected both the deliberations and the outcome. In any event it is impossible to conclude that such disclosure would have had no material effect on the arbitrators, their deliberations and the ultimate outcome.[626]

Having any past or present relationship should not, without any hesitation, lead to dependency or bias.[627] It is necessary to critically assess whether any present or past relationship has an effect.[628]

The purpose of an expert report is primarily not to establish the facts; this is the duty of the counsel and the fact witnesses. The expert, to the degree possible, will provide objective professional comments and opinions on the matter.[629] In line with this, an affirmation by the party-appointed expert of his genuine/honest belief in the opinion is expected.[630] Genuine belief indicates accurate descriptions of the facts he has been provided with and his opinion on the matters. Although this seems a rather formalistic requirement, it can become vital if the expert is acting simultaneously or has acted in another case where he expressed the contrary view. In such a scenario, the opposing counsel could easily highlight this contradiction in front of the tribunal and undermine the expert's opinion.[631]

Indeed, all of these leave much to the 'honour and integrity of an individual expert and provides little in the way of concrete guarantees'.[632]

'At the same time, experts must disclose any circumstance which, in the view of a reasonable and informed person, may give rise to justifiable doubts as to their objectivity and independence.'[633]

624. *Eiser Infrastructure Limited Andenergía Solar Luxembourg S. À R.L. v. Kingdom of Spain (Eiser v. Spain)*, ICSID Case No. ARB/13/36 (11 June 2020) at 188 ff. https://icsid.worldbank.org/cases/case-database/case-detail?CaseNo=ARB/13/36 (accessed 19 November 2022).
625. Zuberbühler et al., *IBA Rules of Evidence*, 138.
626. *Eiser v. Spain*, para. 249.
627. *Nessi* stated that in a confidential ICC arbitration, where an expert was appointed among employees, the tribunal found the findings and opinions of the expert clear and helpful. *See* Nessi, 'Expert Witness: Role and Independence', 100.
628. Zuberbühler et al., *IBA Rules of Evidence*, 138.
629. Zuberbühler et al., 141.
630. O'Malley, *Rules of Evidence in International Arbitration*, 155–156.
631. Zuberbühler et al., *IBA Rules of Evidence*, 142.
632. Blackaby and Wilbraham, 'Practical Issues Relating to the Use of Expert Evidence in Investment Treaty Arbitration', 658.
633. In the Code of Best Practices in Arbitration by the Club Español del Arbitraje, a non-exhaustive list of questions is included that are important to determine the objectivity and independence of party-appointed experts: '1) Are you currently acting as an expert for or against one of the parties in some matter? 2) In the last 10 years, have you acted as an expert for one of the parties or against one of the parties in some matter? 3) Is your firm currently acting as an expert for one

2.6.1.3 *Expertise*

The expert shall attach a CV to the report that outlines his expertise in the field via professional practice and, if present, academic records such as degrees and published works.[634] This part of the opinion forms a core element of why the tribunal shall credit the expert's opinions and incorporate them into the award. The expert is also expected to stipulate areas in which he does not possess any expertise.

2.6.1.4 *Instructions (Terms of Reference)*

The expert's report has to be read together with the instructions on which the opinion was formulated, either with the questions the party counsel asked the expert or by a proactive[635] arbitral tribunal.[636] The report will only be objectively assessable by the tribunal if it understands the basis for the expert's conclusions.[637]

In addition, disclosing the instructions would foster transparency regarding the independence and impartiality of the expert.[638] Disclosure of the instructions is considered necessary and constitutes best practice in international arbitration.[639]

---

of the parties or against one of the parties in some matter, without your involvement? 4) In the last three years, has your firm acted as an expert for one of the parties or against one of the parties in some matter, without your involvement? 5) Is there any other personal or professional relationship, present or past, with either of the parties that you consider you should disclose? 6) Have you, or has your firm, provided advice or issued an opinion on the dispute or on some aspect thereof at any previous time? 7) Can the outcome of the dispute afford you some benefit or occasion you some detriment, financial or otherwise? 8) If you answer yes to any of questions (1) through (5) and (9) through (15), is the other matter or arbitration related to the current arbitration? 9) Are you or your firm currently acting as an expert in another proceeding upon appointment by the same lawyer or law firm that has appointed you in the present arbitration? 10) In the last three years, has your firm acted, without your involvement, as an expert in another proceeding upon appointment by the same lawyer or law firm that has appointed you in the present arbitration? 11) In the last 10 years, have you personally acted as an expert in another proceeding upon appointment by the same lawyer or law firm that has appointed you in the present arbitration? 12) Is there any other personal or professional relationship, present or past, with one of the lawyers for the parties that you consider you should disclose? 13) Is there any personal or professional relationship, present or past, with third-party funders that you consider you should disclose? 14) Is there any other personal or professional relationship, present or past, with witnesses that you consider you should disclose? 15) Is there any personal or professional relationship, present or past, with the arbitral institution that you consider you should disclose?'

634. Blackaby and Wilbraham, 'Practical Issues Relating to the Use of Expert Evidence in Investment Treaty Arbitration', 658; Khodykin and Mulcahy, *A Guide to the IBA Rules on the Taking of Evidence in International Arbitration*, 299; Lew, Mistelis, and Kröll, *Comparative International Commercial Arbitration*, paras 22-80.
635. For the meaning of a proactive arbitral tribunal, *see* section 4.2.1 of Chapter 4.
636. While 97% of respondents in the BCLP Survey responded that the 'expert report should include a description of the instructions given to the expert', only 72% of them 'agreed that a copy of the instructions given to the expert should be annexed to the report'. in 'BCLP 2021 Survey', 14.
637. Elyıldırım, *Hukuk Yargılamasında Uzman Görüşü*, 106; Özbek, 'Uzman Görüşünün Yargılamada Değerlendirilmesi', 85.
638. Khodykin and Mulcahy, *A Guide to the IBA Rules on the Taking of Evidence in International Arbitration*, 299.
639. de Chazournes et al., 'Uses of Experts Before International Courts and Tribunals', 493.

Thus, it is accepted that the instructions from the party concerned should not be privileged (CIArb Protocol Article 5(1)). However, this does not mean that documents for instructions should be disclosed or that experts should be questioned on this issue, unless there is a plausible reason.[640]

If the report does not indicate the questions or is too vague, the tribunal may step in and provide a set of clear instructions or terms of reference (IBA Rules Article 5(2)(b), CIArb Protocol Article 4(d)).[641] However, the tribunal could also act passively and give less weight to the report without engaging in additional endeavour. Nevertheless, it should be more active when an expert opinion is required according to the circumstances of the case, and it wants to refrain from tribunal-appointed experts, which could lengthen the proceedings.

2.6.1.5 Facts and Evidence

The expert's opinion must state a full description of the factual basis and evidence that it has considered and relies on (IBA Rules Article 5(2)(d), CIArb Protocol Article 4(4)(e-f), CBP paragraph 146(d)).[642]

A well-equipped tribunal and counsel for the counterparty will want to know on what circumstances and evidence the opinion was based.[643] This is crucial information that will ensure that everyone in the proceedings is on the same page and that the same matters are addressed.

Where expert evidence refers to photographs, plans, calculations, survey reports or other similar documents, these documents must be provided to the counterparty at the same time as the exchange of reports. If the opinion is based on wrong or irrelevant facts, it can be easily disregarded since the conclusions drawn by it are not applicable to the case at hand.[644] Therefore, the opinion must state on which occasions, facts, and evidence thereto it was produced. The expert shall also make those documents accessible and provide copies, even if some are publicly available or the documents are

640. O'Malley, *Rules of Evidence in International Arbitration*, 155; Khodykin and Mulcahy, *A Guide to the IBA Rules on the Taking of Evidence in International Arbitration*, 300; CIArb Protocol Art. 5(2) stipulates that drafts, working papers, or other documentation created by an expert for the arbitration should be regarded as privileged. For supporting practices that agree with this view, *see* 'BCLP 2021 Survey', 15; Jones, 'Party Appointed Expert Witnesses in International Arbitration: A Protocol at Last', 153; Communications with consulting experts who do not testify remain privileged and non-disclosable, *see* Schäfer and Wilson, 'ICC Bulletin', 2021, 68.
641. Bor, 'Expert Evidence', 514; Blackaby and Wilbraham, 'Practical Issues Relating to the Use of Expert Evidence in Investment Treaty Arbitration', 659; *O'Malley* argues that a line-by-line recitation of the instructions is generally not required, in O'Malley, *Rules of Evidence in International Arbitration*, 155; Schäfer and Wilson, 'ICC Bulletin', 2021, 64.
642. Khodykin and Mulcahy, *A Guide to the IBA Rules on the Taking of Evidence in International Arbitration*, 304; Elyıldırım, *Hukuk Yargılamasında Uzman Görüşü*, 107; Özbek, 'Uzman Görüşünün Yargılamada Değerlendirilmesi', 85.
643. Bor, 'Expert Evidence', 514.
644. Blackaby and Wilbraham, 'Practical Issues Relating to the Use of Expert Evidence in Investment Treaty Arbitration', 659; Webster and Bühler, *Handbook of UNCITRAL Arbitration*, 423; Khodykin and Mulcahy, *A Guide to the IBA Rules on the Taking of Evidence in International Arbitration*, 305.

voluminous[645] (IBA Rules Article 5(2)(d), 5(2)(e), CIArb Protocol Article 4(4)(j)).[646] The failure to do so would have a negative effect on the expert report, potentially being either disregarded or attributed less weight.[647] The tribunal is not bound by the factual basis on which the expert positioned himself but will ultimately establish the facts.[648]

Parties are given the opportunity to comment in writing on the tribunal-appointed expert's report and to examine any document that the expert relied on in the report.[649]

2.6.1.6 *Methodology*

An expert report should indicate which methodology was used while deriving the relevant conclusions (IBA Rules Article 5(2)(e), CIArb Protocol Article 4(4)(j), CBP paragraph 146(c)). This is necessary so that the opinion is independently verifiable or susceptible to peer review.[650]

If the expert uses another expert's opinion, which will be the case in complex construction disputes, e.g., the quantum expert using the scientific expert's opinion, to derive certain conclusions, this should be indicated.

2.6.1.7 *Opinions and Conclusions*

The author of the report should, preferably in a similar style to a judgment's operative part, state explicitly its findings and conclusions as to the questions asked to himself by the parties or the tribunal (IBA Rules Article 5(2)(e), CBP paragraphs 146(e–f)).[651]

---

645. *See Methanex Corporation v. United States of America*, UNCITRAL, Letter from Tribunal (on documents relied upon by Methanex Experts) 10 October 2003, available at https://www.italaw.com/cases/683 (accessed 20 September 2022):

> (1) As previously ordered by the Tribunal, each Disputing Party's Expert Reports are required to comply with Article 5 of the IBA Rules; and in particular each Expert Report is required, by Article 5(2)(b) & (c) of the IBA Rules, to contain a statement of the s on which that Expert Report is based and a description of the evidence and information used in arriving at that Expert Report's conclusions: (2) As also previously ordered by the Tribunal and in accordance with the time-table already established by the Tribunal, each Disputing Party is required by Article 3(1) of the IBA Rules to submit to the Tribunal and the other parties, all documents available to that party on which that party relies, including public documents and those in the public domain (except for any documents that have already been submitted by another party).

646. Blackaby and Wilbraham, 'Practical Issues Relating to the Use of Expert Evidence in Investment Treaty Arbitration', 660; Zuberbühler et al., *IBA Rules of Evidence*, 140; O'Malley, *Rules of Evidence in International Arbitration*, 153; Khodykin and Mulcahy, *A Guide to the IBA Rules on the Taking of Evidence in International Arbitration*, 308.
647. O'Malley, *Rules of Evidence in International Arbitration*, 154; Khodykin and Mulcahy, *A Guide to the IBA Rules on the Taking of Evidence in International Arbitration*, 305.
648. Kesikli, 'Milletlerarası Ticari Tahkimde Delillerin Değerlendirilmesi', 233.
649. Kalpsüz, *Türkiye'de Milletlerarası Tahkim*, 92; Mbengue and Das, 'Rules Governing the Use of Experts in International Disputes', 446.
650. Blackaby and Wilbraham, 'Practical Issues Relating to the Use of Expert Evidence in Investment Treaty Arbitration', 660.
651. Zuberbühler et al., *IBA Rules of Evidence*, 140.

The expert should affirm that he produced the report according to his genuine belief expressed in the report (IBA Rules Article 5(2)(g)).[652] This rule aims to ensure that experts adhere to ethical principles in their discipline.[653] Conclusions should be objective and independent and should not merely reflect the client's case or interests.[654]

Experts should not assume the tribunal's knowledge of any technical matters dealt with or referred to in the report and should explain them and the expert's own view in a 'clear, concise, coherent, organised and simplified manner, without coming across as shallow or unhelpful'.[655] The expert will form his opinion in a simplistic manner. The report should be expressed in a way that explains technical issues to a layman. The opinion will not convince the tribunal if it is not sufficiently simple.[656]

Although not expected in most scenarios, in case the expert could not form an opinion on some points for whatever reason, it shall also state why it was not able to reach an opinion on the matter(s) (CIArb Protocol Article 4(4)(h)).[657] Experts may also include opposing views to show the tribunal that he is conscious of other positions.[658] This could positively impact the perception of an expert's independence and impartiality.[659]

2.6.1.8 Form and Language

Although some arbitration laws provide that the expert's opinion may be in oral or written form, the expert's opinion should be in the form of a firm written report, as this is more in line with due process components (UNCITRAL Arbitration Rules Article 15(2)).[660]

The report should have a clear structure with headings, separate sections or sub-sections, paragraph numbering and simple language that enables arbitrators and other subjects with little or no knowledge of the particular area to understand, summaries and appropriate charts and diagrams.[661]

The expert opinion, in the form of a written report, should generally be submitted to the tribunal with the memorandum in chief, the first submission of the parties,

652. Khodykin and Mulcahy, *A Guide to the IBA Rules on the Taking of Evidence in International Arbitration*, 310. This amendment is criticised with the reason that the 1999 version, which sought 'the truth' rather than 'genuine belief' was more accurate.
653. Kesikli, 'Milletlerarası Ticari Tahkimde Delillerin Değerlendirilmesi', 234.
654. Angoura, *The Impartiality and Independence of Arbitrators in International Commercial Arbitration*, 102; LCIA Ref. No 97/X27, para. 4.3. in 'Challenge Digests', 323–324.
655. Abdel Wahab, 'Party Appointed Experts in International Commercial Arbitration', 189.
656. Roney, 'Cross-Examination of Experts', 114.
657. Khodykin and Mulcahy, *A Guide to the IBA Rules on the Taking of Evidence in International Arbitration*, 306.
658. Khodykin and Mulcahy, 307.
659. Khodykin and Mulcahy, 307, fn. 78.
660. O'Malley, *Rules of Evidence in International Arbitration*, 147; Lim, 'Tribunal-Appointed Experts in International Arbitration', 224.
661. Bor, 'Expert Evidence', 514.

including the statement of claim and evidentiary documents.[662] Nevertheless, depending on the case, it could be submitted at a later stage, especially if document production is necessary or other evidence is anticipated.[663]

As an official document, the expert report shall be signed, indicating the date it was finally produced and also the place (IBA Rules 5(2)(h), CIArb Protocol Article 4(4)(l), CBP paragraph 146(a)).

In case the expert report was originally produced in a language different from the language of the arbitration, a statement should be made in the original language in which it was written (IBA Rules Article 5(2)(f)).[664] The original and translated report should be submitted together so that the tribunal and the counterparty can verify the content and, if necessary, challenge opinions and conclusions in the translated report that do not confirm the original one. Additionally, stating the original language in which the expert report was prepared enables the tribunal to conclude that, in case of loss in translation, this should not be attributed to the expert himself.[665]

2.6.2 Revision of Report and Additional Report

Despite the fact that statutory laws and arbitration rules are silent on the issue, the revision of already adduced expert reports and additional reports ('rebuttal expert reports') is possible in practice (IBA Rules Article 5(3), CIArb Protocol Article 6(1)(f) 6(1)(g)).[666] Based on the parties' right to be heard, this opportunity does not seem restricted; however, durational and scope limitations may be applicable depending on the status of the proceedings.[667]

Perhaps the expert overlooked facts or evidence or that new facts become known, which would lead to a different conclusion from his previous opinions. On that occasion, the tribunal should be made aware, and a revised report should be submitted stating the reasons why the amendment was necessary.[668] Additionally, after the hearings, the tribunal may request that the expert clarify the points in the report and help it understand the issues.[669]

662. O'Malley, *Rules of Evidence in International Arbitration*, 147; Schneider, 'Technical Experts in International Arbitration', 447; Ehle, 'Practical Aspects of Using Expert Evidence in International Arbitration', 79; For acceptance of late submissions *see Enron Corporation and Ponderosa Assets, L.P. v. Argentine Republic*, ICSID Case No. ARB/01/3, para. 188, available at https://www.italaw.com/sites/default/files/case-documents/ita0299.pdf (accessed 1 September 2022).
663. Khodykin and Mulcahy, *A Guide to the IBA Rules on the Taking of Evidence in International Arbitration*, 307.
664. Khodykin and Mulcahy, 309.
665. Zuberbühler et al., *IBA Rules of Evidence*, 141.
666. Khodykin and Mulcahy, *A Guide to the IBA Rules on the Taking of Evidence in International Arbitration*, 313.
667. Zuberbühler et al., *IBA Rules of Evidence*, 142; Webster and Bühler, *Handbook of UNCITRAL Arbitration*, 424.
668. Zuberbühler et al., *IBA Rules of Evidence*, 143.
669. Abdel Wahab, 'Party Appointed Experts in International Commercial Arbitration', 187–188.

After submission, if the expert changes his view on a material matter, such change of view should be communicated to the other side immediately.[670]

It is possible that one party decided not to adduce a party-appointed expert report at the brief interchange phase but changed its mind after seeing the counterparty's expert report or other submissions, despite the fact that parties had to state clearly in their brief if they wanted to adduce an expert report. In that case, the party may submit an expert opinion that responds only to matters 'contained in a witness statement, expert report or other submission of the other party'[671] (IBA Rules 5(3)(a)).

In addition, if new developments occurred that could not have been addressed in a previous Expert Report, then the submission of a revised or additional expert report should be possible (IBA Rules 5(3)(b)).

Thus, a rebuttal of expert reports should only be admissible if it responds to matters contained in a witness statement, party statement or expert report of the other party that has not been previously presented in the proceedings or if new developments occurred that could not have been addressed previously (IBA Rules 5(3)).[672]

2.7 ADMISSIBILITY, ASSESSMENT, AND BINDING NATURE

Sources applicable in international arbitration are mainly silent on the details of admissibility and evidence assessment.[673] The tribunal has great inherent authority to evaluate the admissibility, probative value and materiality of the evidence offered.

Free assessment of evidence is one of the main rules in international arbitration proceedings, where it is rare to find specific and detailed provisions relating to the weighing of evidence or burden of proof in statutes or rules (UNCITRAL Model Law Article 19, MTK Article 8(A), ZPO § 1042 paragraph 4, EAA S. 34(2)(f)).[674]

The UNCITRAL Arbitration Rules set forth this principle by stipulating that the tribunal has the inherent power to determine the admissibility, relevance, materiality,

670. *See The Ikarian Reefer.*

671. Zuberbühler et al., *IBA Rules of Evidence*, 143.

672. O'Malley, *Rules of Evidence in International Arbitration*, 158; Khodykin and Mulcahy, *A Guide to the IBA Rules on the Taking of Evidence in International Arbitration*, 313–314.

673. Redfern et al., 'The Standards and Burden of Proof in International Arbitration', 321; Hacıbekiroğlu, *Milletlerarası Tahkim Hukukunda Deliller ve Delillerin Degerlendirilmesi*, 10; Alfter, *Das Beweismaß in Der Internationalen Handelsschiedsgerichtsbarkeit: Auswirkungen Der Best Practice Der Document Production Auf Den Beweis*, 63 ff.

674. Yeşilirmak, *Türkiye'de Ticari Hayatın ve Yatırım Ortamının Iyileştirilmesi Için Uyuşmazlıkların Etkin Çözümünde Dogrudan Görüşme, Arabuluculuk, Hakem-Bilirkişilik ve Tahkim: Sorunlar ve Çözüm Önerileri*, 114; Wach and Petsch, 'Der Sachverständigenbeweis Im Schiedsverfahren: Grenzen Der Gestaltungsfreiheit von Parteien Und Schiedsgericht', 97; Mbengue and Das, 'Rules Governing the Use of Experts in International Disputes', 450; Patocchi, Paolo Michele and Niedermaier, 'UNCITRAL Rules', 1182; Knoblach, *Sachverhaltsermittlung in Der Internationalen Wirtschaftsschiedsgerichtsbarkeit*, 228–229; Pekcanıtez and Yeşilirmak, 'Tahkim', 2705; Narçin, '4686 Sayılı Milletlerarası Tahkim Uyarınca Deliller', 18; Dülger, *Milletlerarası Tahkimde Hakemlerin Dogal Yetkileri*, 271; Tanrıver, *Medenî Usûl Hukuku*, 2022, II:428; Reiner, 'Austria', 21; Hobér and Sussman, *Cross-Examination in International Arbitration*, 22; Borris et al., 'New York Convention, Article V [Grounds for Refusal of Recognition and Enforcement of Arbitral Awards]', para. 177.

and weight of the evidence offered (UNCITRAL Arbitration Rules Article 27(4), ICSID Arbitration Rule 36(1), IBA Rules Article 9(1)).

Thus, there is wide recognition of the tribunal's discretion in arbitration to admit or reject any evidence, depending on its probative value and full discretion to give evidentiary weight or not to expert reports.[675]

2.7.1 Admissibility

Admissibility of expert evidence is not dealt with in any of the Legal Basis (2.1).[676] Hence, the determination on how to evaluate the admissibility of a party-appointed expert report must be made. Generally, expert opinion, as a means of evidence, is admissible where the subject matter is outside the knowledge or experience of the trier of fact, i.e., the arbitral tribunal, and where such expert opinion can assist the trier in its final determination of an issue.[677]

The inadmissibility of expert evidence relates to the existence of legal or other impediments that prevent the evaluation of the evidence. Arbitral tribunals have great freedom to determine the admissibility of expert evidence and are not bound by court procedure rules in this regard.[678] A tribunal will freely probe the party-appointed expert's report and is free to disregard an expert's opinion if it is considered lacking fundamental qualifications such as being an independent product, impartiality (objectivity) or expertise.

If there is no necessity for an expert opinion, then the opinion is irrelevant or not material and would only impair the cost-efficiency of the proceedings by leading to additional costs and prolonging the hearings.[679] That's why the tribunal should be proactively involved in the case management conference to inform parties about the position of the tribunal, whether it deems an expert opinion is required or not and, if required, the scope and conditions.[680]

There are four requirements for a proposed expert opinion evidence to be admissible: (1) relevance; (2) necessity in assisting the trier of fact; (3) absence of an exclusionary rule; and (4) a properly qualified expert.[681]

---

675. Nessi, 'Expert Witness: Role and Independence', 99; Rosenfeld, 'Country Report: Germany', 185–186.
676. Feutrill and Rubins, 'The Preparation of Expert Evidence in International Commercial Arbitration: Practical Aspects', 313.
677. Silver, 'Back to Burgess: The Impact of the White Burgess Expert Evidence Regime in Alberta Decisions', 5.
678. O'Malley, *Rules of Evidence in International Arbitration*, 203; Schneider and Scherer, 'Art. 184', 2086; However, mandatory provisions of the *lex fori*, including public policy concerns, that restrict the admissibility of the evidence should be given regard; Hobér and Sussman, *Cross-Examination in International Arbitration*, 22.
679. Hobér and Sussman, *Cross-Examination in International Arbitration*, 22; Geisinger, 'Advocacy in International Commercial Arbitration: What For?', 15.
680. Schäfer and Wilson, 'ICC Bulletin', 2021, 64.
681. Godhe, 'Tribunal Duties and the Exclusion of Evidence in International Arbitration: The Tug-of-War of Fairness and Efficiency', 106; *See* Supreme Court of Canada, *R. v. Mohan*; OLG Köln, 19 Sch 7/10, Justiz NRW, para. 58.

Various cases show that there is a thin line between free assessment and unjustly ignoring or not admitting the party's material and relevant expert evidence, thus possibly violating the right to be heard.[682] This is especially true when there are conflicting expert reports.[683]

If the tribunal considers that the expert report or the testimony of the expert is not in accordance with the independence and impartiality declaration, such expert opinion would be either disregarded or attributed very little weight.[684] This is also the case if the expert is not an expert, or the methodology used is fatal.[685]

If the expert fails to comply with the tribunal's directions regarding the submission of a report, the tribunal may bar the expert from testifying or limit it to the material specifically addressed in the report. This is vital because it affects the opposing party's ability to prepare for and present its case at a hearing.[686]

Swiss literature and court decisions stipulate that evidence not offered in due time or form may not be admissible, or the evidence in question is not fit or relevant for proving the facts or arguments or is already accepted to be proven.[687]

2.7.2 Weight of Evidence and Binding Nature

As evaluated above, different jurisdictions categorise experts' and the expert report's legal nature differently. These classifications are primarily based on civil procedure rules before courts. Nevertheless, an arbitral tribunal is not bound by civil procedural law rules on evidence before courts.[688] That is why a separate classification and the binding nature need to be exposed.

682. O'Malley, *Rules of Evidence in International Arbitration*, 203; Knoblach, *Sachverhaltsermittlung in Der Internationalen Wirtschaftsschiedsgerichtsbarkeit*, 265; Tanrıver, *Medenî Usûl Hukuku*, 2022, II:429.
683. Paragraph 3.2.1: 'it is apparent from the award under appeal that, while the sole arbitrator expressly mentions therein the deductions proposed by the expert E.______ (n. 101) and, following him, by the Appellant, he completely ignores them by the following, without providing the slightest explanation in this regard'. (*X.______ v. Y.______*, 4A_669/2012) For the original decision in French *see* Swiss Federal Supreme Court, 4A_669/2012, Bundesgericht.
684. Mbengue and Das, 'Rules Governing the Use of Experts in International Disputes', 451; Lim, 'Tribunal-Appointed Experts in International Arbitration', 213; Khodykin and Mulcahy, *A Guide to the IBA Rules on the Taking of Evidence in International Arbitration*, 291; Ehle, 'Practical Aspects of Using Expert Evidence in International Arbitration', 78.
685. Schäfer and Wilson, 'ICC Bulletin', 2021, 67.
686. Schäfer and Wilson, 67.
687. Nater-Bass and Rouvinez, 'Art. 24 Commentary on Swiss Rules', 266; 'Parties Not Indicated, Tribunal Fédéral, 1ère Cour Civile', 397.
688. Proske, *Expert witness conferencing in Schiedsverfahren*, 6; Liebscher, Mosimann and Schmidt-Ahrendts, 'Handbuch Schiedsgerichtsbarkeit' 379, 395; Rosenfeld, 'Country Report: Germany', 186; Nairn, Szymanski, and Lekakis, 'National Report for England and Wales (2021 through 2023)', 29; Yeşilirmak, *Türkiye'de Ticari Hayatın ve Yatırım Ortamının Iyileştirilmesi Için Uyuşmazlıkların Etkin Cözümünde Dogrudan Görüşme, Arabuluculuk, Hakem-Bilirkişilik ve Tahkim: Sorunlar ve Cözüm Önerileri*, 104; Akıncı, *Milletlerarası Tahkim*, 342; Kalpsüz, *Türkiye'de Milletlerarası Tahkim*, 92; Born, *International Commercial Arbitration*, 2364; Taşkın, *Tahkim Hukukunda Tahkim Anlaşması, Hakem Kurulu ve Tahkim Yargılaması*, 191; Akıncı, 'Usul Kurallarına Aykırılık ve Dinlenilme Hakkı', 50; Liebscher, Mosimann, and Schmidt-Ahrendts, 'Handbuch Schiedsgerichtsbarkeit', 378–379, para. 1141.

In international arbitration, there are no strict rules regarding the binding nature of different evidence, but the free assessment of evidence is predominantly accepted (UNCITRAL Arbitration Rules Article 27(4), ICSID Arbitration Rule 36(1), IBA Rules Article 9(1)). Therefore, whereas the arbitrator is not strictly bound by the expert's opinion, they cannot merely leave the expert's opinion aside without consideration.[689]

As the High Court Judge Justice Foskett from the UK demonstrated, the tribunal can deviate from the expert's view as follows:

> As in any case, I have not seen it as my duty either to accept the whole of the expert opinion of each expert or not to accept it at all. As I shall be observing at one part of the judgment ... an expert can be right about most things but wrong about others.[690]

Arbitrators, who have the power and duty to make findings of fact relevant to the issues between the parties, may also make errors of fact or draw invalid inferences while assessing the expert's opinion. However, without serious irregularity affecting the right to be heard by parties, this is a foreseeable risk not affecting the award.[691]

The expert opinion must be relevant and related to the disputed issues in order to be considered.[692] As laid down in a decision by the Swiss Federal Supreme Court, the examination of evidence may be refused by a arbitral tribunal, without fearing a violation of the right to be heard, if: (1) the evidence is unfit to create conviction; (2) the fact to be proven is already established or irrelevant;[693] or (3) the arbitral tribunal, in an anticipated assessment of the evidence, reaches the conclusion that it is already convinced and that the result of the evidentiary measure requested cannot modify its conviction.[694]

Putting aside the criteria tied to the personality of the expert and the legal nature of it, an expert's opinion will be weighed and credited if it affirmatively assists the tribunal in understanding or establishing facts and rendering the award. The tribunal will decide if it considers that the opinions of the expert agree with the facts of the record, legal provisions and rules of logic.

According to German arbitration law provisions (ZPO § 1042), although the tribunal has the right freely to assess the evidence, including the party-appointed expert, it is

689. Narçin, '4686 Sayılı Milletlerarası Tahkim Uyarınca Deliller', 17. *Atalay* argued similarly for party-appointed experts before state courts in Atalay, 'Pekcanıtez Usûl', 2021, 1959; Atalı, '6754 Sayılı Bilirkişilik Kanunu ve Hukuki Konularda Bilirkişilik', 3279.

690. *England and Wales High Court, Various Claimants v. Giambrone & Law (a firm) & Ors*, [2015] EWHC 1946 (QB), para. 265; *See Hong Kong, Brunswick Bowling & Billiards Corporation v. Shanghai Zhonglu Industrial Co. Ltd. and Chen Rong*, para. 51.
'The issue of quantum is one of the matters submitted to the Tribunal for determination. The Tribunal is not bound by the positions taken by the parties if it can, on the basis of the evidence canvassed, come to a different conclusion.'

691. Similarly, RosenfeldRosenfeld, 'Country Report: Germany', 186.

692. Rosenfeld, 183.

693. Aktepe Artık, *Medeni Usûl Hukukunda Hakem Kararlarının İptali Sebepleri*, 379.

694. Swiss Federal Supreme Court, 4A_440/2010, Bundesgericht, para. 4.1.

clearly attributed less weight, as can be read in the explanatory memorandum, in contrast to a court/tribunal-appointed expert.[695]

The tribunal will freely probe the party-appointed expert's report and is free to ignore an expert's opinion if it is considered immaterial to the award. This, however, should not be a ground for challenge.[696] Reasons should be stipulated in the award if one of the expert's opinions is chosen over the other or the tribunal deviates from the expert's view.[697]

However, especially when the expert report is not challenged by the counterparty and the tribunal sees the evaluation and conclusions of the expert in line with the facts of the record, with legal provisions and the rules of logic, not having any contradictions, there is no reason why it should not adopt it.[698]

Arbitral tribunals must extensively analyse and weigh an expert's views and not directly pre-judge expert evidence based on the personality of the expert. In a case before English courts[699] where the court removed a sole (non-lawyer) arbitrator under section 24 of the EAA, the court did not allow the arbitrary and biased treatment of expert evidence. The key factor of the decision by the court was the relevant explanation of the arbitrator:

> For me, I don't need to hear any of the expert witnesses. I don't think they will add any value. I know what they are saying. They are exceptional people in their fields. They are the best, but I don't need them to say what is normal on a film. I know what is normal on film.

695. Knoblach, *Sachverhaltsermittlung in Der Internationalen Wirtschaftsschiedsgerichtsbarkeit*, 280; Musielak and Voit, *ZPO*, § 1049, para. 11.

    See also Knoblach, *Sachverhaltsermittlung in Der Internationalen Wirtschaftsschiedsgerichtsbarkeit*, 280: 'In jedem Fall zeigen sowohl der Grundsatz des rechtlichen Gehörs § 1042 Abs. 1 S. 2 ZPO als auch die ausdrückliche Erwähnung des Parteisachverständigen in § 1049 Abs. 2 S. 2 ZPO, daß das Schiedsgericht ein Gutachten eines Parteisachverständigen, das den Ausführungen eines vom Schiedsgericht bestellten Sachverständigen widerspricht, nicht leichtfertig ignorieren darf.'
696. O'Malley, *Rules of Evidence in International Arbitration*, 145–146, 201; *See Duke Energy International Peru Investments No. 1 Ltd. v. Republic of Peru*, ICSID Case No. ARB/03/28, Decision on Annulment, 1 March 2011, para. 214, available at https://www.italaw.com/cases/3399 (accessed 11 January 2023):

    > It would not be proper for an annulment committee to re-evaluate that evidence, and nor is it in a position to do so. As it was put in *Rumeli v Kazakhstan*, '[a]n ad hoc committee is not a court of appeal and cannot therefore enter, within the bounds of its limited mission, into an analysis of the probative value of the evidence produced by the parties.'
697. O'Malley, 207; Tanrıver, *Hukukumuzda Bilirkişilik*, 33.
698. O'Malley, *Rules of Evidence in International Arbitration*, 163, fn. 53; A view from Canada: 'I would not go so far as to hold that the expert's independence and impartiality should be presumed absent challenge, my view is that absent such challenge, the expert's attestation or testimony recognizing and accepting the duty will generally be sufficient to establish that this threshold is met', in Supreme Court of Canada, *White Burgess Langille Inman v. Abbott and Haliburton Co.*, para. 47.
699. *H1 & Anor v. W & Ors* [2024] EWHC 382 (Comm).

> Look, if you want to cross examine the expert witness that is fine by me. but I don't think we need to listen to them. I know them all personally extremely well on the insured side. I don't know your expert witnesses. You have an underwriter expert [JY]. But I don't think he adds much.

Party-appointed experts who act as advocates will likely lose credibility before the tribunal. This lack of credibility would undermine a party's case, particularly where the issues on which expert opinion is proffered are central to the dispute.[700] On the other side, the arbitrator would potentially find the expert more credible if he were willing to accept other views.

If the arbitral tribunal decides not to hear a party-appointed expert whose cross-examination was requested, the expert's report can remain on record. However, it is obvious that the arbitral tribunal will have to attribute little weight to such an opinion since the tribunal declined to have the expert examine it.[701]

In case the expert has a long-lasting relationship and is even employed before the subject matter of the dispute, e.g., for a construction project, the expert might be given less value.[702] The US, Canadian, and Australian courts have treated these matters as going exclusively to weight rather than to admissibility.[703]

2.7.3 Proof, Burden of Proof, and Standard of Proof

Proof is the activity carried out by the parties to convince the arbitrator that the facts claimed are in accordance with the conditional facts of the applicable law on which the claim is based and have occurred as claimed.[704] The subject matter of proof is the disputed facts on which the parties cannot agree and which may be effective in the resolution of the dispute.[705]

If there is a technical element in a dispute that needs to be clearly understood, for instance, that the wrong choice of pipes by the respondent was the main cause for occasional floods, then who needs to adduce an expert's opinion to prove its argument, and thus bears the responsibility to prove this argument and what standard is required to have proven its argument? The tribunal shall determine who will bear the burden of proof according to the *lex arbitri*[706] or the *lex causae*.[707]

700. Parlett, 'Parties' Engagement with Experts in International Litigation', 451; Abdel Wahab, 'Party Appointed Experts in International Commercial Arbitration', 194.
701. Zuberbühler et al., *IBA Rules of Evidence*, 148.
702. *See* Nessi, 'Expert Witness: Role and Independence', 99.
703. Supreme Court of Canada, *White Burgess Langille Inman v. Abbott and Haliburton Co.*, para. 39.
704. Atalay, 'Pekcanıtez Usûl', 2021; Özbek, *Tahkim Hukuku*, II:1367.
705. Yeğengil, *Tahkim (L'Arbitrage)*, 302.
706. Knoblach, *Sachverhaltsermittlung in Der Internationalen Wirtschaftsschiedsgerichtsbarkeit*, 217.
707. Schneider and Scherer, 'Art. 184', 2083.

2.7.3.1 *The Burden of Proof and the Burden to Provide Evidence*

When parties commence an arbitration, they must submit (*Iddia yükü, Behauptungslast*) and substantiate their allegations with evidence (*Delil ikame yükü, Beweislast or Beweisführungslast*), unless propositions are so obvious or notorious that proof is not required.[708]

The tribunal generally has limited roles in this process and will generally not intervene, although there could be differences depending on the *lex arbitri*, *lex causae* and the style of the arbitrators.[709] The burden of proof is the concept that foresees in a dispute that the party is responsible for submitting evidence and the consequences for failing to do so (effectively).[710]

The burden of proof plays an important role when a tribunal evaluates a claim and decides whether or not to accept it. While the burden of proof in civil law countries is strictly tied to the right asserted and its material provisions,[711] regarding international arbitration, there is no clear-cut, generally accepted position.

In international arbitration, the general concept and practice is that 'each party has the burden of proving the facts relied on to support its claim or defence', otherwise known as *actori incumbit (onus) probandi*[712] (UNCITRAL Arbitration Rules Article 27(1)).[713]

Some other arbitration rules, such as the Swiss Rules (Article 26), have not directly held the parties responsible for the burden of proof of the claims or defences they

708. Schlaepfer, 'The Burden of Proof in International Arbitration', 127; Yeğengil, *Tahkim (L'Arbitrage)*, 302; Pekcanıtez, Atalay, and Özekes, *Medenî Usûl Hukuku Ders Kitabı*, 356–361; Redfern et al., 'The Standards and Burden of Proof in International Arbitration', 321; *see* Swiss Federal Supreme Court, 4A_597/2013, Bundesgericht, para. 3.2.2.
709. For differences between Germany and the UK *see* Knoblach, *Sachverhaltsermittlung in Der Internationalen Wirtschaftsschiedsgerichtsbarkeit*, 217.
710. Atalay, 'Delil Kavramı Üzerine', 129; O'Malley, *Rules of Evidence in International Arbitration*, 209; Nater-Bass and Rouvinez, 'Art. 24 Commentary on Swiss Rules', 263; Knoblach, *Sachverhaltsermittlung in Der Internationalen Wirtschaftsschiedsgerichtsbarkeit*, 221; Özbek, *Tahkim Hukuku*, II:1367; Kurkela, Turunen, and Conflict Management Institute, *Due Process in International Commercial Arbitration*, 147.
711. Especially civil law jurisdictions foresee the burden of proof rules in their substantive law provisions, whereas common law jurisdictions regard these rules as a matter of procedural law, for details *See* Knoblach, Sachverhaltsermittlung in Der Internationalen Wirtschaftsschiedsgerichtsbarkeit, 222–223; In Tuörkiye, the burden of proof (*'ispat yuökuö'*) is determined according to the applicable substantive law. Thus, if Turkish law is applicable, the tribunal needs to look at the substantive law to decide who has the burden of proof. Budak and Karaaslan, *Medenî Usul Hukuku*, 2022, 262; Hacıbekiroğlu, *Milletlerarası Tahkim Hukukunda Deliller ve Delillerin Degerlendirilmesi*, 12; *See* Nater-Bass and Rouvinez, 'Art. 24 Commentary on Swiss Rules', 262.
712. Also known as onus probandi actori incumbit or Actori incumbit (onus) probation.
713. Amaral, 'Burden of Proof and Adverse Inferences in International Arbitration: Proposal for an Inference Chart', 2; Yeşilirmak, *Türkiye'de Ticari Hayatın ve Yatırım Ortamının Iyileştirilmesi Için Uyuşmazlıkların Etkin Cözümünde Dogrudan Görüşme, Arabuluculuk, Hakem-Bilirkişilik ve Tahkim: Sorunlar ve Cözüm Önerileri*, 114; Webster and Bühler, *Handbook of UNCITRAL Arbitration*, 413; Knoblach, *Sachverhaltsermittlung in Der Internationalen Wirtschaftsschiedsgerichtsbarkeit*, 221; Özbek, *Tahkim Hukuku*, II:1367; Kurkela, Turunen, and Conflict Management Institute, *Due Process in International Commercial Arbitration*, 147; Hacıbekiroğlu, *Milletlerarası Tahkim Hukukunda Deliller ve Delillerin Degerlendirilmesi*, 11; Redfern et al., 'The Standards and Burden of Proof in International Arbitration', 321.

allege. However, they have given the tribunal the discretion to determine in what circumstances each party has the burden of proof.

The burden of proof applies not only to the claiming party but also to the party in defence. Where the claimant will assert and submit evidence that some chain of facts happened, which the law foresees for him a right to claim, the respondent will defend himself by alleging facts and submitting evidence that either the facts did not happen, the evidence submitted is misleading and not accurate, or some other facts occurred which make the claimant's claim fall.[714]

In relation to the experts, if there is a technical/scientific issue that needs to be clarified to the tribunal, both parties, depending on their claim or defence, may bear the burden of proof.[715] If the claiming party asks for damages for the wrong usage of pipes in the infrastructure project, it needs to prove and adduce an expert report from engineers, urban planning and meteorology experts that the respondent had failed to take into account average rainfall statistics and the range of chosen pipes by the respondent were wrong and that floods occurred directly because of this reason.[716] If this is a satisfactory report capable of explaining the concept of average rainfall and its relation to the importance of the diameter of drainpipes and the impact on floods, convincing the tribunal, the defending party will need to counter-argue these allegations with an expert report or other evidence.

The tribunal will then assess and decide which position it agrees with. If neither is persuasive, it must allocate the adverse consequences of the failure to satisfy the burden of proof to the party who bears the burden (claimant or respondent). If the tribunal believes, even without recourse to the defending party's arguments and evidence, that the expert report does not establish the alleged facts, the party will not have fulfilled its burden of proof. Thus, the claim (or the relevant request) will therefore be dismissed.

Some authors have argued that a party's request to the tribunal to appoint an expert is a sufficient means of discharging its burden of evidence.[717]

Instead of stating directly that a particular fact did or did not occur, arbitrators typically conclude that a party has 'failed to provide sufficient evidence' of an alleged fact or has not proven those facts, enabling the right tied to the facts.[718]

2.7.3.2 Standard of Proof

The standard required to determine whether the claiming or defending party has conformed with the burden of proof, i.e., adduced expert evidence that supports the claim and establishes the facts thereto, or not, is regulated by the substantive

714. O'Malley, *Rules of Evidence in International Arbitration*, 211; Amaral, 'Burden of Proof and Adverse Inferences in International Arbitration: Proposal for an Inference Chart', 2.
715. Webster and Bühler, *Handbook of UNCITRAL Arbitration*, 423.
716. Schlaepfer, 'The Burden of Proof in International Arbitration', 133.
717. Contrary to this argument, *see Cemile Demir Gökyayla* in Akıncı and Ekmen, 'Tartışmalar', 201–202.
718. Donoghue, 'Expert Scientific Evidence in a Broader Context', 385.

applicable law (*lex causae*), but sometimes also by the law applicable to the arbitration (*lex arbitri*).[719]

The rules in these provisions generally require proving a fact with full conviction, high probability,[720] or overwhelming probability (also called balance of probabilities or reasonable certainty).[721]

In international arbitration, the standard of overwhelming probability (balance of probability) is generally accepted.[722] This standard calls for a claim to be established if the tribunal is convinced by evidence that the claim is more likely to be true than not.[723]

The tribunal in the ICSID case *Tethyan Copper v. Pakistan* is a good example of this standard:

> The dispute, therefore, appears to concern … whether the valuation method used by Claimant and its expert yields results that are not 'too speculative' or 'too uncertain' but rather enable the Tribunal to assess Claimant's damages 'with reasonable confidence' and reach a 'reliable' conclusion.[724]

The approach is also used in international commercial arbitration: '[U]nder the CISG, the standard of proof is met if the decision maker is convinced with a reasonable degree of certainty that an alleged fact is true.'[725]

These broad rules for both the burden and standard of proof leave great space for the tribunal, which not only deals with the nature and quality of the facts and submitted

---

719. O'Malley, *Rules of Evidence in International Arbitration*, 215; *See* Redfern et al., 'The Standards and Burden of Proof in International Arbitration', 319; For the argument that, in international arbitration, the burden of proof should be determined according to the *lex arbitri*, *see* Knoblach, *Sachverhaltsermittlung in Der Internationalen Wirtschaftsschiedsgerichtsbarkeit*, 227.
720. For the standard for forgery, *see National Bank of Xanadu v. Company ACME*, Final Award, ICC Case No. 17818 in Schill, *ICCA Yearbook Commercial Arbitration 2019*, XLIV:64, para. 114.
721. Redfern et al., 'The Standards and Burden of Proof in International Arbitration', 321; Soria and Schmidt Meyer, 'Weighing Evidence in International Arbitration', 560; Feutrill and Rubins, 'The Preparation of Expert Evidence in International Commercial Arbitration: Practical Aspects', 310; *See* for lower standard of proof for determination of quantum *Distributor v. Manufacturer*, Final Award, ICC Case No. 20065 in Schill, *ICCA Yearbook Commercial Arbitration 2019*, XLIV:308, para. 177; *See* Webster and Bühler, *Handbook of UNCITRAL Arbitration*, 414, paras 27–45; For German law *see* Knoblach, *Sachverhaltsermittlung in Der Internationalen Wirtschaftsschiedsgerichtsbarkeit*, 225–226; Hacıbekiroğlu, *Milletlerarası Tahkim Hukukunda Deliller ve Delillerin Degerlendirilmesi*, 14.
722. Knoblach, *Sachverhaltsermittlung in Der Internationalen Wirtschaftsschiedsgerichtsbarkeit*, 227; Yeşilirmak, *Türkiye'de Ticari Hayatın ve Yatırım Ortamının Iyileştirilmesi Için Uyuşmazlıkların Etkin Cözümünde Dogrudan Görüşme, Arabuluculuk, Hakem-Bilirkişilik ve Tahkim: Sorunlar ve Cözüm Önerileri*, 114; *See Tokios Tokelés v. Ukraine*, ICSID Case No. ARB/02/18, Final Award, 26 July 2007, para. 124, available at https://www.italaw.com/cases/1099 (accessed 1 October 2022).
723. *See* O'Malley, *Rules of Evidence in International Arbitration*, 215 ff.; 'Procedural Efficiency in International Arbitration: Choosing the Best of Both Legal Worlds', 120–122; Nater-Bass and Rouvinez, 'Art. 24 Commentary on Swiss Rules', 264; Redfern et al., 'The Standards and Burden of Proof in International Arbitration', 355.
724. *Tethyan Copper Company Pty Limited v. Islamic Republic of Pakistan*, ICSID Case No. ARB/12/1, Award, 12 July 2019, para. 298, available at https://www.italaw.com/sites/default/files/case-documents/italaw10737.pdf (accessed 12 December 2022).
725. *Buyer (India) v. Seller (Turkey)*, Final Award, ICC Case No. 18981 in Schill, *ICCA Yearbook Commercial Arbitration 2018*, XLIII:201, para. 39; Similarly *Distributor (US) v. Supplier (Germany)*, Final Award, SCC Case No. 2017/164, 27 November 2018 in Schill, *ICCA Yearbook Commercial Arbitration 2020*, XLV:107–113.

evidence but also with the circumstantial perception of the arbitrator, depending on his legal background.[726] Especially when it comes to fraud or corruption allegations, a higher degree of conviction would be necessary due to the seriousness of the allegation.[727]

With respect to quantum issues, there are special issues regarding the burden of proof of fact in many legal systems.[728] Also, UNIDROIT Principles Article 7.4.3 foresee that harm (as a precondition for compensation) can be established with 'a reasonable degree of certainty', and if 'damages cannot be established with a sufficient degree of certainty, the assessment is at the discretion' of the tribunal.

2.8 TESTIMONY AND EXAMINATION

The rules stipulated for the personalities of party-appointed experts and the report may not safeguard the proper functioning of this evidence alone. Therefore, a secondary step is necessary: The testing procedure.

Testing is done at the evidentiary hearing phase via oral examination; be it an examination by the tribunal, direct examination, cross-examination by the counsel or conferencing among the experts.[729] If the expert knows from the outset that he will be examined in various forms, it will motivate him to be diligent and show extra care.[730] It also represents a success for the expert, as his opinion forms part of the foundation of the award.

Unless an expedited procedure or 'documents only' procedure is adopted in an arbitration, or the tribunal orders otherwise or parties have waived to request it, the experts are expected to testify at the hearing and will be examined by the appointing party, counterparty, and arbitral tribunal (IBA Rules Article 5(5)).[731]

---

726. 'Procedural Efficiency in International Arbitration: Choosing the Best of Both Legal Worlds', 121–122; de Chazournes et al., 'Uses of Experts Before International Courts and Tribunals', 494.
727. Feutrill and Rubins, 'The Preparation of Expert Evidence in International Commercial Arbitration: Practical Aspects', 309–310.
728. Webster and Bühler, *Handbook of UNCITRAL Arbitration*, 415.
729. Webster and Bühler, *Handbook of ICC Arbitration: Commentary, Precedents, Materials*, 441; Kesikli, 'Milletlerarası Ticari Tahkimde Delillerin Değerlendirilmesi', 235; Bacanlı, 'Bir Alternatif Uyuşmazlık Cözüm Yolu Olarak Istanbul Tahkim ve Arabuluculuk Merkezi (ISTAC) Tahkim Yargilamasinda Delillerin Ibrazı ve Değerlendirilmesi', 97; Ağırman, *Milli & Milletlerarası Tahkim*, 462–464.Whether these examination methods will be done at the same proceeding is up to the tribunal's decision in each case. For details, *see* Proske, *Expert Witness Conferencing in Schiedsverfahren*, 46.
730. Atalay, 'Pekcanıtez Usûl', 2021, 1962; Pekcanıtez, 'Özel Uzman', 409; Can and Tuna, *Milletlerarası Tahkim Hukuku*, 416; Ağırman, *Milli & Milletlerarası Tahkim*, 464.
731. O'Malley, *Rules of Evidence in International Arbitration*, 161; Knoblach, *Sachverhaltsermittlung in Der Internationalen Wirtschaftsschiedsgerichtsbarkeit*, 191; Raeschke-Kessler, 'The Arbitrator as Settlement Facilitator', 528; For otherwise example *see Karaha Bodas Co LLC and Perusahaan Pertambangan Minyak Dan Gas Bumi Negara*, et al, Final Award, 18 December 2000, Ad Hoc Proceeding, 1976 UNCITRAL, at 10–11 as reported in Caron and Caplan, *The UNCITRAL Arbitration Rules: A Commentary*, 614: 'In case a witness whose presence at the hearing was requested does not show up, his or her written statement shall be disregarded. This rule will not apply to expert's reports.'

The tribunal shall decide whether any testimony or examination will be carried out and in which order.[732] Although arbitrators and parties' counsel are expected to have the necessary intelligence to understand and derive conclusions from a written expert report, it is always helpful to listen to the expert, who will present his opinions, generally in a 30–60 minutes presentation, followed by a question-and-answer phase.[733]

Testimony by the party-appointed expert is key and would definitely affect the tribunal's perception of the report, positively or negatively.[734] In principle, there is no absolute duty of the party-appointed expert to appear before the tribunal.[735] However, the report's gravity would be much higher if the expert presented his report and the parties were granted the opportunity to challenge the expert's opinion.[736]

In rare circumstances, both the parties and the tribunal may not request an examination of the expert but may still give regard to the written report. However, the absence of a request to examine the party-appointed expert does not imply that the tribunal or the parties have agreed to the correctness of the contents of the expert report (IBA Rules Article 5(6)).[737]

The tribunal should not deny an examination if one party or both parties request so, save where the tribunal limits or excludes any appearance of the expert to be irrelevant, immaterial, unreasonably burdensome, duplicative or for grounds of commercial, political or technical confidentiality, considerations of procedural economy, proportionality, fairness or equality of the Parties.

The party has the right to ask the expert supplementary questions. However, as sometimes practised in international arbitration, the receipt of a statement on written

732. Khodykin and Mulcahy, *A Guide to the IBA Rules on the Taking of Evidence in International Arbitration*, 291.
733. Abdel Wahab, 'Party Appointed Experts in International Commercial Arbitration', 185; Bor, 'Expert Evidence', 509; Atalay, 'Pekcanıtez Usûl', 2021, 1961.
734. Pekcanıtez, 'Özel Uzman', 409; Abdel Wahab, 'Party Appointed Experts in International Commercial Arbitration', 186; *See* Schlaepfer and Duvanel, 'Direct and Re-Direct Examination', 73 ff.; Narçin, '4686 Sayılı Milletlerarası Tahkim Uyarınca Deliller', 23.
735. *See Adel A Hamadi Al Tamimi v. Sultanate of Oman*, ICSID Case No. ARB/11/33, Procedural Order No. 8, 18 April 2014, paras 2–4 available at https://jusmundi.com/en/document/other/en-adel-a-hamadi-al-tamimi-v-sultanate-of-oman-procedural-order-no-8-friday-18th-april-2014#other_document_1364 (accessed 11 March 2023):

> the Respondent submitted a letter to the Tribunal in which it stated that the Claimant was refusing to present its party-appointed expert, JAJ Consultants LLC ('JAJ') for cross-examination and had withdrawn the JAJ Expert Report. The Respondent requested that the 'JAJ Report should remain in the record and the Tribunal should draw from it whatever inferences it concludes are warranted in the circumstances'.
>
> …
>
> Mr. Rivkin indicated that the Claimant consented to the Application. The Respondent's Application is therefore granted by consent. JAJ Consultants LLC shall not appear for cross-examination, but its report shall remain in the record and the Tribunal, after receiving further submissions, if any, during the proceedings, may draw whatever inferences, if any, it considers are warranted in the circumstances.

736. Zuberbühler et al., *IBA Rules of Evidence*, 146; Roney, 'Cross-Examination of Experts', 113.
737. O'Malley, *Rules of Evidence in International Arbitration*, 162; Khodykin and Mulcahy, *A Guide to the IBA Rules on the Taking of Evidence in International Arbitration*, 321.

questions should not be considered a violation in this sense. However, the party has the right to ask questions that are supplementary to these written answers.[738]

In *VM Solar & Co. KG and Helmut Vorndran v. Spain*, the request by the Respondent for disqualifying the whole tribunal due to, *inter alia*, refusing to hear the legal expert (on European Union law and Spanish regulatory law) did not lead to the disqualification of the tribunal due to impartiality.[739]

The Tribunal has the discretion to determine specifically how and in what order the examination will occur. In practice, the counsel of the party calling the expert would begin the examination-in-chief.[740] The expert could be asked by the counsel to give a statement in the form of a presentation of the report. If the counsel is not convinced by the expert's presentation or assumes that some points have been left out, they can pose additional questions to the expert.[741] Before the beginning, the expert should be expected to re-affirm that the opinions expressed in the report are his genuine beliefs (IBA Rules Article 8(5)). If the views of the expert have changed during the period between submission and hearing, the expert should clarify his new views and the conclusions thereto.[742] After that, the counterparty to the dispute is given an opportunity to cross-examine the expert. If an expert fails to answer the questions asked, less weight is likely to be given to his opinion.

The scope of the cross-examination would be confined to the personality of the expert and his qualifications (subjective test), as well as written and oral statements (objective test) already made by the experts. Cross-examination will test the veracity of the party-appointed expert evidence by focusing: (1) on the impartiality of the expert; (2) the expert's qualifications; (3) the sources or methodology adopted by the expert to reach his views; (4) whether the expert's views are consistent with the common view expressed in the field and why to adopt it; and (5) whether the expert's own views are consistent and applicable to the case.[743] Additionally, the expert could be asked questions that do not attack the personality or content of the report but serve to affirm the examining party's views.[744]

The party calling the expert could then be asked whether or not to re-examine the expert. Any such re-examination should be shorter and should be limited in scope to

738. Pekcanıtez and Yeşilirmak, 'Tahkim', 2767.
739. *VM Solar Jerez GmbH, M Solar Verwaltungs GmbH, Solarizz Holding Verwaltungs-GmbH, M Solar GmbH & Co. KG, Solarizz Holding GmbH & Co. KG and Helmut Vorndran v. Kingdom of Spain*, ICSID Case No. ARB/19/30, Decision on the Proposal to Disqualify All Members of the Tribunal, 18 October 2022, paras 26, 44, 79.
740. Khodykin and Mulcahy, *A Guide to the IBA Rules on the Taking of Evidence in International Arbitration*, 322; Knoblach, *Sachverhaltsermittlung in Der Internationalen Wirtschaftsschiedsgerichtsbarkeit*, 207.
741. Veeder and et al., 'Act III: Advocacy with Witness Testimony', 606; Abdel Wahab, 'Party Appointed Experts in International Commercial Arbitration', 186; Proske, *Expert witness conferencing in Schiedsverfahren*, 45.
742. Khodykin and Mulcahy, *A Guide to the IBA Rules on the Taking of Evidence in International Arbitration*, 310.
743. Abdel Wahab, 'Party Appointed Experts in International Commercial Arbitration', 200.
744. Abdel Wahab, 201; Kesikli, 'Milletlerarası Ticari Tahkimde Delillerin Değerlendirilmesi', 237; Roney, 'Cross-Examination of Experts', 114.

issues already dealt with in the cross-examination phase. The tribunal may then question the experts.

The arbitral tribunal has the authority to limit or exclude any questions if it considers such question, answer or appearance to be irrelevant, immaterial, unreasonably burdensome or duplicative (Article 8(3) of IBA Rules), taking into account the right to be heard requirements.[745]

Whether an expert must deliver an oath before testimony and examination is a controversial issue. Neither the Model Law nor the major arbitration countries' statutory provisions or arbitration rules have any provision regarding the oath of experts.[746] *Pekcanıtez* argues that party-appointed experts do not need to take an oath, and even if they did, this would not have any effect.[747]

That leaves the tribunal the discretion of whether or not to utilise an oath. Depending on the legal culture of the tribunal, an oath may be required from the party-appointed expert. However, generally, a written affirmation of the genuine belief of the expert is performed and accepted.[748]

For example, arbitral tribunals seated in England or Wales may administer oaths or affirmations for arbitration, but in Germany, there is no oath practice. The question has not yet been settled in Switzerland.[749]

Kantor states that '[m]any international arbitrators do not in any event consider the *administration of an oath* part of international arbitration'.[750] (emphasis added) However, in ICC arbitration, examples of the administration of an oath by experts are also present.[751]

2.9 CHALLENGE OF EXPERTS & EXPERT OPINION

Party-appointed experts, in general, may not be subject to disqualification or exclusion as evidence, as tribunal-appointed experts can in certain situations.[752] In international

745. Khodykin and Mulcahy, *A Guide to the IBA Rules on the Taking of Evidence in International Arbitration*, 291; Ünüvar, 'Experts: Investment Arbitration', para. 29.
746. Öhrström, 'SCC Rules', 840; Poudret and Besson, *Comparative Law of International Arbitration*, 559; Webster and Bühler, *Handbook of UNCITRAL Arbitration*, 423; Hobér and Sussman, *Cross-Examination in International Arbitration*, 21.
747. Pekcanıtez, 'Özel Uzman', 397; Similarly Karadaş, *Ulusal (İç) Tahkim*, 175.
748. O'Malley, *Rules of Evidence in International Arbitration*, 156–157; Elyıldırım, *Hukuk Yargılamasında Uzman Görüşü*, 83; Knoblach, *Sachverhaltsermittlung in Der Internationalen Wirtschaftsschiedsgerichtsbarkeit*, 279; Atalay, 'Pekcanıtez Usûl', 2021, 1960; Boerstra and Bitter, 'The Netherlands', 200.
749. Poudret and Besson, *Comparative Law of International Arbitration*, 559; Berger and Kellerhals, *International and Domestic Arbitration in Switzerland*, 489 ff.; Schneider and Scherer, 'Art. 184', 2093, para. 35.
750. Kantor, 'A Code of Conduct for Party-Appointed Experts in International Arbitration: Can One Be Found?', 327.
751. *See* cases reported in O'Malley, *Rules of Evidence in International Arbitration*, 156, fn. 35.
752. *See, e.g.*, VIAC Rules of Arbitration and Mediation 2021 Art. 23;, Liebscher, 'VIAC Rules', 340; Nessi, 'Expert Witness: Role and Independence', 96; Ehle, 'Practical Aspects of Using Expert Evidence in International Arbitration', 78; Knoblach, *Sachverhaltsermittlung in Der Internationalen Wirtschaftsschiedsgerichtsbarkeit*, 269, 279; Proske, *Expert Witness Conferencing in*

commercial arbitration, under the law applicable to the arbitration procedure, exclusion does not appear on a prima facie scrutiny, because the issue has not been subject to regulation even in the CIArb Protocol or the IBA Rules.[753]

Born states that national procedural law rules regarding the qualifications of party-appointed experts do not apply in international arbitration, and challenges to the authenticity, value or expert character of putatively expert evidence should be relevant only to the weight and credibility of such evidence, not to its admissibility. He further stated that, in practice, arbitrators rarely uphold challenges to the admissibility of party-appointed expert opinions.[754]

However, as arbitration laws[755] and arbitration rules[756] grant the tribunal great autonomy in conducting the proceedings and assessing the evidence, the tribunal might disregard the party-appointed expert, explicitly stating that it will not regard it while deliberating and drafting the award. Alternatively, it could give less weight, depending on the situation.[757]

The reasons for this might be failure to appear despite being ordered to be present at the hearings (section 2.9.1), failing the subjective test, as either a lack of the required impartiality, expertise, or conflict of interest with members of the tribunal (section 2.9.2) or possessing confidential information of the counterparty (section 2.9.3).

2.9.1 Failure to Appear

As stated among the obligations of the party-appointed expert in section 2.5.5.2, the expert is, in principle, expected to appear at the hearing for testimony and examination. Non-appearance of a party-appointed expert at an oral hearing, despite an order to do so, could potentially make the tribunal disregard the expert's written opinion in total (IBA Rules Article 5(5), CIArb Protocol Article 6.1(h&i)).[758]

The CIArb Protocol is strict on testimony, as it dictates that '[e]ach expert who has provided a written opinion in the Arbitration *shall* give oral testimony at an Evidentiary Hearing unless the Parties agree otherwise, and the Arbitral Tribunal confirms that agreement'. (emphasis added)

Schiedsverfahren, 20; Schütze and Thümmel, *Schiedsgericht Und Schiedsverfahren*, 133, para. 21; Tanrıver, *Hukukumuzda Bilirkişilik*, 35.

753. Kesikli, 'Milletlerarası Ticari Tahkimde Delillerin Değerlendirilmesi', 217.
754. Born, *International Commercial Arbitration*, 2449.
755. UNCITRAL Model Law Art. 19(2): 'Failing such agreement, the arbitral tribunal may, subject to the provisions of this Law, conduct the arbitration in such manner as it considers appropriate. The power conferred upon the arbitral tribunal includes the power to determine the admissibility, relevance, materiality and weight of any evidence.'
756. *See, e.g.*, ICC Arbitration Rules Arts 22 and 25.
757. Smiley, 'An Unwanted Intrusion: Challenging the Appointment of Experts in International Arbitration' 368.
758. Bor, 'Expert Evidence', 515; Khodykin and Mulcahy, *A Guide to the IBA Rules on the Taking of Evidence in International Arbitration*, 319; Knoblach, *Sachverhaltsermittlung in Der Internationalen Wirtschaftsschiedsgerichtsbarkeit*, 279; Similarly in Turkish Civil Procedure *See* Tanrıver, *Hukukumuzda Bilirkişilik*, 32; Akıncı, *Milletlerarası Tahkim*, 342; Atalay, 'Pekcanıtez Usûl', 2021, 1961.

Thus, if the CIArb Protocol is applicable, the expert opinion may be excluded and disregarded.[759] The non-appearance of party-appointed experts in Turkish litigation also leads to a disregard of the opinion (HMK m. 293/3).[760] The reasoning behind this is that until it is tested in cross-examination or conferencing, the opinions of the expert have little value.[761]

Another position in this regard is that the mere absence of the expert should not be a reason to disregard the report with prejudice, having also regard to *lex arbitri* provisions, but less weight can be attributed.

Although due process requires that the counterparty have the opportunity to hear and examine the expert,[762] this rule should not be interpreted too rigidly. It is possible that the expert provided an independent and well-established report for a clear understanding of the issue, but the expert cannot attend the hearing due to unanticipated or unplanned occurrences, such as illness, accident, or inability to travel.[763]

Accepting that the party-appointed expert has no absolute duty to appear before the tribunal would definitely negatively affect the gravity of the opinions.[764]

To draw adverse inferences in relation to the non-attendance of the expert should be denied, since it will be difficult to pinpoint a particular inference from a generally non-binary expert opinion.[765]

---

759. Kesikli, 'Milletlerarası Ticari Tahkimde Delillerin Değerlendirilmesi', 236; *Pekcanıtez* argues in the same direction in Pekcanıtez, 'Özel Uzman', 405.
760. Karslı, *Medeni Muhakeme Hukuku*, 624.
761. Khodykin and Mulcahy, *A Guide to the IBA Rules on the Taking of Evidence in International Arbitration*, 320; Karslı, *Medeni Muhakeme Hukuku*, 624.
762. Abdel Wahab, 'Party-Appointed Experts in International Commercial Arbitration', 197; Khodykin and Mulcahy, *A Guide to the IBA Rules on the Taking of Evidence in International Arbitration*, 320.
763. Khodykin and Mulcahy, *A Guide to the IBA Rules on the Taking of Evidence in International Arbitration*, 319.
764. Schütze and Thümmel, *Schiedsgericht Und Schiedsverfahren*, 133, para. 22; *See* Levine, 'Can Arbitrators Choose Who to Call as Witnesses (And What Can Be Done If They Don't Show Up)?', 335–337; *See Adel A Hamadi Al Tamimi v. Sultanate of Oman*, ICSID Case No. ARB/11/33, Procedural Order No. 8 18 April 2014, https://jusmundi.com/en/document/other/en-adel-a-hamadi-al-tamimi-v-sultanate-of-oman-procedural-order-no-8-friday-18th-april-2014#other_document_1364 (accessed 24 September 2025), paras 2–4:

    > the Respondent submitted a letter to the Tribunal in which it stated that the Claimant was refusing to present its party-appointed expert, JAJ Consultants LLC ('JAJ') for cross-examination and had withdrawn the JAJ Expert Report. The Respondent requested that the 'JAJ Report should remain in the record and the Tribunal should draw from it whatever inferences it concludes are warranted in the circumstances'.
    >
    > ...
    >
    > Mr. Rivkin indicated that the Claimant consented to the Application. The Respondent's Application is therefore granted by consent. JAJ Consultants LLC shall not appear for cross-examination, but its report shall remain in the record and the Tribunal, after receiving further submissions, if any, during the proceedings, may draw whatever inferences, if any, it considers are warranted in the circumstances.

765. Khodykin and Mulcahy, *A Guide to the IBA Rules on the Taking of Evidence in International Arbitration*, 321.

2.9.2 Failing the Subjective Test

The expert is expected to have certain personal qualifications, such as impartiality and objectivity, as well as expertise and experience. The expert is also required not to have any status, such as any present or past relation, that would lead to having a conflict of interest with members of the tribunal or the counterparty (and its representatives).[766]

If the expert had served or had a relationship with the party that called the expert, the tribunal usually did not decide that the expert was inadmissible but gave less weight to the opinion.[767]

Whether failing the subjective test should lead to a disqualification or disregard of the expert as evidence is controversial. If the expert seems partial or his expertise is reasonably questioned, then not disqualifying seems more appropriate, but the opinion would have less or even no impact on the matters for which the evidence was provided.[768]

However, if the expert has a conflict of interest with any tribunal member due to an existing or previous relationship,[769] the tribunal should analyse whether allowing the expert would objectively create an improper appearance, taking into account the results to the party who appointed the expert, if the expert is not permitted to the proceedings. Both the tribunal (member) and the expert should disclose such occasions to other members of the tribunal and the parties.[770]

For instance, in the *State General Reserve Fund of Oman v. Bulgaria,*[771] the respondent submitted a report from a quantum expert. The same expert was engaged by the respondent state in an UNCITRAL arbitration in which the party-appointed arbitrator from the claimant acted as counsel for the respondent. In response, the claimant requested that the arbitral tribunal disqualify the expert or that the respondent withdraw the expert from the arbitration proceedings. This offer was declined by the respondent. In a decision by the tribunal in which the concerned party-appointed arbitrator from the claimant did not take part, the remaining arbitrators dismissed the claimant's request for the disqualification of the respondent's expert on damages.[772]

766. Abdel Wahab, 'Party-Appointed Experts in International Commercial Arbitration', 197. In particular, if the expert has been engaged multiple times by the same party, *see* Kamya-Lukoda/Morgan, Role of Expert Witnesses in Construction Arbitration, 79.
767. Schäfer and Wilson, 'Issues for Arbitrators to Consider Regarding Experts', 67.
768. Abdel Wahab, 'Party Appointed Experts in International Commercial Arbitration', 197; Smiley, 'An Unwanted Intrusion: Challenging the Appointment of Experts in International Arbitration', 367.
769. In such a professional relationship, the expert is the employer or vice versa, or the arbitrator is the counsel appointing the expert in another proceeding.
770. Schäfer and Wilson, 'ICC Bulletin', 2021, 68.
771. *State General Reserve Fund of Oman v. Bulgaria,* ICSID Case No. ARB/15/43, available at https://www.italaw.com/cases/8765 (accessed 30 June 2022).
772. Lisa Bohmer, *Newly-Disclosed Award Sheds Light on Attempt to Disqualify Quantum Expert, and on Allocation of Costs in Dispute Between Oman's Sovereign Wealth Fund and Bulgaria,* 22 February 2021, IAReporter, available at https://www.iareporter.com/articles/newly-disclosed-award-sheds-light-on-attempt-to-disqualify-quantum-expert-and-on-allocation-of-costs-in-dispute-between-omans-sovereign-wealth-fund-and-bulgaria/ (accessed 30 June 2022).

It could also be the case that the expert has an interest in the outcome of the dispute. For instance, the contractor's CEO, who is an engineer or architect acting as an expert in the dispute, raises questions about the objectivity of the opinion.[773]

In many arbitrations, challenges against party-appointed experts are encountered, as in *Occidental v. Ecuador*.[774] In the case against Ecuador, the legal expert of Occidental, Hernan Perez Loose, was also co-counsel in a separate claim against Ecuador. However, the tribunal did not accept Ecuador's request for disqualification.[775]

2.9.3 Confidential Information

A party-appointed expert might have a relationship with the counterparty, which he writes an opinion against, where during the relationship, information was obtained that was agreed upon or is, according to the applicable law, confidential or a trade secret. If the report makes use of such information that could deprive the counterparty, the expert should be inadmissible to report or testify. However, if there is no ground for preclusion arising from the agreement of the parties or from the law, the expert should not be dismissed from proceedings.

The arbitral tribunal should give due regard to such a challenge when alleged with detailed reasons.

In investment arbitration, it is encountered in the case law that party-appointed experts are challenged, such as in the *Flughafen Zürich A.G. and Gestión e Ingenería IDC S.A. v. Bolivarian Republic of Venezuela*[776] cases. The investor sought to disqualify the expert from Venezuela based on the confidentiality of information gained by the expert. The Tribunal declined under Article 34(1) of the ICSID Arbitration Rules to disqualify the expert on the basis that, when provided, the claimant had failed to mark any confidential information or make reservations as to the confidentiality of the information.[777]

The Swiss Federal Tribunal has stated that an immediate challenge of experts is as necessary as it is for the challenge of arbitrators:

773. Kamya-Lukoda, 'Role of Expert Witnesses in Construction Arbitration: Delay and Disruption and Quantum Issues', 79.
774. *Occidental Petroleum Corporation Occidental Exploration and Production Company v. Republic of Ecuador*, ICSID Case No ARB/06/11, Award, 5 October 2012, available at https://www.italaw.com/sites/default/files/case-documents/italaw1094.pdf (accessed 30 June 2022). The quantum experts were required to produce a joint expert report using the discounted cash flow method. The tribunal established a procedure for the parties to comment on the joint report. *See Occidental Petroleum v. Republic of Ecuador*, 24–25, paras 80–83.
775. The tribunal declined to disqualify him, finding that his work on a 'family related' dispute 'in no way impacted' his previous work in the case. *See Occidental Petroleum v. Republic of Ecuador*, 153, para. 398, fn. 22.
776. *See Flughafen Zürich A.G. and Gestión e Ingenería IDC S.A. v. Bolivarian Republic of Venezuela*, ICSID Case No ARB/10/19, available at https://www.italaw.com/cases/1524 (accessed 3 August 2022).
777. IAReporter, 'Arbitrators Weigh Disqualification of Venezuela's Damages Expert, but Decide His Earlier Contacts with Claimant Don't Warrant It'. available at https://www.iareporter.com/articles/arbitrators-weigh-disqualification-of-venezuelas-damages-expert-but-decide-his-earlier-contacts-with-claimant-dont-warrant-it/ (accessed 13 October 2022).

> The party intending to challenge an arbitrator must raise the ground for challenge as soon as it becomes aware of it. This rule of case law applies to the grounds for a challenge that the party concerned effectively knew and also to those that it could have known, had they paid due attention (ATF 129 III 445 at 4.2.2.1, p. 465 and references); choosing to remain unaware may be considered in certain cases as an improper maneuver comparable to postponing the announcement of a challenge (judgment 4A_506/2007 of March 20, 2008, at 3.1.2). The aforesaid rule applies the principle of good faith to arbitral proceedings. Pursuant to this principle, the right to invoke the argument drawn from the irregular composition of the arbitral tribunal is forfeited if the party does not raise it immediately because it cannot keep it in reserve only to invoke it if the outcome of the arbitration is unfavorable (ATF 129 III 445 at 3.1, p. 449 and the cases quoted). In view of its general nature, the jurisprudential rule recalled here must also apply to the challenge of an expert.[778]

2.9.4 Exclusion and Its Effects

When the tribunal excludes the expert evidence provided by the party, it makes a decision on the admissibility of the evidence. With this exclusion, the tribunal will not only give no regard to the expert but also exclude the written report from the case file.

Some authors distinguish 'exclusion' from 'gating', where in the latter situation, the tribunal does not require the expert to testify if, for example, his testimony is irrelevant or duplicative.[779] Nevertheless, the expert's report is kept as part of the case record, but the expert is not requested to testify orally.[780]

2.10 LIABILITY

The party expert normally receives a fee for his services, which is usually paid by the instructing party. Accordingly, liability may arise not only for breaches of contractual obligations but also for acts that can be categorised as tort.[781] This will be determined in accordance with the applicable law for the arbitration. In principle, the expert is only liable for intentional wrongdoing or gross negligence.

2.11 INTERIM CONCLUSION

Party-appointed experts have legal basis in various international agreements, arbitration rules (such as ICSID, UNCITRAL, and ICC), the UNCITRAL Model Law, and many acts of state. Additionally, provisions concerning party-appointed experts can be found in soft law elements such as the IBA Rules, the CIArb Protocol, and the ICC Arbitration Commission Report on Controlling Time and Costs.

778. Swiss Federal Supreme Court, 4A_606/2013, Bundesgericht, para. 6.2.
779. Levine, 'Can Arbitrators Choose Who to Call as Witnesses (And What Can Be Done If They Don't Show Up)?', 335–337.
780. Abdel Wahab, 'Party Appointed Experts in International Commercial Arbitration', 199.
781. Proske, *Expert Witness Conferencing in Schiedsverfahren*, 22.

The legal nature of party-appointed experts is categorised differently in various jurisdictions. Often, party-appointed experts are referred to as 'witnesses', relying on the fact that they testify before a tribunal. Some courts and tribunals refer to these experts as 'judicial/adjudicatory assistants' despite being appointed by parties. There is much debate on whether a party-appointed expert can be classified as a (tribunal-appointed) 'expert evidence', a view that is rejected by the majority in various jurisdictions.

Despite some views that consider party-appointed expert opinions to be part of party arguments, the nature of such opinions should not be classified as the same. Party-appointed experts might be classified as evidence assessment tools because the expert mostly does not prove an alleged fact but enables the arbitrator to come to an opinion and derive a conclusion from the other evidence, such as witness statements or documents.[782]

Although court practices are useful for drawing inferences, Article 5(1) of the IBA Rules rightfully regulates that a party-appointed expert is a 'means of evidence'. This indicates that party-appointed experts are neither witnesses nor mere party submissions but have their own classification.[783] This means that they will be assessed freely with other evidence. It is not vital to classify party-appointed experts because international arbitration foresees the free assessment of evidence.[784]

As party-appointed experts directly affect proceedings, this is inherently related to the fundamental principles applicable in arbitration.

Submitting a party-appointed expert opinion as evidence is a way for a party to present its case. As such, expert opinion is part of the right to be heard, and any irregularity could lead to the award being challenged.

The Parties must have equal opportunity to present their claims and defences at all stages of the proceedings. This includes the opportunity to submit expert evidence in equal numbers and, as stressed in *CME Czech Republic B.V. v. The Czech Republic*, cross-examining the parties' experts.[785]

Party autonomy enables the parties to construct the proceedings according to their desire.[786] Parties can adduce whatever evidence they believe would lead them to

782. Özbek, 'Uzman Görüşünün Yargılamada Değerlendirilmesi', 129; Elyıldırım, *Hukuk Yargılamasında Uzman Görüşü*, 56.

783. Zuberbühler et al., *IBA Rules of Evidence*, 136; Münch, *Münchener Kommentar Zur ZPO*, § 1049, para. 39; Schlosser, *ZPO*, § 1049, para. 1.

784. Knoblach, *Sachverhaltsermittlung in Der Internationalen Wirtschaftsschiedsgerichtsbarkeit*, 277.

785. *See CME Czech Republic B.V. v. The Czech Republic*, UNCITRAL, Final Award 14 March 2003, para. 80 available at, https://www.italaw.com/cases/281 (accessed 30 August 2022).

786. Pekcanıtez and Yeşilirmak, 'Tahkim', 2704; Yeşilirmak, *Türkiye'de Ticari Hayatın ve Yatırım Ortamının Iyileştirilmesi Için Uyuşmazlıkların Etkin Cözümünde Dogrudan Görüşme, Arabuluculuk, Hakem-Bilirkişilik ve Tahkim: Sorunlar ve Cözüm Önerileri*, 104; Yeğengil, *Tahkim (L'Arbitrage)*, 295–296; Kuru and Aydın, *Medenî Usul Hukuku El Kitabı*, II:1890; Arslan et al., *Medenî Usul Hukuku*, 829; Budak and Karaaslan, *Medenî Usul Hukuku*, 2019, 434; Knoblach, *Sachverhaltsermittlung in Der Internationalen Wirtschaftsschiedsgerichtsbarkeit*, 48; Karslı, *Medeni Muhakeme Hukuku*, 910; Ekşi, *Hukuku Muhakemeleri Kanunu'nda Tahkim*, 164; Ağırman, *Milli & Milletlerarası Tahkim*, 383, 455.

succeed. Therefore, they are free to adduce an expert opinion.[787] Accordingly, parties may waive the use of party-appointed experts.

Arbitrators, as decision-makers, are expected to know the law to effectively resolve disputes. However, in an international arbitration dispute, more than one or even more laws may be applicable, and the arbitrators may not control every law. Therefore, this situation creates the need for legal experts. Nevertheless, using legal experts does neither harm *iura novit curia* nor, in itself, lead to delegation of decision-making.

On the one hand, the parties enjoy great flexibility[788] in adducing party-appointed experts. On the other hand, permitting the parties to present expert opinions without any limits could adversely affect the proceedings in terms of cost-efficiency,[789] especially when it is unnecessary to have party-appointed experts or experts at all.[790] If the tribunal comprises members who were specifically appointed due to their expertise in specific matters, experts should not be required to take an active part in the proceedings.[791]

When it comes to who must bring an expert to proceedings, no actual provision seems to be found. In international arbitration, the parties are primarily responsible for bringing their evidence, and only a restricted principle of investigation is applicable.[792] Accordingly, the facts relied upon must primarily be established by the parties.[793] This also encompasses the adducing of expert opinion. Although arbitrators generally have the authority to appoint a tribunal-appointed expert depending on the applicable rules of the arbitration, they are not ordinarily obligated to do so.[794] Although there is no doubt that an arbitral tribunal shall not render a decision that it does not fully comprehend, it is also the parties who bear the burden of proof. Therefore, the tribunal's duty of enquiry needs to be considered in conjunction with the maxim of disposition.[795]

In an arbitration proceeding, the parties and their representatives must act according to the principle of truth or good faith. Ideally, the parties have the obligation to submit the facts of the case according to the subjective truth.[796] This principle also extends to

787. Lew, Mistelis, and Kröll, *Comparative International Commercial Arbitration*, 578; Khodykin and Mulcahy, *A Guide to the IBA Rules on the Taking of Evidence in International Arbitration*, 287; Akıncı, *Milletlerarası Tahkim*, 340.
788. Knoblach, *Sachverhaltsermittlung in Der Internationalen Wirtschaftsschiedsgerichtsbarkeit*, 48.
789. Jones, 'Redefining the Role and Value of Expert Evidence', 23; Knoblach, *Sachverhaltsermittlung in Der Internationalen Wirtschaftsschiedsgerichtsbarkeit*, 282; Özekes, *Medenî Usûl Hukukunda Hukukî Dinlenilme Hakkı*, 112.
790. Proske, *Expert witness conferencing in Schiedsverfahren*, 32.
791. Özbek, *Tahkim Hukuku*, II:1456.
792. Curschmann, 'Germany', 143.
793. Tanrıver, *Medenî Usûl Hukuku*, 2022, II:461; Demir Gökyayla, 'Tahkimde Taraflarca Getirilme İlkesi ve Delil İkamesi', 72; Kurkela, Turunen, and Conflict Management Institute, *Due Process in International Commercial Arbitration*, 175; Swiss Federal Supreme Court, 4A_597/2013, Bundesgericht, para. 3.2.2.
794. Akıncı, *Milletlerarası Tahkim*, 339; *Akil* referring to the view echoed in German literatüre *see* Akil, 'Bilirkişi-Uzman Tanık Ayrımı', 175, fn. 20; Demir Gökyayla, 'Tahkimde Taraflarca Getirilme İlkesi ve Delil İkamesi', 86; Özbek, *Tahkim Hukuku*, II:1453; In the same direction in Italy, *see* Cavasola and Paton, 'Italy', 174.
795. Dülger, *Milletlerarası Tahkimde Hakemlerin Dogal Yetkileri*, 95.
796. Pekcanıtez and Yeşilirmak, 'Tahkim', 2704; Tanrıver, *Medenî Usûl Hukuku*, II:430–431.

experts and their opinions. However, an expert's opinion may not reflect the objective truth. Thus, it would be logical to expect experts to provide their opinions according to their 'genuine belief'.

The party-appointed expert's personality should reflect that he is impartial and objective. Independence as a personal qualification cannot be expected from a party-appointed expert because the expert is dependent on the appointing party. Independence should still be a sought qualification, but not from the expert, but the expert opinion, in the sense that it was not drafted solely according to the party's request, and the expert had relative freedom in forming his opinion. Although the expert receives instructions, he will make evaluations based on scientific facts and methods, which will differentiate him from a counsel.[797]

When it comes to the expert appointment procedure, there are no detailed rules. Experts may be engaged prior to the initiation of the proceedings or after the request has been filed. Generally, the expert is interviewed, and if the party deems the expert to support its case, it engages with the expert, and they agree on terms of appointment where the party's instructions can be found. The expert must provide evidence and other documents to support his opinion. He may ask for the party's assistance during that stage. The party-appointed expert will receive his fee directly from the appointing party, which is different from that of the tribunal-appointed expert.

In return, an expert must provide an arguable and convincing expert opinion and, unless directed otherwise, attend the hearings for testimony and examination. An expert must retain confidential information he receives in time of proceedings.

The IBA Guidelines, the CIArb Protocol, and the CBP outline rules that experts should adhere to when drafting their opinions. These rules have been developed over time in practice and present a good example of what qualifications a well-established expert opinion should have. The report shall include the full name and address of the expert, a statement regarding his or her present and past relationship (if any) with any of the parties, their legal representatives, advisors, witnesses and the arbitral tribunal, and a description of his or her background, qualifications, training and experience, including areas outside his or her expertise, a description of the instructions and questions pursuant to which he is providing his or her opinions and conclusions, a declaration of his impartiality and objectivity, a declaration that his opinions are an independent product of his own views and conclusions, a statement that he has received his remuneration before the final production of this report, a statement of the facts on which he is basing his or her expert opinions and conclusions, his expert opinions and conclusions, including a description of the methods, evidence and information used in arriving at the conclusions, if the Expert Report has been translated, a statement as to the language in which it was originally prepared, and the language in which the expert anticipates giving testimony at the hearing, the signature of the expert(s) and its date and place; and if the expert report has been signed by more than one person, an attribution of the entirety or specific parts of the Report to each author.

797. Kesikli, 'Milletlerarası Ticari Tahkimde Delillerin Değerlendirilmesi', 214.

Sources applicable in international arbitration are mainly silent on the details of admissibility and evidence assessment.[798] Free assessment of evidence is one of the main rules in international arbitration proceedings, where it is rare to find specific and detailed provisions relating to the weighing of evidence or burden of proof in statutes or rules. The Model Law and arbitration rules set forth this principle by stipulating that the tribunal has the inherent power to determine the admissibility, relevance, materiality, and weight of the evidence offered (UNCITRAL Arbitration Rules Article 27(4), ICSID Arbitration Rule 36(1), and IBA Rules Article 9(1)).

Generally, expert opinion, as a means of evidence, is admissible where the subject matter is outside the knowledge or experience of the trier of fact, i.e., the arbitral tribunal, and where such expert opinion can assist the trier in its final determination of an issue.[799]

In international arbitration, the general concept and practice is that 'each party has the burden of proving the facts relied on to support its claim or defence' (UNCITRAL Arbitration Rules Article 27(1)).[800] In relation to the experts, if a technical/scientific issue needs to be clarified to the tribunal, both parties, depending on their claim or defence, bear the burden of proof.[801]

The standard required to determine whether the claiming or defending party has conformed with the burden of proof, i.e., adduced expert evidence that supports the claim and establishes the facts thereto, or not, is regulated by the substantive applicable law (*lex causae*), but sometimes also with the law applicable to the arbitration (*lex arbitri*).[802]

The rules in these provisions generally require proof of a fact with complete conviction, high probability, or overwhelming probability. In international arbitration, the standard of overwhelming probability is usually accepted and applied.[803] This standard calls for a claim to be established if the tribunal is convinced by evidence that the claim is more likely to be true than not.[804]

798. Redfern et al., 'The Standards and Burden of Proof in International Arbitration', 321; Hacıbekiroğlu, *Milletlerarası Tahkim Hukukunda Deliller ve Delillerin Degerlendirilmesi*, 10; Alfter, *Das Beweismaß in Der Internationalen Handelsschiedsgerichtsbarkeit: Auswirkungen Der Best Practice Der Document Production Auf Den Beweis*, 63 ff.

799. Silver, 'Back to Burgess: The Impact of the White Burgess Expert Evidence Regime in Alberta Decisions', 5.

800. Yeşilirmak, *Türkiye'de Ticari Hayatın ve Yatırım Ortamının Iyileştirilmesi Için Uyuşmazlıkların Etkin Çözümünde Dogrudan Görüşme, Arabuluculuk, Hakem-Bilirkişilik ve Tahkim: Sorunlar ve Çözüm Önerileri*, 114; Webster and Bühler, *Handbook of UNCITRAL Arbitration*, 413; Knoblach, *Sachverhaltsermittlung in Der Internationalen Wirtschaftsschiedsgerichtsbarkeit*, 221; Özbek, *Tahkim Hukuku*, II:1367; Kurkela, Turunen, and Conflict Management Institute, *Due Process in International Commercial Arbitration*, 147; Hacıbekiroğlu, *Milletlerarası Tahkim Hukukunda Deliller ve Delillerin Degerlendirilmesi*, 11; Redfern et al., 'The Standards and Burden of Proof in International Arbitration', 321.

801. Webster and Bühler, *Handbook of UNCITRAL Arbitration*, 423.

802. O'Malley, *Rules of Evidence in International Arbitration*, 215.

803. Yeşilirmak, *Türkiye'de Ticari Hayatın ve Yatırım Ortamının Iyileştirilmesi Için Uyuşmazlıkların Etkin Çözümünde Dogrudan Görüşme, Arabuluculuk, Hakem-Bilirkişilik ve Tahkim: Sorunlar ve Çözüm Önerileri*, 114.

804. *See* O'Malley, *Rules of Evidence in International Arbitration*, 215 ff.; 'Procedural Efficiency in International Arbitration: Choosing the Best of Both Legal Worlds', 120–122; Nater-Bass and

Testing of the expert and his opinion is done at the evidentiary hearing phase via oral examination, be it examination by the tribunal, direct examination and/or cross-examination by the counsel or conferencing among the experts.[805]

The impartiality of an expert and the independence of the expert's work are two of the most critical areas worth exploring in this regard. If it can be demonstrated during cross-examination that the expert is not objective and impartial or that the expert's work lacks independence, this may result in the tribunal placing little or no weight on the expert's views.[806] Therefore, whereas the arbitrator is not strictly bound by the expert's opinion, he cannot merely leave the expert's opinion aside without consideration.[807]

The expert's qualifications and expertise are also important when assessing weight. For instance, if it can be proven that the expert is testifying in areas falling beyond his scope of expertise, then the whole testimony faces the risk of collapsing without even addressing the substance of the report.

Party-appointed experts, in general, may not be subject to disqualification or exclusion, as tribunal-appointed experts can in certain situations.[808] In international commercial arbitration, depending on the law applicable to the arbitration procedure, no exclusion seems possible at first sight since the issue has not been subject to regulation, not even in the CIArb Protocol or the IBA Rules.[809]

The exclusion of a party-appointed expert is a serious measure that should be a last resort.[810] Wrongful or inappropriate exclusion of an expert may indeed threaten the award to set-aside or denied enforcement due to contended breaches of due process.

Thus, arbitral tribunals are usually very cautious when determining whether or not to exercise their discretionary powers to exclude a party-appointed expert and will

Rouvinez, 'Art. 24 Commentary on Swiss Rules', 264; Redfern et al., 'The Standards and Burden of Proof in International Arbitration', 355.

805. Webster and Bühler, *Handbook of ICC Arbitration: Commentary, Precedents, Materials*, 441; Kesikli, 'Milletlerarası Ticari Tahkimde Delillerin Değerlendirilmesi', 235; Bacanlı, 'Bir Alternatif Uyuşmazlık Çözüm Yolu Olarak Istanbul Tahkim ve Arabuluculuk Merkezi (ISTAC) Tahkim Yargilamasinda Delillerin Ibrazı ve Değerlendirilmesi', 97; Ağırman, *Milli & Milletlerarası Tahkim*, 462–464; Whether these methods of examination will be done at the same proceeding is up to the decision of the tribunal in each case. For details *see* Proske, *Expert Witness Conferencing in Schiedsverfahren*, 46.

806. Abdel Wahab, 'Party Appointed Experts in International Commercial Arbitration', 200–201.

807. Narçin, '4686 Sayılı Milletlerarası Tahkim Uyarınca Deliller', 17. *Atalay* argued similarly for party-appointed experts before state courts in Atalay, 'Pekcanıtez Usûl', 2021, 1959; Atalı, '6754 Sayılı Bilirkişilik Kanunu ve Hukuki Konularda Bilirkişilik', 3279.

808. *See, e.g.*, VIAC Rules of Arbitration and Mediation 2021 Art. 23; Liebscher, 'VIAC Rules', 340; Nessi, 'Expert Witness: Role and Independence', 96; Ehle, 'Practical Aspects of Using Expert Evidence in International Arbitration', 78; Knoblach, *Sachverhaltsermittlung in Der Internationalen Wirtschaftsschiedsgerichtsbarkeit*, 269, 279; Proske, *Expert Witness Conferencing in Schiedsverfahren*, 20; Schütze and Thümmel, *Schiedsgericht Und Schiedsverfahren*, 133, para. 21; Tanrıver, *Hukukumuzda Bilirkişilik*, 35.

809. Kesikli, 'Milletlerarası Ticari Tahkimde Delillerin Değerlendirilmesi', 217.

810. Abdel Wahab, 'Party Appointed Experts in International Commercial Arbitration', 199; Smiley, 'An Unwanted Intrusion: Challenging the Appointment of Experts in International Arbitration', 376.

usually prefer not to exclude it altogether but assess it with caution and potentially credit less weight.[811]

The appointing party or any other party who suffered damages due to the expert opinion may pursue a claim against the expert without forgetting that the expert will be, in principle, only liable for intentional wrongdoing or gross negligence.

811. Abdel Wahab, 'Party Appointed Experts in International Commercial Arbitration', 199; Burianski and Lang, 'Bibliographic Reference "Challenges" to Party-Appointed Experts', 15:272.

CHAPTER 3
Problems Related to Party-Appointed Experts

The prevailing use of party-appointed experts in international arbitration is not without flaws.[812] In practice, there are obvious concerns regarding their fair and efficient use.[813] The critics are not restricted to the realm of international arbitration; they can also be observed in various jurisdictions regarding litigation.[814] Empirical studies have explicitly determined these concerns.

When the studies are reviewed, the problem surrounding the use of party-appointed experts can be classified into two main categories: Problems related to personality and problems related to usage style. These challenges not only discredit the usage of party-appointed experts but also attack the efficiency of arbitration, prolonging proceedings and leading them to cost more.[815]

3.1 EMPIRICAL PROOF OF THE PROBLEMS

For more than 17 years, The Queen Mary University School of International Arbitration, with the financial support of various law firms,[816] has conducted empirical studies

812. Jones, 'Party Appointed Expert Witnesses in International Arbitration: A Protocol at Last', 137; Jones, 'Ineffective Use of Expert Evidence in Construction Arbitration', 1; Samaras and Strasser, 'Managing Party-Appointed Experts in International Arbitration--Analysis of the Current Framework and Best Practice Proposals-', 314.
813. Jones, 'Redefining the Role and Value of Expert Evidence', 23.
814. For the UK *see* Lord Woolf MR, *Access to Justice: Final Report to the Lord Chancellor of the Civil Justice System in England and Wales* (Final Report, 1996); Proske, *Expert witness conferencing in Schiedsverfahren*. Jones, 'Redefining the Role and Value of Expert Evidence', 25–26.
For details in Türkiye *see* Atalı, '6754 Sayılı Bilirkişilik Kanunu ve Hukuki Konularda Bilirkişilik'; Tanrıver, *Hukukumuzda Bilirkişilik*.
815. Jones, 'Party Appointed Expert Witnesses in International Arbitration: A Protocol at Last', 137; Jones, 'Ineffective Use of Expert Evidence in Construction Arbitration', 1; Samaras and Strasser, 'Managing Party-Appointed Experts in International Arbitration--Analysis of the Current Framework and Best Practice Proposals', 314.
816. Like White & Case, PriceWaterhouseCoopers and Pinsent Masons.

that shed light on the developments, trends, and issues faced in international arbitration.[817]

The reports from 2012, 2015, 2018, 2020, 2021, and 2022 indicate statistics regarding experts from which the need for development and change can be derived. In the 2021 report, when asked respondents, as a party or counsel, which procedural options they would leave out in order to have cheaper or faster proceedings, 13 % selected to opt out for party-appointed experts.

Some arbitrators adopted the view that party-appointed experts are sometimes used as 'hired guns'.[818] However, some counsel stated that a tribunal-appointed expert might also become a de facto fourth arbitrator, which, in their view, was undesired.[819]

In the 2018 report, when asked whether arbitration rules should include standards of independence and impartiality of (party) experts, 69 % responded affirmatively, demonstrating a clear need.[820]

It is known in international arbitration that some figures are prominently known not only for their appointment as arbitrators but also for acting as counsel and experts, thus creating the phenomenon known as *double-hatting*.[821]

Double-hatting is a practice in which individuals switch roles as arbitrators, counsel, and experts in different arbitral proceedings. Experienced counsel who actively represent parties before arbitral tribunals may also serve as arbitrators in other cases. In the 2020 report, 57 % of respondents indicated that arbitrators should be allowed to act as experts in other ISDS disputes.[822]

Although more parties are in favour, a substantial number potentially bear the fear that the small-privileged arbitration community could influence each other.

These results are surprising in view of the continued debate on which method is more effective. Respondents' preferences are, in fact, more balanced: 43 % find experts more effective when they are appointed by the parties, while 31 % find tribunal-appointed experts more effective. Consistent with domestic litigation culture, more civil lawyers (43 %) than common lawyers (19 %) find tribunal-appointed experts more effective.

Respondents who preferred tribunal-appointed experts argued that party-appointed experts often act as 'partisan advocates' for the party that appointed them, which regularly leads to the appointment of a third tribunal-appointed expert. According to

---

817. *See* website: https://arbitration.qmul.ac.uk/research/ (accessed 10 March 2022).
818. De Berti, 'Experts and Expert Witnesses in International Arbitration: Adviser, Advocate or Adjudicator ?', 54; Abdel Wahab, 'Party Appointed Experts in International Commercial Arbitration', 191; Waincymer, *Procedure and Evidence in International Arbitration*, 933; This argument is made especially for 'professional' experts, *see* for critics Proske, *Expert witness conferencing in Schiedsverfahren*, 30.
819. '2021 International Arbitration Survey: Adapting Arbitration to a Changing World', 14; 'BCLP 2021 Survey', 17; Can and Tuna, *Milletlerarası Tahkim Hukuku*, 413.
820. '2018 International Arbitration Survey: The Evolution of International Arbitration', 33–34.
821. For instance, Mr Alexandrov in *Tethyan Copper Company v. Islamic Republic of Pakistan*, ICSID Case No. ARB/12/1, and *SolEs Badojoz GmbH v. Kingdom of Spain*, ICSID Case No. ARB/15/38.
822. '2020 International Arbitration Survey: Investor-State Dispute Settlement (ISDS)', 15.

them, a system in which an expert is appointed by the tribunal from the beginning would bring about a more neutral expert opinion and save time and money.[823]

3.2 PROBLEMS RELATED TO THE QUALIFICATIONS OF EXPERTS

Opposed to the understanding of tribunal-appointed experts' personal qualifications of independence and impartiality, it is controversial whether party-appointed experts need to be independent and impartial.

Guidelines, court decisions, arbitral awards, and scholarly writing are not clear when referring to the independence and impartiality of party-appointed experts, and the terms are used interchangeably, leading to confusion.

Below, the relevant terms will be defined and examined on whether and, if so, how they relate to party-appointed experts.

3.2.1 Independence

As elaborated earlier,[824] some soft laws and scholars require not only tribunal-appointed experts to be independent but also party-appointed experts.[825]

Before attributing such a qualification, one must examine the term *independence*. Being independent can be defined as not being dependent, such as not being subject to control by others, not being affiliated with a larger controlling unit, not requiring or relying on something else, not looking to others for opinions or guidance in conduct, and not being bound by or committed to a party.[826] Independence is the first step to ensure neutrality.

According to the comprehensive empirical study conducted by the University of Geneva[827] with arbitrators, counsel, and experts, independence was mentioned as a must-have fundamental attribute of experts by 'all respondents'.[828]

Independence, when related to experts, is the concept in which the expert's position is assessed, whether it has objective links with the party.[829] However, experts view independence slightly differently. According to experts in arbitration, independence is acting in freedom and in the absence of control by the party.[830]

823. '2012 International Arbitration Survey: Present and Preferred Practices in the Arbitral Process', 29.
824. *See* Chapter 2, section 2.4.1–2.4.2.
825. Schütze and Thümmel, *Schiedsgericht Und Schiedsverfahren*, 133, para. 21; Roney, 'Cross-Examination of Experts', 114; Club Español del Arbitraje, Code of Best Practices in Arbitration, Rule 39; Lew, Mistelis, and Kröll, *Comparative International Commercial Arbitration*, 575; Kesikli, 'Milletlerarası Ticari Tahkimde Delillerin Değerlendirilmesi', 215.
826. Merriam-Webster.com Dictionary, 'independent', https://www.merriam-webster.com/dictionary/independent (accessed 6 July 2022).
827. *See* Mbengue and Das, 'Rules Governing the Use of Experts in International Disputes'; de Chazournes et al., 'Uses of Experts Before International Courts and Tribunals'.
828. de Chazournes et al., 'Uses of Experts Before International Courts and Tribunals', 492.
829. de Chazournes et al., 493.
830. de Chazournes et al., 495–496.

The IBA Rules require that the expert not only be independent from the party and its agents but also from the counsel representing the client. In fact, not only the parties but also the legal counsel generally determine the expert to be appointed. It is common for legal counsel and their law firms to reach out to experts whom they occasionally engage for cases. That is why IBA Rules Article 5(2)(c) have foreseen that experts should also be independent of legal advisors.[831]

Neither the IBA Rules nor the CIArb Protocol explain how a party-appointed expert can, in fact, be independent and not just show independence.[832] *Kantor* argued that 'no protocol or code can regulate the ability of a party to hire an expert who is just a good actor or actress and who is able to appear objective while delivering fundamentally partisan evidence'.[833] The declaration of independence, as required by the CIArb Protocol alone, may not ensure independence.[834] The IBA Rules' requirement of the statement on the party-appointed expert's independence is not either. In both rules, it is not clear whether a lack of independence would disqualify or discredit the conclusions submitted by the party-appointed expert.

Party-appointed experts generally work closely with legal counsel when preparing their opinions.[835] If close collaboration prevents independence, it cannot be achieved.

In the US courts, in order to determine the independence of a party-appointed expert, practitioners place greater value on an expert's adherence to scientific methodology and on any relevant standards applied by the expert's profession. If an expert fails to comply with such methodology or standards, this can be revealed during cross-examination.[836]

The views that require party-appointed experts to be independent do not consider the ontology and reality of party-appointed experts. First, party-appointed experts cannot be independent since they are engaged, instructed, and paid by a party. Therefore, it is no surprise that the party-appointed expert was not independent. However, this lack of independence is a natural result when the nature of engagement is considered.[837] According to IBA Rules Article 6(2), tribunal-appointed experts must deliver a statement on their qualifications, background and independence. However, IBA Rules Article 5 does not specify such a right to submit objections to declared independence.[838]

831. Khodykin and Mulcahy, *A Guide to the IBA Rules on the Taking of Evidence in International Arbitration*, 303.
832. Jones, 'Ineffective Use of Expert Evidence in Construction Arbitration', 7.
833. Kantor, 'A Code of Conduct for Party-Appointed Experts in International Arbitration: Can One Be Found?', 335.
834. Parlett, 'Parties' Engagement with Experts in International Litigation', 451.
835. Blackaby and Wilbraham, 'Practical Issues Relating to the Use of Expert Evidence in Investment Treaty Arbitration', 662; IBA Guidelines on Party Representation in International Arbitration Art. 24 provides as follows: 'A Party Representative may, consistent with the principle that the evidence given should reflect the Witness's own account of relevant facts, events or circumstances, or the Expert's own analysis or opinion, meet or interact with Witnesses and Experts in order to discuss and prepare their prospective testimony.'
836. Blackaby and Wilbraham, 658.
837. *Kantor* citing *Prof. Thomas Walde* in Kantor, 'A Code of Conduct for Party-Appointed Experts in International Arbitration – Can One Be Found?', 334.
838. Ünüvar, 'Experts: Investment Arbitration', para. 25.

Rogers also confirmed that 'an expert who is unilaterally selected and compensated by only one party, and who works extensively with that party's counsel, cannot have the same meaning as the requirement that an arbitrator remains "independent" of the parties and their counsel'.[839]

Thus, the following question arises from this perspective: Can the party-appointed expert be literally independent? It is obvious that the party-appointed expert is acting in accordance with the instructions of the party that engaged him.[840] Since an expert is a professional who puts together a 'work', he will be remunerated by the party. Therefore, it cannot be expected that the party-appointed expert will be literally as independent as the tribunal-appointed expert because they do not share the same exact position.[841]

For tribunal-appointed experts, principally, there is the assumption that these experts are already (expected to be) independent due to the appointment procedure.[842] However, party-appointed experts are chosen strategically, even sometimes way before the proceedings, and without interference from the tribunal or the consent of the counterparty.

Not being required to be independent does not mean that they should be biased or partial.[843] Not that the party-appointed expert as a personality should be required to be independent, but the opinion 'must be independent in the sense that it is the product of the expert's independent judgement, uninfluenced by who has retained him or her or the outcome'.[844] The party-appointed expert is not neutral.[845] On the contrary, the tribunal-appointed expert must be neutral and, if not, can be challenged on the same grounds as the arbitrators can.[846]

Thus, independence in relation to party-appointed experts should not be regarded as an admissibility issue but should be evaluated in the context of weight and assessment.[847] That's why, in international practice, even (former) employees and consultants of a party can be seen as experts.[848]

839. Rogers, *Ethics in International Arbitration*, 143.
840. O'Malley, *Rules of Evidence in International Arbitration*, 150; Abdel Wahab, 'Party Appointed Experts in International Commercial Arbitration', 190; Proske, *Expert witness conferencing in Schiedsverfahren*, 21.
841. O'Malley, *Rules of Evidence in International Arbitration*, 150; O'Malley, 150, fn. 15; *Professor Thomas Walde* refers the independence of party-appointed experts as 'fiction' in Kantor, 'A Code of Conduct for Party-Appointed Experts in International Arbitration: Can One Be Found?', 335; Can and Tuna, *Milletlerarası Tahkim Hukuku*, 414.
842. Wach and Petsch, 'Der Sachverständigenbeweis Im Schiedsverfahren: Grenzen Der Gestaltungsfreiheit von Parteien Und Schiedsgericht', 97. This does not mean that they are always independent, but the procedure promises it. Nevertheless, they can be challenged, replaced, or excluded.
843. Kesikli, 'Milletlerarası Ticari Tahkimde Delillerin Değerlendirilmesi', 217.
844. Supreme Court of Canada, *White Burgess Langille Inman v. Abbott and Haliburton Co.*, para. 32.
845. Musielak and Voit, *ZPO*§ 1049, para. 11.
846. Wach and Petsch, 'Der Sachverständigenbeweis Im Schiedsverfahren: Grenzen Der Gestaltungsfreiheit von Parteien Und Schiedsgericht', 103.
847. O'Malley, *Rules of Evidence in International Arbitration*, 152; de Chazournes et al., 'Uses of Experts Before International Courts and Tribunals', 493; That's why, in practice, the party-appointed expert is generally not disregarded, even failing to be independent in 'BCLP 2021 Survey', 21.
848. O'Malley, *Rules of Evidence in International Arbitration*, 151, fn. 17.

Khodykin/Mulcahy stated that it is possible for experts to be independent but partial. That is why what really matters is that they are impartial; however, impartiality is a state of mind that is thorny to detect.[849]

Again, if there is or was a relationship between a party-appointed expert and the counterparty or the arbitral tribunal, this must be critically evaluated.[850] For instance, in *Jan de Nul v. Egypt*, the tribunal was requested by the claimants to disregard the respondent's party-appointed expert report from the case file because the expert had previously been a member of the board of directors for one of the claimants.[851] However, the tribunal concluded that this relationship could not make the expert's opinion inadmissible, but it considered the weight in rendering the decision.[852]

The professionalism and consistency of experts in preparing the report and their testimony at the hearing might be a more determinative factor in whether they are independent (and impartial) than mere links with parties.[853]

As mentioned in *Lord Abinger v. Ashton*:

> [u]ndoubtedly there is a natural bias to do something serviceable for those who employ you and adequately remunerate you. It is very natural, and it is so effectual, that we constantly see persons, instead of considering themselves witnesses, rather consider themselves as the paid agents of the person who employs them.[854]

UNCITRAL Arbitration Rules provide some indication, in the form of appointment, that independence and impartiality are required from a tribunal-appointed expert, not from a party-appointed expert.[855] The party-appointed expert, contrary to the tribunal-appointed one, cannot be rejected.[856]

Misen v. Ukraine is a good example of how the tribunal handled the issue of independence and impartiality.[857] The chair arbitrator, in the decision for a request to disqualify one of the tribunal members, stated:

849. Khodykin and Mulcahy, *A Guide to the IBA Rules on the Taking of Evidence in International Arbitration*, 302.
850. O'Malley, *Rules of Evidence in International Arbitration*, 152.
851. *Jan de Nul N.V. and Dredging International N.V. v. Arab Republic of Egypt*, ICSID Case No. ARB/04/13, Final Award (6 November 2008), para. 28, available at https://www.italaw.com/cases/587 (accessed 24 September 2025).
852. *Jan de Nul N.V. and Dredging International N.V. v. Arab Republic of Egypt*, ICSID Case No. ARB/04/13, Final Award (6 November 2008), para. 28; Similar decision of a UK Court *see Brandeis (Brokers) Ltd v. Black and Ors*, 2001 Arbitration Law Reports and Review at 223–239.
853. O'Malley, *Rules of Evidence in International Arbitration*, 153; Kantor, 'A Code of Conduct for Party-Appointed Experts in International Arbitration: Can One Be Found?', 373.
854. *Lord Abinger v. Ashton* (1873), L.R. 17 Eq. 358, at p. 374 cited in Supreme Court of Canada, *White Burgess Langille Inman v. Abbott and Haliburton Co.*, para. 11.
855. Mbengue and Das, 'Rules Governing the Use of Experts in International Disputes', 433.
856. Wach and Petsch, 'Der Sachverständigenbeweis Im Schiedsverfahren: Grenzen Der Gestaltungsfreiheit von Parteien Und Schiedsgericht', 95, 103; Thomas et al., *Thomas/Putzo ZPO*, § 1049, para. 3.
857. *Misen Energy AB (publ) and Misen Enterprises AB v. Ukraine* (ICSID Case No. ARB/21/15), Decision on the Respondent's Proposal to Disqualify Dr Stanimir A. Alexandrov, para. 104. https://www.italaw.com/sites/default/files/case-documents/italaw170103.pdf (accessed 28 August 2022).

> [I]t is not uncommon for the same expert to appear before the same arbitrator on multiple occasions. Quantum experts specialised in the field, such as Dr. Moselle, are few in number. Some interaction between arbitrators and experts is thus to be expected. As a result, multiple appearances of an expert before an arbitrator are, per se, insufficient to sustain a disqualification decision. This is particularly so considering that in each case, the arbitrator exercises the same independent arbitral function. Thus, something more is required; i.e. that because of the proximity, dependence, intensity and/or materiality, a specific connection between an arbitrator and an expert create an obvious appearance of lack of independence or impartiality.[858]

The matter of proximity, intensity, dependence, and materiality was assessed by *Suez v. Argentina* as follows:

> Proximity: How closely connected is the challenged arbitrator to one of the parties by reason of the alleged connection? The closer the connection between an arbitrator and a party, the more likely that the relationship may influence an arbitrator's independence of judgment and impartiality;
> Intensity: How intense and frequent are the interactions between challenged arbitrator and one of the parties as a result of the alleged connection? The more frequent and intense the interaction by virtue of the relationship between an arbitrator and a party the more probable that such relationship will affect the arbitrator's independence of judgment and impartiality;
> Dependence: To what extent is the challenged arbitrator dependent on one of the parties for benefits as a result of the connection? The more an arbitrator is dependent on a relationship for benefits or advantages the more likely that the relationship may influence the arbitrator's independence of judgment and impartiality; and
> Materiality: To what extent are any benefits accruing to the challenged arbitrator as a result of the alleged connection significant and therefore likely to influence in some way the arbitrator's judgment? Obviously significant benefits derived from a relationship will be more likely to influence an arbitrator's judgment and impartiality than negligible or insignificant benefits.[859]

In *Orazul v. Argentine,* the president arbitrator failed to disclose that she had sat on the *Green Power v. Spain*[860] tribunal together with the respondent's legal expert. This, along with the attitude during questioning and broader conduct during the hearing, led the Claimant to request the disqualification of the president arbitrator. The claimant's and respondent's appointees considered it would have been 'advisable' for the president to disclose that she had sat on the *Green Power v. Spain* with a legal expert

858. *Misen v. Ukraine,* Decision on the Respondent's Proposal to Disqualify Dr Stanimir A. Alexandrov, paras 141–142.
859. Suez, *Sociedad General de Aguas de Barcelona S.A., and InterAgua Servicios Integrales del Agua S.A. v. The Argentine Republic,* ICSID Case No. ARB/03/17, Decision on a Second Proposal for the Disqualification of a Member of the Arbitral Tribunal, 12 May 2008, para. 35. https://jusmundi.com/en/document/decision/en-suez-sociedad-general-de-aguas-de-barcelona-s-a-and-interagua-servicios-integrales-de-agua-s-a-v-argentine-republic-decision-on-a-second-proposal-for-the-disqualification-of-a-member-of-the-arbitral-tribunal-monday-12th-may-2008 (accessed 15 August 2022).
860. *Green Power K/S and Obton A/S v. Spain,* SCC Case No. V 2016/135, available at https://www.italaw.com/cases/9471 (accessed 31 December 2022).

when it became clear that the legal expert would appear at the hearing for cross-examination. However, the arbitrators added that neither party had responded when the *Green Power v. Spain*'s award became public in late June 2022. Considering the attitude to question an expert, the party-appointed arbitrators saw nothing in the president's conduct during the hearing that created an appearance of bias or lack of independence. Consequently, the challenge was dismissed.[861]

3.2.2 Impartiality and Bias

The second problem observed because of the personality of the party-appointed expert is his potential to be impartial, which leads to him being biased or not objective.[862] The main goal of requiring a party-appointed expert to be impartial is to ensure objectivity in the opinion.

The biggest criticism of the party-appointed experts is their lack of impartiality.[863] The impartiality of the arbitrator is an absolute requirement and, as a matter of public policy, cannot be altered by arbitration rules. However, the right to contest the lack of impartiality yields to party autonomy and, therefore, can be waived.[864] In the case of a party-appointed expert, the same level of impartiality cannot be expected.

According to the earlier-referred study, impartiality was also mentioned as a must-have attribute of experts by 'all respondents'.[865] Impartiality refers to a state of mind. Impartiality, in the context of party-appointed experts in international arbitration, means acting without bias in favour of the appointing client.[866] In other words, the party-appointed expert should be objective. Objectivity requires experts to be willing and capable to perform their role according to the truth and report not only favourable matters that help the appointing party but also those adverse to it.[867] The duty of

861. *Orazul International España Holdings S.L. v. Argentine Republic*, ICSID Case No. ARB/19/25, Decision on the Claimant's Proposal to Disqualify Dr. Inka Hanefeld, 11 September 2022, available at https://www.italaw.com/cases/8790 (accessed 15 November 2022).
862. Aygül, *Milletlerarası Ticarî Tahkimde Tahkim Usûlüne Uygulanacak Hukuk ve Deliller*, 270; Van Houtte, 'Party-Appointed Experts and Tribunal-Appointed Experts', 136; Waincymer, *Procedure and Evidence in International Arbitration*, 933; Sachs and Schmidt-Ahrendts, 'Protocol on Expert Teaming: A New Approach to Expert Evidence', 135; Akıncı, 'Milletlerarası Tahkimde Bilirkişi', 78; Balkar, *Milletlerarası Ticari Tahkim ve Etik*, 167; Waincymer, 'Advocacy Training in International Commercial and Investment Arbitration':, 61.
863. Dave, 'Should Experts Be Neutrals or Advocates?', 149; Jones, 'Improving Arbitral Procedure: Perspectives from the Coalface', 94; Sachs and Schmidt-Ahrendts, 'Protocol on Expert Teaming: A New Approach to Expert Evidence', 139; Samaras and Strasser, 'Managing Party-Appointed Experts in International Arbitration--Analysis of the Current Framework and Best Practice Proposals', 314.
864. Angoura, *The Impartiality and Independence of Arbitrators in International Commercial Arbitration*, 185.
865. de Chazournes et al., 'Uses of Experts Before International Courts and Tribunals', 492; *see* for the view that party-appointed experts cannot be impartial in de Chazournes et al., 493.
866. de Chazournes et al., 496; Khodykin and Mulcahy, *A Guide to the IBA Rules on the Taking of Evidence in International Arbitration*, 302; Harry K Woolf, Access to Justice: Final Report to the Lord Chancellor on the Civil Justice System in England and Wales (HMSO, 1996) [13.6].
867. Webster and Bühler, *Handbook of UNCITRAL Arbitration*, 447.

objectivity requires that the expert's fee is not dependent on the outcome of the arbitration.[868]

Kantor stated that parties may prepare their expert to present his arguments in a way that is impartial enough to comply with the impartiality requirements while still supporting the party's case.[869] He believes that rules that address these matters can only address issues related to subconscious bias.[870] However, given the negative consequences, the issue of impartiality cannot be ignored.[871]

The CIArb Protocol Article 4(1) stipulates that '[a]n expert's opinion shall be impartial, objective, unbiased and uninfluenced *by the pressures of the dispute resolution process or by any Party*'. (emphasis added) The IBA Rules do not refer to bias or impartiality as an attribute of the experts or the report.

That the party-appointed expert is naturally not independent does not create problems but dependency that affects impartiality[872] in a way that leads to bias.[873] That is why bias (unobjective) as a concept must be analysed.

Bias can be divided into three categories: Deliberate bias, unconscious bias, and selection bias. In deliberate bias, the party expert deliberately tailors his or her opinion and testimony to support his or her party's case. In more subtle unintentional bias, the expert does not intentionally opine in favour of the appointing party but is nevertheless influenced to opine on favouring points. In case of selection bias, the parties select a party-appointed expert who represents a particular school or method that supports the party's case.[874]

The reality that experts are carefully chosen and paid for by the parties consciously or subconsciously impacts the framing of their view of supporting the party employing them. This does not suggest that experts are directly or purposely biased. However, close engagement may influence them to adopt favourable positions or directions in the light of evidence for the benefit of the appointing party.[875]

Experts are occasionally engaged in an advisory role while counsel structures the claim. It is common knowledge that counsel often collaborate with their experts in fulfilling their task of providing their expert opinion to the tribunal. This leads them to become familiar with the case and counsel of their appointed party, potentially leading to subconscious or unintentional bias.[876] However, the involvement of counsel in the preparation of an opinion may improve its readability and comprehension, as experts

868. Club Español del Arbitraje, Code of Best Practices in Arbitration, 45, paras 134–135.
869. Kantor, 'A Code of Conduct for Party-Appointed Experts in International Arbitration: Can One Be Found?', 335–336.
870. Kantor, 335–336. *Kantor* stated that experts are expected to be partisan to an extent and argued that this partisanship strengthens the adversarial process.
871. Jones, 'Redefining the Role and Value of Expert Evidence', 24.
872. *See Misen v. Ukraine* (ICSID Case No. ARB/21/15), Decision on the Respondent's Proposal to Disqualify Dr Stanimir A. Alexandrov, para. 104.
873. Balkar, *Milletlerarası Ticari Tahkim ve Etik*, 177; Rogers, *Ethics in International Arbitration*, 145.
874. Proske, *Expert Witness Conferencing in Schiedsverfahren*, 22.
875. Jones, 'Redefining the Role and Value of Expert Evidence', 23; Kesikli, 'Milletlerarası Ticari Tahkimde Delillerin Değerlendirilmesi', 214; Akıncı, *Milletlerarası Tahkim*, 340; Schiau, 'An Arbitration Dilemma', 336.
876. Jones, 'Redefining the Role and Value of Expert Evidence', 23.

with no experience before adjudicatory bodies may not always be able to produce clear and understandable reports for non-experts.[877]

Bias can be especially present with full-time experts who are interested in retaining them in future disputes. Bias may also be a particular concern where experts are consistently engaged either by the same counsel or parties on related matters for a particular category of party. A typical example is the constant appointment by a respondent state that received similar claims.[878]

Repeated appointments can be an indicator of bias, especially if the same law firm or party appoints an expert several times.[879] However, if the sought expertise is a niche area in which only a limited pool of experts is available, repeat appointments cannot in themselves be a sign of bias.[880]

An experienced arbitral tribunal is potentially the most important barrier to bias.[881] If there are serious signs recognised by the arbitral tribunal that hint at a partisanship attitude of the party-appointed expert, the tribunal will not credit the expert's opinion and, although it would not exclude his opinion from the record, would deem it de facto inadmissible.[882]

Party-appointed experts are hired and paid by the appointing party. This does not mean that remuneration itself leads to explicit bias. Rather, as *Jones* argued, partiality may exist on a subconscious level.[883] It is, therefore, said to follow that experts naturally feel inclined to use their testimony to 'assist' their appointing party's case.

Although the expert is adduced as evidence by a party that supports its position and pays for it, if the personality does not indicate any signs of partisanship (partiality) and lack of professionalism, and the report is an objectively arguable work that has a scientifically acceptable and reviewable basis, then the party-appointed expert needs to be classified as objective. In other words, if the expert were to be appointed by the counterparty and still would have produced the same exact report, the expert's opinion must be deemed impartial.

It is controversial whether in-house experts can be impartial party-appointed experts. Some views state that in-house (party-appointed) experts are not even technical experts, and seeing them so would be against due process.[884] However,

877. Parlett, 'Parties' Engagement with Experts in International Litigation', 449; Daly and Poon, 'Technical and Legal Experts in International Investment Disputes', 362.
878. Jones, 'Redefining the Role and Value of Expert Evidence', 23.
879. Jones, 'Ineffective Use of Expert Evidence in Construction Arbitration', 3.
880. Jones, 3.
881. 84% of respondents agreed that tribunals are 'generally capable of determining when a party appointed expert is not being objective in their testimony', *see* 'BCLP 2021 Survey', 14.
882. 93% of respondents thought that 'a tribunal should give limited weight to the evidence of a party-appointed expert who breaches his/her duty to remain independent and assist the tribunal'. *See* 'BCLP 2021 Survey', 14; Jones, 'Party Appointed Expert Witnesses in International Arbitration: A Protocol at Last', 137; Samaras and Strasser, 'Managing Party-Appointed Experts in International Arbitration--Analysis of the Current Framework and Best Practice Proposals', 314.
883. *Jones* says that the expert, as a human being, may feel subconsciously indebted to those who are paying their fees and seek repeat business, in Jones, 'Ineffective Use of Expert Evidence in Construction Arbitration', 3.
884. de Chazournes et al., 'Uses of Experts Before International Courts and Tribunals', 493.

various practices appear to allow the use of internal expertise. In *Field v. Leeds City Council,*[885] the English court affirmed that an employee could act as an expert for his employer but warned that there might be circumstances where this would be inappropriate.[886] In *Norbrook Laboratories Ltd v. Tank*, the court ruled as follows:

> The arbitrator was entitled to permit an employee to give expert evidence, provided that he took into account the fact that diminished objectively could reduce the weight properly to be attached to that evidence. Indeed, if he took the view that lack of objectivity was such that no weight should be attached to it, the evidence should not be admitted. No doubt the issue of objectivity could be tested in the course of the hearing. For these reasons I do not consider that the arbitrator can be criticized or bias inferred from his permitting Moulson to rely on Mr Pontefract's evidence simply because he was an employee. It may well be that further investigation of his evidence, possibly in cross-examination, would disclose a lack of objectivity so great as to justify the arbitrator in wholly discounting the witness's technical opinions.[887]

However, one must bear in mind that the arbitrator must strictly evaluate and examine the expert if he is an employee of the appointing party. As demonstrated in *Re Continental Assurance Company*, if the employee is partisan (biased), he should not act as an expert.[888]

Repeat appointments of the same experts, unless they are a very niche subject matter, could be an indication of bias. For instance, when global law firms seek to appoint the same expert regularly, this could be perceived as a potential bias and must be carefully analysed.[889] It can also be argued that a lack of diversity currently exists in the appointment of experts, which could also lead to repeat appointments.[890]

According to some German scholars who handle matters realistically, there is no necessity for the expert to be impartial. On the contrary, the expert will accept orders, will be remunerated and can only present favourable opinions in relation to the appointing party.[891]

Contrary to the tribunal-appointed expert, who has a strict duty of objectivity[892] regardless of the parties' positions, the party-appointed expert, although expected to be objective, does not have the same duty of objectivity in terms of such as the former one. This does not, however, entail the party-appointed expert being a mere advocate for the party.[893] The party-appointed expert is expected to provide a scientific or provable objective opinion.

885. *England and Wales High Court, Field & Anor v. Leeds City Council*, Casemine.
886. Similar views were expressed by Schäfer and Wilson, 'ICC Bulletin', 2021, 65.
887. 'Norbrook Laboratories Ltd v Tank', 665; Bor, 'Expert Evidence', 515–516.
888. England and Wales High Court, Re Continental Assurance Company, Casemine. in Bor, 'Expert Evidence', 511–512.
889. Jones, 'Redefining the Role and Value of Expert Evidence', 23; Jones, 'Ineffective Use of Expert Evidence in Construction Arbitration', 3.
890. Jones, 'Redefining the Role and Value of Expert Evidence', 23.
891. Wach and Petsch, 'Der Sachverständigenbeweis Im Schiedsverfahren: Grenzen Der Gestaltungsfreiheit von Parteien Und Schiedsgericht', 95.
892. Wach and Petsch, 97.
893. Kamya-Lukoda, 'Role of Expert Witnesses in Construction Arbitration: Delay and Disruption and Quantum Issues', 79.

As *Senogles* expresses, when experts are examined, the lack of objectivity is derived because some experts are dogmatic in their opinions, 'unwilling to concede a point made, even in the face of overwhelming logic or contradictory evidence presented. Such attitudes and demeanour, I suggest, are typically easily identified by experienced, vigilant and intelligent tribunal members'.[894]

3.3 PROBLEMS RELATED TO THE USAGE STYLE OF PARTY-APPOINTED EXPERTS

Despite seeing some rules or guidelines for party-appointed experts, it is fair to say that this subject matter is largely unregulated. A code of conduct for professionals acting as party-appointed experts in international arbitration is not present. This leads every arbitral proceeding to be 'another story', and the tribunal is left to deal with the situation without further guidance. Furthermore, the sequential testimony of experts during the hearings and overreliance on experts, as if the case could only be one with a convincing expert opinion, multiplies the problems.

3.3.1 Unregulated Use of Party-Appointed Experts

There are no clear rules in practice besides the soft law elements referred to above. This leads mostly to an unregulated and hence unorganised use of party-appointed experts. Specifically, there are no rules on whom to appoint, how to appoint, or when to appoint. Most institutional rules contain only general provisions for taking evidence or establishing facts, leaving the details to be determined by the tribunal and sometimes the parties.

This generally results in a random flow that creates multiple issues. Appointing experts without being necessary at all or without the direction of the tribunal incurs unnecessary arbitration costs and delays in proceedings. For instance, if no clear rules exist on the engagement of experts, the party may not appoint an expert where it is required or an unrelated or unqualified expert. Additionally, without clear time limits, a party that has not considered engaging an expert may suddenly try to submit an opinion at a later phase in the proceedings, which delays the proceedings.

As the memorial style for written party submissions is generally practised in international arbitration, expert opinions are generally submitted with statements, which prevents them from having a common understanding of how to form opinions and almost inevitably leads to conflicting experts.[895] Having 'conflicting experts' is not the real problem, but the way the experts present diverse opinions creates these issues. The experts will likely have produced opposing opinions relying on different facts, data, and methodologies during the formation. In the end, the arbitral tribunal, which is already not familiar with the matter and requires clear guidance, will not be assisted.

894. Senogles, 'Some Views from the Crucible: The Perspective of an Expert Witness on the Adversarial Principle', 363.
895. Jones, 'Redefining the Role and Value of Expert Evidence', 34.

In addition, the absence of rules for assessing expert opinions can be problematic, at least for inexperienced arbitrators. These challenges lead to prolonged proceedings, increased costs and reduced expert opinion values.[896]

3.3.2 Lack of Code of Conduct and Double-Hatting

Although some arbitral rules and the IBA Guidelines on Conflicts of Interest in International Arbitration regulate the code of conduct for arbitrators,[897] no widely accepted code of conduct in international arbitration that refers to party-appointed experts exists.[898] The Chartered Institute of Arbitrators (CIArb) Protocol appears to be the only soft law element that comprehensively touches on the use of party-appointed experts in international arbitration.[899]

The lack of a code of conduct has led to the same persons acting in various roles in international arbitration, the so-called *double hatting*. Double hatting is an activity describing the situation where actors, such as arbitrators, party counsel, and experts in investor-state dispute resolution proceedings, play various roles in different proceedings with different roles in each proceeding, such as being arbitrators in one proceeding and an expert in another.[900] The challenge of the credibility of quantum experts tends to be the focus of the concerns expressed about such experts.[901]

Double hatting has been criticised for a long period, and the Working Group III of the United Nations Commission on International Trade Law (UNCITRAL) has recently completed the draft code of conduct for arbitrators in international investment dispute resolution, aiming to prevent this phenomenon.[902] The 'Code of Conduct for Arbitrators in International Investment Dispute Resolution and Code of Conduct for Judges in International Investment Dispute Resolution with respective commentary of the United Nations Commission on International Trade Law' was adopted on 7 December 2023 by the General Assembly Resolution in the 45th plenary meeting.[903]

The draft code of conduct for arbitrators aims, among other issues, to reinforce the duty of independence and impartiality and to regulate the practice of arbitrators acting as experts in international investment disputes.

The code of conduct foresees that, as a principle, an arbitrator shall not act concurrently within a period of specified time of years following the conclusion of an

896. Jones, 'Party Appointed Expert Witnesses in International Arbitration: A Protocol at Last', 137; Samaras and Strasser, 'Managing Party-Appointed Experts in International Arbitration--Analysis of the Current Framework and Best Practice Proposals', 314.
897. Balkar, *Milletlerarası Ticari Tahkim ve Etik*, 37.
898. Kantor, 'A Code of Conduct for Party-Appointed Experts in International Arbitration - Can One Be Found?', 323; Balkar, *Milletlerarası Ticari Tahkim ve Etik*, 168.
899. The CIArb Protocol Art. 4(1) foresees that the 'expert's opinion shall be impartial, objective, unbiased and uninfluenced'.
900. *See* Langford, Behn, and Lie, 'The Revolving Door in International Investment Arbitration'; Ünüvar, 'Experts: Investment Arbitration'.
901. Hodgson and Stewart, 'Experts in Investor-State Arbitration: The Tribunal as Gatekeeper', 456.
902. https://unis.unvienna.org/unis/en/pressrels/2023/unisl343.html (accessed 6 May 2023).
903. https://uncitral.un.org/sites/uncitral.un.org/files/media-documents/uncitral/en/2318944_coc_arbitrators_e-book_eng.pdf (accessed 14 February 2024).

international investment dispute as an expert in another international investment dispute involving: (a) the same measures; (b) the same or related parties; or (c) the same provisions of the same treaty.

Double hatting has already been forbidden in the United States-Mexico-Canada Agreement (USMCA) Article 14.D.6(5)(c), such that the arbitrator shall not, for the duration of the proceedings, act as a party-appointed expert in any pending arbitration under USMCA.[904] Additionally, EU-Mexico Modernised Global Agreement Section [X] 'Resolution of Investment Disputes' Article 13(1) foresees that arbitrators, upon appointment, shall refrain from acting as party-appointed expert in any pending or new investment protection dispute under the EU-Mexico Trade Agreement or any other agreement or domestic law.[905]

3.3.3 Sequential Use of Party-Appointed Experts

Parties generally submit expert opinions with their statements. In such a scenario, experts will not have discussed the dispute and how they could engage in the matter. Thus, they base their opinion on different facts, deal with divergent issues, and apply dissimilar methods. This adds to the problem that expert reports do not correspond to each other. In the end, the tribunal will not be in a position to derive conclusions from the reports.[906]

3.3.4 Over-Reliance

Some of the party-appointed experts used in international arbitration may be unnecessary efforts by the parties to bolster their case. The underlying belief is that the number of experts enhances the strength of the case.[907] Alternatively, where either a claimant or respondent did not consider adducing an expert opinion since the case does not explicitly require a technical or expertise-required matter, in order 'not to look weak', the other party also generally submits an expert opinion.[908]

Arbitrators, having 'due process paranoia' in mind, permit lengthy expert testimony, which causes high costs and reduces efficiency in the arbitral process.[909]

904. United States-Mexico-Canada Agreement, entered into force on 1 July, https://ustr.gov/sites/default/files/files/agreements/FTA/USMCA/Text/14-Investment.pdf (accessed 5 May 2023); Ünüvar, 'Experts: Investment Arbitration', para. 37.
905. EU-Mexico Modernised Global Agreement (not in force yet) https://circabc.europa.eu/ui/group/09242a36-a438-40fd-a7af-fe32e36cbd0e/library/9f9e6630-7c43-49df-8a5f-653a23839b94/details (accessed 25 October 2025).
906. Sachs and Schmidt-Ahrendts, 'Protocol on Expert Teaming: A New Approach to Expert Evidence', 139; Proske, *Expert Witness Conferencing in Schiedsverfahren*, 31–32.
907. Jones, 'Ineffective Use of Expert Evidence in Construction Arbitration', 5; Jones, 'Redefining the Role and Value of Expert Evidence', 25.
908. Jones, 'Ineffective Use of Expert Evidence in Construction Arbitration', 5; This problem also arises before Turkish state courts, *see* Atalay, 'Pekcanıtez Usûl', 2021, 1959–1960.
909. Jones, 'Ineffective Use of Expert Evidence in Construction Arbitration', 5; Jones, 'Redefining the Role and Value of Expert Evidence', 25.

Thus, the underlying matter is the determination of whether, how, and when expert assistance is required. For example, if the weather at a particular airport on a particular day is an important element in the factual matrix, it is sufficient to produce a copy of a contemporary report from a newspaper or a weather forecast website rather than to adduce a meteorological expert to provide an opinion.[910]

3.4 PROBLEMS AFFECTING ARBITRAL AWARDS

Undoubtedly, experts will execute important duties during proceedings. Although experts' conclusions are not directly binding upon tribunals, their usage style and opinion may influence the arbitral award's validity and enforcement.[911]

In this section, the problems presented above that impact arbitral awards, either in ICSID annulment proceedings, set-aside[912] proceedings at state courts, or recognition and enforcement proceedings at state courts, will be analysed.

When these decisions are critically evaluated, it becomes obvious that the reasons affecting the validity and enforcement of arbitral awards can be categorised as follows: Refusal to allow parties to adduce or consider the expert opinion, lack of improper notice or inadequate opportunity to comment on expert opinion, delegation of decision-making, challenge based on lack of independence of the expert and quality of evidence, not evaluating conflicting expert opinions and contradicting parties' agreement.

3.4.1 Refusal to Allow Parties to Adduce or Consider Expert Opinions

As illustrated above, the right to be heard and party autonomy grant the parties the right to submit expert evidence and ask the tribunal to consider it.[913] However, rights are not absolute and are not without limits.[914]

As a general principle, no tribunal should refuse to accept expert opinion, which is essential to the dispute.[915] Nevertheless, can an award be set-aside on the grounds of irregularity in the procedure, or can the right to be heard by the parties not be adhered to if a party has been refused to adduce expert opinion or the adduced expert opinion was not considered?

This is up to the applicable arbitration law and the approach adopted by courts to apply a strict or loose threshold for the violation of the fundamental principles of the arbitration procedure. However, some general conclusions can be drawn when various jurisdictions are analysed.

910. Blackaby et al., *Redfern & Hunter on International Arbitration*, para. 6.86.
911. Uluç, *Corruption in International Arbitration*, 163-164.
912. Also referred to in various jurisdictions as *annulment* or *vacatur*.
913. *See* Chapter 2 section 2.3.
914. Khodykin and Mulcahy, *A Guide to the IBA Rules on the Taking of Evidence in International Arbitration*, 289.
915. Rosenfeld, 'Country Report: Germany', 183.

If a tribunal refuses to allow a party to adduce expert opinion to be examined at the hearing, this may amount to a violation of the right to present their case.[916] The limit of the tribunal's discretion is exceeded where it abuses its adjudicatory power by intentionally disregarding the opinion.

One can conclude that the party-appointed expert has been considered if it is seen in the award that the tribunal has evaluated the opinion of the expert in depth.[917]

A reviewing court, whether for annulment or recognition and enforcement proceedings, shall not overturn an award because an arbitral tribunal merely incorrectly credited the expert's opinion (e.g., accepting one party's expert's views over the other), since this would be a matter of materiality of the case and harm the principle of *revision au fond*.[918]

Violation of the right to be heard may serve as grounds to annul an award (Article 34(2)(a)(ii) UNCITRAL Model Law)[919] or occasion for non-recognition or non-enforcement of a foreign or non-domestic award (Article V(1)(b) NYC).[920]

In an ICC arbitration[921] where the IBA Rules were applicable, the Claimant submitted an expert report, which the respondent could not evaluate. However, the arbitral tribunal did so. The award was set-aside by the Turkish Court of Appeal[922] as follows:

> by concealing the relevant assumptions and data being the basis for the financial model of the March 2010 report and also the drafters and the purpose thereof, from the respondent, and by depriving the respondent from the opportunity to cross-examine the experts who drafted the report, the arbitral tribunal acted in violation of IBA Rules ... Finally, it should be emphasized that, by prohibiting the respondent from viewing the March 2010 report, by concealing from the respondent the drafter and purpose thereof, by hiding the financial models based on the preparation thereof from both the respondent and the respondent's valuation expert, the arbitral tribunal not only violated the principles of fair trial such as the equality of the parties and the right to be heard, and not only damaged the principle of impartiality of the arbitrators, but also deprived the respondent of the opportunity to present his case. Pursuant to Article V(1)(b) of the New York Convention, any request for enforcement of an award has to be rejected if the party against whom the award is invoked was not given proper notice of the appointment of the arbitrator or of the arbitration proceedings or was otherwise unable to present his case.[923]

916. Patocchi, Paolo Michele and Niedermaier, 'UNCITRAL Rules', 1187; Sanders, 'Commentary On UNCITRAL Arbitration Rules', 204; Tanrıver, *Medenî Usûl Hukuku*, 2022, II:429.
917. Akil, 'Bilirkişi-Uzman Tanık Ayrımı', 176.
918. O'Malley, *Rules of Evidence in International Arbitration*, 205–206; Patocchi, Paolo Michele and Niedermaier, 'UNCITRAL Rules', 1182.
919. Born, *International Commercial Arbitration*, 3564; Lew, Mistelis, and Kröll, *Comparative International Commercial Arbitration*, 287.
920. Born, *International Commercial Arbitration*, 3863, 3936; Angoura, *The Impartiality and Independence of Arbitrators in International Commercial Arbitration*, 169.
921. ICC Case No. 17586/FM/MHM/EMT available at Lexpera (accessed 25 December 2023).
922. Turkish Court of Appeal, 11. Civil Chamber, Docket No. 2019/2417, Decision No. 2021/1051, 10 February 2021 (Lexpera, accessed 25 December 2023).
923. Esen, 'Violation of the Right to a Fair Trial in Arbitration', 114–116.

The right to be heard requires an arbitral tribunal to obtain an expert opinion if it has to decide on an issue for which technical knowledge is required, which the tribunal does not have.

Accordingly, the Swiss Federal Supreme Court held that if an arbitral tribunal refrains from obtaining such an expert opinion without having the required knowledge, it violates the right to be heard.[924]

However, in a more recent decision, the Swiss Federal Supreme Court stated that, as arbitration proceedings are governed by the principle that it is primarily the task of the parties to present their case (*Verhandlungsmaxime*) and not the arbitral tribunal's task, the arbitral tribunal does not need to remedy failures of the parties and obtain an expert opinion not requested by the parties.[925]

In addition to the submission of expert opinion, the right to be heard requires that the parties have a reasonable opportunity to comment on the presented opinion in the arbitral proceedings.[926]

In a case before the Singapore Court of Appeal, a party claimed that his right to be heard was violated during the arbitration proceedings for reasons such as not granting him the right to extend the time to submit an expert opinion and not accepting the additional expert opinion submitted. In this case, where the allegation of violation was misused, the Singapore Court found that a party's right to be heard is not unlimited and that this right is implicitly limited to fairness and reasonableness.[927]

The Higher Regional Court of Munich had to decide whether a tribunal breached a party's right to be heard by failing to appoint its own expert when the two party-appointed experts reached divergent opinions. The court left it open to determine whether the assessment of evidence by a tribunal that lacks the relevant expertise is tantamount to ignoring the relevant submissions and, for this reason, amounts to a breach of the right to be heard. In any event, the tribunal examined the expert opinions and assessed them with reference to extrinsic considerations that were not arbitrary. The court could rightfully not review whether or not the assessment was correct, as this would have been contrary to the prohibition of a review of the merits.[928]

In another decision by the Higher Regional Court of Hamburg, the court confirmed that a tribunal does not breach the parties' right to be heard if it, by and large, follows an expert's determinations.[929] The right to be heard is also not necessarily violated

924. Arroyo, 'Commentary on Chapter 12 PILS, Article 190 [Finality, Challenge: Principle]', 314; Swiss Federal Supreme Court, 4A_2/2007, Bundesgericht, para. 3.1.
925. Swiss Federal Supreme Court, 4A_597/2013, Bundesgericht, para. 3.2.2.
926. Berger and Kellerhals, *International and Domestic Arbitration in Switzerland*, 414 ff.; Hohler, 'Country Report: Switzerland', 393.
927. *China Machine New Energy Corporation v. Jaguar Energy Guatemala LLC* and *AEI Guatemala Jaguar Ltd* [2020] SGCA 12, 28 February 2020 (https://www.supremecourt.gov.sg/docs/default-source/module-document/judgement/-2020-sgca-12-pdf.pdf (accessed 24 September 2025)), para. 97 in Demirkol, 'Karşılaştırmalı Hukukta Hakem Kararlarının Tenfizinde Hukukî Dinlenilme Hakkı', 197.
928. OLG München, 34 Sch 10/11, 2012, 119383 openJur.
929. OLG Hamburg, 6 Sch 1/16, Rechtstipp24.

where a tribunal uses its own knowledge and dismisses evidentiary offers because it considers the relevant facts to be sufficiently clarified.[930]

Similarly, courts have found that a tribunal does not breach the parties' right to be heard by conducting independent research on the Internet. Where an arbitral tribunal has undertaken such independent research, it should have provided the parties with sufficient opportunity to comment on the result of the findings.[931]

As mentioned above, in *Field v. Leeds City Council*[932] and *Norbrook Laboratories Ltd v. Tank*, English courts have affirmed that an employee can act as an expert for his employer.[933]

Before the TIAL was enacted, the Turkish Court of Appeal considered that not appointing a tribunal-appointed expert when there are technical issues beyond the arbitral tribunal's capacity is grounds for set-aside.[934]

In an older decision by the Turkish Court of Appeal, the award of the arbitral tribunal was set-aside on the grounds that an expert report had not been obtained.[935] During the arbitral proceedings, the tribunal asked the parties whether they would appoint an expert and received a negative response.[936] This approach by the Turkish Court of Appeal was not right, as party autonomy and the knowledge of the arbitral tribunal would enable it to decide without the appointment of experts.[937]

The recent approach by the Turkish Court of Appeal is that not appointing an expert cannot lead directly to annulment.[938] In a case, the Regional Court stated that the matters that restrict or remove the right to defence might be against public policy in accordance with the procedural law and annulled the arbitral award based on the grounds, among others, that the arbitral tribunal did not appoint an expert.

The Regional Court reasoned that under the Turkish International Arbitration Law, the arbitral tribunal had the power to appoint an expert, and according to the applicable arbitration (ITOTAM) rules, the arbitral tribunal had the obligation to safeguard the parties' right to be heard. The court concluded that since the arbitral tribunal did not appoint an expert while there were contradictory expert reports, there was a procedural deficiency affecting the merits of the case, which was directly connected to the right to a fair trial and the right to be heard. It was also connected to public policy and is a ground for annulment.

Upon appeal, the Court of Appeal stated that whether or not obtaining an expert report is a procedural matter not related to public policy, which the law does not list among the grounds for annulment. Hence, it concluded that the contrary contradicts

930. OLG Köln, 19 Sch 6/17, 2018, 7064 openJur.
931. OLG München, 34 Sch 18/06, DISArb.
932. *England and Wales High Court, Field & Anor v. Leeds City Council*, Casemine.
933. 'Norbrook Laboratories Ltd v Tank', 665; Bor, 'Expert Evidence', 515–516.
934. Akıncı, *Milletlerarası Tahkim*, 339; Ağırman, *Milli & Milletlerarası Tahkim*, 461.
935. Turkish Court of Appeal 15th Civil Chamber, Docket No. 1995/4114, Decision No. 1995/4916, 22 September 1995 in Dayınlarlı, *HUMK'da Düzenlenen İhtiyari İç Tahkim*, 79–81.
936. Turkish Court of Appeal 15th Civil Chamber, Docket No. 1995/4114, Decision No. 1995/4916, 22 September 1995 in Dayınlarlı, 79–81.
937. Dayınlarlı, 79–81.
938. Turkish Court of Appeal, 15th Civil Chamber, Docket No. 2019/2474, Decision No. 2019/3640, 26 September 2019 (Yargıtay Karar Arama).

the legislator's general objective and violates the numerous clauses principle under Article 15 of the TIAL. Thus, the court overturned the Regional Court's set-aside decision.

In Switzerland, the Swiss Federal Supreme Court decided that the requesting party must be willing to advance the costs of the expert, it must relate to the relevant facts of the case, the expert opinion must be suitable to have an effect on the outcome of the proceedings, and it must appear necessary. Additionally, the party must expressly request the appointment of an expert on time and in line with the procedural rules of the arbitration. Thus, the court recalled the principles governing a party's (limited) right to request the appointment of an expert by the arbitral tribunal and the circumstances in which the arbitral tribunal could refuse to appoint an expert. Thus, a mere refusal to appoint an expert cannot be a set-aside ground.[939]

In a case before a German court, the respondent objected that the arbitral tribunal did not possess the required knowledge of Italian patent law and, therefore, had violated its duty to call for a tribunal-appointed expert. The court held that the arbitral tribunal's refusal to appoint an expert did not violate the applicant's right to be heard.[940]

Based on this assessment of the facts and the state of the dispute on the basis of the submissions of both parties, the arbitral tribunal came to the conclusion that, in the absence of other available documents, a tribunal-appointed expert would not provide any further reliable findings with regard to the future prognosis to be made. In view of this, the well-founded rejection of the respondent's request for an additional expert opinion cannot be considered an arbitrary exceeding of the arbitral tribunal's authority and, consequently, not a violation of the principle of the right to be heard.

The Higher Regional Court of Köln also confirmed that it was not arbitrary for the tribunal to change its view not to appoint an expert. The arbitral tribunal initially intended to appoint an expert as referred to in its former procedural order, and subsequently, the parties were informed of the change in the (preliminary) assessment (in a later procedural order). The Court ruled that the parties had the opportunity to comment on the matter and raise any objections. The arbitral tribunal was not prevented from changing its initial view.[941]

In a case before the High Court of Delhi, the court decided that it was not an obligation of the arbitral tribunal to call for expert evidence, particularly in cases where the arbitrators themselves were experts in the field.[942]

When appointing a tribunal expert, it is advisable that the role and scope of the expert's duty in arbitral proceedings are clearly defined. In a Singapore case, a party sought to set aside an arbitral award on the grounds that the expert's involvement in the case went beyond what had been agreed upon. The applicant submitted that the

939. Swiss Federal Supreme Court, 4A_277/2017, Bundesgericht, paras 3.2 ff.; *see* Göksu, 'Schiedsgerichtsbarkeit: Anspruch Auf Einholung Eines Gutachtens (BGE 4A_277/2017)'; *see also* Schneider, 'Technical Experts in International Arbitration', 446.
940. BayObLG, 4Z Sch 23/99, CLOUT case 375 UNCITRAL.
941. OLG Köln, 19 Sch 6/17, 2018, 7064 openJur, para. 60.
942. *High Court of Delhi, National Thermal Power Corporation Ltd. v. Wig Brothers Builders and Engineers Ltd.*, paras 55–56, 60.

expert performed tasks that should have been performed by the arbitral tribunal. The court refused this argument and held that 'unless there was strong and clear evidence of irregularity in the manner in which the arbitration was conducted, the integrity of the tribunal should not be questioned'.[943]

The Court of Appeal in New Zealand rejected a challenge to an award based on an alleged violation of the right to be heard. In that case, the party argued that the arbitrator relied solely on his own expertise in rendering the award, as he determined a price for the delivery of natural gas based on a model he had prepared without discussing it with the parties. The Court held that the model prepared by the arbitrator was not an 'expert report' which had to be communicated to the parties. As the arbitrator had been chosen for his expert knowledge and the arbitration agreement expressly provided for the use of such knowledge, the court considered that the refusal to discuss the model with the parties did not constitute a violation of the rules of natural justice.[944]

A Jordan court rendered a similar decision, stating that arbitrators may rely on their personal knowledge and not on expert opinions to assess damages without the threat of having the award set-aside.[945]

A Hong Kong Court decided that if the arbitrators are not experts themselves, they are obliged to appoint an expert and canvassed with the parties the particular provision in the PRC law on the topic and gave them an opportunity to respond:

> [I]n the process of fact finding, arbitrators must have autonomy in drawing inferences as they deem fit and in that respect they are entitled to depart from the positions advanced by the parties. However, on primary factual disputes, they have to act on evidence and give reasonable opportunity to the parties to put forward their respective case on such evidence ... given that we are dealing with an arbitration in Hong Kong, the requirement of contractual validity under PRC law has to be decided on the [expert] evidence before the Tribunal ... the arbitrators were not appointed on account of their expertise in PRC law and the Respondents had no reason to expect the Tribunal to adopt a view on PRC law which had not been canvassed in the course of the arbitration. In such circumstances, *the Tribunal should have canvassed with the parties the particular provision in the PRC law on the topic and gave them an opportunity to respond* before making a decision on the same. The failure of the Tribunal in this regard furnished the Respondents a valid ground of complaint under Article 34(2)(a)(ii).[946] (emphasis added)

In another case before the Hong Kong courts, the court similarly declared that an expert arbitrator could rely on his/her own expert knowledge. However, an 'expert arbitrator should not, in effect, give evidence to himself without disclosing the evidence on which he relies to the parties. But a distinction is made in the cases

943. *Singapore High Court, Luzon Hydro Corp. v. Transfield Philippines Inc.*
944. *New Zealand Court of Appeal, Methanex Motunui Ltd. v. Spellman*, [2004] 3 NZLR 454.
945. UNCITRAL, *UNCITRAL Digest*, 149, fn. 736.
946. *Hong Kong, Brunswick Bowling & Billiards Corporation v. Shanghai Zhonglu Industrial Co. Ltd. and Chen Rong*, paras 26–28.

between general expert knowledge and knowledge of special facts relevant to the particular case'.[947]

In a case before the English High Court, the respondent challenged the award based on not being able to adduce expert evidence due to the tribunal's refusal,[948] where an issue in the case had been the quality of the sold aluminium. The tribunal comprised arbitrators who had extensive knowledge of primary aluminium trading but were not experienced in the trading of secondary aluminium, which the appellant considered material. The English High Court found that the refusal to allow the respondent to adduce expert evidence had been made after careful consideration and did not give rise to a substantial injustice, thus upholding the award.[949]

In the case *JD Wetherspoon v. Jay Mar Estates*, the English High Court set out that an arbitral tribunal can rely on its own expertise; however, it stressed that the arbitrators could not use their expertise to introduce new evidence.[950] In another decision by the Court, unless the parties have agreed otherwise, a tribunal should not feel compelled to appoint an expert where the circumstances do not require it.[951]

Even if the applicable rules of procedural law (arbitration agreement of the parties, arbitration rules, procedural rules issued by the arbitral tribunal) contain a mandatory rule, expert reports should be removed from the record if the party-appointed expert does not appear for testimony. If the arbitral tribunal were not to take the expert report of such a party-appointed expert into consideration, even though it is relevant, this might amount to a violation of the right to be heard, potentially leading to the annulment of the arbitral award.[952]

In *Egmatra AG v. Marco Trading Corporation*, the losing party sought to set-aside the award on the basis that the tribunal had rejected an invitation by that party to permit the introduction of expert opinion to assist the arbitral tribunal. The tribunal declined that request on the basis that it had the necessary expertise. The applicable rules in the arbitration expressly permit the tribunal to allow, refuse or limit the appearance of experts. The Court found that there was no serious irregularity, and the challenge to the award was rejected.[953]

The scenario in which an arbitral tribunal does not sufficiently consider an expert opinion is not considered a ground for refusal. A review of the arbitral tribunal's decision with regard to the question of whether the expert's opinion had been

947. *Fox v. Wellfair Ltd* [1981] 2 Lloyds Representative 514, referred in Hong Kong, para. 23.
948. Bor, 'Expert Evidence', 517; *Queen's Bench Division (Commercial Court), Egmatra AG v. Marco Trading Corporation.*
949. *Queen's Bench Division (Commercial Court), Egmatra AG v. Marco Trading Corporation.*
950. *England and Wales High Court, JD Wetherspoon Plc v. Jay Mar Estates.*
951. *Amego Litho Ltd v. Scanway Ltd* [1994] 1 EGLR 15 reported in Chapter 25: Annulment of International Arbitral Awards (Updated January 2023), in Born, *International Commercial Arbitration* (3rd ed.), fn. 577.
952. Zuberbühler et al., *IBA Rules of Evidence*, 148; In contrast, the violation of any rules or procedural laws mandating removal from the record is not viewed in the case law of the Swiss Federal Supreme Court as a sufficient basis for successfully challenging an arbitral award.
953. *Queen's Bench Division (Commercial Court), Egmatra AG v. Marco Trading Corporation.*

'sufficiently' taken into account would have led to a *révision au fond* and was thus denied by the court.[954]

The problem here is not that the tribunal does not take expert opinion into account but the arbitrary nature of not evaluating it and not giving it consideration.[955] However, if the expert opinion is not material for the resolution of the dispute, an arbitral tribunal may disregard it, and this itself cannot be a violation of the right to be heard.[956]

3.4.2 Lack of Improper Notice or Inadequate Opportunity to Comment on Expert Opinion

It is part of the right to be heard that the parties have an opportunity to comment on the expert opinion.[957] In addition, if the tribunal relies on its own expertise, the parties should be given the opportunity to comment on and object to these views. If the party was not allowed to comment on the expert opinion, this could be grounds for a set-aside or refusal of recognition and enforcement of the arbitral award.[958]

A Hong Kong court set-aside an award on the basis that a party was not given any chance to deal with the tribunal-appointed expert reports relied upon by the arbitral tribunal, which, in effect, prevented the party from presenting its case.[959]

In an ICC arbitration case, the arbitrators appointed an expert to assist the tribunal with technical matters. The tribunal awarded an award. However, no written report of the expert was submitted to the parties for comment. The set-aside application was dismissed on the basis that, among others, the parties would have received a written report if it were made.[960]

3.4.3 Delegation of Decision-Making Skills

As elaborated earlier, decision-making is a power and duty that lies with the arbitral tribunal. It is vital that this power and duty stay with the arbitrators. Especially in international investment arbitration, legal experts are widely employed. Because of this phenomenon, some tribunals may consciously or unconsciously tend to directly adopt the legal position, particularly if a tribunal-appointed expert is present.[961] This is deductible if a legal expert's opinion is heavily embedded in the award.

954. Borris et al., 'New York Convention, Article V [Grounds for Refusal of Recognition and Enforcement of Arbitral Awards]', para. 340.
955. Güvenalp, *Milletlerarası Tahkimde İddia ve Savunma Hakkının İhlali*, 91.
956. Güvenalp, 92.
957. Pekcanıtez, 'Hukuki Dinlenilme Hakkı', 758; Borris et al., 'New York Convention, Article V [Grounds for Refusal of Recognition and Enforcement of Arbitral Awards]', para. 177.
958. Pekcanıtez, 'Hukuki Dinlenilme Hakkı', 767.
959. *Hong Kong, Paklito Investment Limited v. Klockner East Asia Limited*, [1993] 2 HKLR 39, para. 58.
960. *Luzon Hydro Corp v. Transfield Philippines Inc* [2004] 4 SLR 705, https://www.elitigation.sg/gdviewer/s/2004_SGHC_204 (accessed 24 September 2025) in Boo, 'Arbitration', 61.
961. Lew, 'The Need for Expert Evidence?', 253.

In such situations, the parties may challenge the award based on the delegation of the decision-making authority, which is inherent to the arbitral tribunal. Additionally, if it is obvious that the tribunal copy-pasted the expert report into the award, a serious doubt regarding the delegation of authority can be deduced.[962]

Therefore, the recognition and enforcement of an award can be refused if the arbitral tribunal delegates its power to render a decision to an expert.[963]

However, this was decided in the *Price v. Carter* case, if the tribunal has reviewed and evaluated the expert's opinion and nevertheless arrived at the exact conclusion in its award, the argument of delegation cannot succeed.[964]

In an arbitration case, the tribunal appointed an expert to help determine the applicable law without consulting the parties or inviting the parties to a meeting with the expert, which resulted in a challenge to the award. The English High Court held that this behaviour did not amount to an 'irregularity' under the English Arbitration Act and, thus, did not constitute a basis for setting the award aside.[965]

3.4.4 Challenge Based on Lack of Independence/Impartiality of Experts and Non-disclosure

As elaborated, there is generally no requirement under various statutory provisions for party-appointed experts to be independent.[966] However, this does not mean that the opinion can be accepted without recourse to other qualifications, such as impartiality.

As seen in *Brandeis (Brokers) Ltd v. Black and others,*[967] the existence of a party-appointed expert who allegedly was not qualified to give opinion and the tribunal not disqualifying the expert cannot lead in itself to annulment.[968] Given that the tribunal has the discretion not to rely on it, giving its reasons, this procedural issue should not be regarded as a serious irregularity.

In a case before the US courts, the court denied that a mere lack of disclosure between the business or other relationship between the (respondent) party and the party-appointed expert could be a set-aside (vacatur) reason.[969]

The German Federal Court of Justice also decided (in *I ZB 46/18*) that a tribunal-appointed expert can only be challenged if the violation of its duty of disclosure raises

962. Mavrantonakis, *Das Verbot Der Révision Au Fond Im Internationalen Handelsschiedsverfahren: Zur Bindung Des Staatlichen Gerichts an Die Schiedsgerichtlichen Sachverhaltsfeststellungen Und Zu Den Erforderlichen Ausnahmen*, 113; Aktepe Artık, *Medeni Usûl Hukukunda Hakem Kararlarının İptali Sebepleri*, 380–381.
963. Borris et al., 'New York Convention, Article V [Grounds for Refusal of Recognition and Enforcement of Arbitral Awards]', para. 340.
964. *England and Wales High Court, Price & Anor v. Carter* (T/A Ian Carter Building Contractors).
965. *England and Wales High Court, Hussman (Europe) Ltd. v. Al Ameen Dev. & Trade Co. in Bor*, 'Expert Evidence', 522.
966. *See* Chapter 2 section 2.1.4 and section 2.4.1.
967. *Brandeis (Brokers) Ltd v. Black and Ors*, 2001 Arbitration Law Reports and Review.
968. Bor, 'Expert Evidence', 519.
969. *U.S. District Court, Southern District of California, Trevino Hernandez, S. de R.L. de C.V. v. Smart & Final Inc.* at 13.

doubts about his impartiality.[970] Therefore, mere non-disclosure cannot lead to the set-aside of an arbitral award.

3.4.5 Not Evaluating Conflicting Expert Opinions

Experts are being criticised for becoming hired guns or battlers; in addition to counsel who might be expected to some degree to 'battle', they merely argue in favour of the appointing party.[971] Experts are supposed to be presenting something objective in order to assist the arbitrators.

However, arbitrators are generally left to analyse competing and conflicting expert reports.[972] This can sometimes prove to be a very difficult task, even to the extent that the experts are no longer facilitating the proceedings but are making it more complex and burdensome.[973]

It is natural for experts with different backgrounds and experiences to have conflicting opinions and opposing conclusions on complex matters.[974] The problem arises where differences in opinion are due to variations in factual assumptions or experts assuming a partisan position.

As is the case in *Phillip Morris v. Uruguay or Compañía de Aguas del Aconquija S.A.* and *Vivendi Universal S.A. v. Argentine Republic,*[975] there is always the possibility of the involvement of multiple experts from each party who have a difference in opinion. It is also possible that, in addition to conflicting experts, a tribunal-appointed expert may have a different view of the same issues. These lead to questions about what to do or which part to go for the tribunal when there are conflicting experts.

Domestic litigation practices in various jurisdictions will be examined before addressing how to deal with conflicting expert opinions to add value to the analysis.

In Türkiye, according to the Turkish Court of Appeal, to resolve the contradiction between the party-appointed expert and the court-appointed expert opinion in litigation, a new expert should be consulted by the court that established the facts.[976] This approach is, in fact, similar to the Court of Appeal's solution method in the event of a

970. *See* German Federal Court of Justice (BGH), I ZB 46/18, BGH: 'Verletzt ... ein Sachverständiger seine Offenbarungspflicht, kann sich daraus ein selbständiger Grund für seine Ablehnung nur ergeben, sofern der Verstoß für sich bereits Zweifel an seiner Unparteilichkeit weckt.'
971. Nessi, 'Expert Witness: Role and Independence', 72; *see* Swinehart, 'International Law Commons, and the Organizations Law Commons Recommended Citation Recommended Citation Matthew W. Swinehart, Reliability of Expert Evidence in International Disputes'; Unbound and Langbein, 'The German Advantage in Civil Procedure'.
972. Yıldızlı, *Uluslararası Tahkimde Zararın Degerlendirilmesi*, 122.
973. O'Malley, *Rules of Evidence in International Arbitration*, 159.
974. Jones, 'Ineffective Use of Expert Evidence in Construction Arbitration', 4.
975. *Compañía de Aguas del Aconquija S.A. and Vivendi Universal S.A. v. Argentine Republic* (ICSID Case No. ARB/97/3), (Annulment Proceeding) Decision on the Argentine Republic's Request for Annulment of the Award rendered on 20 August 2007, para. 250, available at https://www.italaw.com/sites/default/files/case-documents/ita0221.pdf (accessed 14 December 2022).
976. Kaplan, 'Medenî Usûl Hukukunda Bilirkişi Raporu Ile Uzman Görüşü Arasındaki Celişkinin Giderilmesi', 570; for cases *see* Turkish Court of Appeal, 15th Civil Chamber, Docket No. 2019/748, Decision No. 2019/3857, 9 October 2019 (Lexpera); Turkish Court of Appeal 1. Civil Chamber, Docket No. 2014/1052, Decision No. 2014/17226, 10 November 2014 (Lexpera).

contradiction between two separate court-appointed experts.[977] Scholars argue, in parallel with the practice of the Court of Appeal, that the judge should resolve the contradiction between the party-appointed expert and the court-appointed expert opinion by obtaining a new court-appointed expert report on the same subject matter[978] or order both experts to testify before the court.[979]

The Turkish Court of Appeal deems it crucial that the party-appointed expert opinion be evaluated:

> [T]he party-appointed expert opinion in Article 293 of the HMK is regulated as obtaining information on a subject from a special and technical expert determined by the parties in order to clarify and understand the dispute and to prove the claims and defences. In order to protect the interests of the parties and, in case they are not satisfied with the court-appointed expert report, they may obtain a private expert opinion and submit it to the court in order to ensure that the incident is fully clarified and a correct and fair decision is made. *The court is obliged to consider and evaluate the expert opinion submitted by the party, especially in matters requiring special and technical knowledge, if it is related to the subject of the case.* In this sense, if one of the parties objected to the expert report based on the party-appointed expert opinion and these objections were never taken into consideration by the court and the objections were not met in a reasoned manner, the right to be heard, which is the most important element of the right to a fair trial regulated in Article 27 of the HMK, Article 36 of the Constitution of Türkiye and Article 6 of the European Convention on Human Rights, may be violated. In the expert opinions submitted to the record, findings and opinions contrary to the opinions determined by the court-appointed expert report have been proposed, and the court-appointed expert report and party-appointed expert opinions contain serious contradictions. Expert opinions were not included in the expert report and were not evaluated in the judgement. In terms of resolving the contradiction between the court-appointed expert report and the party-appointed expert opinions, it was not correct to render a judgement without evaluating and discussing the expert opinion.[980] (emphasis added)

977. Kaplan, 570; Turkish Court of Appeal 11. Civil Chamber, Docket No. 2013/16990, Decision No. 2014/18560, 28 November 2014 (Lexpera).
978. Pekcanıtez, 'Özel Uzman', 395; Sarısözen, 'Özel Bilirkişi (Uzman Görüşü)', 1729; Akil, 'Bilirkişi-Uzman Tanık Ayrımı', 175; Işık, 'Uzman Görüşü (Mütalaa)', 93; Özbek, 'Uzman Görüşünün Yargılamada Değerlendirilmesi', 143.
979. Elyıldırım, *Hukuk Yargılamasında Uzman Görüşü*, 178.
980. The original judgment in Turkish: 'Bilindiği üzere 6100 sayılı HMK'nın 293. maddesinde düzenlenen uzman görüşü, tarafların uyuşmazlığın aydınlanabilmesi, anlaşılabilmesi ve iddia ve savunmaların ispatı için kendisinin belirlediği özel ve teknik bilirkişiden bir konuda bilgi alması olarak düzenlenmiş olup, uygulamada özel bilirkişi adı da verilmektedir. Taraflar kendi menfaatlerini koruyabilmek ve alınan bilirkişi raporundan tatmin olmamaları halinde olayın tam olarak aydınlanmasını sağlamak ve doğru ve adil kararın verilmesi için uzman görüşü alıp mahkemeye ibraz edebilecektir. Mahkeme özellikle özel ve teknik bilgiyi gerektiren konularda tarafın sunduğu uzman görüşünü dava konusu ile ilgili olması halinde mutlaka dikkate almak ve değerlendirmek zorundadır. Bu anlamda alınan bilirkişi raporuna, taraflardan biri, uzman görüşüne dayanmak suretiyle itiraz etmiş ve bu itirazlar mahkeme tarafından hiç değerlendirmeye alınmamış ve itirazlar gerekçeli bir şekilde karşılanmamış ise uzman görüşüne dayanan tarafın 6100 sayılı HMK'nın 27, Anayasa'nın 36 ve Avrupa İnsan Hakları Sözleşmesi'nin 6. maddesinde düzenlenen adil yargılanması hakkının en önemli unsuru olan hukuki dinlenme hakkı ihlal edilmiş olabilecektir. Dosyaya ibraz edilen uzman görüşlerinde,

The approach in Germany is similar, where it is suggested that conflicting experts be heard before the court and that a new court-appointed expert be ordered only if the hearing did not result in a resolution of the conflict.[981]

In international arbitration, to decide how to handle all reports submitted by various experts, the tribunal must recognise the reasons for differences in opinion before arriving at a conclusion. In practice, three main conflict scenarios can be observed: (i) experts relying on different factual baselines; (ii) experts advocating rather than acting as experts; and (iii) a genuine difference of opinion between the experts on the same issue.[982]

The first type of conflict can be resolved and even prevented if the tribunal, after submissions, instructs the experts on the questions to be answered with details and scope.[983]

The assumption that experts are analysing objective facts and therefore must come to the same conclusion is misleading.[984] Failure to use common data sets and facts hinders the tribunal's ability to effectively use expert opinions. Had the tribunal asked the experts to have a pre-hearing meeting, common data sets and facts could have been mutually used, and experts may have reached conclusions similar to one another or at least allowed them to narrow the issues in a joint memorandum.[985] The use of different methodologies also leads to similar issues where the tribunal is unable to sufficiently compare expert opinions and assess more persuasive ones.[986]

To deal with the second conflict, the tribunal had to first assess the personality and credibility of the party-appointed experts. It has been suggested that the tribunal should consider the integrity of the experts, whether they are objective, their experience, the extent of work carried out on the issue and whether their opinions would

8.4.2013 tarihli bilirkişi raporu ile tespit edilen görüşlerin aksine tespit ve görüşler ileri sürülmüş olup, bilirkişi raporu ile uzman görüşleri ciddi şekilde çelişkiler içermektedir. Mahkemece alınan bilirkişi raporunda ve gerekçeli kararda uzman görüşlerine hiç yer verilmemiş ve bu görüşler değerlendirilmemiştir. Alınan bilirkişi raporu ile uzman görüşleri arasındaki çelişkinin giderilmesi yönünden de mahallinde keşif yapılıp yeni bir bilirkişi heyetinden rapor alınması yerine esaslı itiraza uğrayan rapora dayanılarak uzman görüşü kararda gerekçeli olarak değerlendirilip tartışılmadan karar verilmiş olması da doğru olmamıştır.' Turkish Court of Appeal 15th Civil Chamber, Docket No. 2020/3360, Decision No. 2021/1893, 22 April 2021. (Yargıtay Karar Arama, accessed 25 December 2023); For similar decisions *see* Turkish Court of Appeal 15th Civil Chamber, Docket No. 2019/748, Decision No. 2019/3857, 9 October 2019, Turkish Court of Appeal 15th Civil Chamber, Docket No. 2017/1782, Decision No. 2017/3805, 6 November 2017; Turkish Court of Appeal 15th Civil Chamber, Docket No. 2015/5127, Decision No. 2016/4635, 10 November 2016.

981. *See* Kaplan, 'Medenî Usûl Hukukunda Bilirkişi Raporu Ile Uzman Görüşü Arasındaki Celişkinin Giderilmesi', 571–572, fn. 67.
982. Abdel Wahab, 'Party Appointed Experts in International Commercial Arbitration', 195.
983. Jones, 'Redefining the Role and Value of Expert Evidence', 25.
984. Jones, 'Ineffective Use of Expert Evidence in Construction Arbitration', 4; Jones, 'Redefining the Role and Value of Expert Evidence', 25.
985. Bernstein, Tackaberry, and Marriott, *Bernstein's Handbook of Arbitration and Dispute Resolution Practice*, para. 2-855; Abdel Wahab, 'Party Appointed Experts in International Commercial Arbitration', 195.
986. Jones, 'Ineffective Use of Expert Evidence in Construction Arbitration', 4; Jones, 'Redefining the Role and Value of Expert Evidence', 25.

have been the same if instructed by the other party.[987] The BCLP Survey shows that tribunals are 'generally capable of determining when no party-appointed expert is being objective in their test testimony'.[988]

For the third occasion, if no issues of factual differences exist or the party-appointed experts do not appear biased or partisan, the tribunal is left to carefully consider all the available evidence and render a decision based on a careful evaluation. In such a scenario, determination is possible because, despite experts' contradictory findings, the arbitral tribunal can still convey knowledge or expertise on the issue. This is not considered inappropriate, and the tribunal can either prefer one expert's report to another or describe its own opinion, stating the reasons for it.[989] Divergent methodological approaches can result in different conclusions, and it is not always possible for the tribunal to discern which, if any, are correct. 'This is particularly the case for expert disciplines where there are multiple accepted methodologies, e.g. delay and disruption expertise.'[990]

In any case, the tribunal should not leave conflicting opinions but should try to resolve the differences or explain the view that it has adopted.[991]

If the matters cannot be decided on without the required knowledge, it might be necessary to appoint a tribunal-appointed expert.[992] However, as recent case law from various jurisdictions has suggested, there is no absolute duty to appoint a tribunal expert.[993]

According to the recent German dominant perspective, in the event of conflicting party-appointed expert opinions, it is at the discretion of the arbitral tribunal to appoint a third expert. If the arbitrators come to the conclusion that it is not necessary due to the expertise of the arbitrators and do not appoint an expert, this cannot automatically constitute a breach of the right to be heard.[994]

In the event of conflicting expert opinions, it is at the discretion of the arbitration tribunal whether to appoint an expert. If it decides that this is not necessarily due to the

987. Bernstein, Tackaberry, and Marriott, *Bernstein's Handbook of Arbitration and Dispute Resolution Practice*, para. 2-856.
988. 'BCLP 2021 Survey', 14.
989. According to Turkish civil procedure, if there are serious differences in opinion of party-appointed experts, the judge needs to appoint ex officio an independent expert. *See* Tanrıver, *Hukukumuzda Bilirkişilik*, 34; Pekcanıtez, 'Özel Uzman', 416; Atalay, 'Pekcanıtez Usûl', 2021, 1959.
990. Jones, 'Redefining the Role and Value of Expert Evidence', 25.
991. Özbek, *Tahkim Hukuku*, II:1465.
992. Bernstein, Tackaberry, and Marriott, *Bernstein's Handbook of Arbitration and Dispute Resolution Practice*, para. 2-857; For civil court practice *see* Pekcanıtez, 'Özel Uzman'.
993. For details *see* Gramlich, 'Widersprüchliche Parteisachverständige: Pflicht zur Bestellung eines schiedsgerichtlichen Sachverständigen?', 233; Saenger, 'ZPO § 1049 Vom Schiedsgericht Bestellter Sachverständiger', para. 5.
994. Musielak and Voit, *ZPO*, § 1049, para. 11; Gramlich, 'Widersprüchliche Parteisachverständige: Pflicht zur Bestellung eines schiedsgerichtlichen Sachverständigen?', 233 ff.; Mavrantonakis, *Das Verbot Der Révision Au Fond Im Internationalen Handelsschiedsverfahren: Zur Bindung Des Staatlichen Gerichts an Die Schiedsgerichtlichen Sachverhaltsfeststellungen Und Zu Den Erforderlichen Ausnahmen*, 98–110.

expertise of the arbitrators, the award does not automatically constitute a violation of the right to be heard.[995]

The High Court in Hong Kong refused enforcement of an award, which was largely based on the report of an expert appointed by the arbitral tribunal, against the objection of the defendant and where the defendant was refused the opportunity to comment on the report. The right to comment on the report of the tribunal-appointed expert has been accepted as a basic right by the court, and enforcement was denied because it was not adhered to.[996]

A challenge before the Superior Court of Ontario was brought against the award by *Nelson v. The Government of the United Mexican States,*[997] with the reasoning that the expert evidence was not evaluated. The court dismissed the application as follows:

> While it may be literally true that the applicants' experts were not mentioned by name in the award, it must be understood that the parties submitted their respective expert evidence as exhibits to their pleadings and their pleadings addressed that expert evidence in detail. ... Throughout the award, the tribunal cited extensively from the applicant's claim and reply. Many of the paragraphs cited by the tribunal expressly address the applicant's expert evidence ... the tribunal set out in great detail what the arguments of each party were and what those arguments were based on. The evidence was not repeated verbatim in the award but detailed and extensive citations were made referring to the parties' positions and evidence on each issue and but the fact is that the experts' arguments are fully referenced and the tribunal's reasons for why it reached its conclusions are set out in detail. No one could reasonably be in any doubt about whether the tribunal considered the applicant's evidence or why the tribunal decided the case the way it did. For the foregoing reasons, the application for relief under Article 34(2)(a)(ii) of the Model Law from the decision of the tribunal in this case is dismissed.[998]

In *Holder-Cowles and Holden v. Worrall*, each party presented expert evidence on technical issues. However, the arbitrator dismissed the claim without referring to the expert's opinion. The court ruled that:

> It was fundamental for the [arbitrator] to have adjudicated upon the conflicting evidence of the experts and to reach a finding as to which expert's opinion he preferred in relation to the issues raised in evidence. A tribunal cannot therefore simply 'sit on the fence' but must be prepared to engage and take a decision on the expert evidence before it, or at least explain why it has been impossible to do so.[999]

995. Musielak and Voit, *ZPO*§ 1049, para. 11; Gramlich, 'Widersprüchliche Parteisachverständige: Pflicht zur Bestellung eines schiedsgerichtlichen Sachverständigen?', 233 ff.
996. *Hong Kong, Paklito Investment Limited v. Klockner East Asia Limited,* [1993] 2 HKLR 39.
997. *Nelson v. The Government of the United Mexican States*, ICSID Case No. UNCT/17/1, Final Award, 5 June 2020 available at https://www.italaw.com/sites/default/files/case-documents/italaw11557_0.pdf (accessed 12 October 2022).
998. *Nelson v. The Government of the United Mexican States,* 2022 ONSC 1193, paras 37 ff. available at https://www.italaw.com/sites/default/files/case-documents/italaw170039.pdf (accessed 9 October 2023); similarly *Oil Basins Ltd v. BHP Billiton LTD* & Ors, [2007] VSCA 255.
999. Referenced in Bor, 'Expert Evidence', 521.

3.4.6 Contradicting Parties' Agreement

Party autonomy is the fundamental basis of arbitration. Therefore, the arbitral tribunal and the parties must follow the framework that the parties have foreseen for the tribunal.[1000] Contradicting the parties' agreement can lead to a challenge to the award.

The Higher Regional Court of Frankfurt am Main set-aside an arbitral award for failure of one of the parties and its appointed expert to adhere to the agreed procedural rules. During the proceedings, the arbitral tribunal issued a procedural order containing detailed directions for the taking of expert evidence. The directions required the parties to disclose all the information that the experts had reviewed in the process of drafting their respective expert reports. This provision had been subject to extensive prior negotiations between the parties and the tribunal and was referred to in the procedural order as an 'agreement by the parties'. Subsequently, a party failed to disclose all the information it had referred to its appointed expert in preparing its opinion. The Court held that the parties' agreement on procedural issues, such as the taking of expert evidence, takes priority over the tribunal's procedural discretion and could not be overridden by the arbitral tribunal.[1001]

Turkish courts concur with the view that the appointment of experts should be left to the discretion of the arbitrators, and failure to appoint an expert should not be considered a deficiency that would affect the arbitral award.[1002]

3.5 INTERIM CONCLUSION

The use of experts in International Arbitration has increased tremendously in recent years. As can be seen in the survey conducted by the LCIA in 2018, experts were involved in almost all three hundred cases.[1003] Statistics based on views from various experienced practitioners and scholars show that there are apparent problems related to the personality and usage style of party-appointed experts.

Due to the above-described problems of the party-appointed expert and the presented opinion, the focus is on improving the use of party-appointed experts. Statistics demonstrate the need for a settled understanding of at least some aspects regarding party-appointed experts.

First, independence and impartiality must be correctly distinguished and evaluated separately. Neither the IBA Rules nor the CIArb Protocol explain how a party-appointed expert can, in fact, be independent and not just show independence.[1004]

1000. *See* Chapter 3 section 3.3 for details.
1001. *See* OLG Frankfurt am Main decision 26 Sch 13/10, dated 17 February 2011. The German Supreme Court, in its judgment of 2 October 2012III ZB 8/11, dismissed the appeal against this decision.
1002. Turkish Court of Appeal, 11. Civil Chamber, Docket No. 2016/1652, Decision No. 2016/2111, 29 February 2016.
1003. LCIA, Experts in International Arbitration, 17 January 2018 available at https://www.lcia.org/News/experts-in-international-arbitration.aspx (accessed 12 March 2022).
1004. Jones, 'Ineffective Use of Expert Evidence in Construction Arbitration', 7.

Although stipulated as requirements in soft laws, due to their status, party-appointed experts cannot and should not be expected to be independent, but their report can be an independent product. More crucially, impartiality, which reflects itself on the outer world as objectivity, must be sought from the party-engaged experts so that the expert report fairly helps the tribunal draw conclusions while rendering a just award.

Moreover, the unregulated use of experts, the lack of a code of conduct, double-hatting, sequential adducing and hearing and reliance on experts, if no assistance is necessary, are adversely affecting and threatening arbitration as an effective dispute resolution mechanism.

When court and annulment decisions are critically evaluated, it becomes obvious that the situations where experts impact the proceedings are as follows: Refusal to allow parties to adduce or consider the expert opinion, lack of improper notice or inadequate opportunity to comment on expert opinion, delegation of decision-making, challenge based on the lack of independence of the expert and quality of evidence, not evaluating conflicting expert opinions, and the failure to reach an agreement between the parties.

The right to be heard and party autonomy grant the parties the right to submit expert evidence and ask the tribunal to consider it.[1005] As a general principle, no tribunal should refuse to admit expert evidence that is essential to the dispute.[1006] If a tribunal refuses to allow a party to examine an expert at a hearing, that may amount to a violation of the right to present their case.[1007] The limit of the tribunal's discretion is exceeded where it abuses its adjudicatory power by intentionally disregarding the opinion. However, one can conclude that the party-appointed expert has been considered if it is seen in the award that the tribunal has evaluated the opinion of the expert in depth.[1008]

It is part of the right to be heard that the parties have an opportunity to comment on the expert opinion.[1009] In case the tribunal is already composed of experts, then the parties should be given the opportunity to comment and object to these views. If the party was not allowed to comment on the expert opinion, this could be a ground for a set-aside or refusal of recognition and enforcement of an arbitral award.[1010]

Although it is allowed to use foreign and international law experts in arbitration, this becomes problematic when a legal expert's opinion is heavily embedded in the award in such a way that the tribunal copy-pasted the expert report into the award. Such a decision risks being set aside or, alternatively, not enforced.[1011]

1005. *See* Chapter 3 section 3.1.
1006. Rosenfeld, 'Country Report: Germany', 183.
1007. Patocchi, Paolo Michele and Niedermaier, 'UNCITRAL Rules', 1187; Sanders, 'Commentary On UNCITRAL Arbitration Rules', 204; Tanrıver, *Medenî Usûl Hukuku*, 2022, II:429.
1008. Akil, 'Bilirkişi-Uzman Tanık Ayrımı', 176.
1009. Pekcanıtez, 'Hukuki Dinlenilme Hakkı', 758; Borris et al., 'New York Convention, Article V [Grounds for Refusal of Recognition and Enforcement of Arbitral Awards]', para. 177.
1010. Pekcanıtez, 'Hukuki Dinlenilme Hakkı', 767.
1011. Borris et al., 'New York Convention, Article V [Grounds for Refusal of Recognition and Enforcement of Arbitral Awards]', para. 340.

As elaborated, there is generally no requirement under various statutory provisions for party-appointed experts to be independent.[1012] However, this does not mean that the opinion can be accepted without recourse to other qualifications, such as impartiality.

As confirmed in *Brandeis (Brokers) Ltd v. Black and others,*[1013] the mere existence of a party-appointed expert who allegedly was not qualified to give opinion and the tribunal not disqualifying the expert cannot lead in itself to annulment.[1014] As the tribunal has the discretion not to rely on expert opinion, this procedural issue should not be regarded as a serious irregularity.

Arbitrators are generally left to analyse competing and conflicting expert reports. This can sometimes prove to be a very difficult task, even to the extent that the experts are no longer facilitating the proceedings but are making it more complex and burdensome.[1015]

In international arbitration, to decide how to handle all reports submitted by various experts, the tribunal must recognise the reasons for differences in opinion before arriving at a conclusion. In practice, three main conflict scenarios can be observed: (i) experts rely on different factual baselines; (ii) experts are advocates rather than experts; (iii) a genuine difference in opinion between experts on the same issue exists.

The first type of conflict can be resolved and even prevented if the tribunal, after submissions, instructs the experts on the questions to be answered with details and scope.

To deal with the second conflict, the tribunal has to assess the personality and credibility of the party-appointed experts. It has been suggested that the tribunal should consider the integrity of the experts, whether they are objective, their experience, the extent of work carried out on the issue and whether their opinions would have been the same if instructed by the other party.[1016]

For the third situation, where there are no issues of factual differences or the party-appointed experts do not appear biased or partisan, the tribunal is left to carefully consider all of the available evidence and render a decision based on its evaluation. The tribunal can either prefer one expert's report over the other one or describe its own opinion, giving reasons for it.[1017]

Last but not least, the tribunal shall give due regard to the parties' agreement on the use of experts. Violation may lead to a set-aside or rejection of enforcement.

1012. *See* Chapter 2 section 2.1.4 and section 2.4.1.
1013. *Brandeis (Brokers) Ltd v. Black and Ors*, 2001 Arbitration Law Reports and Review.
1014. Bor, 'Expert Evidence', 519.
1015. O'Malley, *Rules of Evidence in International Arbitration*, 159.
1016. Bernstein, Tackaberry, and Marriott, *Bernstein's Handbook of Arbitration and Dispute Resolution Practice*, para. 2-856.
1017. According to Turkish civil procedure, if there are serious differences in opinion of party-appointed experts, the judge needs to appoint ex officio an independent expert. *See* Tanrıver, *Hukukumuzda Bilirkişilik*, 34; Pekcanıtez, 'Özel Uzman', 416; Atalay, 'Pekcanıtez Usûl', 2021, 1959.

CHAPTER 4

Possible Solutions to Problems Related to the Use of Party-Appointed Experts

Above, a picture of experts in general, with a special focus on party-appointed experts and their presence in international arbitration, the *raison d'être*, their function, role, qualifications, types and legal basis was presented.

The use of party-appointed experts is directly linked to and affects fundamental rights in arbitration. Although party-appointed experts have a legal basis in primary international and national sources and secondary soft law elements, how they will be used, treated and assessed in proceedings is relatively vague.

The criticisms relating to party-appointed experts are not restricted to international arbitration; they can also be observed in various domestic courts.[1018] The IBA and the CIArb have developed certain standards of conduct for party-appointed experts.[1019] In addition, various recommendations have been proposed over the years for international commercial and investment arbitration and domestic litigation.[1020]

Although 52% of the respondents of the BCLP Survey did not think there should be greater control over the use of party-appointed experts,[1021] international and national arbitration practices reveal that solutions are needed to the above-presented problems arising out of the impartiality and unregulated use of party-appointed experts. A transparent body of rules addressing the duties of party-appointed experts and the way

1018. For critics in Türkiye *see* Tanrıver, 'Yasal Düzenleme ve Teorik Boyutuyla Bilirkişilik'; For critics in the UK *see* Lord Woolf MR, *Access to Justice: Final Report to the Lord Chancellor of the Civil Justice System in England and Wales* (Final Report, 1996); Proske, *Expert Witness Conferencing in Schiedsverfahren*, 13–30; Jones, 'Redefining the Role and Value of Expert Evidence', 25–26.
1019. Jones, 'Ineffective Use of Expert Evidence in Construction Arbitration', 6; Sachs and Schmidt-Ahrendts, 'Protocol on Expert Teaming: A New Approach to Expert Evidence', 137.
1020. *See* Teomete Yalabık, 'Questioning Expert Witnesses in Litigation and International Arbitration: How to Prevent Partisan Expert Reports and "Battle of Experts"'.
1021. Burn, Morel de Westgaver and Clark, 'Expert Evidence in International Arbitration: Saving the Party-Appointed Expert', 9.

their opinions will be dealt with could result in more remedies for the parties and strengthen their role and overall value.

The success of international arbitration has been partly due to its flexibility. That's why some consider not overregulating the issue of experts and instead adapting the process to the nature of each dispute.[1022]

Most institutional arbitration rules only contain general provisions on evidence, leaving the parties and tribunals to determine the details. However, the IBA and CIArb have developed more comprehensive standards of conduct regarding the taking of evidence, including arrangements for party-appointed experts.[1023] Nevertheless, issues regarding admissibility, burden of proof, standard of proof, burden to provide evidence, and style of preparing the opinion and its evaluation are either absent or lack vital nuances.

In the last chapter of this thesis, possible solutions will be analysed, and a single or a combination of solutions will be sought for the problems described. First, from an ethical perspective, the effect of a possible code of conduct for party-appointed experts will be examined. Thereafter, methods/practices for the use of party-appointed experts will be evaluated.

4.1 CODE OF CONDUCT FOR DOUBLE-HATTING

Although some arbitral rules and the IBA Guidelines on Conflicts of Interest in International Arbitration regulate the code of conduct for arbitrators,[1024] no widely accepted code of conduct in international arbitration that refers to party-appointed experts exists.[1025] The CIArb Protocol for the Use of Party-Appointed Expert Witnesses in International Arbitration is the only soft law instrument that comprehensively touches on the use of party-appointed experts in international arbitration.[1026]

The lack of a code of conduct has resulted in 'double hatting'. Double hatting is an activity describing the situation where actors, such as arbitrators, party counsel, and experts in investor-state dispute resolution proceedings, play various roles in different proceedings with different roles in each proceeding, such as being arbitrators in one proceeding and an expert in another.[1027]

Double hatting has been criticised for a long period, and the UNCITRAL Working Group III's work on 'Code of Conduct for Arbitrators in International Investment

1022. Chazournes et al., 'One Size Does Not Fit All-Uses of Experts Before International Courts and Tribunals: An Insight into the Practice' 494; *see* Mbengue/Das, *Rules Governing the Use of Experts in International Disputes*, 447–450; *Plant* critics that rules could limit the core principle of flexibility of international dispute settlement. *See* Plant, 'Expert Evidence and the Challenge of Procedural Reform in International Dispute Settlement', 467–468.
1023. Jones, 'Ineffective Use of Expert Evidence in Construction Arbitration', 6; Sachs and Schmidt-Ahrendts, 'Protocol on Expert Teaming: A New Approach to Expert Evidence' 137.
1024. Balkar, *Milletlerarası Ticari Tahkim ve Etik*, 37.
1025. Kantor, 'A Code of Conduct for Party-Appointed Experts in International Arbitration – Can One Be Found?', 323; Balkar, *Milletlerarası Ticari Tahkim ve Etik*, 168.
1026. The CIArb Protocol Art. 4(1) foresees that the 'expert's opinion shall be impartial, objective, unbiased and uninfluenced'.
1027. *See* Langford, Behn, and Lie, 'The Revolving Door in International Investment Arbitration'.

Dispute Resolution and Code of Conduct for Judges in International Investment Dispute Resolution with respective commentary of the United Nations Commission on International Trade Law' was adopted on 7 December 2023, by the General Assembly Resolution in the 45th plenary meeting.[1028] The draft code of conduct for arbitrators aims, among other issues, to reinforce the duty of independence and impartiality and to regulate the practice of arbitrators acting as experts in international investment disputes.

In the UK, the Ethics Committee of the General Council of the Bar has issued guidance to assist members of the Bar in identifying what is permissible by way of a party-appointed expert preparation. The recommendation emphasises that the counsel plays a proper role in assisting an expert with issues that the expert should address in the report. However, expert reports should be an independent product of the expert in question; therefore, counsels are prohibited from drafting any part of an expert's report. Nevertheless, counsel may annotate a draft report, observations, and questions for the expert to consider in any revisions to the draft.[1029]

A lawyer from the US may be permitted to engage in rehearsals of testimony, including mock cross-examinations, and to take a more interventionist approach to the substance of an expert's opinion, both in terms of written and oral evidence. The expert is coached, which might indicate that the expert is not giving an honest opinion or is not exercising a sufficient degree of independence.[1030] A tribunal can impose cost sanctions or publicly censure a party-appointed expert who breaches his duty to remain impartial and assist the arbitral tribunal.[1031]

The possibility of developing and applying a code of conduct for party-appointed experts is considered generally helpful, but some consider that it should remain in the form of general guidelines rather than a detailed code.[1032]

The goal of a Code of Conduct is to ensure a healthy framework for the use of party-appointed experts. That's why it should address fundamental issues that need to be present before, during, and after the process.

First, it must address who the expert is. The expert must have concrete material qualities. An expert is a professional who has undergone education, experience, and special knowledge or skills that would enable him or her to help the arbitral tribunal to decide on disputed issues. It may be enough for an expert to be appointed by a party due to one or more of the qualifications (CoC-1). The more qualifications are present, the better the expert's credibility would be.

Second, the experts should possess abstract-immaterial qualities. The expert shall only accept the proposal to act as an expert if he is impartial and will remain objective

1028. (accessed 14 February 2024).
1029. Parlett, 'Parties' Engagement with Experts in International Litigation', 450; General Council of the Bar, Ethics Committee, 'Witness Preparation', August 2017, paras 21–23 available at http://www.barcouncil.org.uk/media/411847/witness_preparation.pdf (accessed 10 September 2022).
1030. Parlett, 450.
1031. Burn, Morel de Westgaver and Clark, 'Expert Evidence in International Arbitration: Saving the Party-Appointed Expert', 9.
1032. *See* de Chazournes et al., 'Uses of Experts Before International Courts and Tribunals', 493.

during his service. If the expert senses any reasons that will lead him to prepare a biased opinion, the expert shall not accept his office. An expert shall not accept his duty if he is acting as a mediator or arbitrator in another dispute where the parties or any related parties are the disputants (CoC-2).

Third, the expert's opinion should be an independent product of his own and not influenced by the appointing party (CoC-3). The expert's primary duty and responsibility is to the arbitral tribunal (CoC-4).

To accomplish Rules 3 and 4, the expert's fees for his services shall be paid before the final report has been prepared so that the expert is not pressured by the parties who wish for a pre-ordered report. The expert fees shall not be dependent on the outcome of the case (CoC-5).

The expert will be entrusted with sensitive information. Therefore, he shall maintain the confidentiality of any and all information related to the dispute or the parties that he has gained before, during, or after the proceedings (CoC-6).

An expert shall comply with the Codes of Practice and Guidelines that are foreseen in his profession (CoC-7).

4.2 METHOD AND PRACTICE SOLUTIONS

In addition to the code of conduct and guidelines that may be applicable to the use of experts in arbitration generally, various practices have emerged to address potential concerns regarding the use of party-appointed experts.

4.2.1 Proactive Case Management

The arbitral tribunal has the primary responsibility and authority to determine and direct proceedings.[1033] Not every step or issue can be regulated in statutory provisions or arbitration rules; therefore, the tribunal needs to step in with its procedural orders.[1034]

For tackling the problems and enhancing the usefulness of party-appointed experts, first and foremost, proactive involvement by the arbitral tribunal and reinforcement of the expert's duty to assist the tribunal are required.[1035]

Rather than leaving the use of party-appointed experts to the parties and the expert's discretion, the tribunal, in cooperation with the parties, should determine at an early stage of the proceedings the disciplines for which expert opinion is required and a list of questions that they want the experts to address.[1036] This ensures, from the outset,

1033. Tanrıver, *Medenî Usûl Hukuku*, 20226, II:426; Ağırman, *Milli & Milletlerarası Tahkim*, 393; Kurkela, Turunen, and Conflict Management Institute, *Due Process in International Commercial Arbitration*, 173.
1034. Dülger, *Milletlerarası Tahkimde Hakemlerin Dogal Yetkileri*, 93; Budak, 'Tahkim Yargılamasında İlk Aşama: Görev Belgesi ve 1 Numaralı Usuli Karar', 28.
1035. Jones, 'Redefining the Role and Value of Expert Evidence', 24, 34, 39.
1036. Waincymer, *Procedure and Evidence in International Arbitration*, 452; Ağırman, *Milli & Milletlerarası Tahkim*, 459; Bor, 'Expert Evidence', 509; Blackaby and Wilbraham, 'Practical Issues Relating to the Use of Expert Evidence in Investment Treaty Arbitration', 666–668;

that evidence will be tendered only on relevant issues, thereby preventing excessive proceedings costs.[1037] For example, when a case does not include complex and highly debated legal issues, the arbitral tribunal should inform and direct the parties not to adduce legal experts.[1038] This places a burden on the tribunal in its preparation for a hearing.[1039] The tribunal should not allow legal experts to testify if the tribunal is already an expert in that area of law.[1040]

An arbitral tribunal may decide to bifurcate the proceedings, such as liability and quantum. In *ABH Holdings S.A. v. Ukraine*, the arbitral tribunal bifurcated the case and ruled that this decision would 'promote fairness and procedural efficiency'.[1041] In its ruling, the tribunal underlined the fact that bifurcation would materially reduce the time and cost of the proceedings and had the potential to dispose of the entire case or substantial parts thereof.[1042]

In case of bifurcation, the arbitral tribunal shall address that expert opinions on quantum issues shall only be adduced after the tribunal affirms any liability. This would be more cost-efficient considering the expenses of quantum calculations. Once a finding of liability has been reached, the tribunal is left with an unenviable position of trying to make sense of quantum submissions from experts that have been put in at the beginning without any appreciation of how the liability phase will emerge.

Once relevant disciplines are selected and experts are appointed early in the proceedings, parties have the opportunity to challenge[1043] experts. This contributes to the efficiency of the proceedings, avoiding later challenges and prolonging the assessment of the opinions.[1044]

An expert's duty in providing his opinion in the arbitration is to assist the arbitral tribunal in determining the disputed issues with respect to which expert evidence is adduced.[1045] The tribunal could declare that it will impose cost sanctions regarding a party-appointed expert who breaches his duty to remain impartial and assist the tribunal.[1046]

Pitkowitz and Kathan-Spath, 'The Arbitrator and the Arbitration Procedure, The Vienna Propositions for Streamlining Arbitral Proceedings: Keeping Pace with New Developments and User Expectations', 145; Instructions to the expert should be drafted carefully to ensure that experts deal with all relevant matters, without leading them to adopt a particular line of position.

1037. Jones, 'Redefining the Role and Value of Expert Evidence', 34; For similar practice *see* ICC, 'ICC Arbitration Commission Report on Controlling Time and Costs in Arbitration', 13, para. 62.

1038. Roney, 'Cross-Examination of Experts', 112.

1039. Kalpsüz, *Türkiye'de Milletlerarası Tahkim*, 91; Bor, 'Expert Evidence', 509.

1040. Geisinger, 'Advocacy in International Commercial Arbitration: What For?', 15.

1041. *See ABH Holdings S.A. v. Ukraine*, ICSID Case No. ARB/24/1, Decision on Bifurcation, 12 May 2025, para. 36 available at https://www.iareporter.com/articles/icsid-tribunal-hearing-treaty-claim-against-ukraine-bifurcates-quantum-from-proceedings-on-jurisdiction-and-liability-citing-range-of-possible-liability-findings/ (accessed 20 May 2025).

1042. *ABH Holdings S.A. v. Ukraine*, ICSID Case No. ARB/24/1, Decision on Bifurcation, 12 May 2025, paras 37–44.

1043. *See* Chapter 2 section 2.9.

1044. Jones, 'Redefining the Role and Value of Expert Evidence', 34.

1045. Khodykin and Mulcahy, *A Guide to the IBA Rules on the Taking of Evidence in International Arbitration*, 303.

1046. 'BCLP 2021 Survey', 9.

The arbitral tribunal will be unable to draw conclusions from two opinions that address substantively different questions or matters. Hence, within each expert discipline, the tribunal should establish a common list of questions and issues for the appointed experts to address.[1047] Thus, arbitrators will understand whether there is a genuine difference in methodology or analysis that leads to different opinions. Common questions and issues should be determined, with the assistance of the parties, during the case management conference.[1048]

Disclosure of the instructions the expert received is necessary. In particular, how the counsel formulates instructions may, on their own, help the tribunal understand whether the expert opinion will be helpful or not.[1049]

The tribunal must maintain active oversight over this process, for instance, assisting where parties cannot agree on the questions to be asked.

Another vital point is that an objective analysis is only possible after all the factual evidence has been provided to both experts. A party-appointed expert who has just been provided evidence from the appointing party will not, in fact, be able to create an objective opinion.[1050] Hence, the tribunal must ensure that both their appointed and counterparty experts provide the same factual evidence, and common datasets and expert reports should only be submitted after this has been established.[1051]

Another matter that needs to be addressed is the communication between the party-appointed experts and the arbitral tribunal. Contrary to the proposal in the ICC Arbitration Commission Report on Controlling Time and Costs, where it is advised that the tribunal does not communicate directly with a party-appointed expert, except when the expert is testifying at a hearing,[1052] the direct engagement by the tribunal would affirm the expert's understanding of his duty against the tribunal.

4.2.2 Joint-Appointment

Where some counsels prefer party-appointed experts, others prefer tribunal-appointed experts. A third way could be a joint-appointment.

Joint-appointment is a hybrid method of expert appointment where either both parties nominate the expert who will be appointed by the tribunal or, without the participation of the tribunal, directly appoint a single joint expert.[1053] Alternatively, the

1047. Since the memorial style for written party submissions is generally practised in international arbitration, expert opinions are generally already submitted, which prevents party-appointed experts from addressing the same issues based on the same facts. *See* for critics Jones, 'Redefining the Role and Value of Expert Evidence', 34–36.
1048. Jones, 36.
1049. 'BCLP 2021 Survey', 5.
1050. This is one of the main reasons the Memorial Style of submission is criticised. *See* for details Jones, 'Redefining the Role and Value of Expert Evidence', 36.
1051. Jones, 36.
1052. Schäfer and Wilson, 'ICC Bulletin', 2021, 65.
1053. Sachs and Schmidt-Ahrendts, 'Protocol on Expert Teaming: A New Approach to Expert Evidence', 144; Schäfer and Wilson, 'ICC Bulletin', 2021, 65; Jones, 'Redefining the Role and Value of Expert Evidence', 22, 26; Can and Tuna, *Milletlerarası Tahkim Hukuku*, 414.

parties may propose several experts, and the tribunal may choose one expert from each list.[1054]

If the parties can agree on a single joint expert, this would help reduce costs and streamline the proceedings.[1055] When agreeing on a single joint expert, the parties should clarify in the terms of reference whether they would be bound by the conclusions of the joint expert and the report. Almost half (46%) of the stakeholders in arbitration believe that counsel should consider joint expert reports for better arbitration.[1056]

The parties may apply to the ICC ADR Rules for the Appointment of Experts and Neutrals[1057] for the appointment of experts. The ICC has detailed rules that provide for three different services, which the ICC can provide with respect to experts in a dispute.

As mentioned earlier, CPR Rule 35.7 foresees the usage of a single joint expert. The civil court practice in the UK demonstrates that this method is fruitful.[1058]

Jones rightly stressed that a single joint expert could not find a solution to the problems brought about by the use of party-appointed experts. Relying only on a single expert would lead the tribunal almost blindly to accept the expert's conclusions.[1059]

4.2.3 Expert Teaming

Even if the parties do not jointly appoint an expert, the expert opinion can still be a joint product, at least to a certain degree.

Sachs and *Schmidt-Ahrendts* proposed the 'expert teaming' method, where the tribunal will choose two experts, one from each of the two lists the parties proposed and appoints these experts as a team. In this way, the main aim is to ensure the neutrality and objectivity of experts and to ensure a more qualified proceeding.

1054. In the BCLP survey, the most favoured alternative to the party-appointed expert was a tribunal-appointed expert nominated by the parties (58%), followed by a single joint expert directly appointed by the parties (53%) in 'BCLP 2021 Survey', 9; Webster and Bühler, *Handbook of ICC Arbitration: Commentary, Precedents, Materials*, 446; Jones, 'Ineffective Use of Expert Evidence in Construction Arbitration', 10; Also, the ICC Centre for ADR can be engaged to select experts whose experience is tailored to the parties' particular needs. *See* 'ICC Commission on Arbitration and ADR Report: Resolving Climate Change Related Disputes through Arbitration and ADR' (ICC 2019) ICC Commission on Arbitration and ADR 999 ENG 26, para. 5.32.

1055. Khodykin and Mulcahy, *A Guide to the IBA Rules on the Taking of Evidence in International Arbitration*, 283; Schäfer and Wilson, 'ICC Bulletin', 2021, section D para. (v).

1056. '2015 International Arbitration Survey: Improvements and Innovations in International Arbitration', 30.

1057. Available at https://iccwbo.org/dispute-resolution/dispute-resolution-services/adr/experts/appointment-of-experts-and-neutrals/rules-for-the-appointment-of-experts-and-neutrals/#:~:text=Every%20expert%20or%20neutral%20must,%2C%20availability%2C%20impartiality%20and%20independence. (accessed 8 May 2022).

1058. Yazıcı-Tıktık, 'HMK m. 293'teki Uzman Görüşü Kurumu Ile Anglo-Sakson Hukuk Sistemindeki Uzman Tanık Kurumunun Karşılaştırılması', 86.

1059. Jones, 'Ineffective Use of Expert Evidence in Construction Arbitration', 10–11.

This method allows each party to exchange a list of expert candidates and comments on the other candidates.[1060] The tribunal then selects two experts, one from each list, to form the expert team. The arbitrators and the parties meet with the expert team to establish the terms of reference, outlining the expected issues to be addressed and the style of the report.[1061]

After the exchange of initial reports, parties' experts (within each discipline) can meet to discuss (in a pre-hearing meeting)[1062] the scope of the differences between them and submit a joint report to the tribunal identifying in summary form: (a) assumptions, methodology and opinions on which they agree; and (b) assumptions, methodology and opinions on which they disagree.[1063]

Thereafter, the experts (within each discipline) are to produce individual expert reports on areas of disagreement only and not raise unrelated new matters.[1064] Experts should reply to these expert reports, limiting their replies to what their opinions would be if the counterparty expert's assumptions and methodologies were to be accepted.[1065]

Limiting the scope of individual reports to areas of difference facilitates a better understanding of complex issues for the tribunal and enhances the efficiency of the use of party-appointed experts.[1066]

The expert team would be questioned at the hearing, including by parties' 'expert consultants' (experts hired directly by the parties to address areas of disagreement between the two members of the expert team).[1067]

1060. Sachs and Schmidt-Ahrendts, 'Protocol on Expert Teaming: A New Approach to Expert Evidence', 145–146.
1061. Sachs and Schmidt-Ahrendts, 145–146.
1062. Jones: 'experts are far more likely to find areas of agreement through confidential discussions with each other, before they have formally declared positions in a written report. The tribunal should encourage these discussions to be held in camera without counsel present'. Jones, 'Redefining the Role and Value of Expert Evidence', 37.
1063. Abdel Wahab, 'Party Appointed Experts in International Commercial Arbitration', 195; For problems of instructions from counsel to experts not to agree during the meetings *see* Khodykin and Mulcahy, *A Guide to the IBA Rules on the Taking of Evidence in International Arbitration*, 316 and Jones, 'Party Appointed Expert Witnesses in International Arbitration: A Protocol at Last', 145; Schlaepfer and Duvanel, 'Direct and Re-Direct Examination', 73–74; for content of joint report *see* CIArb Guidelines for Witness Conferencing in International Arbitration, 36, para. 6(b); *see Gold Reserve Inc. v. Bolivarian Republic of Venezuela*, ICSID Case No. ARB(AF)/09/1, Procedural Order No. 2, 25 July 2012, para. 2, available at https://jusmundi.com/en/document/other/en-gold-reserve-inc-v-bolivarian-republic-of-venezuela-procedural-order-no-2-wednesday-25th-july-2012#other_document_17483, (accessed 22 October 2022); *S.D. Myers, Inc. v. Government of Canada*, Procedural Order No. 17, 26 February 2001, para. 12 available at https://jusmundi.com/en/document/other/en-s-d-myers-inc-v-government-of-canada-procedural-order-no-17-and-no-18-monday-26th-february-2001#other_document_1293 (accessed 22 October 2022); *Jones* argues that experts should, as a first step, prepare a joint expert report, and not after the initial report. Jones, 'Redefining the Role and Value of Expert Evidence', 37.
1064. Jones, 'Redefining the Role and Value of Expert Evidence', 37–38.
1065. Jones, 'Ineffective Use of Expert Evidence in Construction Arbitration', 11; Jones, 'Redefining the Role and Value of Expert Evidence', 37–38.
1066. Jones, 'Redefining the Role and Value of Expert Evidence', 37.
1067. Sachs and Schmidt-Ahrendts, 'Protocol on Expert Teaming: A New Approach to Expert Evidence', 145.

Sachs describes this method as providing 'checks and balances' for expert technical findings. It is potentially a way of qualifying experts and ensuring their credibility.[1068]

This method offers an option for addressing the credibility of experts but justifies tribunal-appointed experts. This does not address the process of determining whether a party-appointed expert opinion is credible and should be accepted. Despite its potential advantages, the Sachs method is said to suffer from a lack of application and has not achieved widespread adoption in international arbitration.[1069]

While *Sachs* envisions a solution to a whole host of challenges facing expert evidence by merging the two approaches, there are concerns about the practicality of this proposal with regard to experts' access to relevant documents and information, which would be more readily available to party-appointed experts working closely with counsel.[1070]

4.2.4 Pre-hearing Expert Meeting

4.2.4.1 Definition

A pre-hearing expert conference is a meeting between the party-appointed experts before the main hearing(s) at which they discuss their respective: (a) factual basis, assumptions, methodology and opinions on which they agree; and (b) factual basis, assumptions, methodology and opinions on which they disagree.[1071] Actually, the joint report described and discussed above is a result of this meeting.[1072] Without this meeting, a joint report would be a difficult mission.

The goal of this meeting is to streamline the evidentiary process and make the proceedings cost-efficient.[1073] After the exchange of initial or draft reports, the parties'

1068. Sachs and Schmidt-Ahrendts, 135; *see also* Schmidt-Ahrendts, 'Expert Teaming: Bridging the Divide between Party-Appointed and Tribunal-Appointed Experts', 653.
1069. Jones, 'Redefining the Role and Value of Expert Evidence', 22.
1070. de Chazournes et al., 'Uses of Experts Before International Courts and Tribunals', 493.
1071. Abdel Wahab, 'Party Appointed Experts in International Commercial Arbitration', 195; *see* for problems of instructions from counsel to experts not to agree during the meetings Khodykin and Mulcahy, *A Guide to the IBA Rules on the Taking of Evidence in International Arbitration*, 316. and Jones, 'Party Appointed Expert Witnesses in International Arbitration: A Protocol at Last', 145; Hacıbekiroğlu, *Milletlerarası Tahkim Hukukunda Deliller ve Delillerin Degerlendirilmesi*, 126; Schlaepfer and Duvanel, 'Direct and Re-Direct Examination', 73–74; For the content of a joint report *see* CIArb Guidelines for Witness Conferencing in International Arbitration 36, para. 6(b); *see Gold Reserve Inc. v. Bolivarian Republic of Venezuela*, ICSID Case No. ARB(AF)/09/1, Procedural Order No. 2, 25 July 2012, para. 2, https://jusmundi.com/en/document/other/en-gold-reserve-inc-v-bolivarian-republic-of-venezuela-procedural-order-no-2-wednesday-25th-july-2012#other_document_17483 (accessed 1 September 2022).
    S.D. Myers, Inc. v. Government of Canada, Procedural Order No. 17, 26 February 2001, para. 12. https://jusmundi.com/en/document/other/en-s-d-myers-inc-v-government-of-canada-procedural-order-no-17-and-no-18-monday-26th-february-2001#other_document_1293 (accessed 19 August 2022); *Jones* argues that experts should, as a first step, prepare a joint expert report, and not after the initial report, *see* Jones, 'Redefining the Role and Value of Expert Evidence', 37.
1072. Grenz, *Der Faktor Zeit Im Schiedsverfahren*, 163.
1073. Ehle, 'Practical Aspects of Using Expert Evidence in International Arbitration', 82; Zuberbühler et al., *IBA Rules of Evidence*, 145; Parlett, 'Parties' Engagement with Experts in

experts (within each discipline) meet and discuss the matters on which expert opinions are necessary.[1074]

4.2.4.2 *The Practice of Expert Meetings*

A meeting between the experts early[1075] and before the main evidentiary hearing will be useful to prevent a lengthy and exhausting expert testimony phase in the evidentiary hearings, where the experts may not be willing to let go of their opinions. Almost half (46%) of the stakeholders in arbitration believe that counsel should consider early meetings with experts to improve arbitration outcomes.[1076]

In this meeting, the experts will come together and discuss their understanding of the dispute and their initial approach/view before the expert report is drafted.[1077]

At such meetings, the experts should attempt to come to a common ground on as many issues as possible, record them in writing, and submit a joint report.[1078] For issues where experts have a difference of opinion, they should render their separate views indicating the reasons for their disagreement, and adding to that what their conclusions would be if they were adopting the counter-expert's position.[1079]

The IBA Rules, the CIArb Protocol, and the UNCITRAL Notes encourage pre-hearing meetings between party-appointed experts from the same discipline.[1080] The purpose

International Litigation', 447; Ünüvar, 'Experts: Investment Arbitration', para. 23; Webster and Bühler, *Handbook of UNCITRAL Arbitration*, 424.

1074. *Jones* argues: 'experts are far more likely to find areas of agreement through confidential discussions with each other, before they have formally declared positions in a written report. The tribunal should encourage these discussions to be held in camera without counsel present'. *See* Jones, 'Redefining the Role and Value of Expert Evidence', 37.

1075. *Blackaby and Wilbraham* argue that it will take time before the tribunal (and even the parties) can determine the necessary issues to be discussed with experts in complex investment cases, generally until after the first round of substantive submissions. *See* Blackaby and Wilbraham, 'Practical Issues Relating to the Use of Expert Evidence in Investment Treaty Arbitration', 666; Schäfer and Wilson, 'ICC Bulletin', 2021, 64.

1076. Jones, 'Ineffective Use of Expert Evidence in Construction Arbitration', 11; '2015 International Arbitration Survey: Improvements and Innovations in International Arbitration', 30; Kesikli, 'Milletlerarası Ticari Tahkimde Delillerin Değerlendirilmesi', 218; *see also* Debevoise & Plimpton LLP Protocol to Promote Efficiency in International Arbitration in Waincymer, *Procedure and Evidence in International Arbitration*, 437.

1077. Senogles, 'Some Views from the Crucible: The Perspective of an Expert Witness on the Adversarial Principle', 364; O'Malley, *Rules of Evidence in International Arbitration*, 161; Abdel Wahab, 'Party Appointed Experts in International Commercial Arbitration', 195.

1078. Jones, 'Redefining the Role and Value of Expert Evidence', 37; Grenz, *Der Faktor Zeit Im Schiedsverfahren*, 163.

1079. Senogles, 'Some Views from the Crucible: The Perspective of an Expert Witness on the Adversarial Principle', 364; Wilske and Gack, 'Expert Evidence in International Commercial Arbitration', 95; Jones, 'Ineffective Use of Expert Evidence in Construction Arbitration', 11; Jones, 'Redefining the Role and Value of Expert Evidence', 37.

1080. CIArb Protocol, Art. 6; IBA Rules, Art. 5(4); 2016 United Nations and United Nations Commission on International Trade Law, 'UNCITRAL Notes on Organizing Arbitral Proceedings', paras 97–98; Hodgson and Stewart, 'Experts in Investor-State Arbitration: The Tribunal as Gatekeeper', 459–460; Khodykin and Mulcahy, *A Guide to the IBA Rules on the Taking of Evidence in International Arbitration*, 315.

of these meetings is to attempt to agree and to identify points of difference.[1081] Although indirectly, the Case Management Techniques in the ICC Arbitration Rules also suggest pre-hearing meetings.[1082]

Notably, when multiple quantum experts are engaged by the parties, it would be beneficial for the tribunal to intervene and guide the party-appointed experts to provide views on or even use the methods of the other expert and provide conclusions. The tribunal will make it easier to have a common ground to compare. This method can lead party-appointed experts to disassociate themselves from the parties and their counsel and play a more neutral role. Thus, the need for a tribunal-appointed expert would be diminished, and extensive costs and time loss would be avoided.[1083]

Sachs suggests that such meetings are beneficial because they: (i) clarify technical and factual issues; (ii) outline areas of agreement and disagreement; (iii) focus on relevant points; (iv) narrow down the differences between expert reports; (v) encourage scientific debate and, consequently; (vi) render expert evidence more time-and cost-efficient and effective.[1084]

When practitioners were asked, over half of the respondents (54%) found the practice of experts conferring in advance of the main hearing to be useful, compared to only 7% who do not and 34% who do not exclude the possibility but say that 'it depends on the case'.[1085] Scholars also share the view that these hearings 'almost always do help'.[1086] It is considered useful to engage in discussions with an expert from the other party to identify respective objectives and methods.

Blackaby and *Wilbraham* note that such meetings are likely to be fruitful when they occur between experts of the same qualification who discuss a narrow scope of specific issues and identify the principal issues dividing the experts. This is expected to distil lengthy, complex reports into more digestible ones, thus also assisting parties and the tribunal in preparing more effectively to question experts at the hearing.[1087] However,

1081. Zuberbühler et al., *IBA Rules of Evidence*, 145; Parlett, 'Parties' Engagement with Experts in International Litigation', 447; Webster and Bühler, *Handbook of UNCITRAL Arbitration*, 424; Ünüvar, 'Experts: Investment Arbitration', para. 23; Khodykin and Mulcahy, *A Guide to the IBA Rules on the Taking of Evidence in International Arbitration*, 315; Hodgson and Stewart, 'Experts in Investor-State Arbitration: The Tribunal as Gatekeeper', 459–460; CIArb Protocol, Art. 6; IBA Rules, Art. 5(4); United Nations, 'UNCITRAL Notes on Organizing Arbitral Proceedings', paras 97–98.
1082. ICC Arbitration Rules Appendix IV, para. (b), para. (e).
1083. Blackaby and Wilbraham, 'Practical Issues Relating to the Use of Expert Evidence in Investment Treaty Arbitration', 668; *See Crystallex International Corporation v. Bolivarian Republic of Venezuela*, ICSID Case No ARB(AF)/11/2, Award, 4 April 2016, 31–32, para. 130 https://www.italaw.com/sites/default/files/case-documents/italaw7194.pdf (accessed 9 April 2023).
1084. Sachs and Schmidt-Ahrendts, 'Protocol on Expert Teaming: A New Approach to Expert Evidence', 143–144.
1085. '2012 International Arbitration Survey: Present and Preferred Practices in the Arbitral Process', 31.
1086. de Chazournes et al., 'Uses of Experts Before International Courts and Tribunals', 496.
1087. Parlett, 'Parties' Engagement with Experts in International Litigation', 448; Blackaby and Wilbraham, 'Practical Issues Relating to the Use of Expert Evidence in Investment Treaty Arbitration', 666; *see* Art. 3(1) of the CIArb Protocol.

when the divisions between experts are pivotal to the case, it could be difficult for experts to reach even a partial agreement.[1088]

For instance, in *Hydro Energy 1 and Hydroxana Sweden v. Spain*, initially, the experts' valuation estimates ranged between EUR 4 million and EUR 161 million. Later, the parties filed a joint model designed in collaboration with their experts, with an accompanying memorandum highlighting the remaining areas of disagreement. The tribunal applied this joint model and found a middle ground of EUR 31 million.[1089]

4.2.5 Tribunal-Appointed Expert

As explained, tribunal-appointed experts are generally not preferred over party-appointed experts. Nevertheless, the tribunal may appoint an expert if expertise is required to decide on the disputed matters and the parties have yet to adduce expert opinion.

The tribunal may appoint an expert whose competence is known or approach a specialist institution to help identify expertise or invite the parties to suggest suitable experts. The benefit of this process is that the tribunal will determine the critical issues of the case sufficiently early in the proceedings to allow for the efficient deployment of the expert.[1090]

Additionally, if there are multiple party-appointed experts and the tribunal feels lost due to the complexity of both opinions that do not clarify the required expertise, the tribunal can appoint an expert and resort to him as a guide.[1091] In that case, the expert should preferably deal only with issues with which the party-appointed experts disagree.[1092] This method is viable when the party-appointed experts disagree on a

1088. Blackaby and Wilbraham, 'Practical Issues Relating to the Use of Expert Evidence in Investment Treaty Arbitration', 665.

1089. *Hydro Energy 1 S.à r.l. and Hydroxana Sweden AB v. Kingdom of Spain*, ICSID Case No. ARB/15/42, Award, 5 August 2020, paras 11–13 https://www.italaw.com/sites/default/files/case-documents/italaw170209.pdf (accessed 9 April 2023).

1090. Khodykin and Mulcahy, *A Guide to the IBA Rules on the Taking of Evidence in International Arbitration*, 332; Jones, 'Redefining the Role and Value of Expert Evidence', 21.

1091. Khodykin and Mulcahy, 'Commentary on the IBA Rules on Evidence, Article 5 [Party-Appointed Experts]', 330; Tanrıver, *Hukukumuzda Bilirkişilik*, 34.

1092. O'Malley, *Rules of Evidence in International Arbitration*, 172; Abdel Wahab, 'Party Appointed Experts in International Commercial Arbitration', 196; Lim, 'Tribunal-Appointed Experts in International Arbitration', 214; *See Perenco Ecuador Ltd. v. Republic of Ecuador and Empresa Estatal Petróleos del Ecuador (Petroecuador)*, ICSID Case No. ARB/08/6, Interim Decision on the Environmental Counterclaim, 11 August 2015, para. 585 https://www.italaw.com/sites/default/files/case-documents/italaw6315.pdf (accessed 20 October 2022): 'The Tribunal has now arrived at the point where it has narrowed the counterclaim on the principal issues of law and fact. The Tribunal has set out the main issues of fact and law which have divided the experts. However, with regard to many of the IEMS/GSI differences, the Tribunal does not feel able to prefer one above the other. It seems to the Tribunal that each was attempting to achieve the best result for the party by whom they were instructed, and that they crossed the boundary between professional objective analysis and party representation. It is clear to the Tribunal that the experts were effectively shooting at different targets and this has made the work of this Tribunal most difficult.'

particular point or when the tribunal doubts the neutrality of the party-appointed experts.[1093]

If the tribunal bifurcates the proceedings and the parties have adduced experts only for the merits but not for the quantum stage, the tribunal can appoint a quantum expert.[1094] Some argue that this method could be cost-efficient,[1095] while the contrary experience from some practitioners reveals that tribunal-appointed experts might not be cost- and time-efficient in every case.[1096]

For instance, in *S.D. Meyers v. Government of Canada*, the tribunal decided that a '[t]ribunal expert should be appointed pursuant to Article 27(1) of the UNCITRAL Rules to assist in the *determination of issues that are outstanding as between the Disputing Parties' expert[s]'*.[1097] (emphasis added)

The tribunal should not rely solely on a tribunal-appointed expert if the parties have adduced an expert opinion.[1098]

A tribunal-appointed expert is an alternative to a party-appointed expert and is a less favoured option by practitioners.[1099] Not only does it help out the party with fulfilling the burden of proof, but it also prolongs the case, leads to additional costs, and sometimes does not even solve the issues.[1100] The use of a tribunal-appointed expert is associated with the risk that the tribunal will rely too heavily on the expert's opinion rather than making its own determination. The tribunal may end up delegating key decision-making responsibilities to the expert, especially if it is a legal issue.[1101]

Although not realistic, in theory, a party-appointed expert can become a tribunal-appointed expert with consent from the counterparty.[1102] It should be noted that it is

1093. Wilske and Gack, 'Expert Evidence in International Commercial Arbitration', 893; *see* Van Houtte, 'Party-Appointed Experts and Tribunal-Appointed Experts'.
1094. Khodykin and Mulcahy, *A Guide to the IBA Rules on the Taking of Evidence in International Arbitration*, 283.
1095. Knoblach, *Sachverhaltsermittlung in Der Internationalen Wirtschaftsschiedsgerichtsbarkeit*, 282.
1096. Lehmann and Mazuera, 'LIDW 2022: States as First-Class Citizens? Special Treatment for States in International Disputes'; Hoffmann and Shetty, 'Evidence and Hearings', 215; Bacanlı, 'Bir Alternatif Uyuşmazlık Cözüm Yolu Olarak Istanbul Tahkim ve Arabuluculuk Merkezi (ISTAC) Tahkim Yargilamasinda Delillerin Ibrazı ve Değerlendirilmesi', 97.
1097. *S.D. Myers, Inc. v. Government of Canada*, Procedural Order No. 17, 26 February 2001, para. 12, available at https://jusmundi.com/en/document/other/en-s-d-myers-inc-v-government-of-canada-procedural-order-no-17-and-no-18-monday-26th-february-2001#other_document_1293 (accessed 16 December 2022).
1098. Schlosser, 'Spontan Präsentierte Zeugen Und (Privat-)Gutachten Nach Deutschem Und Österreichischem Recht', 508.
1099. While 41% are in favour, 32% are against it, in 'BCLP 2021 Survey', 9.
1100. Wilske and Gack, 'Expert Evidence in International Commercial Arbitration', 86, 94; *See also* Van Houtte, 'Party-Appointed Experts and Tribunal-Appointed Experts'.
1101. Jones, 'Ineffective Use of Expert Evidence in Construction Arbitration', 10; Knoblach, *Sachverhaltsermittlung in Der Internationalen Wirtschaftsschiedsgerichtsbarkeit*, 282–283; Sachs and Schmidt-Ahrendts, 'Protocol on Expert Teaming: A New Approach to Expert Evidence', 140.
1102. Wach and Petsch, 'Der Sachverständigenbeweis Im Schiedsverfahren: Grenzen Der Gestaltungsfreiheit von Parteien Und Schiedsgericht', 111; In line with IBA Guidelines 2.1 (waivable red list).

not mandatory for the tribunal to appoint an expert if it is not requested in a timely manner.[1103] In addition, if tribunal members consider themselves adequately informed about the subject, they may reject a request to appoint an expert.[1104] When deciding so, in order to prevent any later right to be heard concerns, the arbitral tribunal should expressly highlight the reasons for refusal.[1105]

Parties may not desire the appointment of a tribunal-appointed expert for confidentiality reasons. In ICC Case No. 649,[1106] where corruption allegations were made, the parties objected to the analysis of the documents and records by a tribunal-appointed expert.

4.2.6 Examination

The first five recommendations above for the use of party-appointed experts relate to the formation of an understandable opinion that can be evaluated by the tribunal, which has no understanding of the field.

After the opinion of experts has been brought before the tribunal, the arbitrators will assess the views of the experts and test whether they are credible and worthy of being accepted as the basis of their decisions. As is especially the case in investment arbitration, multibillion-dollar awards are increasingly becoming normal, and it is vital to examine the experts during their damages determination.[1107]

Like witnesses of fact, party-appointed experts are being examined and their opinions cross-examined.[1108] Examination of the opinion(s) can be compared to the safety/homologation tests of new car models before they are allowed on the streets. These tests will determine whether the implants are functioning and safe. It is possible that experts consciously or mistakenly made incorrect assumptions or arithmetical mistakes with the material results.[1109] This can only be revealed through proper oral testimony and examination phase.[1110] Testimony and examination are considered closely related to the right to be heard.[1111]

1103. Swiss Federal Supreme Court, 4A_617/2010.
1104. Bundesgerichtshof (German Federal Court of Justice), III ZR 44/89, Wolters Kluwer.
1105. 'BCLP 2021 Survey', 19.
1106. 'In this case, the Consultant raised a confidentiality objection to disclose when asked to reveal banking documents. These documents allegedly showed deposits into the Consultant's account, deductions from the account, and where money went. The Consultant balked to produce the documents since such "production would jeopardize ... legitimate business secrets and possibly secrets of third parties. To overcome the confidentiality objection, the tribunal appointed an expert witness." Despite resistance, the Consultant ultimately submitted documents illuminating facts at odds with those originally proffered.' in Uluç, *Corruption in International Arbitration*, 163–164; *see* ICC Case No. 6497, Final Award in Van Den Berg, *ICCA Yearbook Commercial Arbitration 1999*, XXIVa:71–79.
1107. Hodgson and Stewart, 'Experts in Investor-State Arbitration: The Tribunal as Gatekeeper', 454.
1108. Wilske and Gack, 'Expert Evidence in International Commercial Arbitration', 79.
1109. Atalay, 'Pekcanıtez Usûl', 2021, 1961.
1110. Hodgson and Stewart, 'Experts in Investor-State Arbitration: The Tribunal as Gatekeeper', 458; Tanrıver, *Hukukumuzda Bilirkişilik*, 32.
1111. Pekcanıtez and Yeşilirmak, 'Tahkim', 2713.

In cases where one of the parties refers to an expert opinion, the other party must be given the opportunity to make explanations against the expert report in accordance with the right to be heard and equality of arms.[1112] Again, if the expert's opinion is erroneous, it will be possible for the other party to prove it by asking questions, revealing contradictions, and asking questions in order to eliminate the doubts of the arbitrator.

If the expert opinion is evaluated only on paper, it may be incomplete in many aspects and may be evaluated without revealing the errors. The ability of the party or the arbitrator to ask expert questions about the opinion prepared and submitted to the arbitral tribunal and to investigate the accuracy of his opinion is not an inconvenience but brings quality and benefit to proceedings. In this way, it is possible to reach a factual truth. Due to examination, experts will be better prepared and will not act arbitrarily.[1113]

The examination phase has been deemed so critical that, for instance, according to the CIArb Protocol, any expert who has provided a written opinion must give oral testimony, unless otherwise agreed by the parties. Failure to appear without a valid reason could cause the tribunal to disregard the expert's written opinion.[1114]

4.2.6.1 Examination by the Tribunal

Many arbitral rules foresee that at the evidentiary hearing, the parties or tribunal may question the experts on issues raised in the expert's report, the parties' submissions, or witness statements.[1115]

The arbitral tribunal will conduct a subjective and objective test on the expert.[1116] The tribunal will decide whether any testimony or examination, and if so, in which order, will be carried out.[1117]

Practitioners view the arbitral tribunal as 'the most important barrier against bias'.[1118] Tribunals are 'generally capable of determining when a party-appointed expert is not being objective in their testimony'.[1119] In cases where the party-appointed expert breaches his duty to be impartial and assists the tribunal, the arbitrators should give limited weight to the testimony and statements.[1120]

1112. Atalay, 'Pekcanıtez Usûl', 2021, 1961.
1113. Tanrıver, *Hukukumuzda Bilirkişilik*, 33.
1114. CIArb Protocol Art. 6.1(h) and (i).
1115. Khodykin and Mulcahy, *A Guide to the IBA Rules on the Taking of Evidence in International Arbitration*, 287; Sarısözen, *Medeni Usul Hukukunda Soru Yöneltme ve Capraz Sorgu*, 349.
1116. *See* Chapter 2 section 2.6.
1117. Khodykin and Mulcahy, *A Guide to the IBA Rules on the Taking of Evidence in International Arbitration*, 291.
1118. 'BCLP 2021 Survey', 14.
1119. 'BCLP 2021 Survey', 14.
1120. Jones, 'Redefining the Role and Value of Expert Evidence', 24; 'BCLP 2021 Survey', 21.

4.2.6.2 *Examination by the Parties*

In addition to the examination by the tribunal, the counsel can also examine the party-appointed experts.[1121] This process has two phases. The first phase is a direct examination, where the counsel examines their own experts to make a case before the tribunal. The second and trickier phase is cross-examination.

There is strong support for the use of cross-examination in international arbitration to test experts. The vast majority of respondents believed that cross-examination was always or usually an effective form of testing the expert (86%).[1122]

An expert who knows that he will be subject to cross-examination through the adversarial process by the opposing counsel is a further check on the process.[1123] Because the counsel will work hard to find any errors in the methodology or application based on the experts' views.

For instance, quantum experts can make incorrect assumptions or arithmetical mistakes based on material results. This should make the expert's testimony not credible.[1124]

Examination of the party-appointed expert by the parties on his evaluations and conclusions strengthens the power of the expert opinion's objectivity.[1125] In practice, the counsel of the party calling the expert would begin the examination-in-chief, followed by cross-examination by the opposing counsel.[1126]

4.2.6.2.1 Direct Examination

Although experts will present their opinions in writing, counsel may want to draw attention to crucial points and nuances of the case in a short presentation.[1127] The direct examination of party-appointed experts can be conducted as an oral presentation, often accompanied by visual aids.

1121. Tanrıver, *Hukukumuzda Bilirkişilik*, 32.
1122. '2012 International Arbitration Survey: Present and Preferred Practices in the Arbitral Process', 26; Abdel Wahab, 'Party Appointed Experts in International Commercial Arbitration', 199; More than two-thirds (69%) of respondents in the BCLP Survey share the view that any potential bias is cancelled out with cross-examination, *see* 'BCLP 2021 Survey', 17; *See* critics regarding cross-examination of party-appointed experts Proske, *Expert Witness Conferencing in Schiedsverfahren*, 31 and Blackaby et al., *Redfern and Hunter on International Arbitration (Student Version)*, 6.138.
1123. Parlett, 'Parties' Engagement with Experts in International Litigation', 451; Aygül, *Milletlerarası Ticarî Tahkimde Tahkim Usûlüne Uygulanacak Hukuk ve Deliller*, 269; Akıncı, *Milletlerarası Tahkim*, 341; Tanrıver, *Hukukumuzda Bilirkişilik*, 32.
1124. Hodgson and Stewart, 'Experts in Investor-State Arbitration: The Tribunal as Gatekeeper', 458.
1125. Tanrıver, *Hukukumuzda Bilirkişilik*, 32.
1126. Khodykin and Mulcahy, *A Guide to the IBA Rules on the Taking of Evidence in International Arbitration*, 322; Knoblach, *Sachverhaltsermittlung in Der Internationalen Wirtschaftsschiedsgerichtsbarkeit*, 207.
1127. Waincymer, 'Advocacy Training in International Commercial and Investment Arbitration':, 72.

Direct examination can be an important medium to acknowledge and address weaknesses in a case.[1128] During the examination, the counsel may only ask 'non-leading' questions to the expert. These are types of questions that do not suggest an answer; however, they leave the expert free to tell what he should tell. Consequently, the tribunal will be educated on a technical matter. In addition, through direct examination of its experts, counsels create the opportunity to enhance the credibility of its case.

The tribunal has the discretion to determine specifically how and in what order the examination will occur.

4.2.6.2.2 Cross-Examination

Cross-examination refers to the process by which an attorney, usually through skilled questioning, seeks to elicit, challenge, and clarify the expert's testimony provided during the hearings.[1129]

This methodical and adversarial approach aims to uncover inconsistencies, biases, and pertinent information that the counter-witness or expert has provided that may impact the resolution of the dispute. Cross-examination enables the testing of an expert's credibility, clarification of ambiguities, and introduction of counter-narratives. Quite occasionally, cross-examination (in addition to the expert conferencing) is suggested to be advisable[1130] or even necessary to have regard to due process.[1131]

The cross-examination of experts requires a high level of understanding of technical matters. The cross-examination of a party-appointed expert is one of the most challenging tasks for attorneys in international arbitration.[1132] When executed effectively, it is an excellent method to test the opinions of experts.[1133]

In fact, in the cross-examination of party experts, the opposing counsel should be familiar with all the details of the case, prepare for the cross-examination in detail before the hearing, and conduct the cross-examination of the party-appointed expert with a disciplined questioning technique.[1134]

Cross-examination aims to shake up the credibility of the expert and his opinion.[1135] If possible, cross-examination should first attempt to shake the credibility of the expert.

1128. Waincymer, 73.
1129. Hobér and Sussman, *Cross-Examination in International Arbitration*, 32–33.
1130. Waincymer, 'Advocacy Training in International Commercial and Investment Arbitration', 72.
1131. Waincymer, *Procedure and Evidence in International Arbitration*, 968; For critics to this view, *see* Proske, *Expert witness conferencing in Schiedsverfahren*, 46.
1132. Beharry and McRae, 'Cross Examination of Expert Witnesses', 187 ff.
1133. Roney, 'Cross-Examination of Experts', 110; Schlaepfer, 'The Burden of Proof in International Arbitration', 129; Ağırman, *Milli & Milletlerarası Tahkim*, 463–464.
Akıncı, Milletlerarası Tahkim, 341.
1134. Kesikli, 'Milletlerarası Ticari Tahkimde Delillerin Değerlendirilmesi', 237.
1135. Kalpsüz, *Türkiye'de Milletlerarası Tahkim*, 93; Kesikli, 'Milletlerarası Ticari Tahkimde Delillerin Değerlendirilmesi', 237; Allen, Jr., 'United States', 289; Waincymer, 'Advocacy Training in International Commercial and Investment Arbitration':, 73.

It can be about his personality, qualifications, or professional attitude. Cross-examination is also considered necessary to uncover contradictions in expert opinions. This can expose inconsistencies between the present and former views of the expert.[1136]

The US practice uses cross-examination to determine whether party-appointed experts adhere to scientific methodology and any relevant standards applied by the expert's profession.[1137]

Before cross-examination, the party-appointed expert and counsel should analyse and identify areas to refute the opinion of the counter-expert. They may also identify matters for seeking an agreement that helps their case.[1138]

Equal opportunity should be given to both parties during examination and cross-examination.[1139] As stressed in *CME Czech Republic B.V. v. The Czech Republic*, the tribunal shall safeguard each party's equal right to present their case, which includes cross-examining the parties' experts.[1140]

In rare circumstances, both parties might not request to cross-examine the expert but still give regard to the written report. However, no request for cross-examination shall not mean that the tribunal or the parties have agreed to the correctness of the contents of the expert report (IBA Rules Article 5(6)).[1141]

4.2.7 Expert Conferencing

4.2.7.1 Definition

Expert conferencing is a method of examination in which two or more party-appointed experts from opposing parties[1142] present their opinions and are questioned by the arbitral tribunal or the counsel during oral hearings jointly and simultaneously rather than sequentially and separately.[1143]

1136. Kalpsüz, *Türkiye'de Milletlerarası Tahkim*, 93; Hunter, 'Expert Conferencing and New Methods', 4, para. 11; Proske, *Expert witness conferencing in Schiedsverfahren*, 45; For the argument that credibility should not be subject at the expert conferencing *See* Raeschke-Kessler, 'Witness Conferencing', 704; Roney, 'Cross-Examination of Experts', 112.
1137. Blackaby and Wilbraham, 'Practical Issues Relating to the Use of Expert Evidence in Investment Treaty Arbitration', 658.
1138. Roney, 'Cross-Examination of Experts', 113.
1139. For more details, *see* Proske, *Expert witness conferencing in Schiedsverfahren*, 42.
1140. *See CME Czech Republic B.V. v. The Czech Republic*, UNCITRAL, Final Award 14 March 2003, para. 80 available at, https://www.italaw.com/cases/281 (accessed 30 August 2022).
1141. O'Malley, *Rules of Evidence in International Arbitration*, 162; Khodykin and Mulcahy, *A Guide to the IBA Rules on the Taking of Evidence in International Arbitration*, 321; Roney, 'Cross-Examination of Experts', 112.
1142. Whereas the method is used mostly for party-appointed experts, it is not excluded when tribunal-appointed experts are also employed. *See* for details Proske, *Expert Witness Conferencing in Schiedsverfahren*, 39–40.
1143. Peter, 'Witness "Conferencing"', 47; For various terms used by different authors, such as expert witness conferencing, conferencing, hot-tubbing or joint conferencing, for the same concept *see* Proske, *Expert witness conferencing in Schiedsverfahren*, 34–37; Townsend, 'Crossing the Hot-Tub: Examining Adverse Expert Witnesses in International Arbitration', 165; Wilske and Gack, 'Expert Evidence in International Commercial Arbitration', 94; Foster,

The salient feature of this method is that it allows experts to interact with each other.[1144] Expert conferencing has not been a recent phenomenon; its application can also be found in domestic litigation in some states.[1145]

4.2.7.2 The Practice of Expert Conferencing

Generally, expert conferencing can be applied in any case where there are complex factual and technical issues involving multiple opposing experts.[1146] Additionally, where experts know each other, what is likely, especially in investment arbitrations, due to its relatively narrow pool of practitioners, or the experts seemingly agree on some points, the method could be practised.[1147] If the issues where expert opinion is sought are highly controversial or the opposing experts did not opine on the same issues, the method may not be viable.[1148]

The expert conferencing method can be helpful on the condition that it is constructed and controlled firmly by the tribunal but is not left solely to the experts or the legal counsel.[1149]

No detailed rules on expert conferencing are found in the arbitration rules.[1150] Therefore, the tribunal, advisably in the first procedural order,[1151] should not only determine and inform the participants of the proceedings how the expert and their

Science and the Precautionary Principle in International Courts and Tribunals: Expert Evidence, Burden of Proof and Finality, 123; Pörnbacher, Duncker, and Baur, 'Gaspreisanpassungs-Schiedsverfahren: Hintergründe und prozessuale Besonderheiten', 298. Weiss and Bürgi Locatelli, 'Der Vom Schiedsgericht Bestellte Experte-Ein Überblick Aus Sicht Eines Internationalen Schiedsgerichts Mit Sitz in Der Schweiz', 482; Proske, *Expert witness conferencing in Schiedsverfahren*, 38; Hwang, 'Witness Conferencing', 3; Hwang and Ong, 'Effective Cross-Examination in Asian Arbitrations', 285; Veeder and et al., 'Act III: Advocacy with Witness Testimony', 605–606; Kesikli, 'Milletlerarası Ticari Tahkimde Delillerin Değerlendirilmesi', 222; Can and Tuna, *Milletlerarası Tahkim Hukuku*, 417; Trittmann and Schardt, 'The Proceedings Before the Arbitral Tribunal, Article 28: Establishing the Facts', 465.

1144. Jones, 'Redefining the Role and Value of Expert Evidence', 32.
1145. *See* for Australia: The New South Wales Uniform Civil Procedure Rules 2005, R 31.23. available at https://legislation.nsw.gov.au/view/html/inforce/current/sl-2005-0418#sec.31.19 (accessed 17 December 2022), Jones, 27–28; *See* for Canada: Federal Courts Rules SOR/98-106, Rule 52.2 Code of Conduct for Expert Witnesses available at https://laws-lois.justice.gc.ca/eng/regulations/sor-98-106/page-118.html#:~:text=1%20An%20expert%20witness%20named,person%20retaining%20the%20expert%20witness (accessed 17 December 2022).
1146. Bor, 'Expert Evidence', 508; Hodgson and Stewart, 'Experts in Investor-State Arbitration: The Tribunal as Gatekeeper', 459–460; Jones, 'Redefining the Role and Value of Expert Evidence', 32; Proske, *Expert Witness Conferencing in Schiedsverfahren*, 52.
1147. Nemeth and Haidostian, 'The "Hot Tub" Method of Taking Expert Testimony Is Gaining Steam: What You Need to Know', 92.
1148. Bor, 'Expert Evidence', 509.
1149. de Chazournes et al., 'Uses of Experts Before International Courts and Tribunals', 496; 'BCLP 2021 Survey', 20; Proske, *Expert Witness Conferencing in Schiedsverfahren*, 38, 40; Bor, 'Expert Evidence', 509; Schütze and Thümmel, *Schiedsgericht Und Schiedsverfahren*, 119, para. 482.
1150. Proske, *Expert Witness Conferencing in Schiedsverfahren*, 48.
1151. Advisably, after consultation and in agreement with the parties. Generally speaking, the tribunal is 'pushing' the parties for conferencing. *See* for details Proske, *Expert Witness Conferencing in Schiedsverfahren*, 49, 51.

opinion should be adduced but also the style and procedure of the examination of the experts, time limits, the stage when the conferencing should take place and whether and how cross-examination will be performed.[1152] If not appropriately regulated early in the proceedings,[1153] expert conferencing will not provide benefits.[1154] Where possible, the tribunal should direct the opposing experts to submit a joint report.

The opposing experts should be placed at the same table in a position that enables them to look into each other's eyes and have a discussion.[1155] The tribunal should limit the matters to be addressed by the experts and should conduct a focused conversation rather than an occasional debate. Translators should be available if necessary.

For the effectiveness of the method, the tribunal should also be well prepared, thoroughly read the written expert opinions, determine the specific matters it needs to understand and explain its opinions.[1156] This method will only bear fruit if the tribunal performs its responsibility to manage the case proactively.[1157]

The arbitral tribunal will be able to ask questions to each expert. After the arbitral tribunal examines the experts, it is imperative to grant the counsels the opportunity to ask supplementary questions to adhere to the parties' right to be heard.[1158] Counsel should ask supplemental questions on issues that still need to be settled or addressed. The tribunal may also directly leave the floor to the party counsel and ask for additional questions where certain points are not clear.

However, counsels should understand that this examination differs from a conventional cross-examination in which they lead the examined expert according to the interests of the party.[1159] Counsel should allow the experts to interact, and the tribunal should intervene if this does not occur.

Whereas one may think that cross-examination is unnecessary when experts already conference, Proske demonstrates in her study that in practice, mainly expert conferencing and cross-examination take place in arbitration, with differences in each regarding their order.[1160]

1152. Proske, *Expert Witness Conferencing in Schiedsverfahren*, 44, 49.
1153. Preferably, during the first case management conference. In case the tribunal can foresee whether the conferencing will be necessary, it should at least foreshadow the possibility.
1154. Proske, *Expert Witness Conferencing in Schiedsverfahren*, 50; Raeschke-Kessler, 'Witness Conferencing', 699.
1155. Blackaby et al., *Redfern & Hunter on International Arbitration*, para. 6.185; Proske, *Expert Witness Conferencing in Schiedsverfahren*, 53; Raeschke-Kessler, 'Witness Conferencing', 701.
1156. Bor, 'Expert Evidence', 509; Foster, *Science and the Precautionary Principle in International Courts and Tribunals: Expert Evidence, Burden of Proof and Finality*, 124; Raeschke-Kessler, 'Witness Conferencing', 698.
1157. *See* Chapter 4 section 4.2.1.
1158. Proske, *Expert witness conferencing in Schiedsverfahren*, 45; Foster, *Science and the Precautionary Principle in International Courts and Tribunals: Expert Evidence, Burden of Proof and Finality*, 123.
1159. *See* for details Proske, *Expert witness conferencing in Schiedsverfahren*, 44; Hwang, 'Witness Conferencing', 3; For the argument by various authors that share the view that expert conferencing is only supplementary to cross-examination *see* Blackaby et al., *Redfern & Hunter on International Arbitration*, para. 6.184; Veeder and et al., 'Act III: Advocacy with Witness Testimony', 609–610.
1160. *Proske* stipulates that expert conferencing is sometimes applied first and sometimes later after cross-examination. *See* Proske, *Expert Witness Conferencing in Schiedsverfahren*, 47.

Cross-examination is considered necessary to uncover contradictions between the former opinions, i.e., published works, and the opinion of a party-appointed expert in the arbitration proceedings or to generally test the credibility of a party-appointed expert.[1161] Quite occasionally, cross-examination (in addition to the expert conferencing) is advisable[1162] or even necessary to have regard to due process.[1163]

Equal opportunity should be given to both parties during examination and cross-examination.[1164] The existence of a different number of party experts per side does not necessarily and automatically lead to unequal treatment of the parties in expert conferencing. The arbitral tribunal should, however, avoid even the impression of favouritism towards one party at any time during the hearing.[1165]

After the expert has presented his opinion orally or when the tribunal and the parties deem it unnecessary, the examination may be conducted by both the tribunal and the counsel by asking questions to the expert(s).[1166]

Where multiple disputed issues from different subject matters need to be addressed by experts, separate conferences should be held.[1167]

4.2.7.3 Evaluation of Expert Conferencing

Over time, with its successful applications, expert conferencing has gained some acceptance in the practice of international arbitration.[1168]

When practitioners were asked their views on expert conferencing, support seems to be mixed. According to the BCLP Survey, only 49% of respondents agreed that conferencing was more effective than sequential hearing.[1169] However, 75% of the respondents agreed that the effectiveness of conferencing was drastically increased when led by the arbitral tribunal in accordance with an agreed protocol.[1170]

This method for obtaining evidence is especially effective in complex arbitrations that have difficult factual and technical issues and in which the parties rely on evidence

---

1161. Hunter, 'Expert Conferencing and New Methods', 4, para. 11; Proske, *Expert Witness Conferencing in Schiedsverfahren*, 45; Hunter, 'Expert Conferencing and New Methods', 4, para. 11; For the argument that credibility should not be subject at the expert conferencing *see* Raeschke-Kessler, 'Witness Conferencing', 704.
1162. Hunter, 'Expert Conferencing and New Methods', 4, para. 11.
1163. Waincymer, *Procedure and Evidence in International Arbitration*, 968; For critic to this view, *see* Proske, *Expert Witness Conferencing in Schiedsverfahren*, 46–47.
1164. For details *see* Proske, *Expert Witness Conferencing in Schiedsverfahren*, 42.
1165. Proske, 43.
1166. Proske, 40; Förstel-Cherng et al., *Beweiserhebung Im Schiedsverfahren*, 83, 174, para. 468, fn. 912.
1167. CIArb Guidelines for Witness Conferencing in International Arbitration, 34, para. 5(1)(a).
1168. Raeschke-Kessler, 'Witness Conferencing', 689; Townsend, 'Crossing the Hot-Tub: Examining Adverse Expert Witnesses in International Arbitration', 165; Webster and Bühler, *Handbook of UNCITRAL Arbitration*, 446; Jones, 'Redefining the Role and Value of Expert Evidence', 32; Some state courts also adopted this method for experts, *see* Federal Court of Australia, Expert Evidence Practice Note 25 October 2016 available at https://www.fedcourt.gov.au/law-and-practice/practice-documents/practice-notes/gpn-expt (accessed 22 December 2022).
1169. 'BCLP 2021 Survey', 20.
1170. 'BCLP 2021 Survey', 20.

from multiple experts.[1171] In such circumstances, the conventional approach of examining experts from each side in a linear fashion does not always lead to a clear understanding for both the tribunal and the counsel and is not cost-efficient.[1172] This is particularly the case when multiple and opposing expert statements are heard in different hearings over a long time span. However, through expert conferencing, the experts can concurrently engage with opposing views and debate, thus enabling a deeper examination of contentious issues.[1173]

It is suggested that the arbitral tribunal examine both party-appointed experts to report on the same issues at the same hearing simultaneously and try to infer an understanding regarding their partiality/objectivity and receive a contrast of the experts (and their opinion), which is more convincing by examining them.[1174] This method is supposedly more effective than traditional hearing, where long presentations and examinations occur sequentially and may even be on different days.[1175]

A perceived advantage of conferencing experts over the traditional method of examination is that it allows expert opinions to be comprehensively explored and tested by another expert before the tribunal and parties. Conferencing experts may also shorten hearing times and are potentially less adversarial. Conferencing experts may not be suitable when experts have not been instructed to opine on the same issues.[1176] However, even when experts present their opinions on different subject matters, if the opinions are strictly interconnected, the method could be useful.[1177]

Expert conferencing can only bear fruit if the tribunal is well prepared and proactive, and a joint-report has been established.[1178]

The dynamics of the process can cause experts to express their own immediate opinions and forget any answers that they might have been expected to give to specific questions. This can further initiate a dynamic conversation, where each expert explains to the arbitral tribunal the reason he disagrees with the views of the other,

1171. Bor, 'Expert Evidence', 508; Hodgson and Stewart, 'Experts in Investor-State Arbitration: The Tribunal as Gatekeeper', 459–460; Jones, 'Redefining the Role and Value of Expert Evidence', 32.
1172. Brown, 'Oral Evidence and Experts in Arbitration', 85; Proske, *Expert Witness Conferencing in Schiedsverfahren*, 31; Grenz, *Der Faktor Zeit Im Schiedsverfahren*, 73–75.
1173. Jones, 'Ineffective Use of Expert Evidence in Construction Arbitration', 7; Knoblach, *Sachverhaltsermittlung in Der Internationalen Wirtschaftsschiedsgerichtsbarkeit*, 280; Townsend, 'Crossing the Hot-Tub: Examining Adverse Expert Witnesses in International Arbitration', 165; Jones, 'Redefining the Role and Value of Expert Evidence', 32.
1174. Wach and Petsch, 'Der Sachverständigenbeweis Im Schiedsverfahren: Grenzen Der Gestaltungsfreiheit von Parteien Und Schiedsgericht', 96; Peter, 'Witness "Conferencing"', 47; Senogles, 'Some Views from the Crucible: The Perspective of an Expert Witness on the Adversarial Principle', 364; Blackaby and Wilbraham, 'Practical Issues Relating to the Use of Expert Evidence in Investment Treaty Arbitration', 667; O'Malley, *Rules of Evidence in International Arbitration*, 159; Abdel Wahab, 'Party Appointed Experts in International Commercial Arbitration', 194, 196; Proske, *Expert Witness Conferencing in Schiedsverfahren*, 26 ff.; Jones, 'Ineffective Use of Expert Evidence in Construction Arbitration', 7.
1175. Wilske and Gack, 'Expert Evidence in International Commercial Arbitration', 95.
1176. Bor, 'Expert Evidence', 509; Abdel Wahab, 'Party Appointed Experts in International Commercial Arbitration', 194, 205; Jones, 'Redefining the Role and Value of Expert Evidence', 33.
1177. Proske, *Expert Witness Conferencing in Schiedsverfahren*, 38.
1178. Jones, 'Redefining the Role and Value of Expert Evidence', 38; Proske, *Expert Witness Conferencing in Schiedsverfahren*, 41.

thereby facilitating the arbitral tribunal's understanding. It may also enable experts to agree on disputed matters.[1179]

The peer pressure and debate that typically result from opposing experts sitting at the same table can also help in rephrasing incorrect or exaggerated previous statements and consequently reducing the number of issues on which experts disagree.[1180]

Nevertheless, these characteristics are derived from various arbitral practices; neither detailed institutional rules nor uniform guidelines regarding the performance of the conference method are present.[1181]

The wording of UNCITRAL Model Law Article 26(2) and many jurisdictions like Türkiye or Germany,[1182] which base their statutes on it, also support expert conferencing.

Whether cross-examination will also be conducted during the expert conferencing or accepted as an alternative to conferencing will be up to the tribunal's decision in each case. Whereas one may think that cross-examination is not necessary when experts already conference, *Proske* demonstrates in her study that in practice, expert conferencing and cross-examination both take place in arbitration, with differences in each regarding their order.[1183]

If the party-appointed expert's credibility is already shaken during the examination by the tribunal or the parties, holding a conference may not be helpful in testing another's lack of independence or qualifications, experience, or expertise.[1184]

4.2.8 Utilising Generative Artificial Intelligence as an Expert

The integration of generative artificial intelligence (GAI) has prompted the arbitration community to explore new avenues for its application, thereby fostering the evolution and enhancement of arbitration proceedings. As technological advancements continue to reshape the landscape of dispute resolution, GAI presents significant potential to streamline processes, improve efficiency, and introduce innovative methods for handling complex arbitration cases. Consequently, arbitration practitioners are actively seeking ways to incorporate GAI tools to optimise procedural practices and advance the overall effectiveness of arbitration.

The question arises of whether the GAI can be used as an expert on matters requiring expertise. Party autonomy and procedural flexibility, as applicable principles in many

1179. Abdel Wahab, 'Party Appointed Experts in International Commercial Arbitration', 205–206.
1180. Jones, 'Ineffective Use of Expert Evidence in Construction Arbitration', 8; '2012 International Arbitration Survey: Present and Preferred Practices in the Arbitral Process', 28; Wilske and Gack, 'Expert Evidence in International Commercial Arbitration', 94; Proske, *Expert Witness Conferencing in Schiedsverfahren*, 38.
1181. Proske, *Expert Witness Conferencing in Schiedsverfahren*, 37.
1182. For the German perspective, *see* Grenz, *Der Faktor Zeit Im Schiedsverfahren*, 154–155; Sachs and Lörcher, 'Experts Appointed by Arbitral Tribunal', 295; Lotz, 'Der Sachvreständige Im Schiedsverfahren', 209; Schütze, *Zivilprozessordnung Und Nebengesetze: Großkommentar*, § 1049, para. 46.
1183. *Proske* stipulates that expert conferencing is sometimes applied first and sometimes later after cross-examination, *see* Proske, *Expert Witness Conferencing in Schiedsverfahren*, 47.
1184. CIArb Guidelines for Witness Conferencing in International Arbitration, 29, para. 3a-b.

jurisdictions, enable parties to agree freely on procedures. For instance, the LCIA Rules Article 14.6(iii) allow the tribunal to employ technology to enhance the efficiency and expeditious conduct of proceedings. Hypothetically, if the parties agree and allow the tribunal to use the GAI rather than appoint an expert, the tribunal can make use of it.

When asked ChatGPT whether and how it could be used in international arbitration as an expert and whether it could replace the use of experts, it gave the following answers:[1185]

> Data Analysis: Generative AI can process and analyse large volumes of data, including expert reports, legal documents, case law, and other relevant information. It can help identify patterns, correlations, and inconsistencies in the information presented by party-appointed experts.
> Comparative Analysis: Generative AI can generate comparative summaries of the methodologies, assumptions, and conclusions presented by different experts. This can help arbitrators and legal teams better understand the differences and similarities between the expert reports.
> Issue Identification: Generative AI can identify key issues and arguments raised by party-appointed experts and provide structured summaries for easier comprehension.
> Alternative Perspectives: By analysing various sources of information, generative AI can help generate alternative viewpoints and arguments that may assist arbitrators in evaluating the expert opinions more comprehensively.
> Legal Precedent: Generative AI can assist in searching for and summarizing relevant legal precedent and past arbitral awards that address similar technical or factual issues, helping arbitrators to make informed decisions.
> Sensitivity Analysis: Generative AI can perform sensitivity analysis based on varying assumptions, allowing arbitrators to understand how changes in assumptions might affect the experts' conclusions.
> However, it's important to note that generative AI is a tool and not a replacement for the expertise and judgement of human arbitrators. It can assist in information processing, analysis, and generating insights, but the final decision-making still rests with the arbitrators. Moreover, the reliability and accuracy of generative AI's output depend on the quality of the input data and the algorithms used.
> Additionally, the use of generative AI in arbitration proceedings may raise concerns about transparency, explainability, and due process. Parties should carefully consider how AI-generated insights will be introduced and utilized within the arbitration process and ensure that all parties have an opportunity to address and challenge the AI-generated content.
> In summary, while generative AI has the potential to provide valuable assistance in addressing issues related to party-appointed experts, its role should be carefully considered, and its outputs should be evaluated in conjunction with expert opinions and other relevant information.
> One of the main problems with party-appointed experts is that they can be biased towards the party that appointed them. This can lead to the expert giving an opinion that is favourable to that party, even if it is not supported by the evidence. A generative AI, on the other hand, is not biased towards any party. It would be able to provide an objective opinion, based on the evidence, regardless of who appointed it.

1185. Text generated by ChatGPT, 27 December 2023, OpenAI, https://chat.openai.com (accessed 24 September 2025).

> Another problem with party-appointed experts is that they can be expensive. A generative AI would be much cheaper to use, as it would not require the same level of expertise as a human expert. This would make it more accessible to parties in arbitration proceedings, who may not have the financial resources to hire a human expert.
>
> Finally, a generative AI could help to speed up the arbitration process. Party-appointed experts can often take a long time to prepare their reports. A generative AI could be programmed to prepare a report much more quickly, which would help to shorten the overall arbitration process.
>
> Of course, there are also some potential drawbacks to using a generative AI in arbitration. One concern is that the AI may not be able to understand the complex legal issues involved in arbitration proceedings. Another concern is that the AI may not be able to provide an opinion that is as persuasive as a human expert.
>
> However, I believe that the potential benefits of using a generative AI in arbitration outweigh the risks. A generative AI could help to solve some of the major problems with party-appointed experts, such as bias, expense, and time delays. As the technology continues to develop, I believe that generative AI will become an increasingly important tool in international commercial and investment arbitration.
>
> One of the main problems with party-appointed experts is that they can be biased towards the party that appointed them. This can lead to the expert giving an opinion that is favourable to that party, even if it is not supported by the evidence. A generative AI, on the other hand, is not biased towards any party. It would be able to provide an objective opinion, based on the evidence, regardless of who appointed it.
>
> Another problem with party-appointed experts is that they can be expensive. A generative AI would be much cheaper to use, as it would not require the same level of expertise as a human expert. This would make it more accessible to parties in arbitration proceedings, who may not have the financial resources to hire a human expert.
>
> Finally, a generative AI could help to speed up the arbitration process. Party-appointed experts can often take a long time to prepare their reports. A generative AI could be programmed to prepare a report much more quickly, which would help to shorten the overall arbitration process.
>
> Of course, there are also some potential drawbacks to using a generative AI in arbitration. One concern is that the AI may not be able to understand the complex legal issues involved in arbitration proceedings. Another concern is that the AI may not be able to provide an opinion that is as persuasive as a human expert.
>
> However, I believe that the potential benefits of using a generative AI in arbitration outweigh the risks. A generative AI could help to solve some of the major problems with party-appointed experts, such as bias, expense, and time delays. As the technology continues to develop, I believe that generative AI will become an increasingly important tool in international commercial and investment arbitration.

In the current state of the art, due to the relative underdevelopment and other concerns regarding GAI tools, it seems a little ahead of time that GAI will make its way into international arbitration proceedings effectively.

First, GAIs come at the risk of bias, which is already a big concern of party-appointed experts. The GAI is primarily controlled and created by humans, and the way they feed the system with specific datasets may lead, although not intentionally, to biased systems.

Second, ChatGPT, as one of the most prominent GAI tools, has limitations in comprehending and contextualising information. This is called 'hallucination'. Hallucination is a problem where the model generates information that is not grounded in reality.

Last but not least, anyone, especially software developers, can build a GAI tool without acquiring proper infrastructure or a duly established company that complies with legal obligations. When information is provided to GAI tools, it is fair to argue that it is highly likely that privacy could be violated. As arbitration is inherently confidential, when using a GAI tool as an expert, sensitive and confidential information will be provided. Because it is not safe for most tools now, if not for bias or hallucination, this concern would deem the use of GAI as experts, at least for now, not possible. As is regulated in most arbitration rules, every person included must keep the information confidential.[1186]

Although it is true that web browsers and other web pages also collect information that could lead to leaks, due to the conversation style with the GAI model, users tend to share more sensitive information, such as identification of confidential information.

Nevertheless, in the near future, enhanced and proven GAI tools will make their way into arbitration practice and enable arbitrators to use them as a valuable tool. However, it is crucial that arbitrators maintain their authority, using GAI as a supportive resource rather than a substitute for human decision-making.

1186. For instance, *see* ISTAC Arbitration Rules Art. 21 or Swiss Rules Art. 44.

CHAPTER 5
Evaluation and Conclusion

Experts clarify disputed issues that impact the outcome of the case and support the tribunal during the decision-making process. Arbitrators in international commercial and investment arbitration mostly originate from a legal background. Due to the limited capability of lawyer arbitrators, technical, legal and quantum experts are heavily involved in international commercial and investment arbitration cases.

Although both are used, data and practice preferences show that party-appointed experts are generally preferred over tribunal-appointed experts. This is understandable, as the parties and their counsel want to have full control over their case. For the tribunal, it is also convenient not to find the exact expert and not to address the costs. The role of experts should always be considered along with the overriding competence and function of the tribunal.

In comparison to a party-appointed expert, the main role of a tribunal-appointed expert is to primarily assist the tribunal. The party-appointed expert is also expected to support or explain the position of the party that appointed the expert. The expert's terms of appointment are defined by the arbitral tribunal; neither party is exclusively responsible for the expert's remuneration, and the tribunal-appointed expert does not receive information exclusively from any particular party. In theory, the absence of a financial incentive and connection with a party increases the likelihood that the expert will be unbiased.[1187]

Expert opinions in international commercial arbitration are crucial to the decision-making process, and it is only logical to classify them as a means of evidence.[1188] The tribunal is not strictly bound by expert opinions and will, therefore, freely appraise them. It may also come to different conclusions.[1189]

1187. Lim, 'Tribunal-Appointed Experts in International Arbitration', 212.
1188. Proske, *Expert Witness Conferencing in Schiedsverfahren*, 26.
1189. Zuberbühler et al., *IBA Rules of Evidence*, 170; ICC Case No. 14079, Procedural Order May 2007, in ICC International Court of Arbitration Bulletin Vol. 25/Supplement (2014): 11; Oetiker, 'Commentary on Art. 26-30 Swiss Rules of Arbitration', 313.

The main difference from a party-appointed expert is that parties have far less control over a tribunal-appointed expert unless the expert has the intention to build some.[1190]

Neither the IBA Rules nor the CIArb Protocol explain how an expert can, in fact, be independent and not merely demonstrate independence.[1191] While the CIArb protocol provides useful guidance for the use of party-appointed experts,[1192] it has been criticised by some practitioners in an international arbitration context for its 'Englishness'.[1193] A clear body of rules addressing the ethical duties and obligations of party-appointed experts would result in more remedies for the parties and, as a consequence, strengthen their role and value in international arbitration.

The prevailing practice, in which the parties present conflicting expert opinions on complex issues, leads to inefficiency in the proceedings, and the arbitration stakeholders are unsatisfied. One of the main reasons for this is the lack of express binding provisions in major international arbitration regulations, such as the UNCITRAL Model Law and arbitration rules. As a result, efforts have been made to overcome these problems through soft law instruments such as the IBA Rules or the CIArb Protocol and recommendations from experienced practitioners.

There is strong empirical proof that bias and the unregulated use of party-appointed experts are crucial problems in international commercial and investment arbitration. This is why the focus is to prevent potential bias while the expert opinion is formed, having a well-structured and transparent process for party-appointed experts, which, in cooperation, simply guides the tribunal without the pressure of pleasing the parties.

To achieve these goals, the arbitral tribunal should first set out rules for party-appointed experts in the first procedural order. The tribunal should set the issues and disciplines for which expert opinion is required and may expressly stipulate that no expert opinion is required for other matters and that they would not be called for testimony or that their costs would not be considered under arbitration costs. The tribunal should address the qualifications of the experts sought and should also inform the parties that it will appoint experts if required.

The tribunal should set out that, especially if it is an investment arbitration case, the expert should not have acted as an arbitrator in another international investment dispute involving: (a) the same measures; (b) the same or related parties; or (c) the same provisions of the same treaty.

The tribunal shall then forward each expert a common set of questions and also the same set of data and evidence to rely on and, if possible, ask the experts within each discipline to meet before the main hearing and produce a joint expert report explicitly mentioning areas of agreement and disagreement, accompanied by an individual report on the disagreed matters only.[1194]

1190. Bennouna, 'Experts Before the International Court of Justice: What For?', 346.
1191. Jones, 'Ineffective Use of Expert Evidence in Construction Arbitration', 7.
1192. Jones, 'Redefining the Role and Value of Expert Evidence', 32.
1193. Kantor, 'A Code of Conduct for Party-Appointed Experts in International Arbitration: Can One Be Found?', 333; *Jones* counter criticises this view, arguing that it 'ignore[s] the need for detailed focus on procedure'. Jones, 'Redefining the Role and Value of Expert Evidence', 32.
1194. Jones, 'Ineffective Use of Expert Evidence in Construction Arbitration', 11.

It is generally considered useful to engage in a discussion with a counterparty expert to identify respective objectives and methods. In that respect, the preparation of a joint report would be very useful, and pre-hearing meetings would be helpful.[1195] These rules should be determined in a procedural order, accompanied by a procedural timetable and should always be reinforced actively by the tribunal.

The tribunal is authorised to appoint an expert on its own. However, a single tribunal-appointed expert, without any party-appointed expert involvement, comes with the risk that arbitrators accept the conclusions of that expert without further analysis.[1196]

To try to find a middle ground, the *Sachs Protocol* envisions a solution to the challenges the expert evidence is facing by merging the benefits of both tribunal and party-appointed experts. Nevertheless, there are concerns regarding experts' access to relevant documents and information, which would be readily available to party-appointed experts working closely with parties and their counsel. Despite its potential merits, the *Sachs Protocol* has not achieved widespread adoption in international arbitration.[1197] Although the *Sachs Protocol* addresses the credibility of experts, it is also criticised for being 'heavily tilted to justifying tribunal-appointed experts'.[1198]

Conferencing experts is often effective because the experts only discuss their professional views before the tribunal and the counsel. Over time, with its successful applications, expert conferencing has gained some acceptance in the practice of international arbitration.[1199] This method attempts to combat the shortcomings of traditional hearing, where long presentations and examinations occur sequentially and may even be on different days, resulting in inefficiency.[1200]

This method for obtaining evidence is especially effective in complex arbitrations that have difficult factual and technical issues and in which the parties rely on evidence from multiple experts.[1201] In such circumstances, the conventional approach of examining experts from each side in a linear fashion does not always lead to a clear understanding for both the tribunal and the counsel.[1202] This is particularly the case

1195. de Chazournes et al., 'Uses of Experts Before International Courts and Tribunals', 496.
1196. Jones, 'Ineffective Use of Expert Evidence in Construction Arbitration', 10–11.
1197. Jones, 'Redefining the Role and Value of Expert Evidence', 22; de Chazournes et al., 'Uses of Experts Before International Courts and Tribunals', 493.
1198. Hodgson and Stewart, 'Experts in Investor-State Arbitration: The Tribunal as Gatekeeper', 461.
1199. Raeschke-Kessler, 'Witness Conferencing', 689; Townsend, 'Crossing the Hot-Tub: Examining Adverse Expert Witnesses in International Arbitration', 165; Webster and Bühler, *Handbook of UNCITRAL Arbitration*, 446; Jones, 'Redefining the Role and Value of Expert Evidence', 32; Some state courts also adopted this method for experts, *see* Federal Court of Australia, Expert Evidence Practice Note 25 October 2016, https://www.fedcourt.gov.au/law-and-practice/practice-documents/practice-notes/gpn-expt (accessed 24 September 2025); Aygül, *Milletlerarası Ticarî Tahkimde Tahkim Usûlüne Uygulanacak Hukuk ve Deliller*, 285; Akıncı, 'Milletlerarası Tahkimde Bilirkişi', 79.
1200. Wilske and Gack, 'Expert Evidence in International Commercial Arbitration', 95.
1201. Bor, 'Expert Evidence', 508; Hodgson and Stewart, 'Experts in Investor-State Arbitration: The Tribunal as Gatekeeper', 459–460; Jones, 'Redefining the Role and Value of Expert Evidence', 32.
1202. Brown, 'Oral Evidence and Experts in Arbitration', 85; Proske, *Expert Witness Conferencing in Schiedsverfahren*, 31; Grenz, *Der Faktor Zeit Im Schiedsverfahren*, 73–75.

when multiple and opposing expert statements are heard in different hearings over a long time span.

However, through expert conferencing, the experts can concurrently engage with opposing views directly, debate and enable a deeper examination of contentious issues.[1203] The conferencing technique is potentially helpful on the condition that it is controlled and managed firmly by the tribunal.[1204] Another advantage of conferencing experts over the traditional examination method is that it allows for an expert's opinion to be fully explored and tested by another expert. Moreover, conferencing experts can potentially shorten hearing times. Conferencing experts may not be suitable when experts have not been instructed to opine on the same issues.[1205] However, even when experts present their opinions on different subject matters, if their opinions are strictly interconnected, this method could be viable.[1206] The spontaneity of the process can lead an expert to express his own sincere opinions and forget any answer he might have been expected to give to specific questions. This further engages the experts in a vigorous conversation, where each expert explains to the arbitral tribunal the reason he disagrees with the views of the other, thereby facilitating the arbitral tribunal's understanding.[1207] Sitting at the same table with a fellow can also help in rephrasing incorrect or exaggerated previous statements and consequently reducing the number of issues on which experts disagree.[1208] If the tribunal is also well prepared and controls the process firmly, then the conferencing would be a dynamic and useful process where expertise issues can be heard and tested in quick time.[1209]

Cross-examination is another vital method for the effective use of party-appointed experts. Through cross-examination, the party counsel will uncover inconsistencies, biases, and pertinent information that the counter-expert has provided that may impact the resolution of the dispute. Cross-examination enables the testing of an expert's credibility, the clarification of ambiguities, and the introduction of counter-narratives. Depending on the flow of the hearing, in addition to the expert conferencing, cross-examination is advisable[1210] or even necessary to have regard to the right to be heard.[1211]

1203. Jones, 'Ineffective Use of Expert Evidence in Construction Arbitration', 7; Knoblach, *Sachverhaltsermittlung in Der Internationalen Wirtschaftsschiedsgerichtsbarkeit*, 280; Townsend, 'Crossing the Hot-Tub: Examining Adverse Expert Witnesses in International Arbitration', 165; Jones, 'Redefining the Role and Value of Expert Evidence', 32.
1204. de Chazournes et al., 'Uses of Experts Before International Courts and Tribunals', 496.
1205. Bor, 'Expert Evidence', 509; Abdel Wahab, 'Party Appointed Experts in International Commercial Arbitration', 205–206; Jones, 'Redefining the Role and Value of Expert Evidence', 33.
1206. Proske, *Expert Witness Conferencing in Schiedsverfahren*, 38.
1207. Abdel Wahab, 'Party Appointed Experts in International Commercial Arbitration', 205–206.
1208. Jones, 'Ineffective Use of Expert Evidence in Construction Arbitration', 8; '2012 International Arbitration Survey: Present and Preferred Practices in the Arbitral Process', 28; Wilske and Gack, 'Expert Evidence in International Commercial Arbitration', 94; Proske, *Expert Witness Conferencing in Schiedsverfahren*, 38.
1209. Senogles, 'Some Views from the Crucible: The Perspective of an Expert Witness on the Adversarial Principle', 364.
1210. Waincymer, 'Advocacy Training in International Commercial and Investment Arbitration', 72.
1211. Waincymer, *Procedure and Evidence in International Arbitration*, 968; For critics to this view, *see* Proske, *Expert Witness Conferencing in Schiedsverfahren*, 46.

Currently, the use of the GAI for replacing experts seems far ahead. Bias, hallucination, and privacy concerns come with the use of the GAI. As of today, these concerns cannot be satisfactorily addressed. Nevertheless, in the near future, GAI and other AI tools will likely streamline quantum work by automating tasks and performing data analysis.

In conclusion, to address the problems arising from the use of party-appointed experts in international commercial and investment arbitration, the aforementioned methods could be helpful, depending on the circumstances. However, the tribunal's active involvement and early determination of the necessity of protocoling the use of party-appointed experts in every detail are indispensable. In particular, designing the examination phase in a conferencing style will enable not only the prevention or disclosure of bias but also accelerate the process for the tribunal to understand the expertise required for technical, legal or quantum issues.

Appendices

APPENDIX I

Rules for the Use of Party-Appointed Experts in International Arbitration

Rule 1: Determining the Requirement

1.1. As soon as the arbitral tribunal receives the case file, it must analyse and decide whether it needs the assistance of experts to resolve the disputed issues.

1.2. If the tribunal decides that assistance is needed, it shall identify the disciplines in need of expert evidence.

Rule 2: Ordering Parties to Submit Expert Opinion

2.1. If the parties have not adduced expert reports, but the arbitral tribunal determined that expertise is necessary in one or more disciplines, it shall order the parties to submit an expert opinion in due time set by the tribunal.

2.2. The tribunal must ensure that all factual evidence from all parties has been provided to all experts in due time.

2.3. Depending on the experience of the arbitral tribunal, it may offer suitable experts whose credibility has been proven in previous arbitration.

Rule 3: Preliminary Analysis of Expert Opinion

3.1. If the parties at that stage have already adduced expert reports in the disputed matters the tribunal had considered requiring expert opinion, the tribunal may analyse the expert opinion to determine whether the opinion addressed the corresponding issues.

Rule 4: Meetings of Experts and Joint Reporting

4.1. If both or one of the expert reports did not address some or all of the issues that the tribunal determined to be addressed, the tribunal shall establish within each discipline a common list of questions and direct the experts to hold meetings and cooperate.

4.2. In this meeting, the experts should produce a joint expert report identifying areas of agreement and disagreement regarding the facts, methodology, and conclusions.

Rule 5: Individual expert reports and report forms

5.1. In cases of disagreement, the tribunal must require experts from each discipline to produce individual expert reports on areas of disagreement. After these reports have been submitted to the tribunal, if it deems it necessary, the experts should produce reply expert reports containing views in the alternative showing what their conclusions would be if the other expert's factual basis and methodologies were accepted.

5.2. The Expert Report shall contain the following information:

(a) the full name and address of the Expert, a statement regarding his/her present and past relationship (if any) with any of the Parties, their legal representatives, advisors, witnesses and the Arbitral Tribunal and a description of his/her background, qualifications, training and experience, including areas outside his/her expertise;

(b) a description of the instructions and questions according to which the respondent provides his/her opinions and conclusions;

(c) a declaration of his/her impartiality and objectivity; and

(d) a declaration that his opinions are an independent product of his/her own views and conclusions;

(e) a statement that he/she received his/her remuneration before the final production of this report;

(f) a statement of the facts on which he/she is basing his/her expert opinions and conclusions;

(g) his/her expert opinions and conclusions, including a description of the methods, evidence, and information used in arriving at the conclusions. Documents and sources on which he/she relies shall be referenced in a way that is easily accessible.

(h) if the Expert Report has been translated, a statement as to the language in which it was originally prepared and the language in which the expert anticipates giving testimony at the hearing; and

(i) the signature of the expert(s), its date, and place; and

(j) if the Expert Report has been signed by more than one person, an attribution of the entirety or specific parts of the Report will be given to each author.

Rule 6: Testimony and Examination

6.1. Experts within each discipline will testify in a conference and will be examined by the tribunal and, where the tribunal deems it necessary, by the party counsel.

6.2. The tribunal shall not allow the hearing of experts if the tribunal has not deemed it necessary to address the expertise-required issues. Nevertheless, if the tribunal considers basing its award on the conclusion of only one expert, it shall order the hearing of the experts to allow the parties to examine the expert.

Rule 7: Evaluation of the Report

7.1. The tribunal shall have the authority to freely assess the experts' reports with all other evidence, including any tribunal-appointed expert's report.

7.2. The tribunal may come to a different conclusion than that presented in the experts' opinion, provided it gives explicit reasons and allows the parties to comment on their views.

APPENDIX II

Code of Conduct

Rule 1:

An expert is a professional who has received specialized education or training, along with practical experience and knowledge, which equips him/her to assist the arbitral tribunal in resolving complex issues that require expertise beyond the tribunal's own understanding.

Rule 2:

The expert shall only accept the proposal to act as an expert if he/she is impartial and will remain objective during his/her service. If the expert senses any reasons that will lead him/her to prepare a biased opinion, the expert shall not accept his/her office. No expert shall accept his duty if he/she acts as a mediator or arbitrator in another dispute where the parties or any related parties are the disputants.

Rule 3:

The expert's opinion shall be an independent product of his/her own and not influenced by the appointing party.

Rule 4:

The expert's primary duty and responsibility is to the arbitral tribunal.

Rule 5:

The expert fees for his services shall be paid before the final report is prepared. The expert fees are not dependent on the outcome of the case.

Rule 6:

The expert shall maintain the confidentiality of any and all information related to the dispute or the parties that he has obtained before, during, or after the proceedings.

Rule 7:

An expert shall comply with his/her Codes of Practice and Guidelines that are foreseen in his/her profession.

Bibliography

'2012 International Arbitration Survey: Present and Preferred Practices in the Arbitral Process'. Queen Mary University of London and White and Case, 2012. https://arbitration.qmul.ac.uk/media/arbitration/docs/2012_International_Arbitration_Survey.pdf (accessed 24 September 2025).

'2015 International Arbitration Survey: Improvements and Innovations in International Arbitration'. Queen Mary University of London and White and Case, 2015.

'2018 International Arbitration Survey: The Evolution of International Arbitration'. Queen Mary University of London and White and Case, 2018. https://arbitration.qmul.ac.uk/media/arbitration/docs/2012_International_Arbitration_Survey.pdf (accessed 24 September 2025).

'2020 International Arbitration Survey: Investor-State Dispute Settlement (ISDS)'. Queen Mary University of London and Corporate Counsel International Arbitration Group (CCIAG), May 2020. https://arbitration.qmul.ac.uk/media/arbitration/docs/QM-CCIAG-Survey-ISDS-2020.pdf (accessed 24 September 2025).

'2021 International Arbitration Survey: Adapting Arbitration to a Changing World'. Queen Mary University of London and White and Case, 2021. https://arbitration.qmul.ac.uk/media/arbitration/docs/LON0320037-QMUL-International-Arbitration-Survey-2021_19_WEB.pdf (accessed 24 September 2025).

'2022 International Arbitration Survey: Future of International Energy Arbitration Survey Report'. Queen Mary University of London & Pinsent and Masons, 2022. https://arbitration.qmul.ac.uk/media/arbitration/docs/Future-of-International-Energy-Arbitration-Survey-Report.pdf (accessed 24 September 2025).

Abdel Wahab, Mohamed S. 'Party-Appointed Experts in International Commercial Arbitration: A Necessity or a Nuisance?' In *Handbook of Evidence in International Commercial Arbitration: Key Concepts and Issues*, edited by Franco Ferrari and Friedrich Jakob Rosenfeld, 181–206. The Netherlands: Kluwer Law International, 2022.

Ağırman, Doğan. *Milli & Milletlerarası Tahkim*. 1. Ankara: Adalet Yayınevi, 2022.

Ahrens, Hans-Jürgen. *Der Beweis Im Zivilprozess*. Köln: Otto Schmidt, 2015.

Akil, Cenk. 'Medeni Yargılama Hukukunda Mahkeme Tarafından Atanan Bilirkişi-Uzman Tanık Ayrımı'. *Ankara Barosu Dergisi*, no. 2 (2011): 171–183.

Akıncı, Ziya. *Milletlerarası Tahkim*. 6. İstanbul: Vedat Kiptaçılık, 2021.

Akıncı, Ziya. 'Milletlerarası Tahkimde Bilirkişi'. In *Milletlerarası Tahkim Semineri 2010*, 69–82. Ankara, n.d.

Akıncı, Ziya. 'Usul Kurallarına Aykırılık ve Dinlenilme Hakkı'. İn *Tahkimde Hukukî Dinlenilme Hakkı*, edited by Ziya Akıncı and Yasin Ekmen, 49–63. Istanbul Tahkim Merkezi (ISTAC) Yayınları, V. İstanbul: On İki Levha Yayıncılık, 2022.

Akıncı, Ziya. 'Usule Uygulanacak Kurallar ve Usule Aykırılığın Sonuçları'. In *Tahkimde Güncel Sorunlar (I-IV)*, edited by Metin Kıratlı et al., 1, 1–12. Türk Tahkim Akademisi. İstanbul: On İki Levha Yayıncılık, 2022.

Akıncı, Ziya, and Yasin Ekmen, eds. 'Tartışmalar'. İn *Tahkimde Hukukî Dinlenilme Hakkı*, 199–203. Istanbul Tahkim Merkezi (ISTAC) Yayınları, V. İstanbul: On İki Levha Yayıncılık, 2022.

Aktepe Artık, Sezin. *Medeni Usûl Hukukunda Hakem Kararlarının Iptali Sebepleri*. İstanbul: On İki Levha Yayıncılık, 2023.

Alangoya, Yavuz, Kamil Yıldırım, and Nevhis Deren-Yıldırım. *Medeni Usul Hukukunun Esasları*. 8. Istanbul: Beta Basım, 2011.

Alfter, Phillipp. *Das Beweismaß in Der Internationalen Handelsschiedsgerichtsbarkeit: Auswirkungen Der Best Practice Der Document Production Auf Den Beweis*. Juridicum – Schriften Zum Zivilprozessrecht. Wiesbaden: Springer, 2019.

Allen, Jr., Ronald R. 'Overview: The Common Law Systems'. In *Evidence in International Arbitration Proceedings*, edited by Peter V. Eijsvoogel and The International Association of Young Lawyers, 15–20. AIJA Law Library. Kluwer Law International; Graham & Trotman/M. Nijhoff, 1994.

Allen, Jr., Ronald R. 'United States'. In *Evidence in International Arbitration Proceedings*, edited by Peter V. Eijsvoogel and The International Association of Young Lawyers, 277–290. AIJA Law Library. Kluwer Law International; Graham & Trotman/M. Nijhoff, 1994.

Allison, Richard C., and Howard M. Holtzmann. 'The Tribunal's Use of Experts'. 269–282. Leiden, The Netherlands: Brill | Nijhoff, 2000. https://doi.org/10.1163/9789004479937_021 (accessed 24 September 2025).

Alvarez, José E. 'The Search for Objectivity: The Use of Experts in Philip Morris v Uruguay'. *Journal of International Dispute Settlement* 9, no. 3 (1 September 2018): 411–422. https://doi.org/10.1093/jnlids/idy015 (accessed 24 September 2025).

Amaral, Guilherme Rizzo. 'Burden of Proof and Adverse Inferences in International Arbitration: Proposal for an Inference Chart'. Edited by Maxi Scherer. *Journal of International Arbitration* 35, no. 1 (2018): 1–30.

Angoura, Stavroula. *The Impartiality and Independence of Arbitrators in International Commercial Arbitration. The Impartiality and Independence of Arbitrators in International Commercial Arbitration*. Nomos, 2022. https://doi.org/10.5771/9783748928140 (accessed 24 September 2025).

'Annual Arbitration Survey 2021: Expert Evidence in International Arbitration Saving the Party-Appointed Expert'. Annual Arbitration Survey 2021: Expert Evidence in International Arbitration Saving the Party-Appointed Expert. BCLP, 2021. https://www.bclplaw.com/en-US/events-insights-news/bclp-arbitration-survey-2021-expert-evidence-in-international-arbitration.html (accessed 24 September 2025).

Arroyo, Manuel. 'Commentary on Chapter 12 PILS, Article 190 [Finality, Challenge: Principle]'. In *Arbitration in Switzerland: The Practitioner's Guide*, edited by Manuel Arroyo, 2, 266–350. Kluwer Law International, 2018.

Arslan, Ramazan et al. *Medenî Usul Hukuku*. 7th ed. Ankara: Yetkin Yayınları, 2021.

Ashford, Peter. *Handbook on International Commercial Arbitration*. 2. New York: JURIS, 2014.

Ashford, Peter. *The IBA Rules on the Taking of Evidence in International Arbitration*. Cambridge: Cambridge University Press, 2013. https://doi.org/10.1017/cbo9781139424714.011 (accessed 24 September 2025).

Aslan, Adem. 'Tahkim Davalarında Hukuk, Dinlenilme Hakkı ve Kamu Düzeni'. İn *Tahkimde Hukukî Dinlenilme Hakkı*, edited by Ziya Akıncı and Yasin Ekmen, 21–47. Istanbul Tahkim Merkezi (ISTAC) Yayınları, V. İstanbul: On İki Levha Yayıncılık, 2022.

Atalay, Oğuz. 'Delil Kavramı Üzerine'. In *Haluk Konuralp Anısına Armağan*, 1:129–137. Ankara: Yetkin Yayınları, 2009.

Atalay, Oğuz. 'Deliller (Tanık, Keşif, Bilirkişi, Uzman Görüşü)'. In *Pekcanıtez Usul: Medenî Usûl Hukuku*, edited by Hakan Pekcanıtez et al., vol. 15. İstanbul: On İki Levha Yayıncılık, 2021.

Atalay, Oğuz. 'İspat'. In *Pekcanıtez Usul: Medenî Usûl Hukuku*, edited by Hakan Pekcanıtez et al., Vol. 15. İstanbul: On İki Levha Yayıncılık, 2021.

Atalı, Murat. '6754 Sayılı Bilirkişilik Kanunu ve Hukuki Konularda Bilirkişilik'. *Ankara Üniversitesi Hukuk Fakültesi Dergisi* 65, no. 4 (2016): 3271–3282.

Atalı, Murat, İbrahim Ermenek, and Ersin Erdoğan. *Medeni Usul Hukuku*. 5. Ankara: Yetkin Yayınları, 2022.

Atlı, Nihal Berker. 'Uluslararası Tahkim Sempozyumu'. İn *Tahkimde Taraf Vekilliği*, 139–144. Ankara: Yetkin Yayınları, 2019.

Australian Centre for International Commercial Arbitration, and FTI Consulting. 'Evidence in International Arbitration Report'. Australian Centre for International Commercial Arbitration, 6 September 2023. https://acica.org.au/evidence-in-international-arbitration-report/ (accessed 24 September 2025).

Aygül, Musa. *Milletlerarası Ticarî Tahkimde Tahkim Usûlüne Uygulanacak Hukuk ve Deliller*. 2. Istanbul: On İki Levha Yayıncılık, 2014.

Bacanlı, Mehmet Rıfat. 'Bir Alternatif Uyuşmazlık Çözüm Yolu Olarak Istanbul Tahkim ve Arabuluculuk Merkezi (ISTAC) Tahkim Yargilamasinda Delillerin Ibrazı ve Değerlendirilmesi'. *Uyuşmazlık Mahkemesi Dergisi*, no. 8 (2016): 75–113.

Baker, C. Mark, and Lucy Greenwood. 'In Search of an Exemplary International Construction Arbitration'. In *Contemporary Issues in International Arbitration and Mediation: The Fordham Papers*, edited by Arthur W. Rovine, 6:173–187. Leiden, Niederlande: Brill | Nijhoff, 2013. https://brill.com/view/serial/CIAM (accessed 24 September 2025).

Balkar, Süheyla. *Milletlerarası Ticari Tahkim ve Etik*. 1. İstanbul: On İki Levha Yayıncılık, 2022.

Beharry, Christina L., and Belinda McRae. 'Cross Examination of Expert Witnesses'. In *International Arbitration in Practice*, edited by Courtney Lotfi et al., 187–196. Kluwer Law International, 2024.

Bennouna, Mohamed. 'Experts before the International Court of Justice: What For?' *Journal of International Dispute Settlement* 9, no. 3 (1 September 2018): 345–351. https://doi.org/10.1093/jnlids/idy009 (accessed 24 September 2025).

Berger, Bernhard, and Franz Kellerhals. *International and Domestic Arbitration in Switzerland*. 4. Verlag C.H., Hart Publishing, Nomos, Nomiki, Stämpfli Publishers, 2021.

Bermann, George A., ed. *Recognition and Enforcement of Foreign Arbitral Awards: The Interpretation and Application of the New York Convention by National Courts*. Ius Comparatum – Global Studies in Comparative Law. Springer, 2017.

Bernardino, Ana Luísa. 'The Discursive Construction of Facts in International Adjudication'. *Journal of International Dispute Settlement* 11, no. 2 (16 March 2020): 175–193. https://doi.org/10.1093/jnlids/idaa008 (accessed 24 September 2025).

Bernstein, Ronald, John A. Tackaberry, and Arthur L. Marriott. *Bernstein's Handbook of Arbitration and Dispute Resolution Practice*. 4. Sweet & Maxwell, 2003.

Blackaby, Nigel et al. *Redfern and Hunter on International Arbitration (Student Version)*. Sixth edition. Oxford: Oxford University Press, 2015.

Blackaby, Nigel et al. *Redfern & Hunter on International Arbitration*. 6th ed. Oxford: Oxford University Press, 2015.

Blackaby, Nigel, and Alex Wilbraham. 'Practical Issues Relating to the Use of Expert Evidence in Investment Treaty Arbitration'. *ICSID Review* 31, no. 3 (2016): 655–669. https://doi.org/10.1093/icsidreview/siw031 (accessed 24 September 2025).

Boerstra, Onno G., and Jan Willem Bitter. 'The Netherlands'. In *Evidence in International Arbitration Proceedings*, edited by Peter V. Eijsvoogel and The International Association of Young Lawyers, 191–201. AIJA Law Library. Kluwer Law International; Graham & Trotman/M. Nijhoff, 1994.

Boo, Lawrence. 'Arbitration', *Singapore Academy of Law Annual Review of Singapore Cases* 5 (2004): 47–63.

Bor, Harris. 'Expert Evidence'. In *Arbitration in England with Chapters on Scotland and Ireland*, edited by Julian D.M. Lew et al., 503–526. Kluwer Law International, 2013.

Born, Gary B. *International Commercial Arbitration*. Kluwer Law International, 2021.

Borris, Christian et al. 'New York Convention, Article V [Grounds for Refusal of Recognition and Enforcement of Arbitral Awards]'. In *New York Convention: Article-by-Article Commentary*, edited by Reinmar Wolff, 2., 231–461. Verlag C.H. Beck oHG, 2023.

Brandeis (Brokers) Ltd v Black and Ors, 2001 Arbitration Law Reports and Review 223 (Commercial Court 2001).

Brown, David W. 'Oral Evidence and Experts in Arbitration'. Edited by Laurent Lévy and Van Vechten Veeder. *Kluwer Law International & ICC*, Arbitration and Oral Evidence, 2 (2004): 77–86.

Budak, Ali Cem. 'Anglo: Amerikan Medeni Yargılama Hukukunda Bilirkişilik (Uzman Tanıklar)'. *Istanbul Barosu Dergisi*, nos 10–12 (1991): 827–841.

Budak, Ali Cem. 'Tahkim Yargılamasında İlk Aşama: Görev Belgesi ve 1 Numaralı Usuli Karar'. In *Tahkimde Güncel Sorunlar (I-IV)*, edited by Metin Kıratlı et al., 1, 13–32. Türk Tahkim Akademisi. İstanbul: On İki Levha Yayıncılık, 2022.

Budak, Ali Cem, and Varol Karaaslan. *Medenî Usul Hukuku*. 3rd ed. Ankara, 2019.

Budak, Ali Cem, and Varol Karaaslan. *Medenî Usul Hukuku*. 6. İstanbul: Filiz Kitabevi, 2022.

Burianski, Markus, and Alexander C Lang. '"Challenges" to Party-Appointed Experts'. *German Arbitration Journal (SchiedsVZ)*, 15, no. 6 (2017): 269-277.

Can, Hacı, and Ekin Tuna. *Milletlerarası Tahkim Hukuku*. 1. Ankara: Seçkin, 2021.

Caron, David D., and Lee M. Caplan. *The UNCITRAL Arbitration Rules: A Commentary*. Oxford Commentaries on International Law. OUP Oxford, 2013.

Cavasola, Pietro, and Andrew G. Paton. 'Italy'. In *Evidence in International Arbitration Proceedings*, edited by Peter V. Eijsvoogel and The International Association of Young Lawyers, 165–174. AIJA Law Library. Kluwer Law International; Graham & Trotman/M. Nijhoff, 1994.

Çayan, Gökhan. *Medeni Usul Hukukunda Bilirkişilik Müessesesi*. İstanbul: Legal Yayıncılık, 2013.

Centner, Björn. *Iura Novit Curia in Internationalen Schiedsverfahren: Eine Historisch-Rechtsvergleichende Studie Zu Den Grundlagen Der Rechtsermittlung*. Tübingen: Mohr Siebeck, 2019.

Cerrahoglu Balssenn, Emine Eda. 'Instructions to Party-Appointed Experts Should Focus on Impartiality'. In *Expert Evidence: Conflicting Assumptions and How to Handle Them in Arbitration*, edited by Sébastien Besson and Harold Frey, 27–34. ASA Special Series 46. Huntington, New York: Juris, 2021.

'Challenge Digests'. *Arbitration International* 27, no. 3 (1 September 2011): 315–474. https://doi.org/10.1093/arbitration/27.3.315 (accessed 24 September 2025).

Chazournes, Laurence Boisson de et al. 'The Expert in the International Adjudicative Process: Introduction to the Special Issue'. *Journal of International Dispute Settlement* 9, no. 3 (1 September 2018): 339–344. https://doi.org/10.1093/jnlids/idy007 (accessed 24 September 2025).

Chazournes, Laurence Boisson de et al. 'One Size Does Not Fit All-Uses of Experts Before International Courts and Tribunals: An Insight into the Practice'. *Journal of International Dispute Settlement* 9, no. 3 (1 September 2018): 477–505. https://doi.org/10.1093/jnlids/idy021 (accessed 24 September 2025).

Cordero-Moss, Giuditta. 'Iura Novit Curia'. In *Handbook of Evidence in International Commercial Arbitration: Key Concepts and Issues*, edited by Franco Ferrari and Friedrich Jakob Rosenfeld, 111–138. Kluwer Law International, 2022.

Cosar, Utku. 'Fraudulent Evidence: Investment Arbitration'. *Max Planck Encyclopedia of International Procedural Law [MPEiPro]* (blog), 2023. https://opil.ouplaw.com/display/10.1093/law-mpeipro/e2769.013.2769/law-mpeipro-e2769?prd = OPIL (accessed 24 September 2025).

Curschmann, Jan. 'Germany'. In *Evidence in International Arbitration Proceedings*, edited by Peter V. Eijsvoogel and The International Association of Young Lawyers, 143–152. AIJA Law Library. Kluwer Law International; Graham & Trotman/M. Nijhoff, 1994.

Daly, Brooks W, and Fiona Poon. 'Technical and Legal Experts in International Investment Disputes'. *Litigating International Investment Disputes* 578 (2014): 323–374. https://doi.org/10.1163/9789004276574_012 (accessed 24 September 2025).

D'Aspremont, Jean, and Makane Moïse Mbengue. 'Strategies of Engagement with Scientific Fact-Finding in International Adjudication'. *Journal of International Dispute Settlement* 5, no. 2 (1 July 2014): 240–272. https://doi.org/10.1093/jnlids/idu004 (accessed 24 September 2025).

Dave, Dushyant. 'Should Experts Be Neutrals or Advocates?' In *ICCA Congress Series No. 15 (Rio 2010): Arbitration Advocacy in Changing Times*, edited by Albert Jan Van Den Berg, 15:149–159. ICCA Congress Series. Rio de Janeiro: ICCA & Kluwer Law International, 2011.

Dayınlarlı, Kemal. *HUMK'da Düzenlenen Ihtiyari Iç Tahkim*. Ankara: Dayınlarlı Hukuk Yayınları, 2004.

Dayınlarlı, Kemal. *Milletlerarası Tahkim Rehberi*. Ankara: Dayınlarlı Hukuk Yayınları, 2014.

Dayınlarlı, Kemal. *UNCITRAL Kurallarına göre Uzlaşma ve Tahkim*. 3. Ankara: Dayınlarlı Hukuk Yayınları, 2012.

De Berti, Giovanni. 'Experts and Expert Witnesses in International Arbitration: Adviser, Advocate or Adjudicator ?' In *Austrian Yearbook on International Arbitration 2011*, edited by Nikolaus Pitkowitz and Alexandre Petsche, 2011:53–63. Manz'sche Verlags- und Universitätsbuchhandlung; Manz'sche Verlags- und Universitätsbuchhandlung, 2011.

Demir Gökyayla, Cemile. 'Tahkimde Taraflarca Getirilme İlkesi ve Delil İkamesi'. In *Tahkimde Güncel Sorunlar (I-IV)*, edited by Metin Kıratlı et al., 1, 71–86. Türk Tahkim Akademisi. İstanbul: On İki Levha Yayıncılık, 2022.

Demirkapı, Ertan. 'Anglo: Amerikan Hukukunda Bilirkişilik Kurumunda Yeni Eğilimler'. *Dokuz Eylül Üniversitesi Hukuk Fakültesi Dergisi* 5, no. 2 (2003): 39–75.

Demirkol, Berk. 'Karşılaştırmalı Hukukta Hakem Kararlarının Tenfizinde Hukukî Dinlenilme Hakkı'. İn *Tahkimde Hukukî Dinlenilme Hakkı*, edited by Ziya Akıncı and Yasin Ekmen, 179–198. Istanbul Tahkim Merkezi (ISTAC) Yayınları, V. İstanbul: On İki Levha Yayıncılık, 2022.

Derains, Yves, and Eric A. Schwartz. *A Guide to the ICC Rules of Arbitration*. 2. Kluwer Arbitration. Kluwer Law International, 2005.

Direnisa, Efe. 'Hukuk Muhakemeleri Kanunu Çerçevesinde Tahkimde Hakem Kararlarının Gerekçesi Üzerine Düşünceler'. *Legal Hukuk Dergisi* 20, no. 233 (2022): 1549–1602.

Donoghue, Joan E. 'Expert Scientific Evidence in a Broader Context'. *Journal of International Dispute Settlement* 9, no. 3 (1 September 2018): 379–387. https://doi.org/10.1093/jnlids/idy011 (accessed 24 September 2025).

Dolzer, Rudolf, Ursula Kriebaum, and Christoph Schreuer. *Principles of International Investment Law*. 3rd ed. Oxford: Oxford University Press, 2022.

Dülger, Ahmet. *Milletlerarası Tahkimde Hakemlerin Doğal Yetkileri*. 1. İstanbul: On İki Levha Yayıncılık, 2023.

Dwyer, Déirdre. *The Judicial Assessment of Expert Evidence*. Cambridge: Cambridge University Press, 2009. https://doi.org/10.1017/cbo9780511575136.007 (accessed 24 September 2025).

Eberl, Walter, ed. *Beweis Im Schiedsverfahren*. 1. Baden-Baden: Nomos, 2015, https://www.beck-shop.de/eberl-hrsg-beweis-schiedsverfahren/product/12575926 (accessed 24 September 2025).

Ehle, Bernd. 'Practical Aspects of Using Expert Evidence in International Arbitration'. Edited by Marianne Roth and Michael Geistlinger. *Yearbook on International Arbitration* II (2012): 75–84.

Eijsvoogel, Peter V. 'General Synthesis Report'. In *Evidence in International Arbitration Proceedings*, edited by Peter V. Eijsvoogel and The International Association of Young Lawyers, 3–14. AIJA Law Library. Kluwer Law International; Graham & Trotman/M. Nijhoff, 1994.

Ekşi, Nuray. *Hukuku Muhakemeleri Kanunu'nda Tahkim*. 2. İstanbul: Beta Basım, 2019.

Elsing, Siegfried H. 'Procedural Efficiency in International Arbitration: Choosing the Best of Both Legal Worlds', 3, 114–123, 2011.

Elsing, Siegfried H., and John M. Townsend. 'Bridging the Common Law-Civil Law Divide in Arbitration'. *Arbitration International* 18, no. 1 (1 March 2002): 1–7. https://doi.org/10.1023/A:1014200908066 (accessed 24 September 2025).

Elyıldırım, Hasan. *Hukuk Yargılamasında Uzman Görüşü (Özel Bilirkişi)*. Ankara: Adalet Yayınevi, 2021.

Erdoğan, Ersin, and Nevin Meral. 'Londra Deniz Ticareti Hakemleri Birliği(LMAA) Tahkimi İlişkin Genel Bir Değerlendirme'. *Yıldırım Beyazıt Hukuk Dergisi* undefined, no. 2 (2022): 1073–1118. https://doi.org/10.33432/ybuhukuk.1105545 (accessed 24 September 2025).

Erdoğan, Ersin, and S. Hilal Üçüncü. 'Bilirkişilik Kurumu ve Bilirkişi Raporunun Delil Değerine İlişkin Bazı Sorunlar'. *Hacettepe Hukuk Fakültesi Dergisi* 10, no. 1 (2020): 354–387. https://doi.org/10.32957/hacettepehdf.747897 (accessed 24 September 2025).

Erdoğan, Ersin, and S. Hilal Üçüncü. 'Bir Davada Alınan Bilirkişi Raporunun Başka Davada Delil Değeri'. *Legal Hukuk Dergisi* 18, no. 208 (2020): 1497–1522.

Erdönmez, Güray. 'Medenî Usîl Hukukuna Hâkim olan İlkeler'. In *Pekcanıtez Usûl Medenî Usûl Hukuku*, edited by Hakan Pekcanıtez et al., 15th ed. vol. I. Istanbul: On İki Levha Yayıncılık, 2021.

Ermenek, İbrahim. 'Tahkimde Hukuki Dinlenilme Hakkının Korunması'. In *Tahkimde Güncel Sorunlar (I-IV)*, edited by Metin Kıratlı et al, 1., 33–52. Türk Tahkim Akademisi. İstanbul: On İki Levha Yayıncılık, 2022.

Eroğlu, Orhan. *Tahkimde Yargılamanın Yenilenmesi*. Ankara: Seçkin, 2022.

Esen, Emre. 'Violation of the Right to a Fair Trial in Arbitration: Analysing the Turkish Court of Cassation's Decision of 10 February 2021'. *Annales de La Faculté de Droit d'Istanbul* 71 (22 September 2022): 99–117. https://doi.org/10.26650/annales.2022.71.0003 (accessed 24 September 2025).

Feutrill, Michael, and Noah Rubins. 'The Preparation of Expert Evidence in International Commercial Arbitration: Practical Aspects'. *International Business Law Journal* 2009, no. 3 (2009): 307–332.

Flannery, Louis. 'The English Statutory Framework'. In *Arbitration in England, with Chapters on Scotland and Ireland*, edited by Julian D.M. Lew and Harris Bor, 207–224. Kluwer Law International, 2013.

Flett, James. 'When Is an Expert Not an Expert?' *Journal of International Dispute Settlement* 9, no. 3 (1 September 2018): 352–360. https://doi.org/10.1093/JNLIDS/IDY014 (accessed 24 September 2025).

Förstel-Cherng, Anna et al., eds. *Beweiserhebung Im Schiedsverfahren*. 2. Wien: Manz'sche Verlags- und Universitätsbuchhandlung, 2021.

Foster, Caroline E. *Science and the Precautionary Principle in International Courts and Tribunals: Expert Evidence, Burden of Proof and Finality*. Cambridge Studies in International and Comparative Law. Cambridge: Cambridge University Press, 2011. https://doi.org/10.1017/CBO9780511973680 (accessed 24 September 2025).

Foster, Caroline E. 'The Role of Adjudicators and the Role of Experts'. In *Science and the Precautionary Principle in International Courts and Tribunals*, 136–182. Cambridge University Press, 2011. https://doi.org/10.1017/cbo9780511973680.005 (accessed 24 September 2025).

Fouchard, Philippe, Emmanuel Gaillard, and Berthold Goldman. *Fouchard, Gaillard, Goldman on International Commercial Arbitration*. Edited by John Savage and Philippe Fouchard. The Hague: Kluwer Law International, 1999.

Freyer, Dana H. 'Assessing Expert Evidence'. In *The Leading Arbitrators' Guide to International Arbitration*, edited by Lawrence W. Newman, and Richard D. Hill, 2, 430–445. Juris, 2008.

Friedland, Paul, and Kate Brown De Vejar. 'Discoverability of Communications Between Counsel and Party- Appointed Experts in International Arbitration'. In *ICCA Congress Series No. 15 (Rio 2010): Arbitration Advocacy in Changing Times*, edited by Albert Jan Van Den Berg, 160–178. ICCA Congress Series 15. Rio de Janeiro: ICCA & Kluwer Law International, 2011.

Friedland, Paul, and Kate Brown De Vejar. 'Discoverability of Communications between Counsel and Party-Appointed Experts in International Arbitration'. *Arbitration International* 28, no. 4 (2012): 1–18. https://doi.org/10.1093/arbitration/28.1.1 (accessed 24 September 2025).

Gautier, Philippe. 'Experts before ITLOS: An Overview of the Tribunal's Practice'. *Journal of International Dispute Settlement* 9, no. 3 (1 September 2018): 433–439. https://doi.org/10.1093/jnlids/idy016 (accessed 24 September 2025).

Geisinger, Elliott. 'Advocacy in International Commercial Arbitration: What For?' In *Advocacy in International Commercial Arbitration*, edited by Elliott Geisinger and Guillaume Tattevin, 3–22. ASA Special Series 36. New York: Juris, 2013.

Geisinger, Elliott, and Pierre Ducret. 'The Arbitral Procedure'. In *International Arbitration in Switzerland: A Handbook for Practitioners*, edited by Elliott Geisinger and Nathalie Voser, 2., 73–106. Alphen aan den Rijn: Kluwer Law International, 2013.

Giray, Faruk Kerem. *Milletlerarası Yatırım Tahkiminde Kamulaştırmadan Doğan Tazminat ve Tazminatın Hesaplanmasında Kullanılan Yöntemler*, 2nd ed. İstanbul: Beta Basım, 2013.

Girsberger, Daniel, and Nathalie Voser. *International Arbitration: Comparative and Swiss Perspectives*. 4th extended ed. Baden-Baden: Zürich: Nomos; Schulthess, 2021.

Godhe, Aleksander. 'Tribunal Duties and the Exclusion of Evidence in International Arbitration: The Tug-of-War of Fairness and Efficiency'. *Arbitration International* 41, no. 1 (2024): 103–117. https://doi.org/10.1093/arbint/aiae037 (accessed 24 September 2025).

Göksu, Tarkan. 'Schiedsgerichtsbarkeit: Anspruch Auf Einholung Eines Gutachtens (BGE 4A_277/2017)'. *Zeitschrift Für Baurecht Und Vergabewesen* 2017, no. 6 (2017): 391.

Görgün, L. Şanal, Levent Börü, and Mehmet Kodakoğlu. *Medenî Usûl Hukuku*. 12. Ankara: Yetkin Yayınları, 2023.

Gramlich, Von Christoph. 'Widersprüchliche Parteisachverständige: Pflicht zur Bestellung eines schiedsgerichtlichen Sachverständigen?' *SchiedsVZ | German Arbitration Journal*, no. 5 (2019): 233–242.

Grando, Michelle T. *Evidence, Proof, and Fact-Finding in WTO Dispute Settlement*. Oxford University Press, 2009. https://doi.org/10.1093/acprof:oso/9780199572649.001.0001 (accessed 24 September 2025).

Grenz, Christoph. *Der Faktor Zeit Im Schiedsverfahren*. Schriftenreihe Der August-Maria-Berges-Stiftung Für Arbitrales Recht. PL Acad. Research, 2013. https://books.google.de/books?id=MLAtnQEACAAJ (accessed 24 September 2025).

Güvenalp, Ferda Nur. *Milletlerarası Tahkimde Iddia ve Savunma Hakkının Ihlali*. İstanbul: On İki Levha Yayıncılık, 2018.

Güvenalp, Ferda Nur. 'Tahkimde Tarafların Eşitliği ve Hukuki Dinlenilme Hakkı'. İn *Tahkimde Hukukî Dinlenilme Hakkı*, edited by Ziya Akıncı and Yasin Ekmen, 103–137. Istanbul Tahkim Merkezi (ISTAC) Yayınları, V. İstanbul: On İki Levha Yayıncılık, 2022.

Hacıbekiroğlu, Ekin. *Milletlerarası Tahkim Hukukunda Deliller ve Delillerin Değerlendirilmesi*. Milletlerarası Uyuşmazlık Çözümü. 6. İstanbul: On İki Levha Yayıncılık, 2012.

Hanağası, Emel. *Medeni Yargılama Hukukunda Silahların Eşitliği*. Ankara: Yetkin Yayınları, 2016.

Hanotiau, Bernard. 'The Conduct of the Hearings'. In *Leading Arbitrators' Guide to International Arbitration*, edited by Lawrence W. Newman and Richard D. Hill, 3rd ed., 633–654. New York: Juris Publishing, Incorporated, 2014. https://books.google.co.in/books?id=0bOIAwAAQBAJ (accessed 24 September 2025).

Harris, Peter, and Mohsun Ali. 'Better Never Than Late?' Edited by Stavros Brekoulakis. *The International Journal of Arbitration, Mediation and Dispute Management* 89, no. 3 (2023): 266–272. https://doi.org/10.54648/amdm2023019 (accessed 24 September 2025).

Haugeneder, Florian. 'The Arbitration Agreement and Arbitrability, Party-Appointed and Tribunal-Appointed Experts in International Arbitration'. In *Austrian Yearbook on International Arbitration 2020*, edited by Christian Klausegger et al. C.H. Beck; Stämpfli Verlag; Manz'sche Verlags- und Universitätsbuchhandlung, 2020.

Hobér, Kaj, and Howard S. Sussman. *Cross-Examination in International Arbitration*. New York: Oxford University Press, 2014.

Hodgson, Mélida, and Melissa Stewart. 'Experts in Investor-State Arbitration: The Tribunal as Gatekeeper'. *Journal of International Dispute Settlement* 9, no. 3 (1 September 2018): 453–463. https://doi.org/10.1093/jnlids/idy006 (accessed 24 September 2025).

Hoffmann, Anne K., and Nish Kumar Shetty. 'Evidence and Hearings'. In *International Arbitration: The Coming of a New Age?*, edited by Albert Jan Van Den Berg, 197–219. ICCA Congress Series 17. Singapore: ICCA & Kluwer Law International, 2012.

Hofmann, Dieter, and Oliver M. Kunz. 'Commentary on the Swiss Rules, Article 27 [Tribunal-Appointed Experts]'. In *Arbitration in Switzerland: The Practitioner's Guide*, edited by Manuel Arroyo, 2, 719–736. Kluwer Law International, 2018.

Hohler, Simon. 'Country Report: Switzerland'. In *Due Process as a Limit to Discretion in International Commercial Arbitration*, edited by Franco Ferrari et al., 375–398. Kluwer Law International, 2020.

Hunter, Martin. 'Expert Conferencing and New Methods'. Edited by Richard E. Walck. *Transnational Dispute Management*, Energy Litigation and Arbitration – Expert Perspectives, 4, no. 3 (June 2007).

Hwang, Michael. 'Witness Conferencing'. In *The Legal Media Group Guide to the World's Leading Experts in Commercial Arbitration*, edited by Jamie McKay, 1–5. Legal Media Group, 2008.

Hwang, Michael, and Andrew Chin. 'The Role of Witness Statements in International Commercial Arbitration'. In *ICCA Congress Series No. 13 (Montreal 2006): International Arbitration 2006: Back to Basics?*, edited by Albert Jan Van Den Berg, 650–660. ICCA Congress Series 13. Montreal: ICCA & Kluwer Law International, 2007.

Hwang, Michael, and Colin Y. C. Ong. 'Effective Cross-Examination in Asian Arbitrations'. In *Take the Witness: Cross-Examination in International Arbitration*, edited by Lawrence W. Newman and Ben H. Sheppard, Jr, 269–290. Juris, 2010. https://books.google.com.tr/books?id=NwT7AwAAQBAJ (accessed 24 September 2025).

IAReporter. 'Arbitrators Weigh Disqualification of Venezuela's Damages Expert, but Decide His Earlier Contacts with Claimant Don't Warrant It'. Investment Arbitration Reporter, 16 September 2012. https://www.iareporter.com/articles/arbitrators-weigh-disqualification-of-venezuelas-damages-expert-but-decide-his-earlier-contacts-with-claimant-dont-warrant-it/ (accessed 24 September 2025).

ICC. 'ICC Arbitration Commission Report on Controlling Time and Costs in Arbitration'. Techniques for Controlling Time and Costs in Arbitration. Paris: ICC, March 2018.

'ICC Commission on Arbitration and ADR Report: Resolving Climate Change Related Disputes through Arbitration and ADR'. ICC Commission on Arbitration and ADR. Paris: ICC, November 2019.

ICC International Court of Arbitration. 'Procedural Decisions in ICC Arbitration'. *ICC Dispute Resolution Bulletin* 25, Supplement (2014).

ICCA Task Force on Standards of Practice in International Arbitration. 'Guidelines on Standards of Practice in International Arbitration'. The ICCA Reports. International

Council for Commercial Arbitration; Permanent Court of Arbitration, 2021. https://www.arbitration-icca.org/icca-reports-no-9-guidelines-standards-practice-international-arbitration (accessed 24 September 2025).

International Law Asociation Committe on International Commercial Arbitration. 'Ascertaining the Contents of the Applicable Law in International Commercial Arbitration'. *Revista Brasileira de Arbitragem* V, no. 20 (August 2008): 163–196.

Işık, Serpil. *MTK ve HMK Kapmasında Hakem Kararlarına Karşı Iptal Davası*. 1. Istanbul: On İki Levha Yayıncılık, 2022.

Işık, Sultan. 'Uzman Görüşü (Mütalaa)'. T.C. Marmara Üniversitesi Sosyal Bilimler Enstitüsü, 2015.

Jones, Doug. 'Ineffective Use of Expert Evidence in Construction Arbitration'. In *Dubai Arbitration Week 2020*, 2020. https://dougjones.info/content/uploads/2017/07/Ineffective-Use-of-Expert-Evidence-in-Construction-Arbitration-1.pdf (accessed 24 September 2025).

Jones, Doug. 'Party Appointed Expert Witnesses in International Arbitration: A Protocol at Last'. *Arbitration International* 24, no. 4 (2008): 137–156. https://doi.org/10.1093/arbitration/24.1.137.

Jones, Doug. 'Redefining the Role and Value of Expert Evidence'. Paris, 2021. https://dougjones.info/content/uploads/2021/12/DJ-ICC-Expert-Evidence-Post-Conference-Updated-Chapter.pdf (accessed 24 September 2025).

Jones, Douglas, S. 'Improving Arbitral Procedure: Perspectives from the Coalface'. In *Stories from the Hearing Room: Experience from Arbitral Practice (Essays in Honour of Michael E. Schneider)*, edited by Bernd Ehle and Domitille Baizeau, 91–102. Kluwer Law International, 2015.

Kalpsüz, Turgut. *Türkiye'de Milletlerarası Tahkim*. 2. Yetkin Yayınları, 2010.

Kamya-Lukoda, Gideon E. 'Role of Expert Witnesses in Construction Arbitration: Delay and Disruption and Quantum Issues'. In *Transnational Construction Arbitration: Key Themes in the Resolution of Construction Disputes*, edited by Renato Nazzini and Anthony J. Morgan. London: Informa Law from Routledge, 2018.

Kantor, Mark. 'A Code of Conduct for Party-Appointed Experts in International Arbitration: Can One Be Found?' *Arbitration International* 26, no. 3 (2010): 323–380. https://doi.org/10.1093/arbitration/26.3.323 (accessed 24 September 2025).

Kaplan, Mikail Bora. 'Medenî Usîl Hukukunda Bilirkişi Raporu Ile Uzman Görüşü Arasındaki Çelişkinin Giderilmesi'. *Türk-Alman Üniversitesi Hukuk Fakültesi Dergisi* 4, no. 2 (2022): 557–586.

Karadaş, İzzet. *Ulusal (Iç) Tahkim*. İstanbul: Adalet Yayınevi, 2013.

Karslı, Abdurrahim. *Medeni Muhakeme Hukuku*. 5. İstanbul: Filiz Kitabevi, 2020.

Kaufmann-Kohler, Gabrielle. 'Globalization of Arbitral Procedure'. *Vanderbilt Journal of Transnational Law Vanderbilt Journal of Transnational Law* 36, no. 4 (October 2003): 1313–1333.

Kaufmann-Kohler, Gabrielle, and Antonio Rigozzi. *International Arbitration: Law and Practice in Switzerland*. Oxford: Oxford University Press, 2015.

Kent, Rachel D. 'Expert Witnesses in Arbitration and Litigation Proceedings'. Edited by Richard E. Walck and Thomas Wälde. *Transnational Dispute Management*, Energy Litigation and Arbitration – Expert Perspectives, 4, no. 3 (2007).

Kesikli, Ömer. 'Milletlerarası Ticari Tahkimde Delillerin Değerlendirilmesi'. Özel Hukuk Anabilim Dalı Doktora Tezi, Galatasaray Üniversitesi, 2023.

Khodykin, Roman Mikhailovich, and Carol Mulcahy. *A Guide to the IBA Rules on the Taking of Evidence in International Arbitration. Commentary on the IBA Rules on Evidence*. Oxford: Oxford University Press, 2019.

Khodykin, Roman Mikhailovich, and Carol Mulcahy. 'Commentary on the IBA Rules on Evidence, Article 5 [Party-Appointed Experts]'. In *A Guide to the IBA Rules on the Taking of Evidence in International Arbitration*, edited by Consultant Editor Nicholas Fletcher QC, 279–322. Oxford University Press, 2019.

Knoblach, Steffen. *Sachverhaltsermittlung in Der Internationalen Wirtschaftsschiedsgerichtsbarkeit*. Schriften zum Prozessrecht. Berlin: Duncker & Humblot, 2003.

Konrad, Sabine, and Robert Hunter. 'LCIA Rules'. In *Institutional Arbitration: A Commentary*, edited by Rolf A. Schütze. C.H. Beck; Hart Publishing; Nomos, 2013.

Korkmaz, Abdullah Harun. 'Güncel Tartışmalar Ekseninde Tahkimde Tanık Delilinin Güvenilirliği'. *Public and Private International Law Bulletin* 42, no. 2 (2022): 643–673. https://doi.org/10.26650/ppil.2022.42.2.1167371 (accessed 24 September 2025).

Kurkela, Matti S., Santtu Turunen, and Conflict Management Institute. *Due Process in International Commercial Arbitration*. 2. Oxford University Press, 2010.

Kuru, Baki. *Medenî Usul Hukuku El Kitabı*. vol. I. Ankara: Yetkin Yayınları, 2020.

Kuru, Baki, and Burak Aydın. *Medenî Usul Hukuku El Kitabı*. vol. II. Ankara: Yetkin Yayınları, 2021.

Lachmann, Jens-Peter. *Handbuch Für Die Schiedsgerichtspraxis*. 3. Köln: O. Schmidt, 2008.

Langford, Malcolm, Daniel Behn, and Runar Hilleren Lie. 'The Revolving Door in International Investment Arbitration'. *Journal of International Economic Law* 20, no. 2 (1 June 2017): 301–331. https://doi.org/10.1093/jiel/jgx018 (accessed 24 September 2025).

Lalive, Pierre (ed.). 'Parties Not Indicated, Tribunal Fédéral, 1ère Cour Civile'. *ASA Bulletin; Kluwer Law International* 10, no. 3 (1992): 381–401.

Lee, N.A. Kyung. 'Selecting the Expert Witness as an Arbitrator in Patent Arbitrations'. *Dispute Resolution Journal* 70, no. 4 (January 2016).

Lehmann, Thomas, and Andres Mazuera. 'LIDW 2022: States as First-Class Citizens? Special Treatment for States in International Disputes'. *Kluwer Arbitration Blog* (blog), 5 June 2022. http://arbitrationblog.kluwerarbitration.com/2022/06/05/lidw-2022-states-as-first-class-citizens/ (accessed 24 September 2025).

Levine, Judith. 'Can Arbitrators Choose Who to Call as Witnesses (And What Can Be Done If They Don't Show Up)?' In *ICCA Congress Series No. 18 (Miami 2014): Legitimacy: Myths, Realities, Challenges*, edited by Albert Jan Van Den Berg, 315–356. ICCA Congress Series 18. ICCA & Kluwer Law International, 2015.

Lew, Julian D.M. 'The Need for Expert Evidence?' *Arbitration International* 39, no. 2 (19 June 2023): 246–253. https://doi.org/10.1093/arbint/aiad030 (accessed 24 September 2025).

Lew, Julian D.M., Loukas A. Mistelis, and Stefan M Kröll. *Comparative International Commercial Arbitration*. Kluwer Law International, 2003.

Liebscher, Christoph. 'VIAC Rules'. In *Institutional Arbitration: Article-by-Article Commentary*, edited by Rolf Arno Schütze. München, Baden-Baden, Oxford: C. H. Beck, Hart, Nomos, 2013.

Liebscher, Christoph, Olivier Luc Mosimann, and Nils Schmidt-Ahrendts. 'Handbuch Schiedsgerichtsbarkeit'. In *Handbuch Schiedsgerichtsbarkeit*, edited by Hellwig Torggler and et al., 2. Deutschland: Nomos; Schulthess; Verlag Österreich, 2017.

Lim, Jonathan W. 'Tribunal-Appointed Experts in International Arbitration'. In *Handbook of Evidence in International Commercial Arbitration: Key Concepts and Issues*, edited by Franco Ferrari and Friedrich Jakob Rosenfeld, 207–228. Kluwer Law International, 2022.

Lörcher, Gino. 'Der Vom Schiedsgericht Bestellte Sachverständige Im Verfahren'. In *Law of International Business and Dispute Settlement in the 21st Century*, edited by Robert Briner et al., 485–496. Köln, Berlin, Bonn, München: Carl Heymanns, n.d.

Lotz, Burkard. 'Der Sachvreständige Im Schiedsverfahren'. Edited by Jörg Risse et al. *SchiedsVZ | German Arbitration Journal* 9, no. 4 (2011): 203–209.

Marriott, Arthur L. 'Evidence in International Arbitration'. *Arbitration International* 5, no. 3 (1 September 1989): 280–290. https://doi.org/10.1093/arbitration/5.3.280 (accessed 24 September 2025).

Mavrantonakis, Emmanouil. *Das Verbot Der Révision Au Fond Im Internationalen Handelsschiedsverfahren: Zur Bindung Des Staatlichen Gerichts an Die Schiedsgerichtlichen Sachverhaltsfeststellungen Und Zu Den Erforderlichen Ausnahmen*. Tübingen: Mohr Siebeck, 2021.

Mbengue, Makane Moïse, and Rukmini Das. 'Rules Governing the Use of Experts in International Disputes'. *Law and Practice of International Courts and Tribunals* 17, no. 3 (2018): 415–454. https://doi.org/10.1163/15718034-12341388 (accessed 24 September 2025).

Meier, Anke. 'Germany'. In *The Healthy Award in International Commercial Arbitration*, edited by Christoph Liebscher, 2. Kluwer Law International, 2023.

Meriç, Nedim. 'Hâkimin Davayı Aydınlatma Yükümlülüğü'. *Dokuz Eylül Üniversitesi Hukuk Fakültesi Dergisi* 11, no. Özel Sayı 2009 (Prof. Dr. Bilge Umar'a Armağan) (2010): 377–424.

Mert, Baver Mazlum, and Süheyla Ahsen Türkmen. 'Milletlerarası Tahkimde Delil İkamesi Hakkında Prag Kuralları ve IBA Kuralları'nın Karşılaştırılması'. İn *Milletlerarası Tahkim ve Usul Hukukuna Ilişkin Güncel Meseleler*, edited by Sibel Özel and Hatice Selin Pürselim, 37–102. İstanbul: On İki Levha Yayıncılık, 2022.

Michell, Paul, and Renu Mandhane. 'The Uncertain Duty of the Expert Witness'. *Alberta Law Review* 42, no. 3 (Special Issue) (31 December 1969): 635–675. https://doi.org/10.29173/alr1281 (accessed 24 September 2025).

Moses, Margaret L. *The Principles and Practice of International Commercial Arbitration*. 3rd ed. Cambridge University Press, 2017. https://doi.org/10.1017/9781316585245.009 (accessed 24 September 2025).

Mosk, Richard M. 'The Role of Facts in International Dispute Resolution (Volume 304)'. In *Collected Courses of the Hague Academy of International Law*. Publications of the Hague Academy of International Law. Brill, n.d. http://referenceworks.

brillonline.com/entries/the-hague-academy-collected-courses/the-role-of-facts-in-international-dispute-resolution-volume-304-A9789004140233_01 (accessed 24 September 2025).

Münch, Joachim. *Münchener Kommentar Zur ZPO*. 6. Beck-Online, 2022.

Munday, Roderick. *Cross & Tapper on Evidence*. 13. Oxford: Oxford University Press, 2018.

Musielak, Hans-Joachim, and Wolfgang Voit. *Zivilprozessordnung Kommentar*. 19. München: Verlag Franz Vahlen, 2022.

Nairn, Karyl, Maximilian Szymanski, and Sophia Lekakis. 'National Report for England and Wales (2021 through 2023)'. In *ICCA International Handbook on Commercial Arbitration*, edited by Lisa Bosman, 1–102. ICCA & Kluwer Law International, 2024.

Narçin, Zelal. '4686 Sayılı Milletlerarası Tahkim Uyarınca Deliller'. *Terazi Hukuk Dergisi* 11, no. 113 (Ocak 2016): 14–29.

Nater-Bass, Gabrielle, and Christina Rouvinez. 'Art. 24 Commentary on Swiss Rules'. In *Swiss Rules of International Arbitration Commentary*, edited by Tobias Zuberbühler, Christoph Müller, and Philipp Habegger, 2. Schulthess Juristische Medien AG, 2013.

Nemeth, J. Christian, and Lisa Haidostian. 'The "Hot Tub" Method of Taking Expert Testimony Is Gaining Steam: What You Need to Know'. *IBA Arbitration News*, February 2014, 91–93.

Nessi, Sebastiano. 'Expert Witness: Role and Independence'. In *New Developments in International Arbitration 2016*, edited by Christoph Müller, Sebastien Besson, and Antonio Rigozzi, 72–105. Geneva/Zurich: Schulthess Juristische Medien AG, 2016.

Newman, Lawrence W., and Rikki Klieman. *Take the Witness: The Experts Speak on Cross Examination*. Juris Pub., 2006. https://books.google.com.tr/books?id=bVRGNTQAlLUC (accessed 24 September 2025).

Nomer, Ergin, Nuray Ekşi, and Günseli Öztekin Gelgel. *Milletlerlarası Tahkim Hukuku*. 4. vol. I. İstanbul: Beta Basım, 2013.

'Norbrook Laboratories Ltd v Tank'. *Arbitration Law Reports and Review* 2006, no. 1 (1 January 2006): 635–667. https://doi.org/10.1093/alrr/2006.1.635 (accessed 24 September 2025).

Oetiker, Christian. 'Commentary on Art. 26-30 Swiss Rules of Arbitration'. In *Swiss Rules of International Arbitration Commentary*, edited by Tobias Zuberbühler, Philipp Habegger, and Christoph Müller, 2. Zürich: Schulthess, 2013.

Öhrström, Marie. 'SCC Rules'. In *Institutional Arbitration: Article-by-Article Commentary*, edited by Rolf Arno Schütze. München, Baden-Baden, Oxford: C. H. Beck, Hart, Nomos, 2013.

O'Malley, Nathan D. *Rules of Evidence in International Arbitration: An Annotated Guide*. 2nd ed. Lloyd's Arbitration Law Library. Abingdon, Oxon; New York, NY: Informa law from Routledge, 2019.

Özbek, Mustafa Serdar. *Tahkim Hukuku*. 1. vol. II. Ankara: Yetkin Yayınları, 2022.

Özbek, Mustafa Serdar. 'Uzman Görüşünün Yargılamada Değerlendirilmesi'. Edited by Metin Suyabatmaz. *Türkiye Noterler Birliği Hukuk Dergisi* 4, no. 1 (2017): 63–162.

Özekes, Muhammet. *Medenî Usûl Hukukunda Hukukî Dinlenilme Hakkı*. Ankara: Yetkin Yayınları, 2003.

Öztek, Selçuk. 'Bilirkişi Raporunun Hâkimi Bağlamaması'. İn *Prof. Dr. Ejder Yılmaz'a Armağan*, 2:1607–1625. Ankara, 2014.

Parlett, Kate. 'Parties' Engagement with Experts in International Litigation'. *Journal of International Dispute Settlement* 9, no. 3 (1 September 2018): 440–452. https://doi.org/10.1093/jnlids/idy018 (accessed 24 September 2025).

Patocchi, Paolo Michele. 'Uluslararası Tahkim Sempozyumu'. In *The Prague Rules on the Efficient Conduct of Proceedings in International Arbitrration: A Step Forward?*, edited by Musa Aygül and Ersin Erdoğan, 145–187. Ankara: Yetkin Yayınları, 2019.

Patocchi, Paolo Michele, and Tilman Niedermaier. 'UNCITRAL Rules'. In *Institutional Arbitration: A Commentary*, edited by Rolf A. Schütze, 1007–1249. Munich/Oxford/Baden-Baden: Bloomsbury Publishing, 2013.

Pekcanıtez, Hakan. 'Hukuki Dinlenilme Hakkı'. İn *Prof. Dr. Seyfullah Edis'e Armağan*, edited by Zafer Gören, 753–791. İzmir: Dokuz Eylül Üniversitesi Yayını, 2000. https://hukuk.deu.edu.tr/wp-content/uploads/2020/01/Pekcanitez.pdf (accessed 24 September 2025).

Pekcanıtez, Hakan. 'Özel Uzman (Bilirkişi) Görüşü ve Değerlendirilmesi'. In *Makaleler*, edited by Hakan Pekcanitez, 2:393–420, İki Levha Yayıncılık, 2016.

Pekcanıtez, Hakan, Oğuz Atalay, and Muhammet Özekes. *Medenî Usûl Hukuku Ders Kitabı*. 11. İstanbul: On İki Levha Yayıncılık, 2023.

Pekcanıtez, Hakan, and Ali Yeşilirmak. 'Tahkim'. İn *Pekcanıtez Usûl: Medenî Usûl Hukuku*, edited by Hakan Pekcanıtez et al., 15. vol. III. İstanbul: On İki Levha Yayıncılık, 2017.

Peter, Wolfgang. 'Witness "Conferencing"'. *Arbitration International* 18, no. 1 (2002): 47–58. https://doi.org/10.1023/a:1014238725055 (accessed 24 September 2025).

Pitkowitz, Nikolaus, and Johanna Kathan-Spath. 'The Arbitrator and the Arbitration Procedure, The Vienna Propositions for Streamlining Arbitral Proceedings: Keeping Pace with New Developments and User Expectations'. In *Austrian Yearbook on International Arbitration 2024*, edited by Christian Klausegger et al., 143–216. Kluwer Law International, 2024.

Plant, Brendan. 'Expert Evidence and the Challenge of Procedural Reform in International Dispute Settlement'. *Journal of International Dispute Settlement* 9, no. 3 (1 September 2018): 464–472. https://doi.org/10.1093/jnlids/idy019 (accessed 24 September 2025).

Pörnbacher, Karl, Philipp Duncker, and Sebastian Baur. 'Gaspreisanpassungs-Schiedsverfahren – Hintergründe und prozessuale Besonderheiten'. Edited by Jörg Risse et al., *SchiedsVZ | German Arbitration Journal* 10, no. 6 (2012): 289–299.

Postacıoğlu, İlhan, and Sümer Altay. *Medeni Usul Hukuku Dersleri*. 7. İstanbul: Vedat Kiptaçılık, 2015.

Poudret, Jean-François, and Sébastien Besson. *Comparative Law of International Arbitration*. 2. Sweet & Maxwell, 2007.

Proske, Caroline Elisabeth. *Expert Witness Conferencing in Schiedsverfahren*. Mohr Siebeck, 2019. https://doi.org/10.1628/978-3-16-158274-5 (accessed 24 September 2025).

Punwar, Philip, and Dustin Appel. 'Weighing the Evidence: Experts and Witnesses Versus Documentary Evidence'. In *The Plurality and Synergies of Legal Traditions in*

International Arbitration: Looking Beyond the Common and Civil Law Divide, edited by Nayla Comair-Obeid and Stavros Brekoulakis, 153–160. Kluwer Law International, 2023.

Raeschke-Kessler, Hilmar. 'The Arbitrator as Settlement Facilitator'. *Arbitration International* 21, no. 4 (1 December 2005): 523–536. https://doi.org/10.1093/arbitration/21.4.523 (accessed 24 September 2025).

Raeschke-Kessler, Hilmar. 'Witness Conferencing'. In *Leading Arbitrators' Guide to International Arbitration*, edited by L.W. Newman and R.D. Hill, 3rd ed., 689–706. New York: Juris Publishing, Incorporated, 2014. https://books.google.co.in/books?id=0bOIAwAAQBAJ (accessed 24 September 2025).

Rawding, Nigel, Gregory Roy Fullelove, and Penny Martin. 'International Arbitration in England: A Procedural Overview'. In *Arbitration in England with Chapters on Scotland and Ireland*, edited by Julian D.M. Lew et al., 361–398. Kluwer Law International, 2013.

Redfern, Allan et al. 'The Standards and Burden of Proof in International Arbitration'. *Arbitration International* 10, no. 3 (1 September 1994): 317–364. https://doi.org/10.1093/arbitration/10.3.317 (accessed 24 September 2025).

Reiner, Andreas. 'Austria'. In *Evidence in International Arbitration Proceedings*, edited by Peter V. Eijsvoogel and The International Association of Young Lawyers, 67–76. AIJA Law Library. Kluwer Law International; Graham & Trotman/M. Nijhoff, 1994.

Reiner, Andreas, and Christian Aschauer. 'ICC Rules'. In *Institutional Arbitration: Article-by-Article Commentary*, edited by Rolf Arno Schütze, 25–202. München, Baden-Baden, Oxford: C. H. Beck, Hart, Nomos, 2013.

Rifkind, Robert. 'Preparing the Witness for Cross-Examination'. In *Take the Witness: Cross-Examination in International Arbitration*, edited by L.W. Newman and B.H. Sheppard, 139–146. Huntington, New York: Juris, 2010.

Risse, Jörg, and Heiko Haller. 'Die "IBA-Regeln" Zur Beweisaufnahme in Der InternationalenSchiedsgerichtsbarkeit'. In *Beweis Im Schiedsverfahren*, edited by Walter Eberl, 1, 115–129. Baden-Baden: Nomos, 2015.

Rogers, Catherine A. *Ethics in International Arbitration. Oxford*. Oxford: Oxford University Press, 2014.

Roney, David. 'Cross-Examination of Experts'. In *The Guide to Advocacy*, edited by Stephen Jagusch, Philippe Pinsolle, and Alexander G. Leventhal, 5th ed., 110–129. London: Law Business Research Ltd., 2021.

Rosenfeld, Friedrich Jakob. 'Country Report: Germany'. In *Due Processs as a Limit to Discretion in International Commercial Arbitration*, edited by Franco Ferrari et al., 177–194. Kluwer Law International, 2020.

Ruhlmann, François, and Olivier Gutkes. 'France'. In *Evidence in International Arbitration Proceedings*, edited by Peter V. Eijsvoogel and The International Association of Young Lawyers, 133–142. AIJA Law Library. Kluwer Law International; Graham & Trotman/M. Nijhoff, 1994.

Sachs, Klaus, and Torsten Lörcher. 'Commentary on the German Arbitration Law (10th Book of the German Code of Civil Procedure), Chapter V: Conduct of the Arbitral Proceeding, § 1049 – Experts Appointed by Arbitral Tribunal'. In *Arbitration in*

Germany: The Model Law in Practice, edited by Patricia Nacimiento, Stefan M Kröll, and Karl-Heinz Böckstiegel, 2, 292–296, 2015.

Sachs, Klaus, and Nils Schmidt-Ahrendts. 'Protocol on Expert Teaming: A New Approach to Expert Evidence'. In *Arbitration Advocacy in Changing Times*, edited by Albert Jan van den Berg, 15:135–148. ICCA Congress Series, Kluwer Law International, 2011.

Saenger, Ingo, ed. 'ZPO § 1049 Vom Schiedsgericht Bestellter Sachverständiger'. In *Zivilprozessordnung*, 9. Beck-Online, 2021.

Samaras, Elena, and Christof Strasser. 'Managing Party-Appointed Experts in International Arbitration--Analysis of the Current Framework and Best Practice Proposals-'. *Zeitschrift Für Schiedsverfahren* 11, no. 6 (2013): 314–329.

Sanders, Pieter. 'Commentary On UNCITRAL Arbitration Rules'. In *ICCA Yearbook Commercial Arbitration 1977*, edited by Pieter Sanders, II:172–224. ICCA & Kluwer Law International, 1977.

Sandifer, Durward V. *Evidence Before International Tribunals*. Revised. Charlottesville: University of Virginia, 1975.

Şanlı, Cemal. *Uluslararası Ticari Akitlerin Hazırlanması ve Uyuşmazlıkların Çözüm Yolları*. 8. İstanbul: Beta Basım, 2023.

Şanlı, Cemal, Emre Esen, and İnci Ataman-Figanmeşe. *Uluslararası Ticari Akitlerin Hazırlanması ve Uyuşmazlıkların Çözüm Yolları*. 9. İstanbul: Beta Basım, 2021.

Sarısözen, M. Serhat. *Medeni Usul Hukukunda Soru Yöneltme ve Çapraz Sorgu*. Ankara: Yetkin Yayınları, 2016.

Sarısözen, M. Serhat. 'Özel Bilirkişi (Uzman Görüşü)'. In *Prof. Dr. Ejder Yılmaz Armağanı*, edited by Emel Hanağası and Mustafa Göksu, 2:1699–1728. Ankara: Yetkin Yayınları, 2014.

Schäfer, Erik, Herman Verbist, and Christophe Imhoos. *ICC Arbitration in Practice*. 2. Alphen aan den Rijn: Kluwer Law International, 2016.

Schäfer, Erik, and David B. Wilson. 'Issues for Arbitrators to Consider Regarding Experts: An Updated Report of the ICC Commission on Arbitration and ADR'. Paris: ICC Commission on Arbitration and ADR, 2021.

Schäfer, Erik, and David B. Wilson. 'Task Force on Guidelines for ICC Expertise or the ICC Rules of Arbitration'. vol. 20. Paris: ICC Commission on Arbitration and ADR, 2009.

Scherer, Maxi, ed. 'A. v. 1. B., 2. C., Federal Supreme Court of Switzerland, 1st Civil Law Chamber, 4A_335/2012, 30 January 2013'. *ASA Bulletin; Kluwer Law International* 32, no. 3 (2014): 570–574.

Scherer, Maxi, ed. 'A. v. B. SA, Federal Supreme Court of Switzerland, 1st Civil Law Chamber, Case No. 4A_572/2015, 6 January 2016'. *ASA Bulletin; Kluwer Law International* 34, no. 1 (2016): 171–177.

Scherer, Maxi, ed. 'Saudi Modern Foods Factory v. Pavan Mapimpianti S.p.A., Federal Supreme Court of Switzerland, 1st Civil Law Chamber, 10 June 1996'. *ASA Bulletin; Kluwer Law International* 22, no. 2 (2000): 764–778.

Scherer, Maxi, ed. 'Society X. v. Z., Federal Supreme Court of Switzerland, 1st Civil Law Chamber, Case No. 4A_277/2017, 28 August 2017'. *ASA Bulletin; Kluwer Law International* 36, no. 1 (2018): 186–192.

Scherer, Maxi, ed. 'X. S.A.L., Y. S.A.L. et A. v. Z. Sàrl, Federal Supreme Court of Switzerland, 1st Civil Law Chamber, 4P.115/2003, 16 October 2003'. *ASA Bulletin; Kluwer Law International* 22, no. 2 (2004): 364–389.

Schiau, Ioan. 'An Arbitration Dilemma: Party-Appointed Experts vs. Tribunal-Appointed Experts'. *Juridical Tribune* 12, no. 3 (14 November 2022). https://doi.org/10.24818/TBJ/2022/12/3.02 (accessed 24 September 2025).

Schill, Stephan W., ed. *ICCA Yearbook Commercial Arbitration 2018*. vol. XLIII. ICCA & Kluwer Law International, 2018.

Schill, Stephan W., ed. *ICCA Yearbook Commercial Arbitration 2019*. vol. XLIV. ICCA & Kluwer Law International, 2019.

Schill, Stephan W., ed. *ICCA Yearbook Commercial Arbitration 2020*. vol. XLV. ICCA & Kluwer Law International, 2020.

Schlaepfer, Anne V., and Vanessa A. Duvanel. 'Direct and Re-Direct Examination'. In *The Guide to Advocacy*, edited by Stephen Jagusch, Philippe Pinsolle, and Alexander G. Leventhal, 5th ed., 70–84. London: Law Business Research Ltd., 2021.

Schlaepfer, Anne-Véronique. 'The Burden of Proof in International Arbitration'. In *ICCA Congress Series No. 18 (Miami 2014): Legitimacy: Myths, Realities, Challenges*, edited by Albert Jan Van Den Berg, 127–133. ICCA Congress Series 18. Miami: ICCA & Kluwer Law International, 2015.

Schlosser, Peter. *Kommentar zur Zivilprozessordnung*. Edited by Friedrich Stein and Martin Jonas. 23. vol. 10. Mohr Siebeck, 2014.

Schlosser, Peter F. 'Spontan Präsentierte Zeugen Und (Privat-)Gutachten Nach Deutschem Und Österreichischem Recht'. In *Festschrift Für Walter H. Rechtsberger Zum 60. Geburstag*, 497–511. Wien: Springer-Verlag, 2005.

Schmidt-Ahrendts, Nils. 'Expert Teaming: Bridging the Divide between Party-Appointed and Tribunal-Appointed Experts'. *Victoria University of Wellington Law Review* 43 (2012): 653–660. https://doi.org/10.26686/vuwlr.v43i4.5017 (accessed 24 September 2025).

Schneider, Michael E. 'Technical Experts in International Arbitration'. *ASA Bulletin; Kluwer Law International* 11, no. 3 (1993): 446–465.

Schneider, Michael E., and Matthias Scherer. 'Art. 184'. In *Baseler Kommentar: Internationales Privatrecht*, edited by Pascal Grolimund, Leander D. Loacker, and Anton K. Schnyder, 4. Basel: Helbing Lichtenhahn Verlag, 2021.

Schütze, Rolf A. 'Beweisaufnahme Nach Civil Law'. In *Beweiserhebung in Internationalen Schiedsverfahren*, edited by Karl-Heinz Böckstiegel, 31. Carl Heymanns, 2001.

Schütze, Rolf A., and Roderich C. Thümmel. *Schiedsgericht Und Schiedsverfahren*. 7th ed. München: C.H. Beck, 2021.

Schütze, Rolf Arno. *Das Internationale Zivilprozessrecht in Der ZPO: Kommentar*. 2. Berlin, New York: De Gruyter, 2011.

Schütze, Rolf Arno. 'Der Beweis Des Anwendbaren Rechts Im Schiedsverfahren Und Die Feststellung Seines Inhalts'. In *Beweis Im Schiedsverfahren*, edited by Walter Eberl, 1., 149–160. Baden-Baden: Nomos, 2015. http://www.nomos-shop.de/_assets/downloads/9783848702787_lese01.pdf (accessed 24 September 2025).

Schütze, Rolf Arno. *Zivilprozessordnung Und Nebengesetze: Großkommentar*. Edited by Bernhard Wieczorek and Rolf Arno Schütze. 4. vol. 11. Großkommentare Der Praxis. Berlin: De Gruyter, 2014.

Schütze, Rolf Arno, Dieter Tscherning, and Walter Wais. *Handbuch Des Schiedsverfahrens: Praxis Der Deutschen Und Internationalen Schiedsgerichtsbarkeit*. 2. Berlin: de Gruyter, 1990.

Schwab, Karl Heinz, and Gerhard Walter. *Schiedsgerichtsbarkeit*. 7. Basel: C.H. Beck: Helbing Lichtenhahn Verlag, 2005.

Schwartz, Eric, and Rocío Digón. 'Witness Statements: Use and Abuse'. In *Leading Arbitrators' Guide to International Arbitration*, edited by L.W. Newman and R.D. Hill, 3rd ed., New York: Juris Publishing, Incorporated, 2014.

Senogles, Geoffrey. 'Some Views from the Crucible: The Perspective of an Expert Witness on the Adversarial Principle'. *Journal of International Dispute Settlement* 9, no. 3 (1 September 2018): 361–366. https://doi.org/10.1093/jnlids/idy008 (accessed 24 September 2025).

Silver, Lisa A. 'Back to Burgess: The Impact of the White Burgess Expert Evidence Regime in Alberta Decisions'. *Alberta Law Review* 57, no. 1 (2019): 1–28. https://doi.org/10.29173/alr2562 (accessed 24 September 2025).

Simmons, Joshua B. 'Valuation in Investor-State Arbitration: Toward a More Exact Science'. *Berkeley Journal of International Law* 30, no. 1 (2012): 196–250.

Smiley, Antoine K.F. 'An Unwanted Intrusion: Challenging the Appointment of Experts in International Arbitration'. *Arbitration: The International Journal of Arbitration, Mediation and Dispute Management* 85, no. 4 (2019): 360–376.

Soria, Santiago, and Manuel Tomas Schmidt Meyer. 'Weighing Evidence in International Arbitration'. In *International Arbitration in Practice*, edited by Courtney Lotfi et al., 559–568. Kluwer Law International, 2024.

Sourgens, Frederic G., Kabir Duggal, and Ian A Laird, eds. *Evidence in International Investment Arbitration*. Oxford: Oxford University Press, 2018.

Spitzer, Martin. 'Der Sachverständigenbeweis Im Österreichischen Zivilprozess'. *Zeitschrift Für Zivilprozess* 131, no. 1 (2018): 25–52. https://doi.org/doi:10.1515/zzp-2018-1310103 (accessed 24 September 2025).

Stampa, Gonzalo. 'The Prague Rules'. *Arbitration International* 35, no. 2 (2019): 221–244. https://doi.org/10.1093/arbint/aiz010 (accessed 24 September 2025).

Swinehart, Matthew W. 'International Law Commons, and the Organizations Law Commons Recommended Citation Recommended Citation Matthew W. Swinehart, Reliability of Expert Evidence in International Disputes'. *Michigan Journal of International Law* 38 (2017). https://repository.law.umich.edu/mjil/vol38/iss2/6/ (accessed 27 October 2025).

Takavut, İbrahim Doğan. *Milletlerarası Ticari Tahkimde Usule Ilişkin Konularda Irade Serbestisi*. Istanbul: On İki Levha Yayıncılık, 2021.

Tanrıver, Süha. 'Hukuk Yargısı Bağlamında Bilirkişilikle Ilgili Temel Problemler ve Çözüm Arayışları'. *Dokuz Eylül Üniversitesi Hukuk Fakültesi Dergisi* 11, no. Özel Sayı 2009 (Prof. Dr. Bilge Umar'a Armağan) (2010): 575–594.

Tanrıver, Süha. *Hukukumuzda Bilirkişilik*. Ankara: Yetkin Yayınları, 2017.

Tanrıver, Süha. *Medenî Usûl Hukuku*. 4. vol. I. Ankara: Yetkin Yayınları, 2021.

Tanrıver, Süha. *Medenî Usûl Hukuku*. 2. vol. II. Ankara: Yetkin Yayınları, 2022.

Tanrıver, Süha. 'Yasal Düzenleme ve Teorik Boyutuyla Bilirkişilik'. vol. 3. Oturum. Lexpera, 2022. https://www.youtube.com/live/F_b6CuiIn1Q?feature=share&t=2 2667 (accessed 24 September 2025).

Tarman, Zeynep Derya. 'Bilirkişilik Sözleşmesinin Hukuki Niteliği ve Bilirkişinin Üçüncü Kişiye Karşı Olan Sorumluluğu'. Yüksek Lisans Tezi, T.C. İstanbul Üniversitesi Sosyal Bilimler Enstitüsü Özel Hukuk Anabilim Dalı, 2005.

Taşdemir, İbrahim Orkun. 'İngiliz ve Amerikan Medenî Yargılamasında Uzman Tanıklık'. Yüksek Lisans Tezi, Galatasaray Üniversitesi Sosyal Bilimler Enstitüsü Özel Hukuk Anabilim Dalı, 2019.

Taşkın, Alim. *Tahkim Hukukunda Tahkim Anlaşması, Hakem Kurulu ve Tahkim Yargılaması (Fransız Tahkim Reformuna Dair Kararname ve Uluslararası Tahkim Kuralları ile Karşılaştırılması)*. Ankara: Yetkin Yayınları, 2019.

Teomete Yalabık, Fulya. 'Questioning Expert Witnesses in Litigation and International Arbitration: How to Prevent Partisan Expert Reports and "Battle of Experts"'. *Medeni Usul ve Icra Iflas Hukuku Dergisi* 16, no. 45 (2020): 133–162.

Theune, Ulrich. 'DIS Rules'. In *Institutional Arbitration: Article-by-Article Commentary*, edited by Rolf Arno Schütze. C.H. Beck, Hart Publishing, Nomos, 2013.

Thomas, Heinz et al. *Zivilprozessordnung*. 44. München: C.H. Beck, 2023.

Tirado, Joseph Manuel, Sherina Petit, and Michelle Keen. 'Factual Evidence'. In *Arbitration in England, with Chapters on Scotland and Ireland*, edited by Julian D.M. Lew et al., 483–502. Kluwer Law International, 2013.

Toraman, Barış. 'Anglo-Amerikan Hukukunda Mahkeme Tarafından Tayin Edilen Bilirkişiler Court-Appointed Experts in Anglo-American Law'. *Anadolu Üniversitesi Sosyal Bilimler Dergisi* 13, no. Hukuk Fakültesi 20. Yıl Özel Sayısı (2013): 115–129.

Toraman, Barış. *Medeni Usul Hukukunda Bilirkişi Incelemesi*. Ankara: Yetkin Yayınları, 2017.

Townsend, John. 'Crossing the Hot-Tub: Examining Adverse Expert Witnesses in International Arbitration'. In *Take the Witness: Cross-Examination in International Arbitration*, edited by L.W. Newman and B.H. Sheppard, 161–166. Juris, 2010.

Trenor, John A., ed. *The Guide to Damages in International Arbitration*. 4. Law Business Research Ltd., 2021.

Trittmann, Rolf, and Boris Kasolowsky. 'Taking Evidence in Arbitration Proceedings Between Common Law and Civil Law Traditions: The Development of a European Hybrid Standard for Arbitration Proceedings'. *University of New South Wales Law Journal*, Forum: Taking Evidence in Arbitration Proceedings, 31, no. 1 (2008): 330–340.

Trittmann, Rolf, and Ramona Schardt. 'The Proceedings Before the Arbitral Tribunal, Article 28: Establishing the Facts'. In *The DIS Arbitration Rules: An Article-by-Article Commentary*, edited by Gustav Flecke-Giammarco et al., 451–472. Kluwer Law International, 2020.

Tuna, Mustafa Oğuz. *Alternative Dispute Resolution in Energy Industries*. Routledge Research in Energy Law and Regulation. Routledge, 2022.

Uluç, İnan. *Corruption in International Arbitration*. Ankara: Yetkin Yayınları, 2021.

Uluç, İnan. *Evidence-Taking in National and International Arbitration: The Reconcili ation of Civil Law and Common Law Traditions*. Ankara: Yetkin Yayınları, 2021.

Unbound, Chicago, and John H. Langbein. 'The German Advantage in Civil Procedure'. 52 *University of Chicago Law Review* 823 (1985). https://chicagounbound.uchicago.edu/journal_articles. (accessed 24 September 2025).

UNCITRAL. *UNCITRAL 2012 Digest of Case Law on the Model Law on International Commercial Arbitration*. Vienna: United Nations Publication, 2012.

United Nations. 'UNCITRAL Notes on Organizing Arbitral Proceedings'. Vienna, 2016. www.uncitral.org.

Ünüvar, Güneş. 'Experts: Investment Arbitration'. *Max Planck Encyclopedias of International Law*, 2021. http://opil.ouplaw.com (accessed 24 September 2025).

Uşan, Fatih. *Uluslararası Tahkim Sempozyumu 25–26 April (Nisan) 2019*. Edited by Musa Aygül and Ersin Erdoğan. Ankara: Yetkin Yayınları, 2020.

Valles, Cherise. 'Different Forms of Expert Involvement in WTO Dispute Settlement Proceedings'. *Journal of International Dispute Settlement* 9, no. 3 (1 September 2018): 367–378. https://doi.org/10.1093/jnlids/idy010 (accessed 24 September 2025).

Van Damme, Isabelle. 'The Assessment of Expert Evidence in International Adjudication'. *Journal of International Dispute Settlement* 9, no. 3 (1 September 2018): 401–410. https://doi.org/10.1093/jnlids/idy013 (accessed 24 September 2025).

Van Den Berg, Albert Jan, ed. *ICCA Yearbook Commercial Arbitration 1988*. vol. XIII. ICCA & Kluwer Law International, 1988.

Van Den Berg, Albert Jan, ed. *ICCA Yearbook Commercial Arbitration 1993*. vol. XVIII. ICCA & Kluwer Law International, 1993.

Van Den Berg, Albert Jan, ed. *ICCA Yearbook Commercial Arbitration 1999*. vol. XXIVa. ICCA & Kluwer Law International, 1999.

Van Den Berg, Albert Jan, ed. *ICCA Yearbook Commercial Arbitration 2012*. vol. XXXVII. ICCA & Kluwer Law International, 2012.

Van Houtte, Vera. 'Party-Appointed Experts and Tribunal-Appointed Experts'. In *Arbitral Procedure at the Dawn of the New Millennium: Reports of the International Colloquium of CEPANI*, edited by Stephen R. Bond, 133–154. Brussels: Bruylant, 2004.

Varga, István. *Beweiserhebung in Transatlantischen Schiedsverfahren: Eine Suche Nach Kompromissen Zwischen Deutscher Und US-Amerikanischer Beweisrechtstradition*. Schriften Des Rechtszentrums Für Europäische Und Internationale Zusammenarbeit. Nomos, 2006. https://books.google.com.tr/books?id=AszEAAAACAAJ (accessed 24 September 2025).

Veeder, Van Vechten et al. eds. 'Act III: Advocacy with Witness Testimony'. *Arbitration International* 21, no. 4 (1 December 2005): 583–612. https://doi.org/10.1093/arbitration/21.4.583 (accessed 24 September 2025).

Voser, Nathalie, and Katherine Bell. 'Expert Evidence in Construction Disputes: Arbitrator Perspective'. edited by Stavros Brekoulakis and Thomas Brynmor, 3, 226–235. London: Law Business Research, 2019.

Voser, Nathalie, and Anna Katharina Mueller. 'Appointment of Experts by the Arbitral Tribunal: The Civil Law Perspective'. *Business Law International* 7, no. 1 (January 2006): 73–82.

Wach, Karl J.T., and Tom Petsch. 'Der Sachverständigenbeweis Im Schiedsverfahren: Grenzen Der Gestaltungsfreiheit von Parteien Und Schiedsgericht'. In *Beweis Im Schiedsverfahren*, edited by Walter Eberl, 1., 91–114. Baden-Baden: Nomos, 2015.

Waincymer, Jeffrey. 'Advocacy Training in International Commercial and Investment Arbitration': In *Advocacy in International Commercial Arbitration*, edited by Elliott Geisinger and Guillaume Tattevin, 57–85. ASA Special Series 36. New York: JURIS, 2013.

Waincymer, Maurice. *Procedure and Evidence in International Arbitration*. Kluwer Law International, 2012.

Webster, Thomas H., and Michael W. Bühler. *Handbook of ICC Arbitration: Commentary, Precedents, Materials*. 5th ed. London: Sweet & Maxwell, 2021.

Webster, Thomas H., and Michael W. Bühler. *Handbook of UNCITRAL Arbitration*. 3rd ed. London: Sweet & Maxwell, 2019.

Weigand, Frank-Bernd, and Antje Baumann, eds. *Practitioner's Handbook on International Commercial Arbitration*. 3rd ed., 2019.

Weiss, Alexandra, and Karin Bürgi Locatelli. 'Der Vom Schiedsgericht Bestellte Experte-Ein Überblick Aus Sicht Eines Internationalen Schiedsgerichts Mit Sitz in Der Schweiz'. *ASA Bulletin* 22, no. 3 (2004): 479–504. https://doi.org/10.54648/asab2004052 (accessed 24 September 2025).

White, Gillian M. *The Use of Experts by International Tribunals*. Syracuse University Press, 1965.

Wiegand, Wolfgang. 'Der Experte im Verfahren Erkenntnisse aus nationalen und internationalen Verfahren vor Schiedsgerichten und staatlichen Gerichten'. In *Modelle für die Einbeziehung von Experten*, edited by Fritz Nicklisch, 15–38. München: C.H. Beck, 2006.

Wilske, Stephan, and Christine Gack. 'Expert Evidence in International Commercial Arbitration'. In *The Comparative Law Yearbook of International Business*, edited by Dennis Campbell and Anita Alibekova, 29:75–97. Alphen aan den Rijn: Wolters Kluwer, 2007.

Wilske, Stephan, and Lars Markert. *Beck'scher Online-Kommentar ZPO*. Edited by Volkert Vorwerk and Christian Wolf. 44. Beck-Online, 2022.

Yazıcı-Tıktık, Çiğdem. 'HMK m. 293'teki Uzman Görüşü Kurumu Ile Anglo-Sakson Hukuk Sistemindeki Uzman Tanık Kurumunun Karşılaştırılması'. *Medeni Usul ve Icra Iflas Hukuku Dergisi* 7, no. 20 (March 2011): 79–99.

Yeğengil, Rasih. *Tahkim (L'Arbitrage)*. İstanbul, n.d.

Yesilirmak, Ali. 'Expert Determination in Turkey'. *ASA Bulletin* 33, no. Issue 2 (1 June 2015): 306–326. https://doi.org/10.54648/ASAB2015024 (accessed 24 September 2025).

Yeşilirmak, Ali. *ICC Tahkim Kuralları ve Uygulaması*. İstanbul: On İki Levha Yayıncılık, 2018.

Yeşilirmak, Ali. *Türkiye'de Ticari Hayatın ve Yatırım Ortamının Iyileştirilmesi Için Uyuşmazlıkların Etkin Çözümünde Doğrudan Görüşme, Arabuluculuk, Hakem-Bilirkişilik ve Tahkim: Sorunlar ve Çözüm Önerileri*. İstanbul: On İki Levha, 2011.

Yıldızlı, Ferhan. *Uluslararası Tahkimde Zararın Değerlendirilmesi*. Ankara: Seçkin, 2020.

Yılmaz, Ejder. *Hukuk Muhakemeleri Kanunu Şerhi*. 2. Ankara: Yetkin Yayınları, 2013.

Yılmaz, Ejder. *Hukuk Muhakemeleri Kanunu Şerhi*. 4. vol. 4. Ankara: Yetkin Yayınları, 2021.

Yılmaz, Ejder. 'Hukukî Dinlenilme Hakkı'. İn *Tahkimde Hukukî Dinlenilme Hakkı*, edited by Ziya Akıncı and Yasin Ekmen, 1–20. Istanbul Tahkim Merkezi (ISTAC) Yayınları, V. İstanbul: On İki Levha Yayıncılık, 2022.

Zhihe, Xu, and Li Tingwei. 'The Use of Expert Witness in Arbitration from the Perspective of SHIAC'. *Kluwer Arbitration Blog* (blog), 29 April 2020. http://arbitrationblog.kluwerarbitration.com/2020/04/29/the-use-of-expert-witness-in-arbitration-from-the-perspective-of-shiac (accessed 24 September 2025).

Zuberbühler, Tobias et al. *IBA Rules of Evidence: Commentary on the IBA Rules on the Taking of Evidence in International Arbitration*. 2. Zürich: Schulthess Juristische Medien AG, 2022.

Table of Court Decisions

1 Australia

Oil Basins Ltd v. BHP Billiton LTD & Ors, [2007] VSCA 255, 158

2 Germany

BayObLG. 4Z Sch 23/99, CLOUT Case 375 UNCITRAL (Bayerisches Oberstes Landesgericht 1999), 149
German Federal Court of Justice (BGH). I ZB 1/16, SchiedsVZ 317 (German Federal Court of Justice (BGH) 2017), 78
German Federal Court of Justice (BGH). I ZB 46/18, BGH (BGH 2019), 25, 153, 154
German Federal Court of Justice (BGH). I ZB 90/18, openJur (German Federal Court of Justice (BGH) 2019), 78
German Federal Court of Justice (BGH). I ZB 7/15, 2016 SchiedsVZ 339–343 (BGH 2016), 78
German Federal Court of Justice (BGH). III ZR 44/89, Wolters Kluwer (BGH 1989), 176
German Federal Court of Justice (BGH). III ZR 169/90, Wolters Kluwer (BGH 1992), 78
German Federal Court of Justice (BGH). III ZB 8/11, Wolters Kluwer (BGH 2012), 159
German Federal Court of Justice (BGH). VI ZB 31/16, BGH, (BGH 2017), 30
OLG Hamburg. 6 Sch 1/16, Rechtstipp24 (Oberlandesgericht Hamburg 2016), 147
OLG Köln. 19 Sch 6/17, 2018, 7064 openJur (Oberlandesgericht Köln 2017), 149
OLG Köln. 19 Sch 7/10, Justiz NRW (Oberlandesgericht Köln 2017), 107
OLG München. 34 Sch 10/11, 2012, 119383 openJur (Oberlandesgericht München 2011), 86, 147
OLG München. 34 Sch 18/06, DISArb (Oberlandesgericht München 2007), 148
OLG Frankfurt am Main, 1 U 104/96, 28 April 2005, 30
OLG Saarland, 5 W 42/08-16, 11 March 2008, 30
OLG Frankfurt am Main, 26 Sch 13/10, 17 February 2011, 159

3 Hong Kong

Hong Kong. Brunswick Bowling & Billiards Corporation v. Shanghai Zhonglu Industrial Co. Ltd. and Chen Rong, No. HCCT 66/2007 (Hong Kong, Court of First Instance, In

4 New Zealand

5 Switzerland

6 Türkiye

7 India

8 UK

9 Canada

10 USA

11 Singapore

Table of Arbitration Cases

ICSID

ICC

UNCITRAL

LCIA

SCC

INTERNATIONAL ARBITRATION LAW LIBRARY

1. Moshe Hirsch, *The Arbitration Mechanism of the International Center for the Settlement of Investment Disputes,* 1993 (ISBN 07-923-1993-1).
2. Aida B. Avanessian, *Iran-United States Claims Tribunal in Action,* 1993 (ISBN 18-533-3902-4).
3. Isaak I. Dore, *The UNCITRAL Framework for Arbitration in Contemporary Perspective,* 1993 (ISBN 18-533-3573-8).
4. Vesna Lazić, *Insolvency Proceedings and Commercial Arbitration,* 1998 (ISBN 90-411-1115-8).
5. Joachim Frick, *Arbitration in Complex International Contracts,* 2001 (ISBN 90-411-1662-1).
6. Katherine Lynch, *The Forces of Economic Globalization: Challenges to the Regime of International Commercial Arbitration,* 2003 (ISBN 90-411-1994-9).
7. Christoph Liebscher, *The Healthy Award: Challenge in International Commercial Arbitration,* 2003 (ISBN 90-411-2011-4).
8. Hamid G. Gharavi, *The International Effectiveness of the Annulment of an Arbitral Award,* 2003 (ISBN 90-411-1717-2).
9. Abdulhay Sayed, *Corruption in International Trade and Commercial Arbitration,* 2004 (ISBN 90-411-2236-2).
10. Gabrielle Kaufmann-Kohler & Thomas Schultz, *Online Dispute Resolution: Challenges for Contemporary Justice,* 2004 (ISBN 90-411-2318-0).
11. Christopher R. Drahozal & Richard W. Naimark (eds), *Towards a Science of International Arbitration: Collected Empirical Research,* 2005 (ISBN 90-411-2322-9).
12. Ali Yeşilirmak, *Provisional Measures in International Commercial Arbitration,* 2005 (ISBN 90-411-2353-9).
13. Christian Bühring-Uhle, *Arbitration and Mediation in International Business,* second revised edition, 2006 (ISBN 978-9-041-12256-8).
14. Bernard Hanotiau, *Complex Arbitrations: Multi-party, Multi-contract and Multi-issue – A Comparative Study,* Second Edition, 2020 (ISBN 978-94-035-1261-7).
15. Loukas A. Mistelis & Julian D.M. Lew (eds), *Pervasive Problems in International Arbitration,* 2006 (ISBN 978-9-041-12450-0).
16. Julian D.M. Lew & Loukas A. Mistelis (eds), *Arbitration Insights – Twenty Years of the Annual Lecture of the School of International Arbitration, Sponsored by Freshfields Bruckhaus Deringer,* 2006 (ISBN 978-9-041-12606-1).
17. Mark Kantor, *Valuation for Arbitration: Compensation Standards, Valuation Methods and Expert Evidence,* 2008 (ISBN 978-9-041-12735-8).
18. Christoph Brunner, *Force Majeure and Hardship under General Contract Principles: Exemption for Non-Performance in International Arbitration,* 2009 (ISBN 978-90-411-2792-1).

19. Loukas A. Mistelis & Stavros L. Brekoulakis (eds), *Arbitrability: International & Comparative Perspectives,* 2009 (ISBN 978-90-411-2730-3).
20. Sam Luttrell, *Bias Challenges in International Commercial Arbitration: The Need for a 'Real Danger' Test,* 2009 (ISBN 978-90-411-3191-1).
21. Monique Sasson, *Substantive Law in Investment Treaty Arbitration: The Unsettled Relationship Between International Law and Municipal Law,* Second Edition, 2017 (ISBN 978-90-411-6103-1).
22. Ileana M. Smeureanu, *Confidentiality in International Commercial Arbitration,* 2011 (ISBN 978-90-411-3226-0).
23. Won Kidane, *China-Africa Dispute Settlement: The Law, Economics and Culture of Arbitration,* 2011 (ISBN 978-90-411-3674-9).
24. Karel Daele, *Challenge and Disqualification of Arbitrators in International Arbitration,* 2012 (ISBN 978-90-411-3799-9).
25. Crina Baltag, *The Energy Charter Treaty: The Notion of Investor,* 2012 (ISBN 978-90-411-3428-8).
26. Alexandra Diehl, *The Core Standard of International Investment Protection: Fair and Equitable Treatment,* 2012 (ISBN 978-90-411-3869-9).
27. Manuel Indlekofer, *International Arbitration and the Permanent Court of Arbitration,* 2013 (ISBN 978-90-411-4766-0).
28. Günther J. Horvath & Stephan Wilske (eds), *Guerrilla Tactics in International Arbitration,* 2013 (ISBN 978-90-411-4002-9).
29. Albert Badia, *Piercing the Veil of State Enterprises in International Arbitration,* 2014 (ISBN 978-90-411-5162-9).
30. Nadja Erk, *Parallel Proceedings in International Arbitration: A Comparative European Perspective,* 2014 (ISBN 978-90-411-5264-0).
31. Simon Vorburger, *International Arbitration and Cross-Border Insolvency: Comparative Perspectives,* 2014 (ISBN 978-90-411-5419-4).
32. Ahmad Ali Ghouri, *Interaction and Conflict of Treaties in Investment Arbitration,* 2015 (ISBN 978-90-411-5417-0).
33. Reto Marghitola, *Document Production in International Arbitration,* 2015 (ISBN 978-90-411-5159-9).
34. Alfonso Gómez-Acebo, *Party-Appointed Arbitrators in International Commercial Arbitration,* 2016 (ISBN 978-90-411-6671-5).
35. Jonas von Goeler, *Third-Party Funding in International Arbitration and Its Impact on Procedure,* 2016 (ISBN 978-90-411-5015-8).
36. Dean Lewis, *The Interpretation and Uniformity of the UNCITRAL Model Law on International Commercial Arbitration: Focusing on Australia, Hong Kong and Singapore,* 2016 (ISBN 978-90-411-6700-2).
37. Stavros Brekoulakis, Julian D.M. Lew & Loukas Mistelis (eds), *The Evolution and Future of International Arbitration,* 2016 (ISBN 978-90-411-7004-0).
38. Rémy Gerbay, *The Functions of Arbitral Institutions,* 2016 (ISBN 978-90-411-6217-5).

39. Maximilian Clasmeier, *Arbitral Awards as Investments: Treaty Interpretation and the Dynamics of International Investment Law*, 2017 (ISBN 978-90-411-8357-6).
40. Tony Cole (ed.), *The Roles of Psychology in International Arbitration*, 2017 (ISBN 978-90-411-5921-2).
41. Pietro Ferrario, *The Adaptation of Long-Term Gas Sale Agreements by Arbitrators*, 2017 (ISBN 978-90-411-8232-6).
42. Jacob B. van de Velden, *Finality in Litigation: The Law and Practice of Preclusion – Res Judicata (Merger and Estoppel), Abuse of Process and Recognition of Foreign Judgments*, 2017 (ISBN 978-90-411-8342-2).
43. Dolores Bentolila, *Arbitrators as Lawmakers*, 2017 (ISBN 978-90-411-8354-5).
44. Giacomo Marchisio, *The Notion of Award in International Commercial Arbitration: A Comparative Analysis of French Law, English Law, and the UNCITRAL Model Law*, 2017 (ISBN 978-90-411-8391-0).
45. Csaba Kovács, *Attribution in International Investment Law*, 2018 (ISBN 978-90-411-9675-0).
46. Mary Mitsi, *The Decision-Making Process of Investor-State Arbitration Tribunals*, 2019 (ISBN 978-90-411-9600-2).
47. Ahmet Cemil Yıldırım, *Interpretation of Contracts in Comparative and Uniform Law*, 2019 (ISBN 978-94-035-1130-6).
48. Beata Gessel-Kalinowska vel Kalisz, *The Legal, Real and Converged Interest in Declaratory Relief*, 2019 (ISBN 978-94-035-1244-0).
49. Maximilian Pika, *Third-Party Effects of Arbitral Awards: Res Judicata Against Privies, Non-mutual Preclusion and Factual Effects*, 2019 (ISBN 978-94-035-1273-0).
50. Yulia Levashova, *The Right of States to Regulate in International Investment Law: The Search for Balance Between Public Interest and Fair and Equitable Treatment*, 2019 (ISBN 978-94-035-0931-0).
51. Flavia Marisi, *Environmental Interests in Investment Arbitration: Challenges and Directions*, 2020 (ISBN 978-94-035-1723-0).
52. Martina Magnarelli, *Privity of Contract in International Investment Arbitration: Original Sin or Useful Tool?*, 2020 (ISBN 978-94-035-2020-9).
53. Xu Qian, *Water Services Disputes in International Arbitration: Reconsidering the Nexus of Investment Protection, Environment, and Human Rights*, 2020 (ISBN 978-94-035-2203-6).
54. Nobumichi Teramura, Ex Aequo et Bono *as a Response to the 'Over-Judicialisation' of International Commercial Arbitration*, 2020 (ISBN 978-94-035-2073-5).
55. Bruno Guandalini, *Economic Analysis of the Arbitrator's Function*, 2020 (ISBN 978-94-035-2265-4).
56. Zena Prodromou, *The Public Order Exception in International Trade, Investment, Human Rights and Commercial Disputes*, 2020 (ISBN 978-94-035-2031-5).

57. Jürg Künzle, *Multiple Contracts and Coordination in International Construction Projects: A Swiss Law Analysis*, 2020 (ISBN 978-94-035-2024-7).
58. Cornel Marian, *The State's Power to Tax in the Investment Arbitration of Energy Disputes: Outer Limits and the Energy Charter Treaty*, 2020 (ISBN 978-94-035-1752-0).
59. Luke Nottage, Shahla Ali, Bruno Jetin & Nobumichi Teramura (eds.), *New Frontiers in Asia-Pacific International Arbitration and Dispute Resolution*, 2021 (ISBN 978-94-035-2855-7).
60. Eva Litina, *Theory, Law and Practice of Maritime Arbitration: The Case of International Contracts for the Carriage of Goods by Sea*, 2021 (ISBN 978-94-035-3035-2).
61. Franco Ferrari & Friedrich Rosenfeld (eds), *Autonomous Versus Domestic Concepts under the New York Convention*, 2021 (ISBN 978-94-035-3173-1).
62. Doğan Gültutan, *Moral Damages under International Investment Law: The Path Towards Convergence*, 2022 (ISBN 978-94-035-4025-2).
63. Simon Foote QC, *The Bona Fide Investor: Corporate Nationality and Treaty Shopping in Investment Treaty Law*, 2022 (ISBN 978-94-035-4185-3).
64. George A. Bermann, *Twilight Issues in International Arbitration: Latent Choice of Law Challenges*, 2023 (ISBN 978-94-035-1746-9).
65. Emmanuel Obiora Igbokwe, *Dealing with Bribery and Corruption in International Commercial Arbitration: To Probe or Not to Probe*, 2023 (ISBN 978-94-035-2066-7).
66. Peter Sester, *Contract Law in International Commercial Arbitration*, 2023 (ISBN 978-94-035-1036-1).
67. Julian Bickmann, *Fact-Finding in International Arbitration: The Emergence of a Transnational* Lex Evidentiae, 2023 (ISBN 978-94-035-1886-2).
68. Giovanna E. Gismondi, *International Environmental Law and International Human Rights Law in Investment Treaty Arbitration: The Contribution of Host States' Argumentation in Re-Shaping International Investment Law*, 2023 (ISBN 978-94-035-3047-5).
69. Fabricio Fortese, *Early Determination of Jurisdiction*, 2024 (ISBN 978-94-035-0268-7).
70. Sabrina Pearson-Wenger, *Good Faith in International Commercial Arbitration: Its Application by Arbitral Tribunals to the Parties' Contract and the Arbitration Agreement*, 2024 (ISBN 978-94-035-0738-5).
71. Charalampos Tagaroulias, *International Investment Law and the Law of the European Union: How Regionalism and Interregionalism Have Shaped the Relationship in the Post-Lisbon Era*, 2024 (ISBN 978-94-035-0708-8).
72. Dan Xie, *Transnational Due Process and Article V(1)(b) of the New York Convention: Grounding Interpretation and Application of the Due Process Defence in the Public International Law Framework for Treaty Interpretation*, 2024 (ISBN 978-94-035-2437-5).
73. Thomas Lehmann, *Investment Arbitration and International Climate Change Law: Revaluing Legitimate Expectations*, 2025 (ISBN 978-94-035-2799-4).

74. Ylli Dautaj, *Sovereign Immunity from Execution and International Arbitration: Theory and Practice*, 2025 (ISBN 978-94-035-0858-0).
75. Satya Talwar Mouland, *Enforcement Jurisdiction in International Law and Arbitration*, 2026 (ISBN 978-94-035-4158-7).
76. Darya Shirokova, *The Fiction of 'State Contract' in the Energy Industry: The Empirical Gap Between the Intentions of the Parties and the Interpretation of Contracts by Arbitral Tribunals*, 2025 (ISBN 978-94-035-2999-8).
77. Viktor Előd Cserép, *Revision of Arbitral Awards Beyond the Model Law: 'Retrial' in Arbitration?*, 2026 (ISBN 978-94-035-3029-1).
78. Claudia Salgado Levy, *The Interpretative Practice of International Investment Arbitral Tribunals*, 2026 (ISBN 978-94-035-4739-8).
79. Ömer Faruk Kafali, *Party-Appointed Experts in International Commercial and Investment Arbitration: Impact on Proceedings, Problems and Solutions*, 2026 (ISBN 978-94-035-4889-0).

www.ingramcontent.com/pod-product-compliance
Lightning Source LLC
LaVergne TN
LVHW010629300926
849162LV00001B/101